DECISION MAKING WITH DEPENDENCE AND FEEDBACK

THE ANALYTIC NETWORK PROCESS

THE ORGANIZATION AND PRIORITIZATION OF COMPLEXITY

SECOND EDITION
EXTENSIVELY REVISED WITH NEW APPLICATIONS

THOMAS L. SAATY

Library of Congress Cataloging-in-Publication Data
Saaty, Thomas L.

Decision Making with Dependence and Feedback: The Analytic
Network Process

CIP 95-069523
ISBN 0-9620317-9-8

1. Priorities 2. Decision Making 3. Analytic Hierarchy Process
(AHP) 4. Analytic Network Process (ANP) 5. Decision Making with
Dependence and Feedback 6. Feedback and Dependence in Decision
Making 7. Economic Priorities 8. Social Priorities 9. Complex
Decision Making

Thomas L. Saaty
University of Pittsburgh
322 Mervis Hall
Pittsburgh, PA 15260
Phone: 412-648-1539

RWS Publications
4922 Ellsworth Avenue
Pittsburgh, PA 15213 USA
Phone: 412-621-4492
FAX: 412-682-7008

THOMAS L. SAATY

University of Pittsburgh

322 Mervis Hall
University of Pittsburgh
Pittsburgh, PA 15260
E-mail: saaty@katz.pitt.edu

The Analytic Hierarchy Process Series - Vol. IX

Dedicated to my boyhood friend and classmate **Philip Rahbany** for his brilliance and sensitivity, and for his exceptionally loving and caring nature.

CONTENTS

Preface

Our lives are the sum of our decisions–whether in business or in personal spheres. Often, *when* we decide is as important as what we decide. Everyday life and history are full of lessons that can help us recognize that critical moment. We learn by trying and by example. Deciding too quickly can be hazardous; delaying too long can mean missed opportunities. In the end, it is crucial that we make up our mind. What we need is a systematic and comprehensive approach to decision making.

Decision making is fundamental to furthering our goal of survival and ensuring the quality of our life. To be a person is to be a decision maker. Life is worth little if we are not free to make our own choices. Today feverish activities surround decision making: multicriteria decision societies, psychological decision-making groups, decision aids, and all kinds of software proliferate. Competing theories of decision making contend for attention in the hope of setting the tone for the future. But a useful theory of decision making needs to be in harmony with human needs and human nature. It should not require long years of training to implement with contrived and massaged techniques that only a fanatic could appreciate.

The Analytic Hierarchy Process (AHP), described in several of my earlier works and now widely used in decision making, is a theory that depends on the values and judgments of individuals and groups. The Analytic Network Process (ANP), developed in detail here, is a generalization of the AHP. The current book is a second-generation book on the ANP. The ANP feedback approach replaces hierarchies with networks and was first described in my book *The Analytic Hierarchy Process*, McGraw-Hill, 1980. In both approaches to decision making, judgments are brought together in an organized manner to derive priorities. A team of experts develops a scale to represent the judgments through which the recommended decision comes out as best, or a group of alternatives is prioritized and resources are allocated in proportion to these priorities.

Science is advanced the furthest when we dare to embrace new ideas that may not fit well with preconceived notions. In fact science is advanced the most by creating new techniques to solve old problems. The use of ratio scales is a technique that enables us to look at decision problems in terms of benefits, costs, opportunities, and risks separately and then combine them appropriately into a single ratio scale. Ratio scales are of our essence.

I have often been asked about my interest in ratio scales. I remember the Archimedes lever principle, which my father brought to my attention when I was 12 years old, and a first course in physics that I took soon after in junior high school. I learned that the ratio of the two weights was traded off as a reciprocal of the ratio of the lengths of the rod on the two sides of the fulcrum ($W_1L_1 = W_2L_2$, $W_1/W_2 = L_2/L_1$). To me it was magic that weight could be compensated for by length, and that ratios permit tradeoff. Following that, I was subconsciously driven for 28 years to study physics, mathematics, chemistry, biology, and even theology with obsessive energy in my search for harmonious compensation, or tradeoff principles. Working in the politics of arms-control negotiations, I had a compelling opportunity to be in a real-life situation that required the tradeoff of weapon systems of mass destruction.

Trading off is the human way of doing things. Nature even makes tradeoffs in the human body by setting up hormones that operate on compensation principles. The brain is empowered to supervise equilibrium by ordering or blocking the secretion of one substance or another to orchestrate the workings of the entire body. I believe the brain itself must operate on a relative principle, as it has no stored scales of measurement to determine the absolute amount of each substance needed to maintain balance.

Tradeoffs can be seen everywhere in the context of hierarchies and network synthesis. This book is about ratio scales and their tradeoffs to attain equilibrium. Its purpose is to show how we can use the intrinsic involvement of the mind with ratio scales in a very general way to connect our experiences and discoveries to our goals.

Science and reason improve our understanding of who we are and in what kind of environment we live. But the facts and understanding we obtain through science and reason are fundamentally related to our values and needs and to the judgments which serve our values. Because values and judgments vary among individuals, we need a new science of judgments and values to help us achieve universality and objectivity. Then we will be able to understand, cooperate, survive, and fulfill ourselves. The Analytic Hierarchy (Network) Process – a mathematical theory of value, reason and judgment based on ratio scales – is developed here and applied extensively to bring scientific and rational findings together, with a myriad of intangibles, to help us synthesize our "qualitative" human nature with the concrete part of our experience captured through science.

I believe that, at least in principle, much of our knowledge and behavior can be explained in terms of relative comparisons expressed in the form of ratios. In the end the intangibles that so far we have had no way to measure and quantify can be measured relatively and meaningfully in terms of other things we understand better: the goals, criteria, and subcriteria that form our value system.

The creative mind is driven by imagination and reasoning ability. Imagination is fragmentary and needs purpose and cohesion for unity. In science, imagination always precedes unity. Synthesizing its creations takes time. A longstanding and troubling observation to me has been the fragmentary and evanescent nature of our knowledge. This is due both to the diversity of our experience and to an absence of goal-oriented thought structures in the form of hierarchies, needed to link knowledge from one set of goals to a higher set and ultimately to our survival.

When I began my work on the AHP in the early 1970's, I had a more religious view of the universe and assumed that the AHP would reveal parts of the underlying order. In time I found that order relates only to our subjective values and that it is mostly our own invention. It does not surprise me that people are holding conferences to argue about Flight from Science and Reason. Many hierarchies can be created for the same purpose with variation, depending on who does the structuring. In time I learned that all hierarchies for a subject could be combined into a higher-order interpretation. At the very macro and very micro levels, we have no experience to relate to our goals; we are best at the intermediate levels, where we live. As we travel to the stars and as we fight viruses, we learn to incorporate the large and the small within our system of values. We are creatures of the physical world, whose impersonal, underlying laws are far removed from our values. We use principles of hierarchic order to capture and generalize information so that it can be applied equally to the small and to the large, to the atoms and molecules as well as to the stars and galaxies. Ratio scales give us the power to understand the human world as we have done with physics. One might say that we did not invent ratio scales, but are born with them. Our minds are intrinsically ratio scalars. As a result, we deal with macro and micro phenomena in bulk, statistically, as if they were random, because we have not been able to relate them one by one to a purpose. Ratio scales are what social scientists need in their research to create and analyze data deriving from judgments along with statistical information.

Decision making places emphasis on value and its priority, which enables us to have a say about our own species' future and how to plan for it both functionally and structurally. Perhaps we achieve this partly by learning about our genetics, thereby creating interaction between two major aspects of our nature: our nervous system, with which we learn about ourselves and transmit knowledge to the future, and our ability to perpetuate our kind and make our progeny more capable of dealing with life proactively.

My interest in setting priorities for decision making dates back to my years in the Arms Control and Disarmament Agency (ACDA) in the Department of State in Washington. It is there that I directed research projects with the participation of some of the world's leading economists and game and utility theorists, three of whom have won the Nobel Prize since: Gerard Debreu, the late John Harsanyi, and Reinhard Selten. I also participated as an observer at some of the negotiations with the former Soviet Union in Geneva during the 1960's. Two things stand out in my mind from that experience. The first is that the theories and models of the scientists were often too general and abstract to be adaptable to particular weapon tradeoff needs. It was difficult for those who prepared the U.S. position to include their diverse concerns within this framework and to come up with practical and sharp answers. The second is that the U.S. position was prepared by lawyers who had a great understanding of legal matters, but were no better than the scientists in assessing the value of the weapon systems to be traded off. It was nobody's fault. What was needed was a realistic and a genuine way to derive priorities that reflect the relative benefits, opportunities, costs, and risks in giving up one system or part of a system in return for what the other side was willing to give. I wrote a book on the subject of arms control and was troubled for years by the lack of a systematic approach that could be used by negotiators to deal with such complex decision problems. I then applied myself to solve this problem. The AHP and ANP are the result of nearly a third of a century's work begun in 1967, and still continues.

I first developed the supermatrix approach of the Analytic Network Process in 1975 and on numerous occasions discussed its implications with my colleague at Wharton, James P. Bennett, who is now at Syracuse University. I valued my interaction with this brilliant scholar, whose social science background and sound training in mathematics left him strong and free of the constraints of my particular mathematical upbringing. In developing a usable theory for practical applications, I was also inspired by the following observations made by two great French scholars. The noted mathematician Emile Borel (as cited by Allais, see below) writes:

> Strictly speaking, a purely logical theory could be established without worrying about the possible existence of its application; however, such a theory would be a purely intellectual game devoid of interest and would not merit the name of science.

The Nobel Prize winner in Economics, Maurice Allais, writes (in Hagen and Wenstop, eds., *Progress in Utility and Risk Theory*, Kluwer Academic Publishers, 1984, p. 114):

> One cannot but deplore the invasion of mathematicians, who are more concerned with the development of pure mathematical models than with their relationship to the real world... It is equally saddening that the *establishment* attaches a higher price to the mathematical skills that are brought to bear than to a pertinent analysis of the facts. The *Foundations of the Theory of Probability* of Kolmogorov, the *Theory of Games* of von Neumann-Morgenstern are but two excellent examples of many.

Again on page 65, he says:

> We should be very wary of the belief that the scientific validity of a theory can be secured merely by basing it on a strict axiomatization. However much needed, axiomatization is truly only secondary by comparison with the critical analysis of the axioms it

is based on and the confrontation of their implications with observed data.

Preface to the Second Edition

The first two chapters of the first edition have been slightly modified and errata removed. Chapters 3 has been completely overhauled and is now a more streamlined exposition of the concepts and mathematics of the ANP. Chapter 4 includes elementary examples to illustrate the ideas. Chapter 5 is the longest, perhaps also the most valuable, and contains numerous observations about the ANP and its uses together with several detailed and well worked- out applications to show the reader step by step how to use the process to make complex decisions with dependence and feedback. The remaining chapters of the first edition have been replaced with completely new material.

Chapter 6 demonstrates that there is both a practical and a theoretical connection between probability theory and Bayesian analysis and the ANP and even more, that probability theory can be presented within the framework of the ANP as a particular case. Chapter 7 provides the necessary linkage of the AHP and ANP measurement of tangibles and intangibles to Euclidean geometry, the basis on which linear programming and resource allocation rest. As it is used in decision making, the ANP needs the combinatorics and optimization framework of linear programming to round out its effectiveness in a diversity of applications. Chapter 8 gives a condensed summary of the Analytic Hierarchy Process. We debated long and hard whether or not to include this chapter. We decided that it has useful material some readers may not know about: the Weber-Fechner law and its relation to the Fundamental Scale, clustering, sensitivity of the eigenvector, additive vs. multiplicative synthesis, and group decision making, There are two appendices in the book. The first is on matrix theory and on graph theory, and the second has been retained from the first edition.

Once more, my gratitude goes to my wife Rozann, to my friend Kirti Peniwati for carefully reading the manuscript and assisting with the production of the final version. Dr. Ozden Bayazit also read the manuscript and helped with the drawing of two figure in chapter 5. The new software for the ANP owes its existence to Rozann and to William Adams, the mathematician who programmed the ANP software in the TclTk language which allows it to run on any platform. The software is immensely improved because of the dedicated efforts of many of my graduate students among whom I would especially like to single out the unique and outstanding Marcel Minutolo. I also owe my gratitude to my diligent student Yeonmin Cho for working with me for many months on two applications in Chapter 5 the first of which was sent to several congressmen and senators in Washington before their decision to grant China permanent trading status in the summer of 2000. Finally, my thanks go to Sarah Lombardo, my many years friend and assistant whose sense of perfection to put a book together is unmatched by anyone else I know.

I am like an alchemist trying to apprehend the non-measurable through the measurable. (Salvador Dali, 1935)

Thomas L. Saaty

Chapter 1

Perspective

1-1. INTRODUCTION

There are two known ways to analyze causal influences and their effects. One is by using traditional deductive logic beginning with assumptions and carefully deducing an outcome from them. This is a linear and piecemeal approach in which several separate conclusions may be obtained and the problem is to piece them together in some coherent way. It needs imagination and experience as logic tells us little or nothing about how to bring the different conclusions into an integrated outcome.

The other is a holistic approach in which all the factors and criteria involved are laid out in advance in a hierarchy or in a network system that allows for dependencies. All possible outcomes that can be thought of are joined together in these structures and then both judgment and logic are used to estimate the relative influence from which the overall answer is derived. This approach requires knowledge and experience with the subject, and is not totally dependent on the ability to reason logically which most people cannot do well anyway and which is not guaranteed to discover the truth; the assumptions may be poor, and the reasoning may be faulty. Feelings and intuition play at least as important a role in deciding the outcome as the ability to reason precisely and deduce unerringly. It may be that some matter of low importance that is determined with logical certainty is found to be cumulatively influential because of its indirect relationship with other important factors. This approach generally leads to a sound overall outcome about the real world.

It would seem that multicriteria logic is the way to view problems in a holistic way. It is a useful and compelling approach for dealing with the outcome of influences in a complex setting.

The purpose of this book is to develop in detail the Analytic Network Process (ANP), extending the Analytic Hierarchy Process (AHP) to problems with dependence and feedback. It is a subject which I first detailed and illustrated in 1975 a few years after developing the AHP. For the convenience of those who are not familiar with the AHP, chapter 2 provides an introduction to the AHP. Chapter 3 contains the basic ANP theory. Chapters 4 and 5 show through many examples and applications the kind of computations required in applying the ANP. Chapters 6 relates the ANP to probability and Bayes theory, Chapter 7 deals with resource allocation involving intangibles, and Chapter 8 is a summary of some central ideas of the Analytic Hierarchy Process. Appendix 1 is about matrices and graphs and Appendix 2 is about rank.

Much has been written on the AHP in the form of books, papers, and reports. The ANP will probably be a subject of much greater interest and awaits new research results. This book is only a beginning.

This book is about real-life decision structures. The reader may think that all decision problems are structured as a hierarchy (see Figures 1-1a and   1-1b)

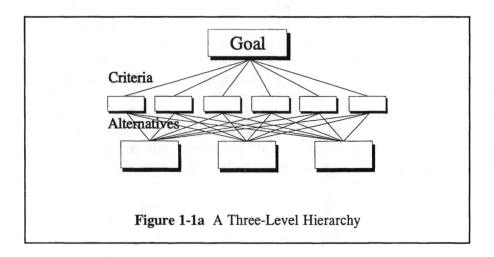

Figure 1-1a A Three-Level Hierarchy

In Figure 1-1a the goal in the first level may be to buy the most suitable car for oneself; some of the criteria in the second level may be cost, style, comfort, and resale value; and the alternatives in the third level may be Chevy Cavalier, Ford Escort, and Honda Civic. The more elaborate Figure 1-1b allows for subcriteria between the criteria and the alternatives, such as methods of financing the car under cost, various possible styles, and several features that offer comfort. Some of the criteria may not have subcriteria. Detailed subcriteria immediately above the alternatives may be specific evaluation factors. However, many decision problems are structured differently and look like the diagrams called **networks** shown in Figure 1-2a and the left side of Figure 1-2b.

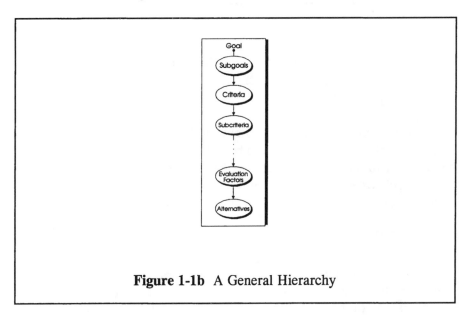

Figure 1-1b A General Hierarchy

In Figure 1-2a each cluster may represent a department in the government or a group in industry or in the population concerned with mitigating the environmental impacts of pollution on animal life. The alternatives may be, for example, to construct a highway near or far from a certain area.

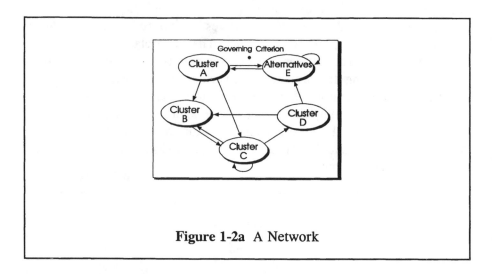

Figure 1-2a A Network

Figure 1-2b shows a control hierarchy with two criteria, Economic and Environmental, which are influenced by either some or all of the clusters. In the figure, environmental influences are described by a network of interactions and feedback, whereas economic influences are hierarchic. The same set of alternative outcomes are governed by both the network and the hierarchy.

INFLUENCE
What is the difference between an influence network and an influence hierarchy and how do we know which structure to use for a decision problem? In general, hierarchies concern the distribution of a property (the goal) among the elements being compared, to judge which one influences or is influenced more or has a greater amount of that property. Networks concern the distribution of the influence of elements on some element with respect to a given property.

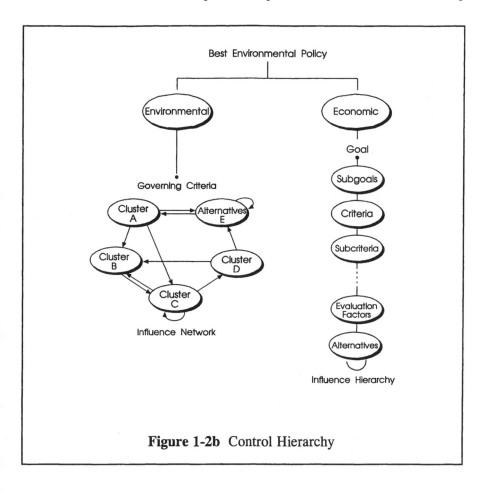

Figure 1-2b Control Hierarchy

An example of an influence network is how the members of the U.S. Congress can influence the president as to what they think he should do about preventing crime or cutting taxes. The question then is: of two members, which one influences the president more and how much more?

The ANP is a theory of measurement generally applied to the *dominance* of *influence* among several stakeholders or alternatives *with respect to an attribute or a criterion,* as just illustrated by the influence of Congress on the President with respect to crime and taxes. The ANP is also applied to evaluate the dominance of criteria with respect to a higher criterion. For example, to improve the economy, should the deficit be decreased, or should trade be increased and in relative terms how strongly? In the setting of a hierarchy, the ANP is applied to evaluate alternatives with respect to a governing criterion or attribute. The governing criterion may be to reduce the budget and the alternatives may be to reduce deficit spending or to cut welfare programs.

DOMINANCE

In general dominance means greater influence with respect to a certain property. To say that one element dominates another is a generic way of saying that it is greater or more important, more preferred, or more likely to occur than another element.

Dominance is a primitive concept used in making comparisons among elements with respect to the possession of an attribute or the fulfillment of conditions as criteria. One asks: Which of two elements has that attribute or meets that criterion more than another element, and how much more? For example we ask: With respect to style, which of two cars is more preferred and hence dominates another car and how strongly does it dominate it? We distinguish between two types of dominance among elements. The first has to do with the possession of a property which we call direct dominance. The second has to do with influencing other elements with respect to a property which we call indirect dominance. For direct dominance we often compare elements in pairs to determine which one has more of a given property and how much more. For indirect dominance we compare elements in pairs to determine the dominance of their influence on a third element with respect to a property. For example: Which of two Congressmen or women influences the President more with respect to health programs and how strongly more than the other does. We shall have more to say about the distribution of influence in Chapter 3.

DIRECT DOMINANCE

Elements, called alternatives, have properties or attributes. They may also satisfy certain standards or conditions called criteria and subcriteria. One question is: Of two alternatives, which is more dominant with respect to a property or with respect to satisfying a criterion? We can also examine one alternative and ask which of two properties possessed by the alternative is dominant with respect to satisfaction or to some standard or goal. For example, is a person a better actor than (s)he is a musician, and how much better? We are all familiar with the situation in which we ask which criterion is more important than the other for attaining a goal. The same concept can be applied in general. With regard to people, for example, we ask which property they exhibit more.

INDIRECT DOMINANCE

Regardless of whether a set of elements possesses a property or not, the elements can influence or make other elements possess that property. For example, the coach of a team can help players become stronger at their sport even though he himself is not strong at it. In making comparisons, we ask which of a pair influences a third element more to possess that property.

To understand the world, we assume that we can describe it, define relations among its parts, and apply judgment to relate the parts according to a goal or purpose that we have in mind. Since the way our minds define and relate the parts is influenced by our experiences and our internal subjective values, there are no absolutely right answers. It cannot be otherwise, because our understanding is in flux and continuously changes. An outcome in real life is the result of the influences and effects of our own actions and those of the environment in which we live. If we plan our actions by considering these influences carefully, we should be able to determine with our thinking minds those outcomes that we can rightfully anticipate.

VALUES

We use values to relate and interpret everything else that we learn and experience. It is the focus of our being. Value is an anchor that binds our energies, our thoughts, and our actions. In a sense, our values are us. It is not something abstract and eternal. Despite some overlap, the values of a tree or those of a bee differ in meaning and substance from our human values. That does not mean that our values are important for the tree; in fact, while the trees and their values are important to us, we and our values are not important to the trees unless we want to destroy them.

Our values help us identify different properties and measure intensities within each property. Our human limitations do not allow an infinitely wide range of intensities. The range of certain measurements in science varies widely over the magnitude of objects and phenomena (from the size of atoms to the size of galaxies). However, the range of human values and feelings is very limited and varies over a few orders of magnitude. For example, our personal values are at their highest in representing our survival and physical needs, to a lesser degree they represent our needs for safety and security, for love and belonging, and for esteem and psychological and social self-realization (in the sense of Abraham Maslow); and at the lower end of the scale they represent our need to know and understand, and finally our aesthetic needs. As members of a group we are concerned about the survival of others, and as part of the environment we are concerned with preserving that environment. There are also group values to which we subscribe that are less instinctive than our personal values and that we learn from experience. Here is a list of some group values to which we subscribe:

Physical:	Health, Exercise, Sports
Educational:	Learning, Communication, Information
Economic:	Money, Property, Manufacturing, Agriculture
Social:	Welfare, Cooperation, Organization
Political:	Power, Influence
Moral:	Order, Honesty, Trust
Ideological:	Religion, Common Belief, Fervor
Technological:	Innovation, Change, Problem Solving
Military:	Security, Force, Defense, Territory
Aesthetic:	Art, Music, Theater
Competition:	Advertising, Quality, Improvement, Reasonable Pricing
Negotiation:	Take and Give
Conflict	
Resolution:	Reconciliation

The science of decision making is concerned with the relation between alternative actions or choices that need to be made and our system of values.

That is why hierarchic and network structures are of essence in this undertaking.

Decision making is a process that leads one to:
• Structure a problem as a hierarchy or as a network with dependence loops.
• Elicit judgments that reflect ideas, feelings, and emotions.
• Represent those judgments with meaningful numbers.
• Synthesize results.
• Analyze sensitivity to changes in judgment.

SCALES AND VALUES

At this point it is useful to define various kinds of scales, and in particular ratio scales. An *ordinal scale* is a set of numbers that is invariant under monotone transformations. Ordinal numbers can neither be multiplied nor added meaningfully. An *interval scale* is a set of numbers that is invariant under linear transformations of the form: $ax+b, a>0, b\neq0$. Different interval scales cannot be multiplied. However, numbers from the same scale can be added. A *ratio scale* is a set of positive numbers that is invariant (that is, their ratio remains the same) under a positive similarity transformation (multiplication by a positive number) of the form: $ax, a>0$. Different ratio scales can be multiplied and divided and still give rise to a ratio scale because the invariance of their products and quotients is derived from the invariance of each one of these scales. Numbers from the same scale can also be added. An *absolute scale* is a set of numbers that is invariant under the identity transformation. Numbers from an absolute scale can both be multiplied and added because the invariance of sums is derivable from the invariance of the scale itself. Note that one cannot multiply numbers from an interval scale because the result is not an interval scale. Thus $(ax_1+b)(ax_2+b) = a^2x^2+ab(x_1+x_2)+b^2$ which does not have the form $ax+b$.

One can take the average of interval scale readings but not their sum. Thus $(ax_1+b)+(ax_2+b) = a(x_1+x_2)+2b$, which does not have the form $ax+b$. However, if we average by dividing by 2 we do get an interval scale value. Similarly, we can multiply interval scale readings by positive numbers whose sum is equal to one and add to get an interval scale result, a weighted average. For a ratio scale, we have $ax_1+ax_2 = a(x_1+x_2) = ax_3$ which belongs to the same ratio scale, and $ax_1bx_2 = abx_1x_2 = cx_1x_2 = cx_3$ which belongs to a new ratio scale. However $ax_1 + bx_2$ does not define a ratio scale and thus we cannot add measurement from different ratio scales.

In the end, whether through learning or through experience, all measurements with instruments that lead to ratio scales are reinterpreted by people in terms of their individual or group values and converted to relative ratio scales so they can be understood and used exactly as needed to serve their goals and values.

RATIO SCALES

Ratio scales enable us to relate alternatives of tangible action to criteria and values that are intangible. These tangibles and intangibles may in turn be related to higher values and goals, which may be related to still higher values and goals and finally to the goal that is the focus of attention for a particular decision. When we have measurements for the alternatives for some tangible criteria, they can be included in relative terms within the structure. For example, in buying a car, the reciprocal of the actual dollar cost of the car can be included because the less costly a car is, the more it is preferred on the criterion of cost. Ratio scales give us power to better understand our values and what derives best from these values.

The human mind, with its limited range of neural firings, miniaturizes experience and creates its own particular framework. Through the use of ratio scales, the mind integrates its assimilation of information to direct the proportionate control of muscular movement and secretion of hormones and enzymes to run the body. Our perceptions need not always be a faithful representation of what reality is. Meaningful thought and imagination must, in turn, be formalized along such proportionality requirements so that they can be arranged and integrated with those subconscious responses that drive our body, to make it stable and better able to cope with its given environment.

The strongest and most general law of nature is not behavior under gravity, but behavior with regard to influence of any kind. The strongest law of human understanding to control an outcome or to change influence is to establish proportionality or ratios among influences and ratios among the responses to these influences. The power of mathematics in the real world is that it helps us establish this proportionality in a precise way and we will always need it for that purpose.

People are in the habit of giving numbers from their head and claiming that these numbers belong to some scale or another. After all, every scale uses numbers and one can claim any scale by selecting a set of numbers. A crucial concern in multicriteria decisions is how to combine the scale generated for one criterion with that for another and still have a meaningful scale. That is not a trivial task because we must be able to tradeoff the measurements from one scale against measurements from another.

By far the best illustration of the idea of tradeoff is given by the Archimedes lever principle mentioned in the preface.

$$w_1 l_1 = w_2 l_2$$

$$\frac{w_1}{w_2} = \frac{l_2}{l_1}$$

The ratio of the weights is equal to the inverse ratio of the corresponding lengths. To raise a larger object, instead of applying more weight on the opposite side, one simply increases the length of the lever on the other side, thus applying a smaller weight and trading off length for weight.

An important aspect of this book is how to deal with the variety of structures encountered in making decisions. Certainly the structure of a decision is as important as the mathematics used to establish priorities for that decision. How to structure a decision and how to apply these structures in real-life problems has been the concern of several of my books. For many decisions a complex hierarchy of more than three levels is the most useful structure. My Ph.D. student Kirti Peniwati showed that the structure and arithmetic operations of decision making should naturally match with our intuitive decision-making processes in such a way that the outcome either represents our expectations well or is sufficiently reliable for us to willingly change our expectations as part of our learning process.

SELECTING A DECISION THEORY

In considering what kind of decision theory to use and when to use it, the reader should examine the two hierarchies in Figures 1-3a and 1-3b. The best test of a decision theory is how well it can be used in prediction. One cannot simply say: I set down the rules, I say how to do the manipulations, I tell you how to establish your decision framework, and you have to take my word for it that you will get the best results. That is arbitrary, short sighted, and worrisome to hide behind subjectivity without justifiable validity.

The AHP is a relatively simple and accessible way to deal with everyday decisions, particularly because of the availability of its user-friendly supporting software *Expert Choice*. The ANP is much broader and deeper than the AHP and can be applied to very sophisticated decisions involving a variety of interactions and dependencies. In general, one would not expect simple everyday decisions to be dealt with as feedback problems that require the ANP. It is mostly the complex corporate or public-sector decisions requiring a large amount of information, interaction, and feedback with a high degree of complexity that would benefit most from this formulation.

For example, the concern may be whether a merger should be made or a subsidiary sold, a new product put on the market, a new activity undertaken, and how best to do it; what kind of legislation is needed and how it should be implemented; where money and other resources should be allocated, and in what amounts. Here the refinements can be handled with greater precision to obtain an answer that is not simply a ranking, as one does in a hierarchy that assumes independence from level to level. It should be possible to include every conceivable concern and every experience and judgment in this approach. The ANP is recommended for cases where the most thorough and systematic analysis of influences needs to be made. The need for simple forms of feedback and dependence will often be encountered when attempting to use a hierarchy to make a decision. It is not a luxury but a core concern to learn about how to deal with dependence in decision making.

How to Decide on the Best Approach to Decision Making

There are nearly half a dozen theories for decision making which give conflicting results with the same data. How do we judge the merits of an approach that is survivable?

Criteria for Judging a Decision Theory

(An Evolutionary Collection)

Theoretical	Applied
•Realistic assumptions in conformity	•Intuitive appeal
•Structural generalizability	•Applicability to both tangible and intangible factors
•Mathematical generalizability	•Simplicity and accessibility to the uninitiated
•Meaningful scale	•No black box effect
•No paradoxes	•Applicability to all areas of decision making without compromise due to limitations of the theory
•Capacity for dealing with dependence	•Capable of both gradual and drastic revision
•Prediction - able to describe the environment of the decision	•Friendly presentation of results
•Accuracy in capturing the decision-maker's preferences	•Facilitates group decision making

Figure 1-3a How to Judge a Decision Theory

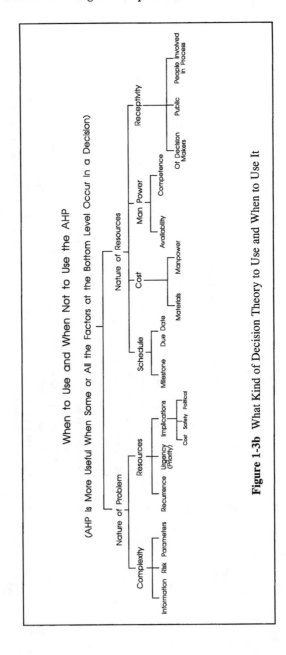

Figure 1-3b What Kind of Decision Theory to Use and When to Use It

Morphological analysis (analysis of form) is the organization of complexity, which is considered one of the four areas of creativity, along with brainstorming, synectics, and lateral thinking. Decision making and morphological analysis have similar concerns: how to structure attributes and criteria in terms of higher goals, how to establish priorities, and how to choose the best alternatives. We will be concerned with these aspects of creative thinking.

1-2. MAKING COMPARISONS IS CRITICAL

There is one and only one way to assign objects meaningful relative magnitudes and that is to compare them in relative terms. By making paired comparisons we can derive a scale of relative measurement among them. To a child a weight of 5 pounds is infinitely heavier to lift than a weight of one pound. Besides, few properties have scales of measurement on which objects can be assigned magnitudes individually. Thus we must deal with all attributes with relative scales of measurement.

Measurement scales tend to be linear and homogenous. But the real world is nonlinear and inhomogeneous. Scales are simply *indicators* of quantity, and it is deceptive to think that there is direct meaning in quantity. We can capture meaning through judgment made precise through numbers and the only way to do this is through comparisons with respect to a common property or goal. Scales of measurement have no intrinsic meaning in themselves.

Speaking of quantity, we know that there are many people in the world who know very little about numbers and about the arithmetic of numbers. Their judgments lead them to make good decisions in their minds with the feelings and understanding that they have. It is not the manipulation of quantity but the synthesis of piecemeal understanding of influences and strengths of influences that leads them to make good decisions. Quality itself is interpreted according to its effects and not according to its precise numerical content or variation on a linear scale. This observation about how the untutored mind works is important. Meaning for people derives from broad and closely connected experiences that are combined into an overall understanding, not from readings on instruments of measurement.

1-3. ON THE FALLIBILITY OF INTUITION ABOUT INFINITE PROCESSES

Were one to ask a person who has not studied the calculus to use his or her intuition to estimate whether the harmonic series

$$1 + \frac{1}{2} + \frac{1}{3} + \frac{1}{4} + \cdots + \frac{1}{n} + \cdots$$

converges to a number or diverges to infinity, the majority would say that because one is adding smaller and smaller numbers, the series must converge to a finite limit. This series may look similar to the geometric series,

$$1 + \frac{1}{2} + \frac{1}{2^2} + \frac{1}{2^3} + \cdots = \sum_{n=0}^{\infty} \frac{1}{2^n} = \frac{1}{1-1/2} = 2$$

whose sum is equal to 2. One might even bet a lot of money that the sum of the first series is not going to be very large. Not even past 10, right? Wrong. The sum becomes infinite. Let us see. The only suspicion of convergence comes from the observation that the partial sums do not increase in total value by very much. We have:

Partial Sums	Sum
1	1.000
$1 + \frac{1}{2}$	1.500
$1 + \frac{1}{2} + \frac{1}{3}$	1.833
$1 + \frac{1}{2} + \frac{1}{3} + \frac{1}{4}$	2.083
$1 + \frac{1}{2} + \frac{1}{3} + \frac{1}{4} + \frac{1}{5}$	2.233
$1 + \frac{1}{2} + \frac{1}{3} + \frac{1}{4} + \frac{1}{5} + \frac{1}{6}$	2.250
$1 + \frac{1}{2} + \frac{1}{3} + \frac{1}{4} + \frac{1}{5} + \frac{1}{6} + \frac{1}{7}$	2.642

$$1 + \frac{1}{2} + \frac{1}{3} + \frac{1}{4} + \frac{1}{5} + \frac{1}{6} + \frac{1}{7} + \frac{1}{8}$$ 2.767

$$1 + \frac{1}{2} + \frac{1}{3} + \frac{1}{4} + \frac{1}{5} + \frac{1}{6} + \frac{1}{7} + \frac{1}{8} + \frac{1}{9}$$ 2.879

$$1 + \frac{1}{2} + \frac{1}{3} + \frac{1}{4} + \frac{1}{5} + \frac{1}{6} + \frac{1}{7} + \frac{1}{8} + \frac{1}{9} + \frac{1}{10}$$ 2.979

It is not credible on intuitive grounds that a series whose partial sums increase so slowly would diverge. Yet it is easy to show that the harmonic series does not converge but diverges. If the terms are grouped as follows:

$$1 + \frac{1}{2} + (\frac{1}{3} + \frac{1}{4}) + (\frac{1}{5} + \frac{1}{6} + \frac{1}{7} + \frac{1}{8}) + (\frac{1}{9} + \cdots + \frac{1}{16}) + (\frac{1}{17} + \cdots + \frac{1}{32}) + \cdots$$

with twice as many terms in a group as in the previous one, the sum of terms in each collection past the second term is greater than one-half. Take the last member of the fourth term, for example, which is 1/8, and note that if we replace each of the other numbers before it with 1/8, we are replacing them by smaller values, and the result is more than 1/2. We can take enough such collections to make the sum arbitrarily large. The Norwegian mathematician Abel wrote in 1828: "Divergent series are the invention of the devil, and it is shameful to base on them any demonstration whatsoever." But this devil makes us think and in the end contributes to the good things we produce.

Assume now that one is examining with logic a sequence of events that influence each other sequentially to a smaller and smaller degree as in the above series. The guess of any person, particularly a learned philosopher, would be that the influence would eventually decline and a certain pet outcome would be targeted and logically shown to be the inexorable result. Clearly that outcome could be estimated erroneously, particularly if the influences estimated numerically exceed term by term the harmonic series. We claim that many real-life situations are of this kind. Their outcomes cannot be correctly identified with linear logical thinking. That is why we do not cope well with political and social influences. They require a process that repeats, or iterates, to obtain the limit. The limit is found to exist often with appropriate organization and estimation of the influences. We need this kind of organized thinking in our real-life problems to arrive at the right outcome. That is the basic concern of the ANP and its specialization to hierarchies, the AHP, to which we turn our attention in Chapter 2.

Prior to continuing our journey into the technical aspects of the subject, I believe that the reader will appreciate the importance of the subject more by reading the following section.

1-4. THE BIG PICTURE

In decision making in particular and life in general, one cannot rely on any one thing exclusively.   All things–judgment, experience, reasoning, logic, intuition–are fallible at times.   It is therefore necessary to make use of a structure within which one can sort through, and give relative weights to relationships, values, and the strength and direction of those relationships. Basically, all that we see, think, and perceive is relative and contextual and is, therefore, subject to error in interpretation at any given time.

We use logic in science to reason in linear chains of ideas, to prove theorems in mathematics, and more generally to study causal relations. We also use logic to structure hierarchies and networks, and use these to extend our understanding to relate nature to our value systems. Science is the study of logical relations and causal connections in collections or structures of homogeneous entities. By homogeneous entities we mean a cluster of nearly similar or close correspondence on related properties with respect to even higher level properties. The relationships are defined through our current understanding. In science, we have assumed so far that the entire universe can be described by a single level of homogeneous clusters connected by common pivots. These pivots enable one to easily extend measurement from one to the next, thus making it possible to measure relationships among them. The outcome of this kind of thinking is the scientific formulas we develop which we assume to be universally true. In reality, our formulas are only true within limited ranges and as yet we have no way to test their validity in the wide ranges to which we believe they apply. These formulas are likely to be good approximations for a range of contiguous closely connected homogeneous structures with fuzzy boundaries. We call these structures patches of understanding and we apply our formulas to these patches whether at the very micro or the very macro levels. In the AHP, we have the belief that the universe is stratified into a continuum of homogeneous structures, but that these structures are related among themselves in a manner similar to the relations which occur within each homogeneous structure.

Science is a human interpretation of what we perceive reality to be in terms of our own vision and experience. It is not possible to define the purpose and meaning of reality outside such a framework. Any tests we conduct use some means or instruments improvised by us to appeal to our senses and minds in ways that extend our own imagination from our very own perceptions derived from our will and understanding of survival. Figure 1-4 gives us a wide view of the world and where the symbolism and thinking we use to understand it fall in this scheme of things. Our brain and creative mind, themselves part of nature, are the seat from which a sense of purpose emerges with the hope that there is a meaningful underlying reality. That sense of reality shapes our attitude in art, science and humor to investigate the world and ourselves with the appropriate tools for understanding. We search for that understanding and it shapes our orientation for further search, a never-ending cycle.

It is only with imagination that we attempt to relate inhomogeneous patches of structure with the help of logic. We tend to assume that the same kind of logic that we apply to construct single patches with deductive logic also applies across the patches. But such chain-like linear thinking has gaps in it because the very small (quantum theory) cannot be linked with meaningful measurement to the very large (astrophysics). We need a holistic approach. For that purpose, we need hierarchies and networks and ratio-scale thinking to study influences in which our own goals and purposes are involved in the analysis of relations between inhomogeneous clusters, thus connecting the very small to the very large according to the purpose we envision they have.

We can use chain-like logical thinking to explain activities in homogenous structures, and for the more general activities between inhomogeneous structures we can use hierarchies and networks. This process is inherent in nature's design of our neural brain. Our perception of reality is better represented through hierarchies and networks which enable us to more accurately understand, control, and predict happenings in the world around us. The thoughts and insights we obtain from our neural network give rise to the kind of thinking we do, which is characteristic of our kind of biology and has no necessary intrinsic relationship to some underlying truth but rather to how we can survive better. We are a form of existence with consciousness, a scheme of evolution from plant life to lower and higher forms of animal life. All life forms have apparently kaleidoscopic ways to sense and fit themselves in a very large and complex world and to successfully control their environment to satisfy their own perceptions of what they must do to survive. It is plausible that the physical world is very different from what human science tells us it is for many reasons, not the least of which is that we do not have all the necessary senses to capture all conceivable phenomena. For example, the way we survive is fundamentally different from that of plants. It is also true that we are "hard-wired" and may not have the connections in our brains that bring sensations and abstractions of sensations in all the important ways needed to distill significant truth from reality. The result is that we have only a limited capacity to grasp and to interpret. The Buddhist religion extends far beyond the thinking of science, identifying five major attributes of existence: form, feeling, memory, thinking and spirit. The processes that determine plant biology and survival (presumably form and spirit) have been effective in making plants proliferate to fill the earth. This form of existence, as a way of coping with the reality of the environment, has done well for plants. It is a process of integration of physical creation with sensory or perceptive creation for surviving in an environment. Success in knowing what it takes to survive leads to success in proliferating physically even if the latter is a random process of evolution "seeking" to capture the more survivable essence of our nature. Our ability to track reality in very broad and comprehensive terms thereby facilitates the conditions and circumstances of our survival. Our physical and mental needs will probably lead to proliferation similar to that of plants where we might eventually fill the universe with our kind just as the plants have filled the earth with theirs. The purpose of that may be to introduce our kind of organization and order into the scheme of things; like taming the universe to support and serve our collective nature.

Five Part Environment

	The Biosphere	The Self (Mind & Body)	People (Socioeconomic) (Physical Minds and Bodies)
1. Physical Universe (Matter, Energy, Information)	←	←	←
2. Science, Engineering, Exploration, Procreation, Sports (From Thought and Observation to Total Participation)	Biology, Environmental Science	Psychology, Human Anatomy, Medicine	Social Science, Behavioral Science, Business, Politics
3. Artistic Expression Art, Music, Painting, Sculpture, Dance, Poetry, Prose	Scientific Expression Language, Philosophy, Logic, Mathematics, Hierarchies and Networks ←		Humor
4.	Search for Purpose Unity, Order Religion ←		
5.	The Mind (Neuroscience) Mind, Thought, Feeling, Emotion, Interpretation Stability, Chaos ←		

Figure 1-4 The Mind with a Purpose uses Expression as Appropriate to Understand the World

Chapter 2

Decision Making: Hierarchies

2-1. THE ANALYTIC HIERARCHY PROCESS

The Analytic Hierarchy Process is a general theory of measurement. It is used to derive ratio scales from both discrete and continuous paired comparisons in multilevel hierarchic structures. These comparisons may be taken from actual measurements or from a fundamental scale that reflects the relative strength of preferences and feelings. The AHP has a special concern with departure from consistency and the measurement of this departure, and with dependence within and between the groups of elements of its structure. It has found its widest applications in multicriteria decision making, in planning and resource allocation,[1] and in conflict resolution.[2,3] It has also been applied to a variety of prediction problems.[4] In its general form, the AHP is a nonlinear framework for carrying out both deductive and inductive thinking without use of the syllogism by taking several factors into consideration simultaneously and allowing for dependence and for feedback, and making numerical tradeoffs to arrive at a synthesis or conclusion.

Many decision problems involve both physical and psychological attributes. By physical, we mean the realm of what is fashionably known as the tangibles, insofar as they constitute some kind of objective reality outside the individual conducting the measurement. In contrast, the psychological is the realm of the intangibles, comprising the subjective ideas, feelings, and beliefs of the individual and of society as a whole. The question is whether there is a coherent theory that can deal with both these worlds of reality without compromising either. The AHP is a method that can be used to establish measures in both the physical and the social domains.

In using the AHP to model a problem, one needs a hierarchic or a network structure to represent that problem, as well as pairwise comparisons to establish relations within the structure. In the discrete case these comparisons lead to dominance matrices, and in the continuous case to kernels of Fredholm Operators,[5] from which ratio scales are derived in the form of principal eigenvectors, or eigenfunctions, as the case may be. These matrices, or kernels, are positive and reciprocal, e.g., $a_{ij} = 1/a_{ji}$. In particular, special effort has been made to characterize these matrices.[2,6] Because of the need for a variety of judgments, considerable work has also been done to deal with the process of synthesizing group judgments.[7]

2-2. ABSOLUTE AND RELATIVE MEASUREMENT AND STRUCTURAL INFORMATION

Cognitive psychologists have recognized for some time that there are two kinds of comparisons, absolute and relative. In absolute comparisons, alternatives are compared with a standard in one's memory that has been developed through experience; in relative comparisons, alternatives are compared in pairs according to a common attribute. The AHP has been used with both types of comparisons to derive ratio scales of measurement. We call such scales absolute and relative measurement scales. Relative measurement w_i, $i = 1, ..., n$, of each of n elements is a ratio scale derived by comparing the elements in pairs with the others. In paired comparisons two elements i and j are compared with respect to a property they have in common. The smaller, i, is used as the unit and the larger, j, is estimated as a multiple of that unit in the form $(w_i/w_j)/1$, where an estimate of the ratio w_i/w_j is taken from a fundamental scale of absolute values.

Absolute measurement (sometimes called scoring or rating) is applied to rank the alternatives in terms of the criteria or else in terms of ratings (or intensities) of the criteria; for example: excellent, very good, good, average, below average, poor, and very poor; or A, B, C, D, E, F, and G. After priorities are set for the criteria (or subcriteria, if there are any), pairwise comparisons are also made between the ratings themselves to set priorities for them under each criterion, and each of their priorities is divided by the largest alternative. The scores thus obtained for the alternatives can, in the end, be normalized by dividing each one by their sum.

Absolute measurement has been used, for example, to rank cities in the United States according to nine criteria as judged by six different people. Another appropriate use for absolute measurement is to select students for school admission.[8] Most schools set their criteria independently of the performance of the current crop of students seeking admission. Their priorities are then used to determine whether a given student meets the standard set of qualifications. In that case, absolute measurement should be used to determine which students qualify for admission.

The AHP includes four axioms. Informally they are concerned with reciprocal relation, comparison of homogeneous elements, hierarchic and systems dependence, and expectations about the validity of the rank and value of the outcome and their dependence on the structure and its extension.

An important question in decision making is whether adding new alternatives to a decision structure should or should not affect the rank of the old ones. It was once thought that irrelevant alternatives should not affect their rank. But experiments reported in the literature have shown that rank reversal can occur for many different reasons. The decision to preserve rank depends on whether the number of alternatives added, and how good they are, influences preference among the old ones. The AHP has a procedure to preserve rank, as in buying a best computer even if there are many like it, and another to allow rank to change, as in buying a beautiful tie if there are many like it.[7]

2-3. THE FUNDAMENTAL SCALE

Paired comparison judgments in the AHP are applied to pairs of homogeneous elements. When the elements are inhomogeneous, they are separated into clusters of homogeneous elements with a common element shared by two

Table 2-1 The Fundamental Scale

Intensity of Importance	Definition	Explanation
1	Equal Importance	Two activities contribute equally to the objective
2	Weak	-----between Equal and Moderate
3	Moderate importance	Experience and judgment slightly favor one activity over another
4	Moderate plus	-----between Moderate and Strong
5	Strong importance	Experience and judgment strongly favor one activity over another
6	Strong plus	-----between Strong and V. Strong
7	Very Strong or demonstrated importance	An activity is favored very strongly over another; its dominance demonstrated in practice
8	Very, very strong	-----between V. Strong and Extreme
9	Extreme importance	The evidence favoring one activity over another is of the highest possible order of affirmation
Reciprocals of above	If activity *i* has one of the above nonzero numbers assigned to it when compared with activity *j*, then *j* has the reciprocal value when compared with *i*	If x is 5 times y, i.e., x = 5y, then y = x/5 or y = 1/5x
Rationals	Ratios arising from the scale	If consistency were to be forced by obtaining *n* numerical values to span the matrix

consecutive clusters.[7]   The fundamental scale of absolute values for representing the strength of judgments is shown in Table 2-1.

NOTE: In the AHP/ANP instead of using pairwise comparison judgments to form the comparison matrix, we can use measurements from a ratio scale – if one exists for the property being measured. In that case one's judgment would be replaced by measuring each of the two items being compared using ratio scale and forming the ratio of the two measurements. The derived scale (the eigenvector) from a pairwise comparison matrix composed in this way from actual measurements would be the same as one would obtain by normalizing the direct measurements of the items to one.

This scale was derived from the basic mathematics of neural firing that leads to the well-known logarithmic law of stimulus response(see Chapter 8). In addition the scale has been validated for effectiveness in many applications and also compared with other scales by applying it in real life situations where measurements are already known. *The numbers are used to represent how many times the larger of two elements dominates the smaller one with respect to a property or criterion they have in common.* The smaller element has the reciprocal or inverse value with respect to the larger one. Thus if x is the number of times the larger element dominates the smaller one, then the smaller is x^{-1} times the larger, so that $x^{-1}x = xx^{-1} = 1$. Hence, the fundamental operation of inversion originates in our ability to make paired comparisons. The process of inversion to solve equations in mathematics is a generalized reciprocal relation and a basic relation in problem solving.

In many situations elements are close or tied in measurement and the comparison must be made not to determine how many times one is larger than the other, but to determine how close the larger one is to the smaller. In other words there are comparisons to be made between 1 and 2, and what we want is to estimate verbally the values such as 1.1, 1.2, ..., 1.9. Making the comparisons by directly estimating the numbers is no problem. Our proposal is to continue the verbal scale to make these distinctions so that 1.1 is a "tad" more, 1.3 indicates moderately more, 1.5 strongly more, 1.7 very strongly more, and 1.9 extremely more than one. This type of refinement can be used in any of the intervals from 1 to 9 and for further refinements if one needs them; for example, between 1.1 and 1.2 and so on. For better accuracy, elements so close with respect to a criterion can be directly compared with other more different elements from which their own relative weights are obtained. A theorem assures us that small errors in judgment lead to small errors in the derived (ratio) scale.

2-4. WHAT QUESTION TO ASK AND HOW TO ASK IT WHEN MAKING COMPARISONS

The paired comparison matrix attempts to capture the relative dominance of one element over another with respect to an attribute that they have in common. In fact the real world, to the observing mind, is a set of stimuli that give rise to neural firing. The best knowledge of neural science today holds that neural firing is distinguishable in terms of frequency and amplitude. The entire human experience is mapped into these types of signals. It is not surprising then that, at higher levels, brain signals become interchangeable or "tradeoffable" in terms of goals like the Archimedean lever example given in the preface. The concrete objects of the real world as well as the strategic concepts of the mind can be decomposed in terms of common attributes, and these, in turn, in terms of finer attributes, and so on. In a sense then, all properties can be reduced to very simple attributes associated with the firing of a single neuron in terms of amplitude and frequency. In particular two apples can be compared with respect to redness as a common property. However, redness itself may be compared with respect to the intensity it stimulates in the brain. In addition redness and greenness may be compared according to the relative intensity they each stimulate in a single neuron or in separate neurons as judged by neurons that do such distinctions at higher levels. There is no prior reason why this process needs to be stopped because someone is unable to accept that such things do take place in the nervous system.

Take an individual with his or her variety of attributes and ask: Is this individual more experienced as a teacher or as a brick layer and how much better is this individual in doing one activity than the other? It is clear that the mind of the judge has to be trained at recognizing a good teacher or a good bricklayer from a poor teacher or a poor bricklayer. It is the range of experience that enables one to make such fine distinctions, which one must do because an individual may actually be striving to be many things and has achieved different levels of virtuosity in each. Once the major principle of capturing the dominance of any two attributes with respect to a common source is understood, one then needs to exercise care in answering the question of dominance. Given an apple that is mostly red but a little green in one patch, it is clear that this apple is more red than green, and one is seeking a comparison of the total redness to the total greenness in that apple. The diverse examples given in the book show that this can be done. The validity of the results are clearly demonstrated in the predictions that have been made in the area of economics, in sports and other types of competition, and in social and political situations whose outcomes became known later. To the brain, tangibles and intangibles produce similar responses because both cause neurons to fire, thereby enabling us to make distinctions in quality and intensity among them, whether we have measurements for them or not. Both knowledge and experience are matters of social and psychological interpretation.

I shall illustrate these ideas with simple examples and follow them with brief theoretical explanations.

RELATIVE MEASUREMENT: CHOOSING THE BEST HOUSE

A family of average income wanted to buy a house and identified eight factors, or criteria, that were important for them to select a best house. These factors fall into three categories: economic, geographic, and physical. Although one might begin by examining the relative importance of these three clusters, the family feels they want to prioritize the relative importance of all eight factors. The problem is to decide which of three candidate houses to choose. In applying the AHP, the first step is *decomposition*, or the structuring of the problem into a hierarchy (see Figure 2-1). On the first (or top) level is the overall goal of *Satisfaction with House*. On the second level are the eight factors or criteria that contribute to the goal, and on the third (or bottom) level are the three candidate houses to evaluate in terms of the criteria on the second level. The definitions of the factors and the pictorial representation of the hierarchy follow.

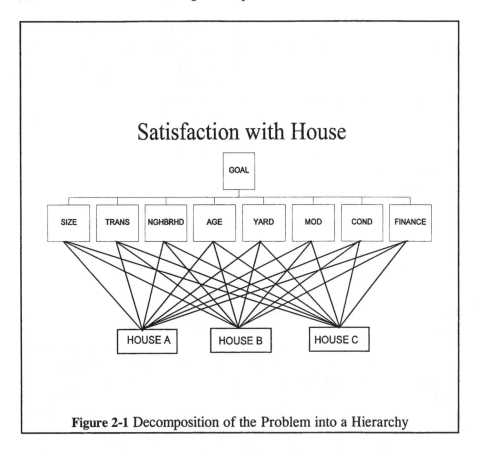

Figure 2-1 Decomposition of the Problem into a Hierarchy

The factors important to the individual family are:

1. *SIZE* - Size of House: storage space, size of rooms, number of rooms, total area of house.
2. *TRANS* - Transportation: convenience and proximity of bus service.
3. *NGHBRHD* - Neighborhood: degree of traffic, security, view, taxes, physical condition of surrounding buildings.
4. *AGE* - Age of House: how old house is.
5. *YARD* - Yard Space: front, back, and side space, and space shared with neighbors.

6. *MOD* - Modern Facilities: dishwashers, garbage disposals, air conditioning, alarm system, and so on.
7. *COND* - General Condition: extent to which repairs are needed; condition of walls, carpet, drapes, wiring; cleanliness.
8. *FINANCE* - Financing: availability of assumable mortgage, seller financing, or bank financing.

The next step is *comparative judgment*. Arrange the elements on the second level into a matrix and elicit from the people buying the house judgments about the relative importance of the elements with respect to the overall goal, *Satisfaction with House.*

The questions to ask when comparing two criteria are of the following kind: Of the two criteria or factors being compared, which is considered more important by the family buying the house, and how much more important is it with respect to satisfaction with the house?

The matrix of pairwise comparisons of the factors given by the home buyers in this case is shown in Table 2-2, along with the resulting vector of priorities. The judgments are entered using the Fundamental Scale, first verbally as indicated in the scale and then by associating the corresponding number. The priorities derived from the judgments are measured on a ratio scale and give the relative importance of the factors (on a ratio scale.) In this case financing has the highest priority, with 33% of the influence. Later, in Section 2-9, we will discuss how to derive these priorities and also refer to the items λ_{max}, C.I., and C.R. which appear in Table 2-2.

In Table 2-2, we indicate the dominance of the factor on the left over the factor on top using judgments from the Fundamental Scale in Table 2-1. If the factor on the left is not dominant, the reciprocal value is used. For example, the entry of 5 in the first row and second column corresponds to the judgment that with respect to satisfaction, the size of the house is strongly more important than convenience of transportation. The reciprocal 1/5 is automatically entered in the second-row, first-column position.

Table 2-2 Pairwise Comparison Matrix for Level 1 with respect to the Goal (Entries show Dominance of Factor on Left over Factor on Top)

Factor	Size	Trans	Nghbrhd	Age	Yard	Mod	Cond	Finance	Priority Vector
Size	1	5	3	7	6	6	1/3	1/4	.175
Trans	1/5	1	1/3	5	3	3	1/5	1/7	.062
Nghbrhd	1/3	3	1	6	3	4	1/2	1/5	.103
Age	1/7	1/5	1/6	1	1/3	1/4	1/7	1/8	.019
Yard	1/6	1/3	1/3	3	1	1/2	1/5	1/6	.034
Mod	1/6	1/3	1/4	4	2	1	1/5	1/6	.041
Cond	3	5	2	7	5	5	1	1/2	.221
Finance	4	7	5	8	6	6	2	1	.348

λ_{max} = 8.811   C.R. = .083

We now move to the pairwise comparisons of the houses on the bottom level, comparing them pairwise with respect to how much better one is than the other in satisfying each criterion on the second level. Thus there are eight 3 × 3 matrices of judgments since there are eight elements on level two, and three houses to be pairwise compared for each element. The matrices in Table 2-3 contain the judgments of the family involved. For a better understanding of the judgments, a brief description of the houses follows:

House A: This house is the largest of them all. It is located in a good neighborhood with little traffic and low taxes. Its yard space is comparably larger than that of houses B and C. However, its general condition is not very good, and it needs cleaning and painting. Also, the financing is unsatisfactory because the mortgage would have to be financed through a bank at a high rate of interest.

House B: This house is a little smaller than house A and is not close to a bus route. The neighborhood gives one the feeling of insecurity because of traffic conditions. The yard space is fairly small, and the house lacks basic modern facilities. On the other hand, its general condition is very good. Also an assumable mortgage is obtainable, which means the financing is good with a rather low interest rate. There are several copies of house B in the neighborhood.

Table 2-3 Pairwise Comparison Matrices for Alternatives

Size of House	A	B	C	Normalized Priorities	Idealized Priorities
A	1	5	9	.743	1.000
B	1/5	1	4	.194	0.261
C	1/9	1/4	1	.063	0.085
				C.R. = .07	

Transportation	A	B	C	Normalized Priorities	Idealized Priorities
A	1	4	1/5	.194	0.261
B	1/4	1	1/9	.063	0.085
C	5	9	1	.743	1.000
				C.R. = .07	

Neighborhood	A	B	C	Normalized Priorities	Idealized Priorities
A	1	9	4	.717	1.000
B	1/9	1	1/4	.066	0.092
C	1/4	4	1	.217	0.303
				C.R. = .04	

Age of House	A	B	C	Normalized Priorities	Idealized Priorities
A	1	1	1	.333	1.000
B	1	1	1	.333	1.000
C	1	1	1	.333	1.000
				C.R. = .00	

Yard Space	A	B	C	Normalized Priorities	Idealized Priorities
A	1	6	4	.691	1.000
B	1/6	1	1/3	.091	0.132
C	1/4	3	1	.218	0.315
				C.R. = .05	

Modern Facilities	A	B	C	Normalized Priorities	Idealized Priorities
A	1	9	6	.770	1.000
B	1/9	1	1/3	.068	0.088
C	1/6	3	1	.162	0.210
				C.R. = .05	

General Condition	A	B	C	Normalized Priorities	Idealized Priorities
A	1	1/2	1/2	.200	0.500
B	2	1	1	.400	1.000
C	2	1	1	.400	1.000
				C.R. = .00	

Financing	A	B	C	Normalized Priorities	Idealized Priorities
A	1	1/7	1/5	.072	0.111
B	7	1	3	.650	1.000
C	5	1/3	1	.278	0.430
				C.R. = .06	

House C: House C is very small and has few modern facilities. The neighborhood has high taxes but is in good condition and seems secure. The yard space is bigger than that of house B but is not comparable to house A's spacious surroundings. The general condition of the house is good, and it has a pretty carpet and drapes. The financing is better than for A but not better than for B.

Table 2-3 gives the matrices of the houses, the alternatives in this decision, and their local priorities with respect to the elements on level two.

The next step is to synthesize the priorities. In order to establish the composite or global priorities of the houses, we lay out in a matrix (Table 2-4) the local priorities of the houses with respect to each criterion. We multiply each column of vectors by the priority of the corresponding criterion and add across each row, which results in the composite or global priority vector of the houses.

Table 2-4 Distributive and Ideal Synthesis

Criteria Weights	Size (.175)	Trans. (.062)	Nghbd (.103)	Age (.019)	Yard (.034)	Modrn (.041)	Cond (.221)	Finance (.345)	Overall
				(Distributive Mode)					
A	.743	.194	.717	.333	.691	.770	.200	.072	.346
B	.194	.063	.066	.333	.091	.068	.400	.649	.369
C	.063	.743	.217	.333	.218	.162	.400	.279	.285
				(Ideal Mode)					
A	1.000	.261	1.000	1.000	1.000	1.000	.500	.111	.315
B	.261	.085	.092	1.000	.132	.088	1.000	1.000	.383
C	.085	1.000	.303	1.000	.315	.210	1.000	.430	.302

In Table 2-4 in the distributive mode House B is preferred (.369); there the number and quality of the other houses is allowed to influence the decision. This mode, also known as the dominance mode, is used when one is concerned with the extent to which each alternative dominates all other alternatives. If, on the other hand, we select the best house on its performance with respect to a benchmark ideal without regard to the number and quality of the other houses (ideal or performance mode), then house B (.383) is also preferred. Here each column is obtained by dividing the column above it by the largest value in that column. Sometimes a dummy alternative that ranks best on every criterion is used for the benchmark. In statistical trials with 10 criteria and 3 alternatives, the two modes gave the same best choice 92% of the time.[7]

ABSOLUTE MEASUREMENT: EVALUATING EMPLOYEES FOR RAISES

The AHP is both a descriptive theory and a normative theory of measurement. In its pairwise comparisons, it is descriptive. However, it is normative by requiring expert judgment to create intensity scales for rating alternatives one at a time. The latter approach is known as absolute measurement. Here is how it works:

Employees are evaluated for raises. The criteria are Dependability, Education, Experience, and Quality. Each criterion is subdivided into intensities, standards, or subcriteria as shown in Figure 2-2. Priorities are set for the criteria by comparing them in pairs, and these priorities are then given in a matrix. These derived priorities appear with the criteria to which they correspond. In this example, dependability received the highest priority, .4347. The intensities are then pairwise compared according to priority with respect to their parent criterion (as in Table 2-5), and their priorities are divided by the largest intensity for each criterion (second set of columns of priorities in Figure 2-2). Finally, each individual is rated in Table 2-6 by assigning the intensity rating that applies to him or her under each criterion. The scores of these subcriteria are weighted by the priority of their criterion and summed to derive a total ratio scale score for the individual. This approach can be used whenever one can set priorities for intensities of criteria, which is usually possible when sufficient experience with a given operation has been accumulated. Salary raises can be made proportionately to the final priorities. The criteria do not need to have the same number of intensities as they do here.

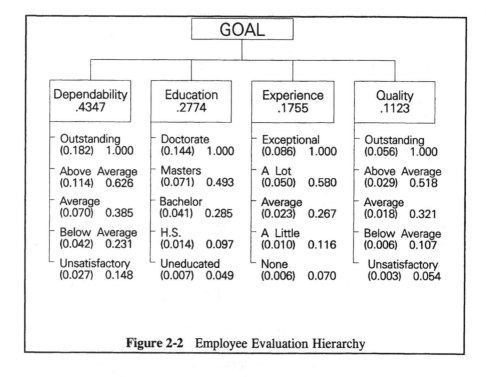

Figure 2-2 Employee Evaluation Hierarchy

Table 2-5 Illustration of Paired Comparisons of Intensities under Dependability

DEPENDABILITY	Outstanding	Above Average	Average	Below Average	Unsatisfactory	Priorities
Outstanding	1.0	2.0	3.0	4.0	5.0	0.419
Above Average	1/2	1.0	2.0	3.0	4.0	0.263
Average	1/3	1/2	1.0	2.0	3.0	0.630
Below Average	1/4	1/3	1/2	1.0	2.0	0.097
Unsatisfactory	1/5	1/4	1/3	1/2	1.0	0.062
Inconsistency Ratio = 0.015						

Table 2-6 Rating Alternatives using Intensities

	Dependability .4347	Education .2774	Experience .1755	Quality .1123	Total
1. Adams, V	Outstanding	Bachelor	A Little	Outstanding	0.646
2. Becker, L	Average	Bachelor	A Little	Outstanding	0.379
3. Hayat, F	Average	Masters	A Lot	Below Average	0.418
4. Kesselman, S	Above Average	H.S.	None	Above Average	0.369
5. O'Shea, K	Average	Doctorate	A Lot	Above Average	0.605
6. Peters, T	Average	Doctorate	A Lot	Average	0.583
7. Tobias, K	Above Average	Bachelor	Average	Above Average	0.456

THE ROLE OF AN IDEAL ELEMENT

If a set of alternatives is mutually exclusive and exhaustive, then one can use relative measurement to determine which is the best among them, and it would be the best possible alternative. However, if the alternatives are not exhaustive and there may be others that are better or worse, then one may think that absolute measurement is the only way to deal with the situation, but that is not so. One needs to identify the best possible alternative which may or may not yet be in the set, known as the ideal, and use it as a benchmark to compare each of the other alternatives with it. This would yield a rank order of these alternatives that is not affected even if one introduces others later or deletes some of the existing ones. The ideal can conceivably be more than an order of magnitude better than what we have. If it is, then we need other alternatives to link with the existing set by comparing them one at a time in decreasing order until we obtain the appropriate linkage.

In reality a benchmark alternative may be best on one criterion, but not on another and the problem remains how to combine the different rankings on the benchmarks. And we are back to the need for a fictitious or composite benchmark. In absolute measurement if one does not have an alternative that is best on every criterion, then a fictitious ideal is created that is best on every criterion. This is done by dividing the priorities of all the alternatives by the ideal's priority for each criterion. Thus the ideal gets the value 1 on each criterion and the other alternatives get proportionate values.

Absolute measurement brought to the ideal setup <u>always</u> preserves rank, but that is not necessarily a law we should take for granted. Let us see.

2-5. RATIO SCALES REVISITED

By now the reader has seen how we *derive* a ratio scale from a numerical dominance (as distinct from profile, proximity, or conjoint) paired comparison matrix. Actually, it does not matter what numbers we use, we always get a ratio scale as the principal eigenvector. But how valid is such a scale as far as giving a careful rather than an arbitrary representation of reality? Some derived ratio scales are not worth while. So far as the validity of measurements with ratio scales, there are four kinds of derived ratio scales:

1) An *absolute ratio scale* whose paired comparisons are based on an absolute fundamental scale as in the AHP. The ratio scale contains information about the relative magnitudes of the elements measured. The most valid ratio scale is derived from a consistent set of absolute fundamental scale values used to make paired comparisons.

2) A *ratio ratio scale* whose paired comparisons are based on a ratio fundamental scale. Here one simply gets the original ratio scale back. The scale is as valid as the fundamental ratio scale used. We find an example of the use of ratio scales in physics in the measurment of length, mass and time. If we use such measurements to derive a scale, we get them back.

3) An *ordinal ratio scale* whose comparisons are based on numbers from fundamental scale intended to express relative dominance with attention to monotonicity but not absolute or ratio magnitudes. Such a derived ratio scale could represent order relations but has little or no ratio scale validity as far as the actual ratio scale of magnitudes between elements is concerned. It cannot be legitimately used for multicriteria purposes. Example: Replacing the fundamental scale by a set of powers of a certain number.

4) A *chaotic ratio scale* is a ratio scale derived from an arbitrary set of numerical paired comparisons without regard to dominance. Example: using random numbers to represent judgments violating reciprocity.

2-6. OBSERVATIONS ON ADDITIVE VERSUS MULTIPLICATIVE COMPOSITION IN THE AHP

There are serious problems with raising priorities to the powers of the priorities of their criteria and then multiplying them to obtain the overall weights of the alternatives. To see this consider two criteria whose measurements are given in dollars as costs. The overall cost of an alternative is obtained by adding its dollar value for each criterion. We can then normalize the result for all the alternatives. To obtain this result after normalizing the two columns of alternatives for both criteria, we must first assign each criterion the ratio of the sum of the dollars under it to the total dollars for both criteria. This yields priorities for both criteria which we use to weight the normalized vectors and add to get the normalized dollar vector obtained before. We would obtain the wrong result if we multiply the alternatives' priorities to the power of the corresponding criterion priority and multiply.

We need to keep the following in mind:

1) Homogeneity and clustering are essential for making comparisons to transit gradually from the small to the large to integrate the measurements of our perceptions. When we compare one thing with another we find it easy and natural to estimate how many times the larger has a property more than the smaller used as the unit. From such comparisons we derive ratio scales of relative magnitudes. We would find it difficult to assign a meaning to saying what power of the smaller we need to assign the larger. We have no advance knowledge of these relative magnitudes for many things being compared.

2) Unlike measurements in astronomy and in quantum physics, the human range of values is limited with a few orders of magnitude.

3) While formulas are used in science to cover ranges from zero to infinity, one cannot do that directly with perception. Absolute measurement of physics will not coincide with our perception of the meaning of those measurements. In addition, we cannot yet measure the very large or the very small with sufficient accuracy to know how well our formulas work there.

4) T. G. Fechner proposed that a psychophysical law expressed as a logarithmic relationship applies between real world measurement from zero to infinity assuming that the intensity of our perception also extends from zero to infinity. On the other hand, based on a large number of psychophysical experiments, S.S. Stevens and his co-workers advocated power functions as more suitable. Because of 1) above and its resulting aggregation, we do not need to use a psychophysical law to cover wide ranges. It is already built into the AHP homogeneity and decomposition approach.

5) The supermatrix approach for representing dependence and feedback requires composition of ratio scales with limiting operations involving infinite iterative steps. Additive composition is mathematically the only reasonable way to do this and is closely related to similar practices in matrix and graph theories.

6) If subcriteria are to be regarded as decompositions of their parent criteria, the sum of their global weights (each obtained by multiplying their local weights by the weight of the criterion) is a more appropriate way to recover the weight of the criterion than the product of these weights.

7) Our natural tendency is to instinctively look wider and deeper to obtain more detailed knowledge about the world. This implies that hierarchic structures, which represent our perceptions of reality with their multielements and multilevels, are appropriate for that purpose. Also, the composite priorities at the bottom level should approach closer and closer to the measurement of the truth we seek. Additive composition gives rise to multilinear forms which are the simplest kind of nonlinear functions whose density in various mathematical spaces assures us that in fact we can work with wide and deep hierarchies to get as close as we want to the underlying truth. It is interesting and puzzling to note that classical physics with its sophisticated power formulas uses only primary and secondary variables to represent the diverse phenomena with which it deals. It seems to me that the physical world needs structures no less wide and deep than the hierarchic structures we encounter so abundantly in human affairs. These structures, according to some theories that ignore the role of synergy, are only a subset of the physical world.

8) Additivity in the AHP takes the form $\sum_{i=1}^{n} a_i w_i$. Some people have been inclined to propose using logarithms after deriving the eigenvector. They would then multiply by the corresponding priority of the criterion, add across the criteria, and in the end take the antilog. We can mechanically write

$$\sum_{i=1}^{n} a_i \log w_i = \sum_{i=1}^{n} \log w_i^{a_i} = \log \prod_{i=1}^{n} w_i^{a_i}$$ and if we take the antilog we obtain

the multiplicative result $\prod_{i=1}^{n} w_i^{a_i}$. What is wrong with this transformation as far as the meaning of the quantities involved is that we cannot derive $\log w_i$ directly from paired comparisons. Transforming with the logarithm adds nothing to and in fact distorts the final answer. Besides, by decomposing a problem into homogeneous groupings in deriving w_i, we can capture the meaning inherent in the judgments, thus obtaining real or valid results about the world as it appears to our system of values.

The multilinear forms obtained through additivity play a special role in capturing meaning from judgments in hierarchic and in feedback structures converging to our holistic understanding of complexity. In that way, in a step-by-step, fashion we can expand the detail and accuracy of our search for meaning.

2-7. THE FALLACY OF RANK PRESERVATION

Some researchers have said that the AHP allows rank reversal, and allowing for rank reversal is a weakness of the AHP. On the contrary, allowing for rank reversal is a strength of the AHP, or I might add, is *the* strength of the AHP because in reality rank reversals do take place in many situations involving choice.

Rank reversal is the process of a change in rank among already-ranked alternatives on a set of criteria, when a new alternative is added to the group or an old one is deleted, and no additional criteria are introduced or deleted.

There are two schools of thought about preserving rank or allowing it to change. One school argues that rank must always be preserved. The other argues that rank reversals do occur in practice and any theory or model should reflect that fact.

The following examples illustrate two scenarios in which rank reversal can take place. In the first scenario, rank reversal takes place because of the discovery of an abundance of an existing alternative. In the second scenario, rank reversal occurs because of the addition of a high-quality alternative.

1. **Quantity**: Suppose someone finds a large nugget of shiny, gold-colored metal and, thinking it is gold, carefully hides it away for use during more austere times. Now suppose that one day that person finds a mound of the same metal in another city. Because of its abundance, the metal no longer provides a feeling of security. The person's preference for it declines relative to his or her other possessions. In other words, the existence of the metal in large quantities has decreased its importance and therefore also its rank order relative to other existing possessions.

2. **Quality**: Consider two cars, A and B. Car A is inexpensive and not very durable, but it is operational. Car B is more expensive and also more durable. Because one may be unable to estimate how much the extra durability is worth, one may decide to buy car A. Now suppose a company declares that it will make car C. Car C is more durable than car B but is also *far more* expensive than car B. Now we have a better perspective on what durability is worth. Car B can become a better option than car A. In other words, the addition of a new alternative, car C, has reversed the preference ordering for cars A and B.

Rank reversal has been documented in the literature of psychology, among others, and noted researchers such as Tversky [9] have experimentally shown that it does occur. It is not difficult to construct decisions in which rank should be preserved, but on changing the names of the criteria and the alternatives but not any of the judgments, rank needs to be allowed to reverse. Thus it is up to the decision maker to determine whether to preserve rank or not.

2-8. COMMENTS ON COST/BENEFIT ANALYSIS

Often the alternatives are associated with both costs and benefits. In such a case it is useful to construct separate costs and benefits hierarchies, with the same alternatives on the bottom level of each. Thus one obtains both a costs-priority vector and a benefits-priority vector. The benefit/cost vector is obtained by taking the ratio of the benefits priority to the costs priority for each alternative, with the highest ratio indicating the preferred alternative. In the case where resources are allocated to several projects, benefit-to-cost ratios or the corresponding marginal ratios prove very valuable. When a single decision is made, benefits and low costs can often be combined in the same hierarchy.

For example, in evaluating three types of copying machine, one represents in the benefits hierarchy the good attributes, and one represents in the costs hierarchy the pain and economic costs that would be incurred in buying or maintaining the three types of machine. Note that the criteria for benefits and the criteria for costs need not be simply opposites of each other but may be totally different. Also note that each criterion may be regarded at a different threshold of intensity, and that such thresholds may themselves be prioritized according to desirability, with each alternative evaluated only in terms of its highest-priority threshold level. Similarly, four hierarchies can be used to assess *(benefit $\times$ opportunity)/(cost $\times$ risk)* outcomes.

In doing benefit/cost analyses, one needs to ensure that benefits and costs are sufficiently commensurate so that their ratio is meaningful. Since the criteria in each hierarchy are homogeneous, it is sufficient to ordinally match the economic benefits with the economic costs. If either is negligible when compared with the other, the corresponding hierarchy and its priorities are left out of the analysis, and only costs or only benefits are combined with risk. Of course the benefits may be in billions of dollars and the costs in millions, which we still cannot afford, and so both benefits and costs should be considered. On the other hand, if the costs are measured simply in tens of dollars or in pennies, then we need consider only the benefits.

In general we can rate benefits, costs, opportunities and risks one at a time with respect to still higher level criteria whose concern is the overall importance of the particular decision being made. One then proceeds to evaluate the respective hierarchies and compare the weights of the alternatives. One uses the normalized vector of the reciprocals of the costs and the risks vectors as the contribution of these two hierarchies along with benefits and opportunities. The rating vector of benefits, costs, opportunities and risks is used to weight the corresponding vectors of priorities of the alternatives and add to obtain the overall ranking of the alternatives. One way to deal with uncertainty is to use risk scenarios in both benefit and cost hierarchies, thus affecting the evaluation of the alternatives in terms of such scenarios. No risk hierarchy is needed in that case. This new approach with four hierarchies is an effective way to make decisions (See Chapter 5).

POSITIVES AND NEGATIVES

Consider a problem of rating projects according to their benefits. One of the criteria may be financial gain, which may have a range that includes negative values. The question would be, whether the negative gain should or should not belong in the benefits hierarchy. If the decision maker is able to pairwise compare the intensities without difficulty and get priorities with acceptable inconsistency, then there is no reason to say that the negative intensity should not be in the benefits hierarchy. If, on the other hand, the decision maker finds himself judging all the other positive benefits as extremely more important than all the negative ones, then they should not belong in the same hierarchy. If this happens, he must consider the negative financial gain as a criterion in a costs hierarchy. Since a project can only have either a positive financial gain or a negative one, a profitable project will be evaluated as zero under the financial "gain" in the costs hierarchy. The opposite is true for a project which is a loss. In general, it is not necessary that criteria for a rating model must be possessed by all the alternatives. The same type of reasoning applies to qualitative intensities. By pairwise comparisons one can place them in hierarchies of benefits or costs and use their priorities to rate alternatives.

EXAMPLE 1: THE BOSTON CHIPPENDALE SECRETARIAL DESK PROBLEM

Bartley in Easton, MD, is a one-of-a-kind, do-it-yourself traditional American furniture manufacturer. The pieces of furniture they make are of the best-quality wood conceivable: Honduras mahogany, Pennsylvania cherry and walnut. For the furniture lover, the prices they charge and their financing are very attractive. They do not skimp. They cut the wood and supply the customer with glue, sandpaper, filing dust paste to fill gaps, and flexible braces to hold the glued parts. They have even perfected an easy method of stain finish that is superlative. For the connoisseur, they offer special-edition posters, design plans, and tempting reductions. Their latest offer is a copy of a Boston Chippendale secretarial desk circa 1765. It is a most attractive piece offered at $300 less to the earlybirds. This author has assembled and finished several pieces from Bartley, but the house is rather full of such attractive furniture. Should he take the latest offer? Figure 2-3 and 2-4 are the two hierarchies, one for the benefits and one for the costs, of making the decision to buy or not to buy. Tables 2-7 through 2-11 contain results of the pairwise comparisons. The final outcome is lukewarm in favor of not buying as shown in the normalized benefits/costs column of Table 2-11; No = .52, Yes = .48.

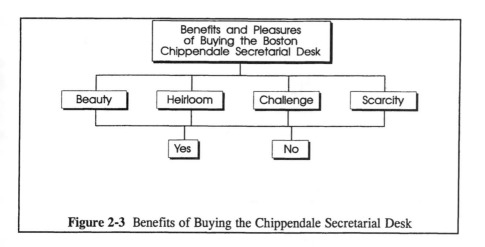

Figure 2-3 Benefits of Buying the Chippendale Secretarial Desk

Table 2-7 Paired Comparisons of Criteria

	B	H	C	S	
Beauty	1	5	7	1/5	0.25
Heirloom	1/5	1	3	1/6	0.08
Challenge	1/7	1/3	1	1/9	0.04
Scarcity	5	6	9	1	0.63

Inconsistency = 0.12

Table 2-8 Paired Comparisons of Alternatives

Beauty	Y	N	
Y	1	6	.86
N	1/6	1	.14

Heirloom	Y	N	
Y	1	3	.75
N	1/3	1	.25

Challenge	Y	N	
Y	1	2	.67
N	1/2	1	.33

Scarcity	Y	N	
Y	1	6	.86
N	1/6	1	.14

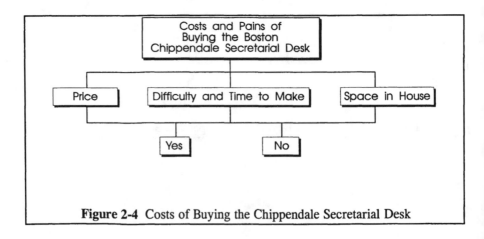

Figure 2-4 Costs of Buying the Chippendale Secretarial Desk

Table 2-9 Paired Comparisons of Criteria

	P	D	S	
Price	1	1/5	1/3	.097
Difficulty and Time	5	1	5	.701
Space	3	1/5	1	.202

Inconsistency = 0.12

Table 2-10 Paired Comparisons of Alternatives

Price	Y	N			Difficulty	Y	N			Space	Y	N	
Y	1	4	.8		Y	1	7	.88		Y	1	4	.8
N	1/4	1	.2		N	1/7	1	.12		N	1/4	1	.2

Table 2-11 Benefit/Cost Ratios

	Benefits	Costs	Benefits/Costs	Benefits/Costs (Normalized)
Yes	.841	.853	0.99	0.48
No	.159	.147	1.08	0.52

Sometimes one assumes that the goal of a decision hierarchy is sufficient to define the problem. However, in many problems the entire hierarchy defines the problem, including its assumptions. In this example we have seen that the high priority of Difficulty under costs implies that the decision maker assumes that he alone would be assembling the piece, but the low priority for the dollar costs indicates that one would not mind giving up dollars to trade off Difficulty, and Challenge has low priority. As a result, the author contacted a furniture maker in Pittsburgh and found that he could assist in finishing the project for a relatively small fee. The revised problem changed the outcome.

When the priority of Difficulty is reduced to 0.37 and Price increased somewhat disproportionately relative to Space with respective priorities 0.25

and 0.38, the benefit-cost ratio of *yes* becomes 1.02 and that of *no* 0.93. Further reducing Difficulty increases this trend. The decision, still close, was to buy the desk and to hire help to assemble the complicated piece.

EXAMPLE 2: THE WISDOM OF A TRADE WAR WITH CHINA OVER INTELLECTUAL PROPERTY RIGHTS

This example was developed jointly with the author's colleague Jen S. Shang in mid-February 1995 to understand the issues when the media were voicing strong conflicting concerns prior to the action to be taken in Beijing later that month. Many copies of the analysis were sent to congressmen and senators and to the chief U.S. negotiator, Mickey Kantor, in Washington, and to several newspapers in the U.S. and in China. We do not claim any credit for influence on what happened later; still, we feel extremely satisfied that the outcome of the decision was along the lines of our recommendation. In fact I received a call soon after February 26 from Mr. Kantor's office congratulating us on the outcome, which coincided with the agreement. I have kept the tense of the writing as it was when the paper was written to better convey the sense of urgency in which we wrote it:

There are many strong, conflicting opinions about what to do with Chinese piracy of U.S. technology and management know-how. Should the U.S. sanction China on February 26? The basic arguments in favor of imposing tariffs derive from the U.S. perceived need not to allow China to become a runaway nation with an inward-oriented closed economy. Some also argue convincingly that a nation whose economy will equal that of the U.S. in three decades must be taught to play by the rules. We have made a brief study of the decision to impose tariffs on Chinese products in the U.S. It is not the immediate small injury to U.S. corporations from such an action that is of major concern, but what might happen in the future. The effect of the tariffs will be decisively more intangible with long-term results that can aggravate trade in the Pacific.

Our findings, based on benefits, costs, and risks and on all the factors we could bring to bear on the outcome, conclude in a definite and very decisive *No*, which means that it is not in the best overall interest of the U.S. to take strong action against China. Since we are not usually told much about what China says, we also summarize some arguments gleaned from Chinese newspapers. We explain our analysis and offer the reader the opportunity to perform a similar evaluation based on the factors given here plus others we may have overlooked. In our opinion, the costs are too high to treat China in the same style as an outlaw nation, even though China can and should do better as a member of the world community.

The war of intellectual property is just a reflection of the contention between the two sides. Several factors drive this friction between China and the U.S. Among the issues are human rights, weapons proliferation, the independence of Taiwan and the trade deficit. In the ten years leading to 1994, China's exports to the U.S. grew from $3.1 billion to $38 billion, whereas U.S. exports to China grew from $3 billion to only $8.5 billion. Because of this deficit, the U.S. has come to believe that China should open its markets in return.

According to the *Economist* magazine of February 11, 1995, the official trade deficit figures have been overstated. On the one hand, those figures count Chinese goods re-exported through Hong Kong to the U.S. as imports from China. On the other hand, the value of American goods exported to China through Hong Kong was not added to the American export figures. As a result, U.S. statistics have overestimated the U.S. bilateral deficit with China since 1990 by about one-third. Another telling point is that cheap Chinese labor has persuaded firms from Hong Kong and Taiwan to move their labor-intensive production to China. Goods that were once imported from Taiwan and Hong Kong now count as Chinese. The U.S. deficit with the three countries combined rose by less than 10% between 1987 and 1992; but its deficit with China alone grew by a whopping 550% in that period. When capital can cross borders freely, it appears that bilateral deficits are misleading. Despite these facts, the perception of a huge trade deficit makes it difficult for the U.S. to see China's benefits from violating U.S. intellectual property rights as being a small part of the trade.

It is important that China follow global commercial practices. However, many Chinese do not recognize sufficiently the leadership role the U.S. has taken in international trade. They feel that it is arrogant for the U.S. to act as a judge, a policeman, or an umpire and to sanction other nations, who then would retaliate for loss of dignity. Many Chinese officials believe that if they accept the sanctions quietly, China would be perceived as passive to actions against its own sovereignty and dignity, just as in the colonial era. To save face, so far they have cancelled a $97-million purchase of corn and threaten to disengage from a deal of more than $2 billion with Boeing. It is evident that they are not going to yield to intimidation.

China's per capita income is $2946. There is still a huge gap between China and the advanced industrialized nations. For decades officials and citizens in China have not known what intellectual property rights are. Did Chinese officials overtly indulge in encouraging piracy, or is it one of the many difficulties a newly arrived developing country encounters in the course of development? According to Chinese newspapers, the Chinese government has tried to control piracy but on the surface appears not to have been effective and not to have been given credit for trying.

Political entanglements also exist between central and local governments in China, and between the judicial and legislative systems. Usually, local governments frown upon punishing piracy because it would result in less taxable income and higher unemployment. That is one reason why they have not tried hard to implement the law. In turn, the courts are not serious about piracy because their finances and personnel are all constrained by the local government. Many of those who profit from the piracy are sons and daughters of senior comrades, army officers, and provincial bureaucrats. Top officials are too embarrassed by their children's behavior to touch that issue. Even if China were to make an agreement with the U.S., the immediate benefits of such an agreement are in doubt. According to the *Wall Street Journal* of February 6, few Chinese can actually afford $14 CDs or $150 Windows disks, which raises some doubt about the numbers being tossed around for lost sales in China. The pirates are awakening appetites that did not exist a decade ago. However, punishing China will not automatically increase U.S. exports of such items.

To arrive at a rational decision, we considered the factors shown in Figure 2-5 as they influence the outcome of the decision. They are arranged in three hierarchies: one for the benefits of implementing such a sanction, one for the costs, and a third for the risks and uncertainties that can occur. Each hierarchy has a goal followed by the criteria that affect the performance of the goal. The alternatives are listed in the last level of the hierarchy. They are: *Yes – to sanction China*, and *No – not to sanction China*.

We then determined the relative importance of the criteria contributing to the goal by comparing them in pairs. For example, in the benefits hierarchy we asked the question: How much more important is protecting American interests than teaching China to follow international business practices?

Apparently, from the U.S. standpoint, protecting American rights is more important, and there is dependence between these two factors. If China does not follow the international copyright law, more American products will be pirated. However, so long as the U.S. ensures that China does not pirate its technology, the U.S. would benefit even if China does not strictly follow the rules in dealing with other countries. From the U.S. viewpoint, protecting American copyrights is more important than teaching China to be responsible. We assigned a higher priority to the former in our comparison. The rest of the comparisons are examined in the same manner.

A scale of relative importance is derived for the factors from the pairwise comparison judgments. We then proceed to the third level of the hierarchy to compare the alternatives under each factor. For example, under the costs hierarchy, *Yes* is judged to be extremely more important in contributing to retaliation than *No* and is given the value 9 when compared with *No*. The other values in each of the three hierarchies were assigned in a similar fashion. We gave *Yes* the same priority as *No* in terms of the "Harder to justify China joining WTO" factor. This is because from the U.S. viewpoint, whether sanctions are made or not, China does not qualify to receive World Trade Organization (WTO) membership at the current level of protecting copyrights, patents, and trademarks.

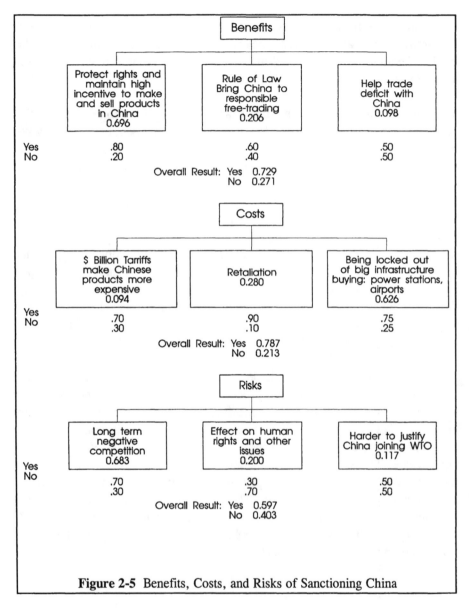

Figure 2-5 Benefits, Costs, and Risks of Sanctioning China

The results are shown below.

$$\frac{Benefits}{Costs \times Risks}: \ Yes = \frac{.729}{.787 \times .597} = 1.55; \ No = \frac{.271}{.213 \times .403} = 3.16$$

In each hierarchy we synthesize the values for *Yes* and for *No* by multiplying each alternative's priority with the importance of its parent criterion and adding to obtain the overall result for *Yes* and for *No*. A user-friendly computer software program, Expert Choice, was used to do all the calculations. To combine the results from the three hierarchies, we divide the benefit results for *Yes* by the costs and by the risks for *Yes* to obtain the final outcome. We do the same for *No* and select *Yes* or *No* depending on which has the larger value. While *Yes*'s benefits are high, the corresponding costs and risks are also high. Its ratio is less than that of the *No* decision. *No* dominates *Yes* both when no risk is considered and also when projected risk is taken into account. Including risk by using possible scenarios of the future can be a powerful tool in assessing the effect of the decision on the future.

To ensure that the outcome not be construed as a result of whimsical judgments, we performed a comprehensive sensitivity analysis. Sensitivity analysis helps the decision maker discover how changes in the priorities affect the recommended decision. The *Yes* and *No* weights are fixed because they are our best judgments based on the facts. So we fixed the *Yes* and *No* judgments as shown in Figure 2-5 and varied the importance of each factor. A policy maker may choose from a wide range of admissible priority values for each factor. Our sensitivity analysis covers all the reasonable priorities a politician might choose. We changed each factor's importance from the value indicated in the hierarchy to the near extreme values 0.2 and 0.8. This gave us six variations in each hierarchy, because there are three factors in each. With three hierarchies, we generated 216 (6*6*6) data points. In this simulation we found that it is only when long-term negative competition is thought to be unimportant that sanctions would be justified. From Figure 2-6 depicting the 216 possibilities, we see that *No* dominates *Yes* appreciably. Regardless of the weights one assigns to the factors, over 90% of the cases lead to *No*, not to sanction China.

If a trade war becomes inevitable and the U.S. follows the *Yes* option, both sides would be affected. There is the possibility that the U.S. might then be locked out of major Chinese infrastructure business, and China would have a hard time joining GATT and WTO. It is also possible that because both countries share many common interests, should the war start, it may not last long. The U.S. has previously been engaged in trade wars with the Europeans and the Japanese, all of which ended with last-minute bargaining.

Deng Rong, the daughter of Deng Xiaoping, the most senior elder statesman of China, said recently, "Sanctions are never the best way to resolve a dispute. One should talk things over and consider the interests of the people." Our analysis seems to support this attitude.

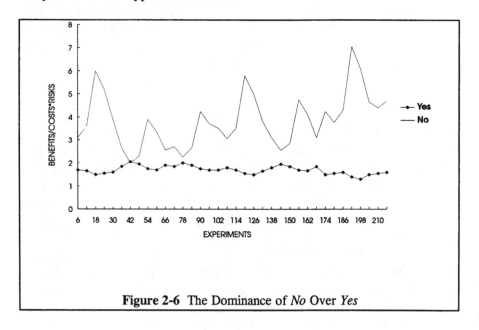

Figure 2-6 The Dominance of *No* Over *Yes*

2-9. THE EIGENVECTOR SOLUTION FOR WEIGHTS AND CONSISTENCY

We now look at some of the technical aspects of the AHP as they relate to deriving the priorities and assessing their consistency. There are an infinite number of ways to derive the vector of priorities from the reciprocal matrix of comparisons $A = (a_{ij})$. Only one of them is the correct one, and that has been proven mathematically. Allowing for a degree of inconsistency, and the need to capture dominance, lead to an eigenvalue formulation. Good decision making should have a single justifiable procedure for getting the right answer.

If a_{ij} represents the importance of alternative i over alternative j and a_{jk} represents the importance of alternative j over alternative k, then a_{ik}, the importance of alternative i over alternative k, must equal $a_{ij}a_{jk}$ for the judgments to be consistent. If we do not have a scale, or cannot read it conveniently, as in the case of some measuring devices, we cannot give the precise values of $a_{ij}=w_i/w_j$ but can only provide an estimate. Now,

$$
\begin{pmatrix}
w_1/w_1 & w_1/w_2 & \cdots & w_1/w_n \\
w_2/w_1 & w_2/w_2 & \cdots & w_2/w_n \\
\vdots & \vdots & & \vdots \\
w_n/w_1 & w_n/w_2 & \cdots & w_n/w_n
\end{pmatrix}
\begin{pmatrix}
w_1 \\
w_2 \\
\vdots \\
w_n
\end{pmatrix}
= n
\begin{pmatrix}
w_1 \\
w_2 \\
\vdots \\
w_n
\end{pmatrix}
$$

Here w_i, $i=1,\ldots,n$ are the derived scale values. If the judgments are not consistent, instead of solving $Aw=nw$, our problem becomes $A'w' = \lambda_{max}w'$ where λ_{max} is the largest or principal eigenvalue of $A' = (a'_{ij})$, the perturbed value of $A = (a_{ij})$ with $a'_{ji} = 1/a'_{ij}$ forced. To simplify the notation we shall continue to write $Aw = \lambda_{max}w$ where A is the matrix of pairwise comparisons.

The solution is obtained by raising the matrix to a sufficiently large power (the Power Method), then summing over the rows and normalizing (dividing each row sum by the total) to obtain the priority vector $w = (w_1, \ldots, w_n)$. The process is stopped when the difference between components of the priority vector obtained at the kth power and at the $(k + 1)$st power is less than some predetermined small value.

An easy way to get an approximation to the priorities is to normalize the geometric mean (the nth root of the product of the elements) in each row. This result coincides with the eigenvector for $n \leq 3$. A second way to obtain an approximation is by normalizing the elements in each column of the judgment matrix and then averaging over each row. The crudest approximation is obtained by normalizing the sum of each row.

We would like to caution that for important applications one should use only the eigenvector derivation procedure because approximations can lead to the wrong ranks and also one loses the measure of inconsistency.[10]

A simple way to obtain λ_{max} when w is known is to add the numbers in each column of A and multiply the resulting vector by the normalized priority vector w.

The problem now is, how good is the principal eigenvector estimate w? Note that if we obtain $w = (w_1, \ldots, w_n)^T$, by solving this problem, the matrix whose entries are w_i/w_j is a consistent matrix, which is our consistent estimate of the matrix A. The original matrix A itself need not be consistent. In fact the entries of A need not even be transitive; i.e., A_1 may be preferred to A_2 and A_2 to A_3, but A_3 may be preferred to A_1. What we would like is a measure of the error due to inconsistency. It turns out that A is consistent if and only if $\lambda_{max} = n$, and that we always have $\lambda_{max} \geq n$.

The consistency index of a matrix of comparisons is given by C.I. $= (\lambda_{max} - n)/n$-1. It is interesting to note that $(\lambda_{max}-n)/(n-1)$ is the variance of the error incurred in estimating a_{ij}. This can be shown by writing $a_{ij} = (w_i/w_j)\varepsilon_{ij}$, $\varepsilon_{ij} > 0$ and $\varepsilon_{ij} = 1 + \delta_{ij}$, $\delta_{ij} > -1$ and substituting in the expression for λ_{max}. It is δ_{ij} that concerns us as the error component and its value $|\delta_{ij}| < 1$ for an unbiased estimator. The measure of inconsistency can be used to successively improve the consistency of judgments. The consistency ratio (C.R.) is obtained by comparing the C.I. with the appropriate one of the set of numbers shown in Table 2-12 below, each of which is an average random consistency index derived from a large sample of randomly generated reciprocal matrices using the scale 1/9, 1/8, ..., 1, ..., 8, 9. The resulting vector is accepted if C.R. is about 0.10 or less (0.20 may be tolerated, but not more). For $n=3$, it is 0.05, and for $n=4$, it is 0.08. If it is not less than 0.10, study the problem and revise the judgments. The AHP has a systematic procedure for better judgments.

Table 2-12 Table of Random Inconsistency for Different Size Matrix

n	1	2	3	4	5	6	7	8	9	10
Random Consistency Index (R.I.)	0	0	.52	.89	1.11	1.25	1.35	1.40	1.45	1.49

The AHP includes a consistency index for an entire hierarchy.

2-10. MULTILINEAR FORMS: THE NONLINEARITY OF HIERARCHIC COMPOSITION

The composite priorities of each alternative at the bottom level of a hierarchy may be represented as a multilinear form:

$$\sum_{i_1,\dots,i_p} x_1^{i_1} x_2^{i_2} \cdots x_p^{i_p}$$

Using the concept explained on page 39, consider a single term of this sum and for simplicity denote it by $x_1, x_2, \dots, x_p$. We have

$$x_1 x_2 \cdots x_p = e^{\log x_1 x_2 \cdots x_p} = \prod_{i=1}^{p} e^{\log x_i} = e^{\sum_{i=1}^{p} \log x_i} \rightarrow e^{\int \log x(\alpha) d\alpha}$$

a product integral. Also

$$x_1 x_2 \cdots x_p + y_1 y_2 \cdots y_p + \cdots + z_1 z_2 \cdots z_p \rightarrow \int_\Lambda e^{\int \log u_i du_i}_{\omega(\lambda)} \, d\mu(\omega(\lambda))$$

This is the same result as one obtains from the continuous formulation of hierarchic composition with eigenfunctions

$$\int w_{n-1,n}(x_{n-1},x_n) \int w_{n-2,n-1}(x_{n-2},x_{n-1}) \cdots \int w_{1,2}(x_1,x_2) w_1(x_1) dx_1 dx_2 \cdots dx_n$$

$$= \int\int \cdots \int w_{n-1,n}(x_{n-1},x_n) \cdots w_{1,2}(x_1,x_2) w_1(x_1) \, dx_1 \cdots dx_n$$

$$= \int\int \cdots \int e^{\sum \log w_{i-1,i}(x_{i-1},x_i)} \, dx_1 \cdots dx_n$$

$$\rightarrow \int\int \cdots \int e^{\int \log a_i \, da_i} \, dx_1 \cdots dx_n$$

$$\rightarrow \int_{\Lambda_1} e^{\int \log a_i da_i}_{\omega(\lambda)} \, d\mu_1(\omega_1(\lambda)) \qquad \lambda \in \Lambda_1$$

2-11. HOW TO STRUCTURE A HIERARCHY

Lest the reader by now think that all decision hierarchies dealt with through the AHP can have only three levels, Figure 2-7 is an example of a multilevel hierarchy and its priorities. We worked on it with a team of hospital staff to choose the best way to treat terminal cancer patients.[11]

Perhaps the most creative part of decision making and one that has a significant effect on the outcome is modeling the problem. In the AHP, a problem is structured as a hierarchy. This is then followed by a process of prioritization. Prioritization involves eliciting judgments in response to questions about the dominance of one element over another when compared with respect to a property. The basic principle to follow in creating this structure is always to see if one can answer the following question: *Can I compare the elements on a lower level meaningfully in terms of some or all of the elements on the next higher level?*

A useful way to proceed is to come down from the goal as far as one can and then go up from the alternatives until the levels of the two processes are linked so as to make comparison possible. Here are some suggestions for an elaborate design:

1. Identify overall goal. What are you trying to accomplish? What is the main question?
2. Identify subgoals of overall goal. If relevant, identify time horizons that affect the decision.
3. Identify criteria that must be satisfied to fulfill subgoals of the overall goal.
4. Identify subcriteria under each criterion. Note that criteria or subcriteria may be specified in terms of ranges of values of parameters or in terms of verbal intensities such as high, medium, low.
5. Identify actors involved.
6. Identify actor goals.
7. Identify actor policies.
8. Identify options or outcomes.
9. For yes-no decisions take the most preferred outcome and compare benefits and costs of making the decision with those of not making it.
10. Do benefit/cost analysis using marginal values. Because we are dealing with dominance hierarchies, ask which alternative yields the greatest benefit; for costs, which alternative costs the most. Proceed similarly if a risks hierarchy is included.

The software program Expert Choice[12] incorporates the AHP methodology and enables the analyst to structure the hierarchy and solve the problem using relative or absolute measurement, as appropriate.

2-12. CAVEAT EMPTOR*

The outcome of arithmetic operations performed in the AHP can be expected to have greater validity about the real-life situation if the structure has

---

*Buyer Beware

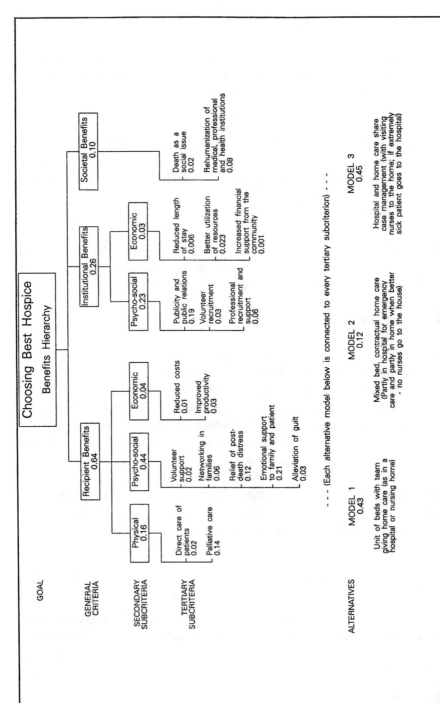

Figure 2-7 Hierarchy for Benefits of Choosing a Best Hospice

incorporated all the essential factors. The arithmetic by itself cannot be assumed to always do that because it works on what one puts in the structure. For example, three secretaries apply for a job, one is good at English but is a poor typist, the second is good at typing but poor at English and the third is balanced between the two but is never better than what the other two are better at. The composition process would never choose the balanced secretary unless being good at English, being good at typing and being good at both were to be included as criteria. Thus our expectations cannot be satisfied fully by applying arithmetic operations to an arbitrary structure. The structure itself must carefully represent all the qualities expected in the formulation and solution.

2-13. GROUP DECISION MAKING

To combine group judgments and satisfy the reciprocal property for the group in comparing two items in the AHP, one must use the geometric mean.[13, 14] The same unique procedure is used to combine final ranking outcomes. Aczel and Roberts[15] have studied possible ways for combining individual judgments into a group judgment and found them to be few if we want meaningful statements involving the merged functions. The conditions are symmetry, linear homogeneity, and agreement. The symmetry axiom specifies that the merging function does not change if the functions giving individual judgments are interchanged. The agreement axiom says that if all individuals agree, then the group agrees with all the individuals. Linear homogeneity means that if every member of the group multiplies his preference by a constant r, then the resulting group preference is also multiplied by r. In many cases the arithmetic mean and the geometric mean are the only possible merging functions, but they are not the only ones. Aczel and Saaty[16] have shown that symmetry, agreement, and homogeneity together with reciprocity and separability (decomposition into individual judgments) uniquely imply the geometric mean.

In group voting, people usually use *yes* and *no* instead of actual weights. Majority voting can produce an opposite outcome to what one would obtain by combining individual-generated priorities with the geometric mean. In fact the AHP can make it possible to pool together the benefits, costs, opportunities and risks and have individuals fill out the agreed upon hierarchies with their own judgments and obtain their own overall preferences for the outcomes.   If there is a single outcome one can use absolute measurement for it according to each voter. The results are then combined by applying the geometric mean to the final outcomes of the different people. The result is very likely to differ from the yes or no majority vote and would include everybody's contribution to the final outcome and not just of those who voted yes in the majority vote. We hope that someday in the near future people will learn to use this approach in dealing with complex decisions rather than resorting to the traditional and minorit- preference-blind method of voting of today. I have already written a paper on this idea with my colleague Jen Shang and illustrated it with an example.

When a group of individuals want to make a collective choice, they would each express their own individual choices and one would then combine their choices into a group choice. One way to do this is to see what alternative has the most votes followed by the one with the next most vote and so on. But there are other ways of deriving a group choice from individual choices. It seems reasonable that no matter how we aggregate individual into group choice, if all the people prefer one alternative over another, then the group also should. This is called Pareto optimality. It is possible when there are more than two choices, the group ordering of choices may be intransitive, and thus it would be impossible to say which is the most preferred choice. This is known as the Condorcet paradox. Borda's answer to this paradox is for each individual to number his choices from 1 to n and the group choice is made by summing the numbers assigned by the individuals to each alternative. In case of a tie, the alternatives involved are arbitrarily ordered among themselves. An objection to Borda's scheme is why use equidistant numbers when one alternative may be much preferred by one person but a little by another.[7] Kenneth Arrow[17,18] proved that in general it is impossible to arrive at a rational group choice from individual *ordinal* preferences. Rationality implies that four conditions should be satisfied:

1. No dictatorship: no single individual determines the group order.
2. Decisiveness: the aggregation procedure must produce a group order.
3. Pareto optimality: if every individual prefers A to B, then so does the group.

4. Independence of irrelevant alternatives: the group choice between two alternatives must be based on the individual preferences only between that pair of alternatives.

Arrow's impossibility is made possible by using cardinal numbers as in the AHP, as shown by my student Kirti Peniwati in her Ph.D. dissertation. The forgoing conditions are satisfied in the AHP if one aggregates the separate orderings by the individuals using the geometric mean. However, in the AHP one can also aggregate judgments to obtain a group choice. If these judgments are inconsistent, the individuals need to work on improving inconsistency. The resulting group order may be different from the previous order, but also satisfies the above four conditions.

2-14. A COMPATIBILITY METRIC

In addition to consistency, one can speak of the compatibility of different results in the AHP. Actually, when dealing with the judgment matrix of a single individual, compatibility of the judgments and resulting eigenvector and the consistency of the judgments are closely related. In group decision making, the two concepts are distinct.

Given the vector $w = (w_1, \ldots, w_n)$ where all the w_i belong to the same scale, we consider the matrix of all possible ratios $A = (a_{ij}) = (w_i/w_j)$. This matrix is reciprocal, that is $a_{ji} = 1/a_{ij}$. The Hadamard product of a reciprocal matrix A and its transpose A^T is given by:

$$A \circ A^T = \begin{pmatrix} w_1/w_1 & \cdots & w_1/w_n \\ \vdots & & \vdots \\ w_n/w_1 & \cdots & w_n/w_n \end{pmatrix} \circ \begin{pmatrix} w_1/w_1 & \cdots & w_n/w_1 \\ \vdots & & \vdots \\ w_1/w_n & \cdots & w_n/w_n \end{pmatrix} = \begin{pmatrix} 1 & \cdots & 1 \\ \vdots & & \vdots \\ 1 & \cdots & 1 \end{pmatrix} = \begin{pmatrix} 1 \\ \vdots \\ 1 \end{pmatrix} (1 \ \cdots \ 1) \equiv ee^T$$

The sum of the elements of a matrix A can be written as $e^T A e$. In particular $e^T A \circ A^T e = n^2$.

If we assume that two vectors $w = (w_1, ..., w_n)$ and $u = (u_1, ..., u_n)$, whose coordinates are measured on the same ratio scale, differ by a perturbation matrix $E = (\epsilon_{ij})$ *so that* $\dfrac{u_i}{u_j} = \dfrac{w_i}{w_j} \epsilon_{ij}$ and if their corresponding matrices are

$A = (\dfrac{w_i}{w_j})$ and $B = (\dfrac{u_i}{u_j})$, the Hadamard product we want is $A \circ B^T = (\varepsilon_{ij})$. We

are concerned with the closeness of $e^T A \circ B^T e = \displaystyle\sum_{i,j=1}^{n} \dfrac{w_i \, u_j}{w_j \, u_i}$ to its minimum

value n^2 or with the closeness of the normalized vectors $w_i / \displaystyle\sum_{i=1}^{n} w_i$ and

$u_i / \displaystyle\sum_{i=1}^{n} u_i$ to each other. It is easy to prove the first three theorems below.

Theorem 2-1: *If* $A = (\dfrac{w_i}{w_j})$ *then* $A = vw$, $v = (\dfrac{1}{w_1}, ..., \dfrac{1}{w_n})^T$,

$w = (w_1, ..., w_n)$.

Corollary: *If* $\displaystyle\sum_{i=1}^{n} w_i = 1$ *then* $e^T A e = e^T v$.

Theorem 2-2: $e^T A \, e = e^T v w e = \displaystyle\sum_{j=1}^{n} \dfrac{1}{w_j} \cdot \displaystyle\sum_{i=1}^{n} w_i$.

We define compatibility between two ratio scales w and u as $c(w,u) = e^T A \circ B^T e$.

Ratio scales have no zero value but only a zero origin. The following theorem is analogous to the first axiom of a metric.

Theorem 2-3: $c(w,u) = n^2$ if and only if $w=u$.

Proof: If $A=B$ then $A^T=B^T$ and $e^T A \circ B^T e = n^2$ or $c(w,u) = n^2$. Conversely, assume that $c(w,u) = n^2$. The sum of the elements of the reciprocal matrix $A \circ B^T$ can be represented in pairs of terms of the convex form $x + 1/x$ each of which has a minimum value of 2. Since the sum of the elements is equal to n^2, each term $x + 1/x$ must be equal to 2 which is attained if and only if $x=1$. If we let $x = \dfrac{w_i}{w_j} \dfrac{u_j}{u_i}$, it follows that $\dfrac{w_i}{w_j} = \dfrac{u_i}{u_j}$ for all i and j and hence $w = u$.

A special case of this theorem is that of $n = 1$, in other words the comparison of two ratio scales rests on the comparison of a single measurement from each. If we define $d(w,u) = log\ c(w,u)$ we obtain the first axiom of an ordinary metric in geometry.

One can generate a relative ratio scale when a set of attributes are being compared in a test. What should one do when there is only one attribute and how do we compare two measurements of the same attribute. There are two ways to obtain measurement for a single attribute. One is through relative comparisons with a known ideal state of that attribute obtained from memory. This is the only way to create measurement when one deals with an intangible attribute. The other, useful mostly for physical measurement, is to create a scale with a unit for measuring that attribute. It is a special case of relative measurement. Physical measurement is related to the idea of distance and more abstractly to a metric and geometry. Measurement on a physical scale may or may not belong to a ratio scale. If it does, one can sometimes directly form ratios of such measurements on such a scale or alternatively use the measurements to develop relative measurements or create new ratios from them through judgment. Alternatively one can take the differences of two measurements on a difference scale each of whose readings is itself the logarithm of a ratio scale measurement. These are the two possible ways to create physical measurement that are compatible with the fundamental process of relative measurement.

Lemma: $\sum_{i=1}^{n} a_i b_i \leq (\sum_{i=1}^{n} a_i)(\sum_{i=1}^{n} b_i)$ $a_i, b_i \geq 0,$ $i = 1,...,n.$

Proof: Note that each term on the right is positive and that the left side is included in the right side.

Theorem 2-4: $c(w,v) \leq c(w,u)\, c(u,v)$

Proof: $e^{T}A \circ C^{T}e = e^{T}A \circ B^{T} \circ B \circ C^{T}e \leq e^{T}A \circ B^{T}e\, e^{T}B \circ C'e$
$$= c(w,u)\, c(u,v)$$
having used the lemma.

We note that if we have to compare a single reading from a ratio scale with a standard value on the same scale we simply take their ratio for the Hadamard product of their two single element matrices. Thus if one reading is p and the other is q we have $c(p,q) = p/q$ and
$$d(p,q) = log\ c(p,q) = log\ p/q.$$
If P and Q are vectors defined by a set of coordinates in cartesian space, we can use one of the many possible norms for that vector to form the ratio p/q.

The transformation $d(w,u) = log\ c(w,u)$ for $n = 1$ satisfies the two axioms of a metric: 1) given in Theorem 2-3 with $n = 1$ and 2) the triangular inequality derived from Theorem 2-4. In addition, it is easy to show that 3) $d(w,u) = d(u,w)$, 4) $d(w,u)$ is a continuous function of w and u, 5) if u lies on a line between w and v then $d(w,v) = d(w,u) + d(w,v)$ (the geodesic property), and 6) $d(\alpha w, \alpha u) = d(w,u)$, $\alpha > 0$, for all w and u (invariance with respect to the ratio scale property). A second metric $d'(w,u) = k\,d(w,u)$ for some $k > 0$ also satisfies all these conditions. The space of all w's and u's endowed with the metric $d(w,u)$ is a hyperbolic space.[19]

What is a good bound to place on compatibility as defined by $e^{T}A \circ B^{T}e$? First we divide by n^2 and note from arguments dealing with the measurement of acceptable inconsistency that perturbations which increase the original by not more than one order of magnitude can be considered as acceptable when compared with the original. Perturbations that are as large (of the same order of magnitude or more) as the number itself are unacceptable. Thus an admissible bound for compatibility can be set at 1.100. It is in accord with the idea that a 10% deviation is at the upper end of acceptability.

COMPATIBILITY AND CONSISTENCY

Consistency is concerned with the compatibility of a matrix of the ratios constructed from a principal right eigenvector with the matrix of judgments from which it is derived. Compatibility is concerned with two different vectors. If the matrix of judgments is inconsistent, is it compatible with the matrix of eigenvector ratios? The following theorem and the table following it show that there is a relation between consistency and compatibility. Comparison of the two indices suggests that for the cases of $n = 3,4,5$ the Compatibility Index should have a smaller value than 1.1.

Let $W = (w_i/w_j)$ be the matrix of ratios of the principal right eigenvector $w = (w_1,...,w_n)$ of the positive reciprocal matrix A and λ_{max} be the corresponding principal eigenvalue and let $\sum_{i=1}^{n} w_i = 1$. We define the Compatibility Index (S.I.) of a matrix of judgments and the matrix of derived eigenvector ratios as S.I. $= \dfrac{1}{n^2} e^T A \circ W^T e$.

Theorem 2-5 : $\dfrac{1}{n^2} e^T A \circ W^T e = \dfrac{\lambda_{max}}{n}$

Proof: From $Aw = \lambda_{max} w$ we have

$$\sum_{j=1}^{n} a_{ij} w_j = \lambda_{max} w_i \text{ and}$$

$$\frac{1}{n^2} e^T A \circ W^T e = \frac{1}{n^2} \sum_{i=1}^{n} \sum_{j=1}^{n} a_{ij} \frac{w_j}{w_i} = \frac{\lambda_{max}}{n}$$

Table 2-13 gives information on compatibility and consistency for different size judgment matrices.

Table 2-13 Relationship Between Consistency and Compatibility for a Different Number of Elements

Number of Elements (n)	Compatibility Index (S.I.)	λ_{max}	$C.I. = \dfrac{\lambda_{max} - n}{n-1}$	R.I.	$C.R. = \dfrac{C.I.}{R.I.}$
3	1.017	3.052	0.026	0.52	0.05
4	1.053	4.214	0.071	0.89	0.08
5	1.089	5.444	0.111	1.11	0.10
6	1.104	6.625	0.125	1.25	0.10
7	1.116	7.810	0.135	1.35	0.10
8	1.123	8.980	0.140	1.40	0.10
9	1.129	10.160	0.145	1.45	0.10
10	1.134	11.341	0.149	1.49	0.10
11	1.137	12.510	0.151	1.51	0.10
12	1.141	13.694	0.154	1.54	0.10
13	1.144	14.872	0.156	1.56	0.10
14	1.146	16.041	0.157	1.57	0.10
15	1.147	17.212	0.158	1.58	0.10

EXAMPLES

Consider the Hadamard product:

$$
\begin{pmatrix} 1 & 2 & 4 \\ 1/2 & 1 & 2 \\ 1/4 & 1/2 & 1 \end{pmatrix} \circ \begin{pmatrix} 1 & 1/3 & 1/5 \\ 3 & 1 & 3/5 \\ 5 & 5/3 & 1 \end{pmatrix} = \begin{pmatrix} 1 & 2/3 & 4/5 \\ 3/2 & 1 & 6/5 \\ 5/4 & 5/6 & 1 \end{pmatrix}
$$

We have
$$
\frac{1}{n^2} e^T A \circ B^T e = \frac{9\frac{1}{4}}{9} = 1.028
$$

The ratio scale vectors corresponding to the two matrices are $\left[\frac{4}{7}, \frac{2}{7}, \frac{1}{7}\right]^T$ and $\left[\frac{3}{4.6}, \frac{1}{4.6}, \frac{.6}{4.6}\right]^T$ which by this measure are considered close.

Again

$$
\begin{pmatrix} 1 & 2 & 4 \\ 1/2 & 1 & 2 \\ 1/4 & 1/2 & 1 \end{pmatrix} \circ \begin{pmatrix} 1 & 1/3 & 1/9 \\ 3 & 1 & 1/3 \\ 9 & 3 & 1 \end{pmatrix} = \begin{pmatrix} 1 & 2/3 & 4/9 \\ 3/2 & 1 & 2/3 \\ 9/4 & 3/2 & 1 \end{pmatrix}
$$

from which we have

$$
\frac{1}{n^2} e^T A \circ B^T e = \frac{10\frac{1}{36}}{9} = 1.114
$$

The ratio scale vectors in this case are

$$\left[\frac{4}{7}, \frac{2}{7}, \frac{1}{7}\right]^T \quad and \quad \left[\frac{9}{13}, \frac{3}{13}, \frac{1}{13}\right]^T$$

whose closeness may be considered as a borderline case.

An example of a large perturbation of a matrix is:

$$\begin{pmatrix} 1 & 2 & 4 \\ 1/2 & 1 & 2 \\ 1/4 & 1/2 & 1 \end{pmatrix} \circ \begin{pmatrix} 1 & 1/9 & 1 \\ 9 & 1 & 9 \\ 1 & 1/9 & 1 \end{pmatrix} = \begin{pmatrix} 1 & 2/9 & 4 \\ 9/2 & 1 & 18 \\ 1/4 & 1/18 & 1 \end{pmatrix}$$

from which we have

$$\frac{1}{n^2} e^T A \circ B^T e = \frac{30.027}{9} = 3.336$$

The ratio scale vectors of the two matrices are respectively

$$\left(\frac{4}{7}, \frac{2}{7}, \frac{1}{7}\right)^T \quad and \quad \left(\frac{1}{11}, \frac{9}{11}, \frac{1}{11}\right)^T$$

which by any measure are not close. We also note that from

$$\begin{pmatrix} 1 & 2 & 4 \\ 1/2 & 1 & 2 \\ 1/4 & 1/2 & 1 \end{pmatrix} \circ \begin{pmatrix} 1 & 2 & 4 \\ 1/2 & 1 & 2 \\ 1/4 & 1/2 & 1 \end{pmatrix} = \begin{pmatrix} 1 & 4 & 16 \\ 1/4 & 1 & 4 \\ 1/16 & 1/4 & 1 \end{pmatrix}$$

we have $$\frac{1}{n^2} e^T A \circ B^T e = \frac{27\frac{9}{16}}{9} = 3.063$$

The two vectors of A and B are

$$\left(\frac{4}{7}, \frac{2}{7}, \frac{1}{7}\right)^T \quad and \quad \left(\frac{1}{7}, \frac{2}{7}, \frac{4}{7}\right)^T$$

which are not close.

Finally, consider the following two cases of 4 × 4 matrices constructed to test compatibility with the vector $[.05 \ .15 \ .30 \ .50]^T$ of:

(a) with a close vector $[.08 \ .22 \ .25 \ .45]^T$

$$\begin{pmatrix} 1 & \frac{.05}{.15} & \frac{.05}{.30} & \frac{.05}{.50} \\ \frac{.15}{.05} & 1 & \frac{.15}{.30} & \frac{.15}{.50} \\ \frac{.30}{.05} & \frac{.30}{.15} & 1 & \frac{.30}{.50} \\ \frac{.50}{.05} & \frac{.50}{.15} & \frac{.50}{.30} & 1 \end{pmatrix} \circ \begin{pmatrix} 1 & \frac{.22}{.08} & \frac{.25}{.08} & \frac{.45}{.08} \\ \frac{.08}{.22} & 1 & \frac{.25}{.22} & \frac{.45}{.22} \\ \frac{.08}{.25} & \frac{.22}{.25} & 1 & \frac{.45}{.25} \\ \frac{.08}{.45} & \frac{.22}{.45} & \frac{.25}{.45} & 1 \end{pmatrix} = \begin{pmatrix} 1.00 & 0.92 & 0.52 & 0.56 \\ 1.09 & 1.00 & 0.57 & 0.61 \\ 1.92 & 1.76 & 1.00 & 1.08 \\ 1.77 & 1.63 & 0.93 & 1.00 \end{pmatrix}$$

with $$\frac{1}{n^2}e^T A \circ B^T e = \frac{17.36}{16} = 1.085$$

which is tolerable; and

(b) with a not so close vector $[.03 \ .25 \ .10 \ .62]^T$.

$$\begin{pmatrix} 1 & \dfrac{.05}{.15} & \dfrac{.05}{.30} & \dfrac{.05}{.50} \\[2mm] \dfrac{.15}{.25} & 1 & \dfrac{.15}{.30} & \dfrac{.15}{.50} \\[2mm] \dfrac{.30}{.05} & \dfrac{.30}{.15} & 1 & \dfrac{.30}{.50} \\[2mm] \dfrac{.50}{.05} & \dfrac{.50}{.15} & \dfrac{.50}{.30} & 1 \end{pmatrix} \circ \begin{pmatrix} 1 & \dfrac{.25}{.03} & \dfrac{.10}{.03} & \dfrac{.62}{.03} \\[2mm] \dfrac{.03}{.25} & 1 & \dfrac{.10}{.25} & \dfrac{.62}{.25} \\[2mm] \dfrac{.03}{.10} & \dfrac{.25}{.10} & 1 & \dfrac{.62}{.10} \\[2mm] \dfrac{.03}{.62} & \dfrac{.25}{.62} & \dfrac{.10}{.62} & 1 \end{pmatrix} = \begin{pmatrix} 1.00 & 2.77 & 0.55 & 2.07 \\ 0.36 & 1.00 & 0.20 & 0.74 \\ 1.80 & 5.00 & 1.00 & 3.72 \\ 0.48 & 1.34 & 0.27 & 1.00 \end{pmatrix}$$

and
$$\frac{1}{n^2} e^T A \circ B^T e = \frac{22.99}{16} = 1.437$$

which is not tolerable.

THE CASE OF SEVERAL RATIO SCALES

Consider now the case of two vectors $p = (p_1, ..., p_n)$ and $q = (q_1, ..., q_n)$ each of which consists of single readings each on one of n scales as in the case of a patient who takes several tests measured in different ways. How should we judge how close are p and q? Here we first consider the ratios $\dfrac{p_i}{q_i}$. We consider the sum $\dfrac{1}{2n} \displaystyle\sum_{i=1}^{n} (\dfrac{p_i}{q_i} + \dfrac{q_i}{p_i})$ and require that it be close to one. If on the other hand we can determine through paired comparisons that the properties have different priorities given by a normalized vector $\alpha = (\alpha_1, ..., \alpha_n)$, then we require that $\dfrac{1}{2} \displaystyle\sum_{i=1}^{n} \alpha_i(\dfrac{p_i}{q_i} + \dfrac{q_i}{p_i})$ be close to one. If we have multiple readings on each property, we could use the same analysis for each as in the previous discussion for a single attribute and add the outcomes and require the total not to exceed 1.10. For a mixed vector with several readings each on a different property some of which are measured on the same ratio scale, we compare these readings as before. Finally we add the different indices derived for the different ratio scales and take their average for an overall index which should be no more than 1.10.

The foregoing discussion assumes that the measurements are independent of one another. If there is dependence among the factors it can be captured in part through α_i above. Measurements from several different ratio scales may be multiplied to form a single new ratio scale. This product may be compared with a similar product by forming the expression

$$\frac{1}{2} \left[\frac{p_1\, p_2\, \cdots\, p_n}{q_1\, q_2\, \cdots\, q_n} + \frac{q_1\, q_2\, \cdots\, q_n}{p_1\, p_2\, \cdots\, p_n} \right]$$

which should be close to one.

USES OF COMPATIBILITY

Compatibility can be used to assess how close the composite outcome of a set of alternatives by an individual is from that of a group composite outcome. The latter can be obtained by taking the geometric mean of the composite outcome of several individuals. After assessing the compatibility of the matrix of ratios of each individual with that of the group, one can suggest to each individual which of his ratios is the most incompatible with that of the group and propose changes in his overall thinking to make it more compatible. Through such revision and recalculation of the group outcome, one may be able to obtain a group decision that is compatible with each member. A similar approach may be applied to test the compatibility of individual outcomes with that of a group whose outcome is derived by combining individual judgments in each matrix. There is opportunity to fine tune such an approach.

2-15. THE AHP AND LINEAR PROGRAMMING

The AHP is a process which converts multidimensional complexity to an integrated unidimensional scale of priorities. It is argued that in order for all measurements to have meaning, they must connect to our system of values measured by priorities of importance or preference. The AHP derives priorities underlying each of the scales in multidimensionality by decomposing complexity into a hierarchy of goals, criteria and subcriteria and then composing the resulting priority scales. As long as we can fathom and understand magnitudes in terms of our value systems (our ultimate frames of reference), we can transform magnitudes of each measurement dimension to corresponding priorities. While we can reduce multidimensional scales to a unidimensional one, we cannot reverse this process. One may be able to define relationships that can be used to convert the composite unidimensional priority scale to multidimensional measurements.

Linear programming is a multidimensional activity. How do we relate it to the AHP through priorities? A linear programming problem takes the form

maximize $\quad\quad\quad cx$

subject to $\quad\quad\quad b_2 \leq Ax \leq b_1$
$\quad\quad\quad\quad\quad\quad x \geq 0.$

The nonnegativity condition on the variables is well-suited for deriving ratio scale results. In some problems one would like to optimize an answer involving intangibles by examining a large number of possible combinations. Linear programming works well only with absolute measurements and we need to make it work also for intangibles with relative measurement.

There are two types of paired comparisons we must make. The first type is on alternatives represented by the unknowns with respect to a hierarchy of a criterion and its subcriteria to obtain the vector c of the objective function and also the coefficients of the matrix A. For example, we can pairwise compare the alternatives with respect to profit or cost per unit of each with maximization or minimization in mind. For the coefficients in the constraints, for example, in a diet problem we can compare the relative contribution to several health criteria. In this manner, for each criterion we obtain the left hand side of a constraint. If the criteria have weights, we can use each of these to weight the corresponding coefficients of A.

Again each constraint is bounded above and below by vectors b_1 and b_2, respectively, corresponding to required maximum and minimum amounts of a nutrient for example. Note first that we can divide each two-sided inequality by the sum of all the upper bounds, the coefficients of b_1 thus reducing the right side to relative numbers. If we then multiply and divide each entry on the left by the sum of the coefficients of b_2 we obtain on the left normalized values of these coefficients each multiplied by the same constant that is the ratio of the sum of the coefficients of b_2 divided by the sum of the coefficients of b_1. In the middle, each component of the unknown vector x would also be divided by the sum of the coefficients of b_1. The question then is how to determine the relative values of the upper and lower bounds. In the diet problem one must consider a certain size and age individual at a prescribed level of activity and determine the relative value of each type of nutrient that is needed. Here we need a hierarchy to assess the relative amounts of nutrients the person needs for better health performance according to weight, cell regeneration, health appearance, energy level (calories), stamina, immunity to disease (vitamins), and resistance to temperature (fat). We would recognize carbohydrates, proteins and minerals by tasting different grains, meats, vegetables and fruits. Pairwise comparison of these gives relative numbers. The resulting vector of ratios must be converted to an absolute vector b_1 by multiplying by a constant. How?

Note that because we have determined the coefficients of b_1 proportionately, if we multiply these coefficients by a constant, we can then also multiply each variable x on the left by the same constant. Thus, the solution would belong to a ratio scale. In the end one can increase the solution values of the unknowns proportionately until a level of satisfaction is reached. Herbert Simon's idea of *satisficing* has a significant scientific validation from this perspective because the determination of b_1 depends on what values are suitable at a given time and have no intrinsic meaning deriving from the mathematical structure of the problem. Yet their proportionality is an intrinsic factor. Here we see that linear programming is only meaningful with ratio scales and has intimate connection with the AHP. Consideration of the dual problem in linear programming gives further validation to the foregoing observations.

AN EXAMPLE

The diet problem in linear programming is a good illustration of how one might use judgments based on experience to construct a linear programming problem. Of course our object is to deal with intangibles by learning what to do when measurements are available. Suppose we have the following information shown in Table 2-14 on choosing among nine foods to consider for a daily diet to minimize the costs and satisfy three constraints on the amount of calories from carbohydrates, amount of protein and of fat as required in the column under b_1. Here the costs are determined from a hierarchy with three criteria: price, flavor, and cooking time whose priorities from paired comparisons are 0.674, 0.226, and 0.101 respectively. The costs in the table are the composite values obtained by using the actual costs per unit of the food under price, and the values with respect to the other two criteria obtained through judgments. The priorities under b_1 were also obtained through paired comparisons made by a dietitian. The priorities were so close to the actual values that we simply use the relative values of the latter for accuracy. The real problem here is to determine the a_{ij} for each food and each of the three kinds of requirements. The values given in Table 2-14 were obtained from the literature where they are given in calories per 100 grams. This requires that the relative solution to the resulting linear programming problem be converted to absolute values by multiplying by both 100 and 2300 (the maximum calories per day). Let us make an observation here about how the a_{ij} could be determined through paired comparisons. An experienced person could conceivably design observational experiments in which the foods would be compared first as to the amount of energy derived from them. They can also be compared as to the muscle tone they provide as protein and also as to how much they contribute to body size and fatness thus obtaining the relative values of the a_{ij}. Of course in this problem we have the values and do not need this kind of exercise, but in reality the problem may involve intangible criteria for which something like this has to be done. Furthermore, all these criteria can be combined in a single hierarchy and prioritized according to the importance of their contribution to overall health, in the end yielding a composite vector for a single inequality in the a_{ij}. The single coefficient of b_1 would then also be obtained by weighting by the corresponding criteria and adding. In this case a linear programming problem takes a simpler form involving a single constraint.

We do not recommend this procedure because it assumes that all the constraints are interchangeable, and in this case they definitely are not.   One often encounters the objection in the literature that all the constraints of a linear programming problem are assumed to be equally binding.   We see here that using a hierarchy, the constraints can be combined and the complexity of the problem reduced, at least in theory.   How valid the final answer may be requires investigation, which appears to be a fertile area for research.   The AHP would give one the single most preferred compromise food in which some of the requirements may be completely absent.

Table 2-14 Diet Problem Mostly Treated as Intangible

Foods	Cheese	Fish	Margarine	Chicken	Flakes	Eggs	Vegetables	Bread	Milk	b_1
Variables	x_1	x_2	x_3	x_4	x_5	x_6	x_7	x_8	x_9	
Costs	0.218	0.199	0.122	0.113	0.099	0.092	0.078	0.044	0.034	
Carbohydr.	0	0	0	0	252	0	32	240	20	0.58
Protein	88	80	0	8	52	48	4	40	12	0.30
Fat	216	27	900	45	36	108	0	0	27	0.12
Solution	0	0.001	0	0	0	0.001	0	0.002	0	
Absolute	0	242.6	0	0	0	194.89	0	555.83	0	

2-16. APPLICATIONS IN INDUSTRY AND GOVERNMENT

The AHP has been applied in a variety of areas. It has been used extensively in the economics/management area for auditing, database selection, design, architecture, finance, macro-economic forecasting, marketing (consumer choice, product design and development, strategy), planning, portfolio selection, facility location, forecasting, resource allocation (budget, energy, health, project), sequential decisions,policy/strategy, transportation, water research, and performance analysis. In political problems, the AHP has been used in such areas as arms control, conflicts and negotiation, political candidacy, security assessments, war games, and world influence. For social concerns, it is applied in education, behavior in competition, environmental issues, health, law, medicine (drug effectiveness, therapy selection), population dynamics (interregional migration patterns, population size), and public sector. Some technological applications include market selection, portfolio selection, and technology transfer.

Example: To Build or Not to Build a Stadium

Decomposing the analysis of a complex decision in terms of benefits, opportunities, costs and risks can be of considerable value. It may well be that using some but not all of these forms of considerations would lead to a different decision than would using all forms. This approach was used to decide whether a baseball club should or should not build a new stadium. The benefits hierarchy included an economic criterion with subcriteria: city use, funds infused, and build tax base, and a social criterion with subcriteria: first class city status, civic identity, and recreation and entertainment. The opportunities hierarchy included the criteria: the team would stay in the city, additional jobs, more business, developing areas of city not in use, tie in to games and for concerts and conventions. The costs hierarchy included the criteria: increased tax on tax payers, improving infrastructure to facilitate new stadium, lost funds for other programsd, cost of land for a new stadium and lost revenue from old stadium. The risks hierarchy included the criteria: city's bond rating suffers, team leaves town anyway after a while, voter alienated by process, lost identity of parties involved, debt assumed by local problems such as parking and crime. The outcome of the analysis was as follows:

	Benefits	Oppor-tunities	Costs	Risks	Standard B/C	Pessimistic B/(CxR)	Realistic (BxO)/(CxR)
Build	0.696	0.815	0.769	0.576	0.905	1.571	1.280
Don't build	0.304	0.185	0.231	0.424	1.310	3.104	0.574

It is an interesting postscript to note that the new stadium (in Pittsburgh) in fact was built. If one had only considered benefits and costs, or benefits, costs and risks, the recommendation would have been not to build. Opportunities here made the difference.

Additional applications are discussed in Golden et al.[20]; R.F. Dyer and E.H. Forman[21]; and Saaty and Vargas, *Decision Making in Economic, Political, Social and Technological Environments*.[22] For a popular and readable description of the AHP and its applications, see *Decision Making for Leaders*.[23]

REFERENCES

1. Saaty, T.L. and K. P. Kearns, 1985, *Analytical Planning: The Organization of Systems*, International Series in Modern Applied Mathematics and Computer Science 7, Pergamon Press, Oxford, England.

2. Saaty, T.L., 1990, *The Analytical Hierarchy Process*, RWS Publications, Pittsburgh, PA (first published: McGraw Hill, New York, 1980).

3. Saaty, T.L. and J. Alexander, 1989, *Conflict Resolution*, Praeger, New York.

4. Saaty, T.L. and L.G. Vargas, 1991, *Prediction, Projection and Forecasting*, Kluwer Academic, Boston.

5. Saaty, T.L. and L.G. Vargas, 1993, "A Model of Neural Impulse Firing and Synthesis," *Journal of Mathematical Psychology* 37, 200-219.

6. Saaty, T.L., 1993, "What is Relative Measurement? The Ratio Scale Phantom," *Mathematical and Computer Modelling* 17/4-5, 1-12.

7. Saaty, T.L., 1994, *Fundamentals of Decision Making and Priority Theory*, RWS Publications, 4922 Ellsworth Ave., Pittsburgh, PA.

8. Saaty, T.L., J.W. France and K.R. Valentine, 1991, "Modeling the Graduate Business School Admissions Process," *Socio-Economic Planning Sciences* 25/2, 155-162.

9. Tversky, A., P. Slovic and D. Kahneman, 1990, The Causes of Preference Reversal, *The American Economic Review* 80/1, 204-215.

10. Saaty, T.L. and L.G. Vargas, 1982, *The Logic of Priorities, Applications in Business, Energy, Health, Transportation*, Kluwer-Nijhoff Publishing, Boston.

11. Saaty, T.L., 1994, "How to Make a Decision: The Analytic Hierarchy Process," *Interfaces* 24/6, 19-43.

12. Expert Choice Software, 1993, Expert Choice, Inc., 4922 Ellsworth Ave., Pittsburgh, PA 15213.

13. Schrage, M., 1995, *No More Teams! Mastering the Dynamics of Creative Collaboration*, Currency Doubleday, New York.

14. Guzzo, R.A., E. Salas, et. al., 1995, *Team Effectiveness and Decision Making in Organizations*, Jossey-Bass Inc., San Francisco, CA.

15. Aczel, J. and F.S. Roberts, 1989, "On the Possible Merging Functions", *Mathematical Social Sciences* 17, 205-243.

16. Aczel, J. and T.L. Saaty, 1983, "Procedures for Synthesizing Ratio Scale Judgments", *Journal of Mathematical Psychology* 27, 93-102.

17. Fishburn, P.C., 1973, *The Theory of Social Choice*, Princeton University Press, Princeton, NJ.

18. Fishburn, P.C., 1990, "Multiperson Decision Making: A Selective Review", Chapter 1 in: J. Kacprzyk and M. Fedrizzi (eds.), *Multiperson Decision Making Using Fuzzy Sets and Possibility Theory*, 3-27, Kluwer Academic Publishers, Netherlands.

19. R.C. Lyndon, Groups and geometry, *London Mathematical Society Lecture Note Series 101*, Cambridge University Press, Cambridge, England (1985).

20. Golden, B.L., P.T. Harker and E.A. Wasil, 1989, *Applications of the Analytic Hierarchy Process*, Springer-Verlag, Berlin.

21. Dyer, R.F. and E.H. Forman, 1989, *An Analytic Framework for Marketing Decisions: Text and Cases,* Prentice-Hall, Englewood Cliffs, NJ.

22. Saaty, T.L. and L.G. Vargas, 1994, *Decision Making in Economic, Political, Social and Technological Environments*, RWS Publications, 4922 Ellsworth Ave., Pittsburgh, PA.

23. Saaty, T.L., 1990, *Decision Making for Leaders* (RWS Publications, 4922 Ellsworth Ave. Pittsburgh, PA (orig.pub.Wadsworth, Belmont, CA, 1982).

24. Saaty, T.L. and J.S. Shang, 1996, "The Analytic Hierarchy Process and the Voting System," *Proceedings of the Fourth International Symposium on the Analytic Hierarchy Process*, July 12-15, Simon Fraser University, Vancouver, B.C. pp. 505-517. (Request copies of Proceedings from www.expertchoice.com)

Chapter 3

Feedback Network

3-1. INTRODUCTION

Many decision problems cannot be structured hierarchically because they involve the interaction and dependence of higher-level elements on lower-level elements. Not only does the importance of the criteria determine the importance of the alternatives as in a hierarchy, but also the importance of the alternatives themselves determines the importance of the criteria. Two bridges, both strong, but the stronger is also uglier, would lead one to choose the strong but ugly one unless the criteria themselves are evaluated in terms of the bridges, and strength receives a smaller value and appearance a larger value because both bridges are strong. Feedback enables us to factor the future into the present to determine what we have to do to attain a desired future.

The feedback structure does not have the linear top-to-bottom form of a hierarchy but looks more like a network, with cycles connecting its components of elements, which we can no longer call levels, and with loops that connect a component to itself. It also has sources and sinks. A **source** node is an origin of paths of influence (importance) and never a destination of such paths. A **sink** node is a destination of paths of influence and never an origin of such paths. A full network can include source nodes; intermediate nodes that fall on paths from source nodes, lie on cycles, or fall on paths to sink nodes; and finally sink nodes. Some networks can contain only source and sink nodes. Still others can include only source and cycle nodes or cycle and sink nodes or only cycle nodes. A decision problem involving feedback arises often in practice. It can take on the form of any of the networks just described. The challenge is to determine the priorities of the elements in the network and in particular the alternatives of the decision. Because feedback involves cycles, and cycling can be an infinite process, the operations needed to derive the priorities become more demanding than has been familiar with hierarchies.

Unraveling their intricacies is challenging to the intellect and is essential for making the computations precise.

At present, in their effort to simplify and deal with complexity, people who work in decision making use mostly very simple hierarchic structures consisting of a goal, criteria, and alternatives. Yet, not only are decisions obtained from a simple hierarchy of three levels different from those obtained from a multilevel hierarchy, but also decisions obtained from a network can be significantly different from those obtained from a more complex hierarchy. We cannot collapse complexity artificially into a simplistic structure of two levels, criteria and alternatives, and hope to capture the outcome of interactions in the form of highly condensed judgments that correctly reflect all that goes on in the world. We must learn to decompose these judgments through more elaborate structures and organize our reasoning and calculations in sophisticated but simple ways to serve our understanding of the complexity around us. Experience indicates that it is not very difficult to do this although it takes more time and effort. *Indeed, we must use feedback networks to arrive at the kind of decisions needed to cope with the future.*

To test for the mutual independence of elements such as the criteria, one proceeds as follows: Construct a zero-one matrix of criteria against criteria using the number one to signify dependence of one criterion on another, and zero otherwise. A criterion need not depend on itself as an industry, for example, may not use its own output. For each column of this matrix, construct a pairwise comparison matrix only for the dependent criteria, derive an eigenvector, and augment it with zeros for the excluded criteria. If a column is all zeros, then assign a zero vector to represent the priorities. The question in the comparison would be: For a given criterion, which of two criteria depends more on that criterion with respect to the goal or with respect to a higher-order controlling criterion?

In this chapter we lay out the theoretical foundations for the kinds of structures and matrices of derived ratio scales associated with feedback networks from which we obtain the priorities for a decision.

3-2. THE SUPERMATRIX OF A FEEDBACK SYSTEM[1]

Assume that we have a system of N components where the elements in each component interact or have an influence on some or all of the elements of another component with respect to a property governing the interactions of the entire system, such as energy or capital or political influence (see Figure 3-1). *Note that the network connecting the components of a decision system must always be connected. It cannot be divided into two or more disconnected parts, otherwise they cannot communicate with each other and it is pointless to ask for the influence of one part on another because there can never be any.* There are three kinds of components in Figure 3-1.

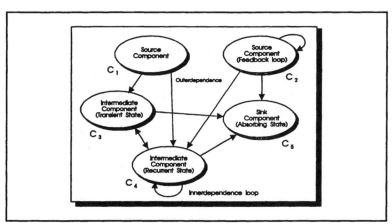

Figure 3-1 Feedback Network

Those components which no arrow enters are known as **source** components such as C_1 and C_2. Those from which no arrow leaves are known as **sink** components such as C_5; and finally those which arrows both enter and exit leave are known as **transient** components such as C_3 and C_4. In addition C_3 and C_4 form a **cycle** of two components because they feed back and forth into each other. C_2 and C_4 have **loops** that connect them to themselves. They are **inner dependent**. All other connections represent dependence between components which are thus known to be **outer dependent**. An example of dependence between components is the input-output of materials among industries. The electric industry supplies electricity to other industries including itself. But it depends more on the coal industry than on its own electricity for operation and also more on the steel industry for its turbines.

In general, a network consists of components and elements in these components. But in creating structures to represent problems there may be larger parts to consider than components. According to size, we have a **system** that is made up of **subsystems,** with each subsystem made up of **components,** and each component made up of **elements.** We might consider that the whole need not be equal to the sum of its parts but may, due to synergy be larger or smaller in the sense of contributing to a goal. Sometimes we refer to a set of objects contained in a larger one as elements when in fact they may be components. The context would make this clear.

We denote a component of a decision network by C_h, $h = 1, \ldots m$, and assume that it has n_h elements, which we denote by $e_{h1}, e_{h2}, \ldots, e_{hm_h}$. The influences of a given set of elements in a component on any element in the system is represented by a priority vector derived from paired comparisons in the usual way of the AHP. It is these derived vectors, how they are grouped and arranged, and then how to use the resulting structure which turns out to be a matrix, that interests us here. This matrix is thus used to represent the flow of influence from a component of elements to itself as in the loop which flows back to C_4 above, or from a component from which an arrow is directed out to another component. Sometimes, as with hierarchies, one is concerned with the influence of the component at the end of an arrow on the component from which the arrow begins; one must decide on one or the other. The influence of elements in the network on other elements in that network can be represented in the following **supermatrix:**

$$
W \;=\;
\begin{array}{cc}
& \begin{array}{cccc}
\quad C_1 & \quad C_2 & \cdots & \quad\; C_m \\
e_{11}e_{12}\cdots e_{1n_1} & e_{21}e_{22}\cdots e_{2n_2} & & e_{m1}e_{m2}\cdots e_{mn_m}
\end{array} \\[2ex]
\begin{array}{cc}
C_1 & \begin{array}{c} e_{11} \\ e_{12} \\ \vdots \\ e_{1n_1} \end{array} \\
C_2 & \begin{array}{c} e_{21} \\ e_{22} \\ \vdots \\ e_{2n_2} \end{array} \\
\vdots & \vdots \\
C_m & \begin{array}{c} e_{m1} \\ e_{m2} \\ \vdots \\ e_{mn_m} \end{array}
\end{array}
&
\begin{bmatrix}
W_{11} & W_{12} & \cdots & W_{1m} \\[2ex]
W_{21} & W_{22} & \cdots & W_{2m} \\[2ex]
\vdots & \vdots & \vdots\vdots\vdots & \vdots \\[2ex]
W_{m1} & W_{m2} & \cdots & W_{mm}
\end{bmatrix}
\end{array}
$$

A typical entry W_{ij} in the supermatrix, is called a **block** of the supermatrix. It is a matrix of the form

$$
W_{ij} \;=\;
\begin{bmatrix}
w_{i_1 j_1} & w_{i_1 j_2} & \cdots & w_{i_1 j_{n_j}} \\[1ex]
w_{i_2 j_1} & w_{i_2 j_2} & \cdots & w_{i_2 j_{n_j}} \\[1ex]
\vdots & \vdots & \vdots\vdots\vdots & \vdots \\[1ex]
w_{i_{n_i} j_1} & w_{i_{n_i} j_2} & \cdots & w_{i_{n_i} j_{n_j}}
\end{bmatrix}
$$

Each column of W_{ij} is a principal eigenvector of the influence (importance) of the elements in the *ith* component of the network on an element in the *jth* component. Some of its entries may be zero corresponding to those elements that have no influence. Thus we do not need to use all the elements in a component when we make the paired comparisons to derive the eigenvector, but only those that have a non-zero influence. Figures 3-2 and 3-3 and their

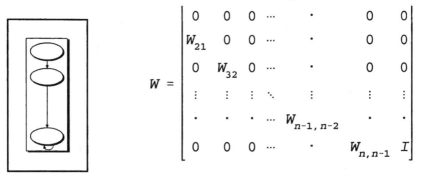

$$W = \begin{bmatrix} 0 & 0 & 0 & \cdots & \cdot & 0 & 0 \\ W_{21} & 0 & 0 & \cdots & \cdot & 0 & 0 \\ 0 & W_{32} & 0 & \cdots & \cdot & 0 & 0 \\ \vdots & \vdots & \vdots & \ddots & \vdots & \vdots & \vdots \\ \cdot & \cdot & \cdot & \cdots & W_{n-1,\,n-2} & \cdot & \cdot \\ 0 & 0 & 0 & \cdots & \cdot & W_{n,\,n-1} & I \end{bmatrix}$$

Figure 3-2 The Structure and Supermatrix of a Hierarchy

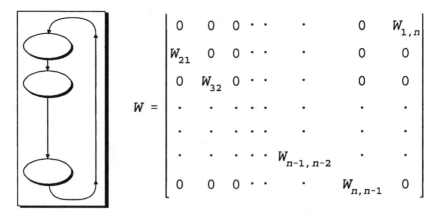

$$W = \begin{bmatrix} 0 & 0 & 0 & \cdot & \cdot & \cdot & 0 & W_{1,\,n} \\ W_{21} & 0 & 0 & \cdot & \cdot & \cdot & 0 & 0 \\ 0 & W_{32} & 0 & \cdot & \cdot & \cdot & 0 & 0 \\ \cdot & \cdot & \cdot & \cdot & \cdot & \cdot & \cdot & \cdot \\ \cdot & \cdot & \cdot & \cdot & \cdot & \cdot & \cdot & \cdot \\ \cdot & \cdot & \cdot & \cdot & W_{n-1,\,n-2} & \cdot & \cdot \\ 0 & 0 & 0 & \cdot & \cdot & \cdot & W_{n,\,n-1} & 0 \end{bmatrix}$$

Figure 3-3 The Structure and Supermatrix of a Holarchy

accompanying supermatrices represent a hierarchy and a holarchy of *m* levels. As with any supermatrix, an entry in each of the foregoing two supermatrices is a block W_{ij} positioned where the *i*th component or level is connected to and influences the *j*th level immediately above. The entry in the last row and column of the supermatrix of a hierarchy is the identity matrix *I*. It corresponds to a loop at the bottom level, used to show that each element depends only on itself, is a necessary aspect of a hierarchy (or any sink) when viewed within the context of the supermatrix. The entry in the first row and last column of a holarchy is nonzero because the top level depends on the bottom level. Again we did not use identity matrices on the diagonal to make easier to see later on how cycling takes place through   powers of the matrix. Both types of supermatrices will occur again in the book.

A network may be generated from a hierarchy by increasing the hierarchy's connections gradually so that pairs of components are connected as desired and some components have an inner dependence loop. This suggests the following classification of hierarchies modified to become networks with feedback. This classification is not used in this book but may serve some need in the future.

A CLASSIFICATION OF HIERARCHIES

We introduce the following terminology for special kinds of hierarchies and their modifications to a feedback system. A *hierarchy* is a structure with a goal at the top. A *suparchy* (Figure 3-4a) is a structure that is like a hierarchy except that it has no goal but has a feedback cycle between the top (superior) two levels. An *intarchy* (Figure 3-4b) is a hierarchy with a feedback cycle between two consecutive intermediate levels. A *sinarchy* (Figure 3-4c) is a hierarchy with a feedback cycle between the last two (bottom or sink) levels. We also use the terms neosuparchy, neointarchy, and neosinarchy for a hierarchy whose top, middle, or lower levels, no matter how many, are connected in such a way that they form a cycle.

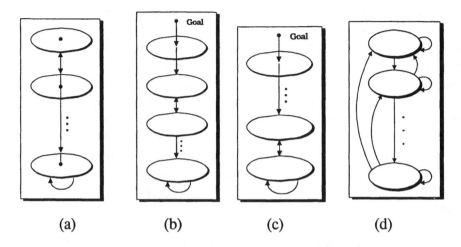

(a)   (b)   (c)   (d)

Figure 3-4 (a) A Suparchy, (b) An Intarchy, (c)A Sinarchy and (d) A Hiernet

A *hiernet* is a network arranged vertically to facilitate remembering its levels (Figure 3-4d). It is possible for a system to have interactive components, which as a whole influence another such interactive system of components as in Figure 3-5. In this figure we have a reducible network because there is no path that connects the bottom group of two components to the top group of three components.

Note that wherever there is a cycle in a network, its priorities take precedence over whatever leads into it, and that the priorities of what leads into a cycle may be ignored and that part of the structure discarded for limit results. However, a cycle can lead into noncycling terminal nodes or portions of a hierarchy, and its priorities have an effect on the limit priorities of the outcome. To summarize, an intarchy and a sinarchy can be truncated and the top parts discarded. Thus for a sinarchy it is sufficient to simply compute the supermatrix for the bottom two levels. Similar observations apply to neo structures.

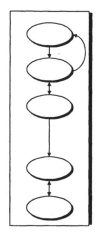

Figure 3-5 A Reducible System of Two Irreducible Parts

3-3. THE CONTROL HIERARCHY AND WHAT QUESTION TO ASK

For clarity and greater precision, the influence represented in all the derived eigenvectors of priorities entered in a supermatrix must be measured according to a single criterion, such as economic influence. Another supermatrix may represent social influence, and so on. We call such criteria with respect to which influence is represented in individual supermatrices **control criteria**. Because we need to combine all such influences obtained from the limits of the several supermatrices in order to obtain a measure of the priority of **overall influence,** we need to group the control criteria in a structure that allows us to derive priorities for them and use these priorities to weight the corresponding individual supermatrix limits and add. Such a structure of control criteria may itself be elaborate as examples in Chapter 5 will show. For simplicity we call the structure of control criteria a **control hierarchy**. Analysis of priorities in a system can be thought of in terms of a control hierarchy with dependence among its bottom-level alternatives arranged as a network (Figure 3-6). Dependence can occur within the components and between them. A control hierarchy at the top may be replaced by a control network with dependence among its components. More generally, one can have a cascading set of control networks, the outcome of one used to synthesize the outcomes of what it controls. For obvious reasons relating to the complexity of exposition, apart from a control hierarchy, we will not discuss such complex control structures here. A control hierarchy can also be involved in the networks of its criteria with feedback involved.

A component in the ANP is a collection of elements whose function derives from the synergy of their interaction and hence has a higher-order function not found in any single element. A component is like the audio or visual component of a television set or like an arm or a leg, consisting of muscle and bone, in the human body. A mechanical component has no synergy value but is simply an aggregate of elements and is not what we mean by a component. The components of a network should generally be synergistically different from the elements themselves. Otherwise they would be a mechanical collection with no intrinsic meaning.

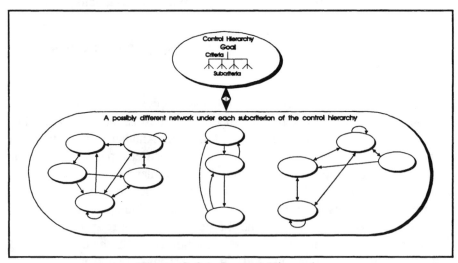

Figure 3-6 A Control Hierarchy

The criteria in the control hierarchy that are used for comparing the components are usually the major parent criteria whose subcriteria are used to compare the elements in the component. Thus the criteria for comparing the components need to be more general than those of the elements because of the greater functional complexity of the components.

There are two types of control criteria (subcriteria). A control criterion may be directly connected to the structure as the goal of a hierarchy if the structure is in fact a hierarchy. In this case the control criterion is called a comparison-"linking" criterion. Otherwise a control criterion does not connect directly to the structure but "induces" comparisons in a network. In that case the control criterion is called a comparison-"inducing" criterion.

The **generic question** to be answered by making pairwise comparisons is: Given a control criterion (subcriterion), a component (element) of the network, and given a pair of components (element), how much more does a given member of the pair influence that component (element) with respect to the control criterion (subcriterion) than the other member?

The material from here on is essential for our purpose but is of a highly technical nature and is included in the book for completeness of the story of the ANP. It explains how a supermatrix that is either positive or non-negative and stochastic is central to obtaining priorities in decision making with dependence and feedback. There are also some interesting theorems about hierarchies. The reader anxious to see how the theory is applied, may wish to move on directly to Chapter 4 and skip this material.

3-4. THE BENEFITS, COSTS, OPPORTUNITIES AND RISKS AND THEIR MERIT RATINGS

Any decision has several favorable and unfavorable **concerns** to consider. Some of these are sure things, others are less certain and have a likelihood of materializing. The favorable sure concerns are called **benefits** while the unfavorable ones are called **costs**. The uncertain concerns of a decision are the positive **opportunities** that the decision might create and the negative **risks** that it can entail. Each of these four concerns utilizes a separate structure for the decision, beginning with a benefits control structure and the network of interdependencies that belongs under each benefit control criterion, and ending with a risks control structure. We refer to the four concerns collectively as **BOCR**, having used the initials of the positive ones (benefits and opportunities) before the initials of the negative ones (costs and risks). Each of these concerns contributes to the merit of a decision and must be evaluated (rated) individually on a set of (prioritized) criteria that is used to also rate any other decision. We call these ratings **merits** and refer to the evaluation criteria to derive them as **merit criteria**. Examples of merit criteria are: satisfaction, happiness, convenience, fulfillment, order, harmony, peace, power, efficiency, social good, progress, wealth and so on. They must themselves be prioritized for frequent use in all decisions. In this manner we can synthesize the outcome of the alternatives for each of the BOCR structures, to obtain their **overall synthesis**. We note that for costs and risks one must ask which is more costly and which is more risky (not which is less costly and which is less risky) because in paired comparisons we can only estimate how much more the dominant member of a pair has a property as a multiple of how much the less dominant one has it and not the other way around. The priorities of the alternatives are now obtained from the reciprocals of their final synthesized values in the costs and the risks structures. This is in conformity with using actual measurement such as dollars on several criteria and inverting the final outcome. The computer program for the ANP does this automatically after all the judgments have been made.

3-5. PRIORITIES IN THE SUPERMATRIX

We are interested in deriving limit priorities of influence from the supermatrix. To obtain such priorities the supermatrix must first be transformed to a matrix each of whose columns sums to unity, known as a *column stochastic* or simply a **stochastic** matrix. *If the matrix is stochastic, the limit priorities can be viewed in a way to depend on the concepts of reducibility, primitivity, and cyclicity of the matrix.*

The question arises as to whether there is a natural way (a scientific on top of a mathematical justification) to transform a given supermatrix whose columns usually sum to more than one, to a stochastic matrix. The priority of an element in a component is an inadequate indicator of its priority in the entire set of components. The highest priority element in a component need not be the highest priority element in the set of components. This is obvious because each component has a highest ranked element and they cannot all be first in the system. Thus we need to compare the components themselves according to their influence on each component in the supermatrix with respect to a higher order "control" criterion. The comparisons give rise to a derived vector of priorities of the influence of all the components (on the left of the supermatrix) on each component on top. This is done as many times as there are components. The resulting vectors are each used to weight the blocks of matrices that fall in the column under the given component. The first entry of the vector is multiplied by all the elements in the first block of that column, the second by all the elements in the second block of the column and so on. In this manner we weight the blocks in each column of the supermatrix. The result is known as the **weighted supermatrix** which is now stochastic. It is this stochastic matrix that we can work with to derive the desired priorities by transforming it to a **limit matrix** described below. This matrix yields the long-run or limit priority of influence of each element on every other element.

Remark: By way of further elaboration on rendering the supermatrix stochastic we note that it may be that only some elements of a component have an influence on some elements of another component in which case zeros are entered where there is no influence. Or it may even be that no element of a component influences a given element of another (there would be zeros for all the priorities represented by that vector) or only some elements influence it (there would be zeros for the priorities of the elements that do not influence it in the priority vector). In the case where an entire vector, but not all vectors in that component, is zero, the weighted column of the supermatrix must be renormalized. It is appropriate to say here that if all the elements of a component have zero influence on all the elements of a second component, the priority of influence of the first component itself on the second must also be equal to zero. However, this is not true when some or all the elements of the first component have an influence on some or all of those of the second. That is why the renormalization of some columns is essential and natural in making the weighted supermatrix stochastic.

We note that if the component of the alternatives of a decision is a sink of the network, and the other components do not depend on it, it need not be included in the supermatrix, and its priorities are used in the process of synthesis after limit priorities have been obtained for the relevant components of the supermatrix. This enables one to ensure rank preservation when desired by using the ideal mode of the AHP. If the component of alternatives is not a sink then it must be kept in the supermatrix whose priorities are analogous to the distributive mode and hence rank may legitimately be allowed to reverse.

ON THE LIMIT SUPERMATRIX AND ITS CESARO SUM

Why do we need to raise the supermatrix to powers? It is because we wish to capture the transmission of influence along all possible paths of the supermatrix. The entries of the weighted supermatrix itself give the direct influence of any element on any other element.   But an element can influence a second element indirectly through its influence on some third element and then by the influence of that element on the second. There are potentially many third elements. One must consider every such possibility of a third element. All indirect influences of pairs of elements through an intermediate third element   are obtained by squaring the weighted supermatrix (see the theorem on the number of paths in a matrix of a graph or network in Appendix 1). Again the influence of one element on another can occur by considering a third element that influences a fourth element, which in turn influences the second element. All such influences are obtained from the cubic power of the matrix, and so on. Thus we have an infinite sequence of influence matrices: the matrix itself, its square, its cube, etc., denoted by W^k k=1,2,... . If we take the limit of the average of a sequence of N of these powers of the

supermatrix (known as the Cesaro sum), $\lim_{k \to \infty}(1/N)\sum_{k=1}^{N} W^k$, does the result

converge and is the limit unique? How do we compute this limit to obtain the desired priorities? It is known in mathematical analysis that if a sequence converges to a limit then its Cesaro sum converges to the same limit. Since the sequence is defined by the powers of the matrix, it is sufficient to find out what the limit of these powers is. It may well be that the sequence does not converge to a unique limit but its Cesaro sum averages out over the different limits of the sequence obtaining a unique limit. As we shall see, both these cases occur for our supermatrix when it is raised to powers. First we note from the Jordan

Canonical Form of a stochastic matrix W, that $\lim_{k \to \infty} W^k$ generally exists. It

is known that W is similar to its Jordan matrix J if there is a nonsingular matrix P such the $J=PWP^{-1}$. Thus raising W to limiting powers is equivalent to raising J to limiting powers. So what does J look like? With every square matrix is associated a unique Jordan matrix that has the following form: It consists of square blocks whose principal diagonals lie on its principal diagonal. All entries that lie outside these blocks are equal to zero. All entries that lie in a block are zero except for the principal diagonal all of whose entries are the same and are equal to an eigenvalue of W, and all entries in the diagonal immediately above the principal diagonal are equal to one. The matrix W is said to be the direct sum of its Jordan blocks. Without too much detail, it is clear

that $\lim_{k \to \infty} W^k$ exists if, (a) no eigenvalue of W has modulus greater than one,

(b) W has no eigenvalue of modulus one other than $\lambda = 1$, and if $\lambda = 1$ is an eigenvalue as it is with the stochastic matrix W, it has only 1-by-1 blocks in the Jordan Canonical Form. In fact one can define a limit in the sense of Cesaro when case (b) is not satisfied. To know that the limit exists and to derive that limit are different matters. We now derive this limit.

3-6. UNFOLDING THE COMPLEXITY OF $f(W)$

There are five parts to the mathematics of this story; four are described in this chapter and the fifth is discussed in my book, *The Brain: Unraveling the Mystery of How it Works* (RWS Publications, 2000). The first has to do with matrices eigenvalues and eigenvectors, discussed both in this chapter and in the Appendix, the second with functions of matrices discussed in the chapter, the third with the characterization of a nonnegative matrix, its principal eigenvalue and eigenvector, the fourth with stochastic matrices and Markov chains, and the fifth and final one with Dirac type distributions (generalized functions) and neural firings which is discussed in my book on the brain.

Three leading mathematicians of the last century laid the foundations for the theory of matrices by generalizing on the solvability of systems of linear algebraic equations. They were the Irish mathematician William Rowan Hamilton (1805-1865) and the two English mathematicians James Joseph Sylvester (1814-1897) and Arthur Cayley (1821-1891). Hamilton, at the age of 21, became the Royal Astronomer of Ireland, holding the position until his death. Sylvester was a poet, a wit, and one of the great creators of terms in mathematics. During his stay (1877-1883), he gave Johns Hopkins University in Baltimore its reputation in mathematics. Cayley followed an early career as a lawyer with a chair in mathematics at Cambridge. A famous result, known as the Hamilton-Cayley theorem, will be used later. Sylvester gave us his powerful formula to represent a function $f(W)$ of a matrix W, and in particular $f(W) = W^\infty$.

The two names that need to be mentioned in the third part of the story are those of the German mathematicians Oskar Perron (1880-1975) and Georg Ferdinand Frobenius (1849-1917). The first proved in 1907 that a matrix of positive entries always has a real positive and simple eigenvalue λ_{max} called the principal eigenvalue of the matrix, which strictly dominates in modulus all the other eigenvalues. With this eigenvalue is associated a principal eigenvector that is positive and unique to within multiplication by a positive constant. In 1912 Frobenius extended and amplified Perron's result. He arrived at a similar conclusion for a nonnegative matrix that is irreducible, except that now the principal eigenvalue need not strictly dominate the moduli of the other eigenvalues but may be equal to them, and the corresponding eigenvector is nonnegative.

The fourth part of our story derives from the study of Markov chains and processes. Andre Andreevich Markov (1856-1922) was probably the first person to draw attention to stochastic matrices because of his work on probabilistic chains of transition (known as Markov chains) among the different states of a system. In this type of analysis one is often interested in steady state or limiting probabilities when they exist and in how to obtain them.

The theory of eigenvalues is essential for characterizing the different cases that arise in calculating W^∞. Here are some useful facts that one needs to know. The principal eigenvalue λ_{max} of a nonnegative matrix lies between the maximum and the minimum of the row sums. Because the eigenvalues are the same for a given matrix and for the transpose of that matrix, λ_{max} also lies between the maximum and the minimum of the column sums. Thus if a nonnegative matrix is column stochastic (each of its columns sums to one), as is the supermatrix, its maximum and minimum column sums are equal to one and hence its maximum eigenvalue is one. If it is nonnegative but not everywhere positive, then the moduli of some of the other eigenvalues may be equal to one. If the matrix is irreducible, then the theorem of Frobenius assures us that $\lambda_{max} = 1$ is a simple root; but if the matrix is reducible, then $\lambda_{max} = 1$ may be a simple or a multiple root.

To see that one is an eigenvalue of a stochastic supermatrix W we note that the vector $e=(1,\ldots,1)$ is a left eigenvector of such a matrix with eigenvalue one. An eigenvalue can be obtained by summing each column of the matrix thus obtaining a vector whose scalar product with the corresponding normalized eigenvector yields the desired eigenvalue. Thus from

$$\sum_{j=1}^{n} a_{ij}w_j = \lambda w_i, \quad i=1,\ldots,n$$

we have on summing with respect to i and interchanging sums and remembering that the sum of the w_j is equal to one, we have:

$$\sum_{i=1}^{n} w_j \sum_{i=1}^{n} a_{ij} = \lambda$$

For a column stochastic matrix, we may take w as the vector e normalized so that $w_j = 1/n$ and the second sum on the left is equal to one and thus summing over j gives the desired result $\lambda=1$. Because the maximum and minimum column sums of a column stochastic matrix are equal to one, $\lambda=1$ must be its maximum or principal eigenvalue.

On The Roots of Unity [1]

If the characteristic equation of a nonnegative matrix A has the form $\lambda^n - 1 = 0$, or even if it factors into the product of several factors one of which is $\lambda^k - 1 = 0$, the roots of the characteristic polynomial have a special property.

By the fundamental theorem of algebra, $\lambda^n - 1 = 0$ has exactly n roots. By De Moivre's theorem for the representation of a complex number z we have:

$$z = a + bi = r(\cos\theta + i\,\sin\theta) = re^{i\theta}$$

$$r = \sqrt{a^2 + b^2}$$

$$\theta = \arctan\frac{b}{a}$$

We can show by series expansion that we also have $z = re^{i\theta}$. We can represent each root of unity (of $\lambda^n - 1 = 0$) in the polar form $\lambda = re^{i\theta}$, from which we have $\lambda^k = r^k e^{i\theta k}$. Consider a complex number z whose representation is given by

$$z = \cos\frac{2\pi}{n} + i\sin\frac{2\pi}{n} = e^{2\pi i/n}$$

where z is an nth root of unity since:

$$z^n = (\cos\frac{2\pi}{n} + i\sin\frac{2\pi}{n})^n = (e^{\frac{2\pi i}{n}})^n = e^{2\pi i} = \cos 2\pi + i\sin 2\pi = 1$$

For every integer m we have $(z^m)^n = (z^n)^m = 1$, and z^m is also an nth root of unity. In particular $z, z^2, ..., z^{n-1}, z^n$ are all distinct nth roots of unity. If, for example, two powers of z are the same, we have $z^s = z^t$, $t > s$, and we have

$$1 = z^{t-s} \equiv z^p = \cos\frac{2\pi p}{n} + i\sin\frac{2\pi p}{n}, \quad \cos\frac{2\pi p}{n} = 1, \quad \sin\frac{2\pi p}{n} = 0$$

having equated real and imaginary parts. Since $\sin\frac{2\pi p}{n} = 0$, it follows that

$\frac{2\pi p}{n}$ is a multiple $q\pi$ of π, and substitution yields $\cos q\pi = 1$, which

implies that q is an even integer, $q = 2r$, from which we have $\frac{2p}{n} = 2r$ or

$p = nr$. But $1 \le p = t - s \le n - 1$, and we have a contradiction. Thus $z, z^2, ..., z^{n-1}, z^n$ are distinct and are all the roots of $\lambda^n = 1$. The moduli of all these n roots are equal to one. In general, when there are c such roots, they are given as follows: $\lambda_1 = \lambda_{max}$, $\lambda_2 = \lambda_{max}z$, ..., $\lambda_c = \lambda_{max}z^{c-1}$ where

$z = e^{2\pi i/c}$ and $i = \sqrt{-1}$.

ON THE MULTIPLICITY OF A ROOT

We will be concerned with the multiplicity of $\lambda_{max} = 1$ for our stochastic supermatrix W. If λ_{max} is a multiple root of multiplicity k of a characteristic polynomial, then $(\lambda - \lambda_{max})^k$ is one of the factors of that polynomial. One way to find k is to apply the derivative over and over again to the point where λ_{max} is no longer a root of the resulting polynomial. Thus if λ_* is a root of multiplicity k of a polynomial $f(\lambda)$, then on differentiating f with respect to λ once we have

$$[f'(\lambda) = (\lambda - \lambda_*)^k g'(\lambda) + k(\lambda - \lambda_*)^{k-1} g(\lambda)$$

$$= (\lambda - \lambda_*)^{k-1} [(\lambda - \lambda_*) g'(\lambda) + k g(\lambda)]$$

and the quantity in brackets is not divisible by $\lambda - \lambda_*$ and thus $f'(\lambda)$ has λ_* as a root of multiplicity k-1. The process can be continued k times, until λ_* disappears as a root and we would then know the multiplicity k.

3-7. HOW TO COMPUTE FUNCTIONS OF A MATRIX[2]

Many real-life problems are solved mathematically by considering functions of an operator. The classic example is solving a system of linear inhomogeneous equations given in matrix operator form as $Ax = y$. Solving such a system requires that a certain function of A, namely its inverse A^{-1} should exist. Using it we have for the solution: $x = A^{-1}y$. In the case of the supermatrix W, what we want is the limit of W^k as $k \to \infty$. This is another kind of function. Thus it is useful to have a general way to calculate a function of a matrix A.

Consider the polynomial

$$f(x) = a_n x^n + a_{n-1} x^{n-1} + \cdots + a_1 x_1 + a_0$$

The function $f(x)$ is completely determined by its values for $n+1$ or more arbitrary but distinct values of x. The $n+1$ values of x and the $n+1$ corresponding values of $f(x)$ lead to a system of $n+1$ linear equations in a_i, $i=0,1,...,n$, making it possible to obtain a unique solution to the system of $n+1$ coefficients and thus determine $f(x)$ uniquely. If two polynomials of degree n coincide in $n+1$ or more values, then they must be identical. Otherwise their difference is a polynomial of degree no more than n and, by the fundamental theorem of algebra, cannot have more than n roots, contradicting the fact that this difference has at least $n+1$ roots.

The following representation of a polynomial is known as the Lagrange interpolation formula (identity), named after Joseph Louis Lagrange (1736-1813), a mathematician of Italian-French ancestry who worked in the court of Frederick the Great and moved to Paris after Frederick's death. This formula enables one to compute the values of a polynomial $f(x)$ of degree not more than n at any point by simply knowing its values at $n+1$ points, $x_1, ..., x_{n+1}$:

$$f(x) = \sum_{i=1}^{n+1} f(x_i) \frac{(x-x_1)\cdots(x-x_{i-1})(x-x_{i+1})\cdots(x-x_{n+1})}{(x_i-x_1)\cdots(x_i-x_{i-1})(x_i-x_{i+1})\cdots(x_i-x_{n+1})}$$

$$= \sum_{i=1}^{n+1} f(x_i)\prod_{j\neq i}(x-x_j)/\prod_{j\neq i}(x_i-x_j)$$

It has a form that is a polynomial of degree n in x, and by the foregoing discussion, uniquely represents $f(x)$. If the degree of $f(x)$ does not exceed $n-1$, the upper limit of the sum would be n, which is its usual form in the literature. Note on the right that only $f(x_i)$ depends on the form of f and not its multiplying factor, which is a polynomial of degree $n-1$.

If instead of the variable x we use a matrix A, then because of the analogy between the algebras of the two polynomials we can write for a polynomial in A of degree less than or equal to n

$$f(A) = \sum_{i=1}^{n+1} f(x_i)\prod_{j\neq i}(x_j I - A)/\prod_{j\neq i}(x_j-x_i)$$

For matrices the x_i are the eigenvalues λ_i.

Sylvester showed that this relation holds for the general case of an entire function of A (an analytic function whose power series expansion converges in the entire plane). He observed that a power A^k of A, when represented in this way, is for each term a polynomial of degree n-1 in A, and the sum simplifies to a polynomial in A. Thus a power series that converges everywhere can also be represented by this expression.

Traditionally this formula for distinct roots of a matrix and more generally for a diagonizable matrix is written as follows:

$$f(A) = \sum_{i=1}^{n} f(\lambda_i) Z(\lambda_i)$$

where
$$Z(\lambda_i) = \frac{\prod_{j \ne i}(\lambda_j I - A)}{\prod_{j \ne i}(\lambda_j - \lambda_i)}$$

The $Z(\lambda_i)$ can be shown to be complete orthogonal idempotent matrices of A; that is, they have the properties

$$\sum_{i=1}^{k} Z(\lambda_i) = I, \quad Z(\lambda_i)Z(\lambda_j) = 0, \quad i \ne j, \quad Z^2(\lambda_i) = Z(\lambda_i),$$

where I and 0 are the identity and null matrices, respectively. The first relation follows by substituting I for $f(A)$ above. The second follows from the observation that two such products involve all the factors of the characteristic polynomial in A which vanishes by the Hamilton-Cayley theorem. The Hamilton-Cayley theorem says that the characteristic equation is identically equal to the zero matrix if λ is replaced by A, and the constant term is multiplied by the identity matrix I, thus yielding a matrix equation.

It is not difficult to show, as in the Hamilton-Cayley theorem, that a polynomial in a single variable with scalar coefficients and the same polynomial with a square matrix replacing the variable have analogous algebras. Thus it is meaningful to form a polynomial in a matrix and treat the polynomial much as one does polynomials in a single variable.

On multiplying both sides of the first equation successively by each of the n $Z(\lambda_i)$, each time applying the orthogonality condition, the third relation (idempotence)   follows.

If $f(A) = A^k$ and all eigenvalues are distinct, we have:

$$A^k = \sum_{i=1}^{n} \lambda_i^k Z(\lambda_i) = \sum_{i=1}^{n} \lambda_i^k \frac{\prod_{j \neq i}(\lambda_j I - A)}{\prod_{j \neq i}(\lambda_j - \lambda_i)}$$

In this formula each term consists of a product of a function of one of the characteristic roots and of a polynomial of degree at most $(n-1)$ in A. Thus, for example, if we want to evaluate W^k as $k \to \infty$, it is sufficient to examine what happens to $\lim_{k \to \infty} \lambda_i^k$, $i = 1, \ldots, n$. In each of these terms we may replace an eigenvalue by its complex number representation $re^{i\theta}$. In that case we would be concerned with r^k as $k \to \infty$, since $e^{i\theta k} = \cos\theta \, k + i \sin\theta \, k$, which oscillates and is bounded. Thus in the limit the outcome depends on the value of r. Now as $k \to \infty$ we have

$$r^k = \begin{cases} 0 & r < 1 \\ 1 & r = 1 \\ \infty & r > 1 \end{cases}$$

Now $\lambda_{max} = 1$ may be a simple or a multiple root. The case of multiple roots is covered by another form of Sylvester's formula which we now give.

Note that in Lagrange's formula the terms involving $(x - x_i)$ in the numerator and $(x_i - x_i)$ in the denominator were excluded only once because the values x_i were all distinct. If x_i is a repeated value of multiplicity k, how do we exclude it k times? Obviously, to exclude it $k-1$ additional times, we must differentiate the right side $k-1$ times and divide by $(k-1)!$. This is done for each multiple root.

We have for multiple characteristic roots what is known as the confluent form of Sylvester's theorem:

$$f(A)=\sum_{i=1}^{k} T(\lambda_i)=\sum_{i=1}^{k} \frac{1}{(m_i-1)!} \frac{d^{m_i-1}}{d\lambda^{m_i-1}} f(\lambda)(\lambda I-A)^{-1} \left. \frac{\prod\limits_{i=1}^{n}(\lambda-\lambda_i)}{\prod\limits_{i=m_{i+1}}^{n} (\lambda-\lambda_i)}\right|_{\lambda=\lambda_i}$$

where k is the number of distinct roots and m_i is the multiplicity of the root λ_i. Now what to do about $(\lambda I-A)^{-1}$?

From the relation of the inverse of A to the adjoint of A, i.e., $A^{-1} = \dfrac{adj\,A}{\det A}$, or $A\ adj\,A = (\det A)I$, we may similarly write, using $F(\lambda)$ for the adjoint of $(\lambda I - A)$:

$$(\lambda I - A)\,F(\lambda) = \Delta(\lambda)I, \ \ \Delta(\lambda) = (\lambda-\lambda_1)\cdots(\lambda-\lambda_n)$$

$$\text{and } (\lambda I-A)^{-1} = \frac{F(\lambda)}{\Delta\lambda}$$

Thus

$$T(\lambda_i) = f(\lambda_i)Z_{m_i-1}(\lambda_i) + f'(\lambda_i)Z_{m_i-2} + \frac{f''(\lambda_i)}{2!}Z_{m_i-3}(\lambda_i) + \cdots + \frac{f^{m_i-1}(\lambda_i)}{(m-1)!}Z_0(\lambda_i)$$

$$Z_{m_i}(\lambda_i) = \frac{1}{m_i!} \frac{d^{m_i}}{d\lambda^{m_i}} \frac{F(\lambda)}{\Delta_{m_i}(\lambda)} \Bigg|_{\lambda=\lambda_i}$$

where

$$F^{(m)}(\lambda_i) = m!(-1)^{n-m-1}(\lambda_i I-A)^{m_i-m-1} \prod_{j\neq i}(\lambda_j I-A)$$

gives the mth-order derivative of F, and

$$\Delta_{m_i}(\lambda) = \prod_{j \neq i}(\lambda - \lambda_j)$$

Note, for example, that

$$Z_1(\lambda) = \frac{d}{d\lambda}\frac{F(\lambda)}{\Delta(\lambda)} = \frac{\Delta(\lambda)F'(\lambda) - F(\lambda)\Delta'(\lambda)}{[\Delta(\lambda)]^2}$$

For distinct roots we have:

$$(\lambda I - A)^{-1} = \frac{F(\lambda)}{\Delta(\lambda)} = \frac{C_1}{\lambda - \lambda_1} + \frac{C_2}{\lambda - \lambda_2} + \cdots + \frac{C_n}{\lambda - \lambda_n}$$

The right side is a rational fraction decomposition of the middle term. If we multiply the two sides of the last equation by $\lambda - \lambda_i$, we obtain

$$C_i = \frac{F(\lambda_i)}{\Delta'(\lambda_i)}, \quad \Delta'(\lambda_i) = \frac{d\Delta(\lambda)}{d\lambda}\Big|_{\lambda = \lambda_i}$$

where $\Delta'(\lambda)$ is the derivative of $\Delta(\lambda)$.

We have for $(\lambda I - A)^{-1}$, known as the resolvent of A:

$$(\lambda I - A)^{-1} = \sum_{i=1}^{n} \frac{F(\lambda_i)}{\Delta'(\lambda_i)(\lambda - \lambda_i)}$$

We also have

$$f(A) = \sum_{i=1}^{n} \frac{f(\lambda_i)F(\lambda_i)}{\Delta'(\lambda_i)}$$

This result, together with the relation $F(\lambda) = (\lambda I - A)^{-1}\Delta\lambda$, is suggestive of a similar representation for a function of a general operator other than a matrix.

In that case the multiplicity of roots is not the main concern, but, with regard to the existence of $(\lambda I - A)^{-1}$, what kind of spectral values there are and where they are located in the complex plane are the serious concerns.

3-8. THE VALUES OF $\lim\limits_{k \to \infty} W^k$

The theory reveals what one must do to obtain the limit of W^k. There are essentially three cases to consider: 1) $\lambda_{max} = 1$ is a simple root and there are no other roots of unity, or, 2) there are other roots of unity that cause cycling, whether $\lambda_{max} = 1$ simple or multiple, and 3) $\lambda_{max} = 1$ is a multiple root.

The concept of an irreducible–reducible matrix is due to Frobenius. A nonnegative matrix (a_{ij}) is irreducible if the graph (with as many nodes as the order of the matrix, and for any pair of nodes i and j there is an arc directed from i to j if $a_{ij} > 0$, otherwise there is no arc from i to j) corresponding to that matrix is strongly connected (there is a sequence of arcs, often called a path, from any node to any other node.) Thus an irreducible matrix cannot have source or sink nodes. Algebraically, a nonnegative matrix W is **irreducible** if it cannot be reduced or decomposed into the form

$$\begin{bmatrix} W_1 & 0 \\ W_2 & W_3 \end{bmatrix}$$

where W_1 and W_3 are square submatrices. Otherwise, it is said to be **reducible**. W is irreducible if and only if $(I + W)^n > 0$ (for proof see Appendix 1). An irreducible matrix has a largest eigenvalue λ_{max} that is simple. If W is stochastic then we know that $\lambda_{max} = 1$. An irreducible matrix is either primitive (some power of W is positive; $W^{n^2-2n+1} > 0$ always), or cyclic, which means that it has other eigenvalues that are roots of one; cases 1) or 2) above. If W is reducible, $\lambda_{max} = 1$ may be simple with no other roots of unity, and case 1) applies, or multiple with no other roots of unity, and case 3) applies; otherwise if there are other roots of unity, then case 2) applies.

The limit priorities are found in the row corresponding to the element they represent. They are normalized for the elements in each component to determine their relative priorities. We now state what the solution is in the three cases.

1) When there are no other roots of unity and $\lambda_{max} = 1$ is the dominant (in modulus) simple root, and because $f(\lambda) = \lambda^k$, the only root to the power k that does not tend to zero as $k \to \infty$ in Sylvester's formula is $1^k \to 1$. We have

$$W^k \to \frac{\prod\limits_{j \ne i}(\lambda_j I - W)}{\prod\limits_{j \ne i}(\lambda_j - \lambda_i)} = \frac{Adjoint(I - W)}{\Delta'(1)}$$

A more convenient, better known, and simpler outcome for case 1) is obtained as we now show.

If the nonnegative matrix W is primitive then[3] $\lim\limits_{k \to \infty} W^k = we^T$ where to form the matrix we^T, w is the (column) right principal eigenvector of W and because W is stochastic $e^T = (1,...,1)$ is its (row) left principal eigenvector. Thus again we have the answer for $\lambda_{max} = 1$ when W is primitive. This outcome can be shown to be the same as the previous one involving the adjoint of W. What is most characteristic of this outcome is that it is a stochastic matrix all of whose columns are identical i.e., all the entries in any single row are the same. If we multiply we^T on the right by the stochastic matrix W we still obtain we^T indicating that the limit has been attained. With a computer, and particularly because the product of stochastic matrices is stochastic, it is sufficient to raise the primitive stochastic matrix W to large powers to get a good approximation to the limit outcome.

2) Let us first show with an example what cycling means. We have:

$$W = \begin{bmatrix} 0 & W_{12} & 0 \\ 0 & 0 & W_{23} \\ W_{31} & 0 & 0 \end{bmatrix}; \quad W^2 = \begin{bmatrix} 0 & 0 & W_{12}W_{23} \\ W_{23}W_{31} & 0 & 0 \\ 0 & W_{31}W_{12} & 0 \end{bmatrix}$$

$$W^3 = \begin{bmatrix} W_{12}W_{23}W_{31} & 0 & 0 \\ 0 & W_{23}W_{31}W_{12} & 0 \\ 0 & 0 & W_{31}W_{12}W_{23} \end{bmatrix}$$

$$W^{3k} = \begin{bmatrix} (W_{12}W_{23}W_{31})^k & 0 & 0 \\ 0 & (W_{23}W_{31}W_{12})^k & 0 \\ 0 & 0 & (W_{31}W_{12}W_{23})^k \end{bmatrix}$$

$$W^{3k+1} = \begin{bmatrix} 0 & (W_{12}W_{23}W_{12})^k W_{12} & 0 \\ 0 & 0 & (W_{23}W_{31}W_{12})^k W_{23} \\ (W_{31}W_{12}W_{23})^k W_{31} & 0 & 0 \end{bmatrix}$$

$$W^{3k+2} = \begin{bmatrix} 0 & 0 & (W_{12}W_{23}W_{31})^k W_{12}W_{23} \\ (W_{23}W_{31}W_{12})^k W_{23}W_{31} & 0 & 0 \\ 0 & (W_{31}W_{12}W_{23})^k W_{31}W_{12} & 0 \end{bmatrix}$$

In this case we do not have a single limit answer because by raising the matrix W to powers, it passes through the three different cyclic forms or phases shown, each of which tends to its own limit that is different from the other two. What we do then for a limiting outcome is to take the average of the three limits which is their Cesaro sum.

Let us compute the average limit value for the case of a cycle of length c by taking the average over large powers of each of the consecutive phases of the cycle. We have formally

$$\frac{1}{c}[(W^c)^\infty + (W^{c+1})^\infty + \cdots + (W^{c+c-1})^\infty] = \frac{1}{c}(I + W + \cdots + W^{c-1})(W^c)^\infty \quad c \geq 2$$

which is the answer for case 2).

Although a computer can be programmed to go through a cycle by raising the matrix to powers, it may be useful to show what the theory has to say about finding c.

Assume that there are c such roots, let W be irreducible, and let

$$\lambda^n + a_1 \lambda^{n_1} + a_2 \lambda^{n_2} + \cdots + a_k \lambda^{n_k}$$

be the characteristic polynomial of W where $n > n_1 > n_2 > \cdots > n_k$ and $a_t \neq 0$, $t = 1, 2, ..., k$.

Now consider $c = \text{g.c.d.}(n - n_1, n_1 - n_2, ..., n_{k-1} - n_k)$ where g.c.d. stands for the greatest common divisor.

Note that if $n_k = 0$, then $a_k \lambda^{n_k} = a_k$, and the last term in the g.c.d. is n_{k-1}.

If, for example, the characteristic polynomial of W is given by:

$$\lambda^{13} + 2\lambda^{10} + 5\lambda^4$$

then $c=3$ since 13-10=3 and 10-4=6. However, if the characteristic polynomial is

$$\lambda^{13} + a_1\lambda^{10} + a_2\lambda^4 + a_3, \quad a_1, a_2, a_3 \neq 0$$

then $c=1$.

3) If the stochastic matrix W is reducible, then $(I+W)^{n-1} > 0$ does not hold, and we need the characteristic equation to determine if $\lambda_{max} = 1$ is a simple or a multiple root. In the former case we would still have the same answer as in case 1). In the latter, the limit priorities are obtained by using Sylvester's formula with $\lambda_{max} = 1$ a multiple root of multiplicity n_1. We have:

$$W^\infty = n_1 \frac{d^{(n_1-1)}}{d\lambda^{(n_1-1)}}(\lambda I - W)^{-1}\Delta(\lambda) / \frac{d^{n_1}}{d\lambda^{n_1}}\Delta(\lambda)|_{\lambda=1} =$$

$$n_1 \sum_{k=0}^{n_1} (-1)^k \frac{n_1!}{(n_1-k)!} \frac{\Delta^{(n_1-k)}(\lambda)}{\Delta^{(n_1)}(\lambda)}(\lambda I - W)^{-k-1}|_{\lambda=1} =$$

$$n_1 \sum_{k=n_1-1}^{n-1} \sum_{h=0}^{k-n_1+1} \frac{(k-h)!}{(k-n_1+1-h)!}p_h W^{n-1-k} / \sum_{h=0}^{n-n_1} p_h \frac{(n-h)!}{(n-n_1-h)!}$$

where

$$\Delta(\lambda) \equiv Det(\lambda I - W) = \lambda^n + p_1\lambda^{n-1} + \ldots + p_n$$

and the limit outcome is a polynomial in W. It is a sufficient but not a necessary condition. We shall see in the next section that with hierarchies the power can be much less than prescribed by the above formula. This approach for raising matrices to powers was developed more than a century ago when computers had not yet been invented. Although we have given an algorithm in the Appendix 1 for computing the characteristic polynomial and another for calculating the eigenvalues, it is tedious to do that in general. Isaacson and Madsen,[4] in writing about use of the direct approach to obtain limit results in the reducible case, say, "Actually for many examples it is almost impossible" (p. 92). They then develop a special procedure to deal with the problem.

We note that in this particular case of dealing with limits, if we multiply both sides of the reducible case by $\lim_{k \to \infty} W^k$, we would still have $\lim_{k \to \infty} W^k$ on the left. On the right, a large power of W, because it converges to a limit, would absorb the other factors involving powers of W. It would thus factor out leaving a finite sum of terms that is a constant multiplier which we can ignore because we are only interested in the proportionality of the limit outcome in the resulting matrix. It is thus again computationally sufficient when W is reducible and acyclic to raise it to large powers.

The excellent ANP software *Super Decisions* developed by Rozann W. Saaty and William Adams does these calculations automatically without having to go through the different cases. It first tests for irreducibility, and unless there is cyclicity for which the Cesaro sum would be calculated, they obtain the outcome for primitivity as the limit powers of W. If irreducibility fails, they again raise W to large powers. The result is that in all cases the matrix is raised to powers with the Cesaro sum used when there is cycling, recognized by noting that successive powers of the matrix yield different limit outcomes.

Our analysis narrows the possibilities to two cases for computation. We raise the stochastic matrix W to large powers and read off the priorities. If the powers do not converge to a single matrix whose successive values improve in accuracy, we know that the outcome belongs to a cycle whose length is determined by taking successive large powers of W. In that case, we take the average (Cesaro sum) of the successive matrices of an entire cycle for the final priorities.

3-9. APPLICATION TO HIERARCHIES

Let us look at hierarchies.

Lemma: *The supermatrix W of a hierarchy is reducible.*

Proof: Its graph is not strongly connected because there is no path from the bottom to the top.

Theorem 3-1 *The characteristic polynomial of the n by n supermatrix W of a hierarchy is given by* $\lambda^{n_c}(\lambda-1)^{n_a}$, $n_c+n_a=n$,*where* n_c *is the number of elements above the level of alternatives, and* n_a *is the number of alternatives in a hierarchy.*

Proof: Consider row cofactor expansion of the determinant. By the lemma, all elements above the main diagonal in *W* are zero, and this is also the case for $\lambda I - W$. Thus, except for λ in the 1,1 position, all elements in the first row are zero, and hence they and their cofactors make no contribution to the determinant. If we strike out the first row and first column, then the top row of the surviving cofactor again has λ in its $(1,1)$ position and zeros for the remaining elements in the row. In this manner the process is continued. Note that the diagonal elements corresponding to the alternatives are each equal to $(\lambda\text{-}1)$, and all elements to its right in that row are again zero. Thus the determinant of $(\lambda I\text{-}W)$ has the form given in the theorem.

Corollary: $\lambda_{max} = 1$ *is a multiple root of the supermatrix of a hierarchy whose multiplicity is equal to the number of alternatives.*

Theorem 3-2 *The composite vector of a hierarchy of n levels is the entry in the* $(m,1)$ *position of* W^k, $k \geq m\text{-}1$.

Proof: The supermatrix of a hierarchy of *m* levels (Figure 3-2) is stochastic, reducible, and acyclic. In this case it is easy to see that the formula in case 3) simplifies to $W^\infty = W^k$, *for* $k \geq m\text{ -}1$, *where*

$$W^k = \begin{bmatrix} 0 & 0 & \cdots & 0 & 0 & 0 \\ 0 & 0 & \cdots & 0 & 0 & 0 \\ \vdots & \vdots & \vdots & \vdots & \vdots & \vdots \\ 0 & 0 & \cdots & 0 & 0 & 0 \\ W_{m,m-1}W_{m-1,m-2}\cdots W_{32}W_{21} & W_{m,m-1}W_{m-1,m-2}\cdots W_{32} & \cdots & W_{m,m-1}W_{m-1,m-2} & W_{m,m-1} & I \end{bmatrix}$$

It is easy to show by induction on multiplying blocks while raising *W* to powers that when the power $k=m\text{-}1$ is reached, further multiplication does not produce a new outcome. Because the number of components far exceeds the total number of elements in each component, this number is always less than the number $n - n_a$ assured by the outcome we gave for Sylvester's formula.

The foregoing theorem shows that hierarchic composition is a result of raising W to powers. It also shows that to obtain the final priorities, the submatrices of the supermatrix corresponding to higher levels of the hierarchy are arranged from right to left as influence is transmitted from top to bottom. This leads us to the observation that the submatrices on a path leading to a cycle in a network would be multiplied on the right by the submatrices corresponding to the blocks in the cycle and eventually by their limit. Since this limit is stochastic with identical columns, the outcome of multiplying it matrix on the right by a stochastic matrix is the limit itself. Thus in a feedback network with cycles, influence along a path leading into a cycle is cancelled by the influences in that cycle and the paths from source nodes have no effect on the outcome priorities of the network. For a path leading to a sink (such as the alternatives of a decision) from a cycle, the opposite is true.   This is because the influence matrices of the blocks on the path multiply the limit matrix of the cycle on the left and thus makes a contribution to the outcome.

AN EXAMPLE OF A REDUCIBLE MATRIX WITH A MULTIPLE ROOT: HIERARCHIC COMPOSITION FROM THE SUPERMATRIX

Our simplest example of the multiple root (and hence reducible) case is a hierarchy. In practice the structure of a decision problem is often a hierarchy or a simple modification of a hierarchy, so that a feedback cycle is required at some point as in the holarchy in Figure 3-3. In a hierarchy when one is using time periods for projection purposes, the time periods both influence and depend on the criteria in the level under them. A cycle between the two top levels of the hierarchy is then needed. In that case it is simpler to first evaluate the limit outcome of the cycle between the two levels, and then use the resulting weights of the criteria to proceed downward in the hierarchy. Consider the first supermatrix W of a hierarchy with two criteria and two alternatives below on the left and the supermatrix $\lambda I - W$ on the right.

$$\begin{pmatrix} 0 & 0 & 0 & 0 & 0 \\ 0.2 & 0 & 0 & 0 & 0 \\ 0.8 & 0 & 0 & 0 & 0 \\ 0 & 0.1 & 0.6 & 1 & 0 \\ 0 & 0.9 & 0.4 & 0 & 1 \end{pmatrix} \quad \begin{pmatrix} \lambda & 0 & 0 & 0 & 0 \\ -0.2 & \lambda & 0 & 0 & 0 \\ -0.8 & 0 & \lambda & 0 & 0 \\ 0 & -0.1 & -0.6 & -1+\lambda & 0 \\ 0 & -0.9 & -0.4 & 0 & -1+\lambda \end{pmatrix}$$

We know that we are in case 3) because the supermatrix of a hierarchy is reducible, and has no cycles. We have two ways to get the limit. The first is to multiply the matrix by itself. Since it has three components (goal, criteria and alternatives), it is enough to square it to get the answer. We can get the same outcome with Sylvester's formula. It can take more work because for this case it turns out that we need to cube the matrix.

We have$\Delta(\lambda) = \lambda^5 - 2\lambda^4 + \lambda^3$, and

$$(\lambda I - W)^{-1} = \begin{pmatrix} \dfrac{\lambda^2 - 2\lambda^3 + \lambda^4}{\lambda^3 - 2\lambda^4 + \lambda^5} & 0 & 0 & 0 & 0 \\[2ex] \dfrac{0.2\lambda - 0.4\lambda^2 + 0.2\lambda^3}{\lambda^3 - 2\lambda^4 + \lambda^5} & \dfrac{\lambda^2 - 2\lambda^3 + \lambda^4}{\lambda^3 - 2\lambda^4 + \lambda^5} & 0 & 0 & 0 \\[2ex] \dfrac{0.8\lambda - 1.6\lambda^2 + 0.8\lambda^3}{\lambda^3 - 2\lambda^4 + \lambda^5} & 0 & \dfrac{\lambda^2 - 2\lambda^3 + \lambda^4}{\lambda^3 - 2\lambda^4 + \lambda^5} & 0 & 0 \\[2ex] \dfrac{-0.5\lambda + 0.5\lambda^2}{\lambda^3 - 2\lambda^4 + \lambda^5} & \dfrac{-0.1\lambda^2 + 0.1\lambda^3}{\lambda^3 - 2\lambda^4 + \lambda^5} & \dfrac{-0.6\lambda^2 + 0.4\lambda^3}{\lambda^3 - 2\lambda^4 + \lambda^5} & \dfrac{-\lambda^3 + \lambda^4}{\lambda^3 - 2\lambda^4 + \lambda^5} & 0 \\[2ex] \dfrac{-0.5\lambda + 0.5\lambda^2}{\lambda^3 - 2\lambda^4 + \lambda^5} & \dfrac{-0.9\lambda^2 + 0.9\lambda^3}{\lambda^3 - 2\lambda^4 + \lambda^5} & \dfrac{-0.4\lambda^2 + 0.4\lambda^3}{\lambda^3 - 2\lambda^4 + \lambda^5} & 0 & \dfrac{-\lambda^3 + \lambda^4}{\lambda^3 - 2\lambda^4 + \lambda^5} \end{pmatrix}$$

The formula for case 3) gives

$$\frac{2B^{(1)}(\lambda)}{\Delta^{(2)}(\lambda)}\bigg|_{\lambda=1} = W^3 = \begin{pmatrix} 0 & 0 & 0 & 0 & 0 \\ 0 & 0 & 0 & 0 & 0 \\ 0 & 0 & 0 & 0 & 0 \\ 0.5 & 0.1 & 0.6 & 1 & 0 \\ 0.5 & 0.9 & 0.4 & 0 & 1 \end{pmatrix}$$

The last two rows are precisely the hierarchic composition we obtain by raising W to the second power because the matrix remains the same for $k > 2$.

For the house buying example of Chapter 2, we have:

Supermatrix for Buying a House

$W =$ 0	0	0	0	0	0	0	0	0	0	0	0
0.175	0	0	0	0	0	0	0	0	0	0	0
0.062	0	0	0	0	0	0	0	0	0	0	0
0.103	0	0	0	0	0	0	0	0	0	0	0
0.019	0	0	0	0	0	0	0	0	0	0	0
0.034	0	0	0	0	0	0	0	0	0	0	0
0.041	0	0	0	0	0	0	0	0	0	0	0
0.221	0	0	0	0	0	0	0	0	0	0	0
0.345	0	0	0	0	0	0	0	0	0	0	0
0	0.743	0.194	0.717	0.333	0.691	0.770	0.2	0.072	0	0	0
0	0.194	0.063	0.066	0.333	0.091	0.068	0.4	0.649	0	0	0
0	0.063	0.743	0.217	0.334	0.218	0.162	0.4	0.279	0	0	0

$(I-W) =$ 1	0	0	0	0	0	0	0	0	0	0	0
-0.175	1	0	0	0	0	0	0	0	0	0	0
-0.062	0	1	0	0	0	0	0	0	0	0	0
-0.103	0	0	1	0	0	0	0	0	0	0	0
-0.019	0	0	0	1	0	0	0	0	0	0	0
-0.034	0	0	0	0	1	0	0	0	0	0	0
-0.041	0	0	0	0	0	1	0	0	0	0	0
-0.221	0	0	0	0	0	0	1	0	0	0	0
-0.345	0	0	0	0	0	0	0	1	0	0	0
0	-0.743	-0.194	-0.717	-0.333	-0.691	-0.770	-0.2	-0.072	1	0	0
0	-0.194	-0.063	-0.066	-0.333	-0.091	-0.068	-0.4	-0.649	0	1	0
0	-0.063	-0.743	-0.217	-0.334	-0.218	-0.162	-0.4	-0.279	0	0	1

$$
(I\text{-}W)^{-1} =
\begin{matrix}
1 & 0 & 0 & 0 & 0 & 0 & 0 & 0 & 0 & 0 & 0 & 0 \\
0.175 & 1 & 0 & 0 & 0 & 0 & 0 & 0 & 0 & 0 & 0 & 0 \\
0.062 & 0 & 1 & 0 & 0 & 0 & 0 & 0 & 0 & 0 & 0 & 0 \\
0.103 & 0 & 0 & 1 & 0 & 0 & 0 & 0 & 0 & 0 & 0 & 0 \\
0.019 & 0 & 0 & 0 & 1 & 0 & 0 & 0 & 0 & 0 & 0 & 0 \\
0.034 & 0 & 0 & 0 & 0 & 1 & 0 & 0 & 0 & 0 & 0 & 0 \\
0.041 & 0 & 0 & 0 & 0 & 0 & 1 & 0 & 0 & 0 & 0 & 0 \\
0.221 & 0 & 0 & 0 & 0 & 0 & 0 & 1 & 0 & 0 & 0 & 0 \\
0.345 & 0 & 0 & 0 & 0 & 0 & 0 & 0 & 1 & 0 & 0 & 0 \\
0.346 & 0.743 & 0.194 & 0.717 & 0.333 & 0.691 & 0.770 & 0.2 & 0.072 & 1 & 0 & 0 \\
0.369 & 0.194 & 0.063 & 0.066 & 0.333 & 0.091 & 0.068 & 0.4 & 0.649 & 0 & 1 & 0 \\
0.285 & 0.063 & 0.743 & 0.217 & 0.334 & 0.218 & 0.162 & 0.4 & 0.279 & 0 & 0 & 1
\end{matrix}
$$

By consulting chapter 2 we find that the final priorities of the alternatives coincide with the last three entries of the first column of this matrix. We also obtain this outcome for the alternatives by simply squaring the matrix. We have:

$$
W^2 =
\begin{matrix}
0 & 0 & 0 & 0 & 0 & 0 & 0 & 0 & 0 & 0 & 0 & 0 \\
0 & 0 & 0 & 0 & 0 & 0 & 0 & 0 & 0 & 0 & 0 & 0 \\
0 & 0 & 0 & 0 & 0 & 0 & 0 & 0 & 0 & 0 & 0 & 0 \\
0 & 0 & 0 & 0 & 0 & 0 & 0 & 0 & 0 & 0 & 0 & 0 \\
0 & 0 & 0 & 0 & 0 & 0 & 0 & 0 & 0 & 0 & 0 & 0 \\
0 & 0 & 0 & 0 & 0 & 0 & 0 & 0 & 0 & 0 & 0 & 0 \\
0 & 0 & 0 & 0 & 0 & 0 & 0 & 0 & 0 & 0 & 0 & 0 \\
0 & 0 & 0 & 0 & 0 & 0 & 0 & 0 & 0 & 0 & 0 & 0 \\
0 & 0 & 0 & 0 & 0 & 0 & 0 & 0 & 0 & 0 & 0 & 0 \\
0.346 & 0.743 & 0.194 & 0.717 & 0.333 & 0.691 & 0.770 & 0.2 & 0.072 & 1 & 0 & 0 \\
0.369 & 0.194 & 0.063 & 0.066 & 0.333 & 0.091 & 0.068 & 0.4 & 0.649 & 0 & 1 & 0 \\
0.285 & 0.063 & 0.743 & 0.217 & 0.334 & 0.218 & 0.162 & 0.4 & 0.279 & 0 & 0 & 1
\end{matrix}
$$

INNER DEPENDENCE OF CRITERIA

Consider a three-level hierarchy with a goal, criteria, and alternatives. Assume that the criteria are dependent among themselves. The supermatrix representation is given by:

$$
W = \begin{pmatrix} 0 & 0 & 0 \\ X & Y & 0 \\ 0 & Z & I \end{pmatrix}
$$

where X is the column vector of priorities of the criteria with respect to the goal, Y is the matrix of column eigenvectors of interdependence among the criteria, and Z is the matrix of column eigenvectors of the alternatives with respect to each criterion. W is a column stochastic matrix obtained by appropriate weighting of the matrices corresponding to interactions between levels.

The kth power of W that captures rank dominance along paths of length k is given by:

$$W^k = \begin{pmatrix} 0 & 0 & 0 \\ Y^{k-1}X & Y^k & 0 \\ Z\sum_{i=0}^{n-2} Y^iX & Z\sum_{i=0}^{n-1} Y^i & I \end{pmatrix}$$

and the priorities are obtained from the limit of W^k as $k \to \infty$. We have:

$$W^\infty = \begin{pmatrix} 0 & 0 & 0 \\ 0 & 0 & 0 \\ Z(I-Y)^{-1}X & Z(I-Y)^{-1} & I \end{pmatrix}$$

Note that if $Y=0$, and hence the criteria are independent among themselves, the weights of the alternatives are given by ZX, the result of the additive model obtained by hierarchic composition. Also when Y is not zero but is a small perturbation in a neighborhood of the null matrix, the additive model would be a good representation of the limit priorities, and hierarchic composition is still valid. It is only when Y is a large perturbation away from zero that the supermatrix solution should be used. In general, unless there are strong dependencies among the criteria, the additive model is an adequate estimate of the priorities in a hierarchy. Otherwise the criteria should be redefined to ensure the independence of the new set.

3-10. THE CONSISTENCY OF A SYSTEM

We want to represent both the inconsistency in paths beginning with a goal and the inconsistency in cycles. For paths we want the initial, not the limit, priorities of the elements. For cycles we want the limit priorities of the elements. We need to weight inconsistency by the weight of the corresponding elements. Also we need the influence priority of a component containing an element used to compare elements in another component, on that component. In the end we need to weight by the priorities K_C of the supercriteria in the control hierarchy.

$$C_S = \sum_{\substack{control \\ criteria}} K_C \sum_{\substack{all \\ chains}} (\sum_{j=1}^{h} \sum_{i=1}^{n_{ij+1}} w_{ij}\, \mu_{ij+1} + \sum_{\substack{control \\ criteria}} K_C \sum_{k=1}^{S} \sum_{j=1}^{n_k} w_{jk} \sum_{h=1}^{|C_h|} w_{(k)(h)}\mu_k(j,h)$$

where $n_j = j = 1, 2, ..., h$ is the number of elements in the jth level and μ_{ij+1} is the consistency index of all elements in the $(j+1)^{st}$ level with respect to the ith criterion of the jth level. In the second term, $w_{(k)(h)}$ is the priority of the influence of the hth component on the k component and w_{jk} is the limit priority of the jth element in the kth component. In the case of a hierarchy, there are no cycles and the second term is equal to zero. As in the measurement of consistency of a hierarchy, this index must be divided by the corresponding index with random inconsistencies.

3-11. JUDGMENTS: THEIR QUALITY AND NUMBER

The number of judgments and their validity are two constant concerns particularly to users of the ANP. One would prefer not to tax the energy of the decision maker. One may be willing to spend more time on an important decision but may not have the desire to confirm the obvious by putting forth too much effort. This kind of concern is legitimate. Also, no one would argue that with less information provided, the decision may not be as certain as it would be if an exhaustive analysis were made. Sometimes it should be possible to do a back-of-the-envelope estimation to determine whether a certain outcome is worth pursuing. Then the staff can spend more time verifying and validating the decision with a thorough development. What methods can we use to expedite decision making without loss of validity? That will be our concern in this section.

The following ideas can be used to control the number of judgments in the model:
1. Good results are the outcome of good judgments, and there is no good, ready-made substitute for that knowledge. The more complex the problem, the more complex its structure and the more judgments are needed. Patience is a virtue in any creative effort.
2. Make a smaller model.
3. Reduce the number of components.
4. Reduce the number of elements in each component.
5. Pairwise compare the control criteria and subcriteria and eliminate those with small priorities, since there is no feedback among them.
6. Pairwise compare the components influence on each component and compute the limit priorities of the resulting supermatrix. Drop those components whose limit weight is very small relative to the others.
7. Assign priorities geometrically using the software by adjusting the relative length of bars associated with the elements. It can also be done arithmetically by assigning them numbers that are then normalized and introduced into the supermatrix.
8. With confidence in the accuracy of the knowledge available, in each set of paired comparisons one can fill in the judgments in one row of the matrix or fill in any set of n-1 judgments that form a spanning tree.
9. Distribute the judgment effort among experts specialized in those parts of the problem. Only the most important parts of the problem should be considered by the entire group.
10. Combine benefits, costs, and risks in each judgment and use only one model.

The most scientific approach would be to apply Harker's algorithm for incomplete judgments and use our ratio scale metric to add the next most important judgments until diminishing returns indicate that one should stop. Here is a description of that procedure.

A METHOD FOR INCOMPLETE COMPARISONS

Harker[5],[6] suggests the following:

- Have the decision maker provide judgments such that at least one judgment is answered in each column, yielding a matrix with some unknown ratio elements.

- Enter zero for any missing judgment in that matrix and add the number of missing judgments in each row to the diagonal element in the row, producing a new matrix A.

- Calculate the weight w:

$$\lim_{k \to \infty} \frac{A^k e}{e^T A^k e} = cw$$

- Use the resulting w_i/w_j as a suggested value for the missing judgments to make it consistent with the judgments already provided.

- Guide the decision maker to make additional judgments that have the greatest influence on the weight w. One chooses for the next judgment that entry (i,j), with the largest sum of the absolute values of the coefficients of the gradient of w with respect to (i,j) calculated using the following formula:

x: right principal eigenvector $= w$, in AHP notation
           $Ax = \lambda_{max} x$

y: left principal eigenvector $y^T A = \lambda_{max} y$

$$D_{\lambda_{max}}^A = \left[\frac{\partial \lambda_{max}}{\partial_{ij}} | i,j \right],$$

$$= \left[(y_i x_j) - (y_j x_i)/a_{ij}^2 \quad j > i \right]$$

where y is normalized so that $y^T x = 1$. When an original $a_{ij} = 0$, it is replaced by the corresponding ratio w_i/w_j from w.

Then $D_x^A = \left[\frac{\partial x}{\partial_{ij}} | j > i \right]$ is the matrix of gradients for the

weights x and is given by:

$$\left[\left(\tilde{A} - \lambda_{\max} \tilde{I} \right)^{-1} \right] \left[\tilde{D}_{\lambda_{\max}}^A x - \tilde{z} \right]$$

where $\quad\quad\quad e \quad\quad\quad\quad 0$

$I = n \times n$ identity matrix

$e = n$ dimensional row vector of ones

$z = (z_k) = n$ dimensional column vector defined by:

$$z_k = \begin{cases} x_j & \text{if } k = i \\ -x_i/a_{ij}^2 & \text{if } k = j \\ 0 & \text{otherwise} \end{cases}$$

$\sim$ denotes the matrix or vector with its last row deleted.

D_x^A is a column vector whose elements can either be positive or negative, and their sum is zero.

- We then follow this process. Identify an element of the gradient which is too large in proportion with its corresponding eigenvector element. For example, adding a large negative gradient value to a small eigenvector element may give a negative value. If such an element exists, decide on a proportion (say, 50%) and apply it to all gradient elements for all missing entries.

- If the number of gradient elements that require adjustment is more than one, choose that with the smallest proportion to apply to all gradient elements. This ensures the nonnegativity of the elements of the new eigenvector to be computed next.

- Compute the potentially new eigenvector for each missing entry by adding elementwise the gradient vector to the most recent eigenvector.

- Compute compatibility between each of the potentially new eigenvector representing each missing entry (say p_{ij}) and the most recent eigenvector w, as follows:
  - Construct the matrix of ratios for p_{ij} and w.

- Compute the metric for each missing entry.

$$\text{Metric } (i,j) = \frac{1}{n^2} e^T P_{ij} \circ W^T e$$

where n = the number of elements in the component
            e = a column vector of 1's
            P_{ij} = the matrix of ratios for p_{ij}
            W^T = the transpose of the matrix of ratios for w
            e^T = a row vector of 1's

- Rank the missing entries according to their metric

- Guide the decision maker to provide a judgment for the entry with the largest metric.

The decision maker may decide to stop the questioning or continue according to whether the metric comparison of the new and old eigenvector is less than a predetermined value such as 1.1. One should keep in mind that redundancy is needed to ensure that the outcome has practical validity and hence one may need to add more than a single additional judgment.

AN EXAMPLE

Consider the matrix of Table 3-1 with initial judgments:

Table 3-1 Initial Judgment Set

	A	B	C	D
A	1	2	1/7	5
B	1/2	1	0	0
C	7	0	1	0
D	1/5	0	0	1

Applying the Harker's ideas above to this matrix, we have for the initial calculations, shown in Table 3-2:

Table 3-2 Initial Calculations

Element	Gradient Absolute Sum	Ratio Metric
(1,2)	0.0271	1.0081
(1,3)	0.8739	1.8466
(1,4)	0.0104	1.0013
(2,3)	**1.4241**	**8.4838**
(2,4)	0.0111	1.0051
(3,4)	0.0025	1.0000

Here the user is invited to provide a judgment in the (2,3) position which has the largest metric value. Assume that the judgment is 1/5 which gives the following new matrix (Table 3-3).

Table 3-3 New Judgment Set

	A	B	C	D
A	1	2	1/7	5
B	1/2	1	1/5	0
C	7	5	1	0
D	1/5	0	0	1

The new calculations are exhibited in Table 3-4. This shows that the next judgment is in the (3,4) position because we already have a judgment in the (1,4) position. Assume that the judgment is 8 for this position. Compute the eigenvector and check its compatibility with the previous eigenvector. If they are acceptably close, stop. Otherwise, continue. The process needs refinements to make it work successfully all the time.

Table 3-4 New Calculations

Element	Gradient Absolute Sum	Ratio Metric
(1,2)	0.4261	15.0431
(1,3)	1.2518	1.4560
(1,4)	0.3994	2.9926
(2,3)	0.6131	1.1385
(2,4)	0.3859	2.2172
(3,4)	**0.3962**	**2.9019**

3-12. FEEDBACK CAN CAUSE AN UNIMPORTANT ELEMENT TO BECOME IMPORTANT

The following example illustrates how an element e_{12} that has low priority in its component (Table 3-5) but has high priority of influence on elements in other components obtains a high overall priority in the limit (Table 3-6). The idea is that intuitively one may assume that at first glance that element is unimportant relative to its component, and therefore perhaps unimportant overall, but finds with the ANP that it is the most important element. Here we give the initial and the limit supermatrices. We also learn from this example that while in a hierarchy we can proceed downward by ignoring the judgments of subcriteria and alternatives under a low priority criterion, we cannot do the same in a feedback process because an initially unimportant criterion may become more important in the cycling and limit operations.

Table 3-5 The Supermatrix of Column Eigenvectors

	e_{11}	e_{12}	e_{13}	e_{21}	e_{22}	e_{31}	e_{32}	e_{41}	e_{42}
e_{11}	0.021	0.025	0.028	0.025	0.018	0.022	0.026	0.020	0.028
e_{12}	0.005	0.005	0.005	0.189	0.245	0.243	0.225	0.241	0.246
e_{13}	0.223	0.220	0.217	0.119	0.071	0.068	0.082	0.073	0.059
e_{21}	0.219	0.214	0.222	0.000	0.000	0.277	0.277	0.222	0.250
e_{22}	0.031	0.036	0.028	0.000	0.000	0.056	0.056	0.111	0.083
e_{31}	0.208	0.214	0.214	0.266	0.276	0.000	0.000	0.250	0.286
e_{32}	0.042	0.036	0.036	0.067	0.056	0.000	0.000	0.083	0.048
e_{41}	0.188	0.219	0.219	0.278	0.278	0.267	0.278	0.000	0.000
e_{42}	0.063	0.031	0.031	0.056	0.056	0.067	0.056	0.000	0.000

Table 3-6 The Limit Supermatrix

	e_{11}	e_{12}	e_{13}	e_{21}	e_{22}	e_{31}	e_{32}	e_{41}	e_{42}
e_{11}	0.024	0.024	0.024	0.024	0.024	0.024	0.024	0.024	0.024
e_{12}	0.159	0.159	0.159	0.159	0.159	0.159	0.159	0.159	0.159
e_{13}	0.125	0.125	0.125	0.125	0.125	0.125	0.125	0.125	0.125
e_{21}	0.183	0.183	0.183	0.183	0.183	0.183	0.183	0.183	0.183
e_{22}	0.047	0.047	0.047	0.047	0.047	0.047	0.047	0.047	0.047
e_{31}	0.187	0.187	0.187	0.187	0.187	0.187	0.187	0.187	0.187
e_{32}	0.044	0.044	0.044	0.044	0.044	0.044	0.044	0.044	0.044
e_{41}	0.193	0.193	0.193	0.193	0.193	0.193	0.193	0.193	0.193
e_{42}	0.038	0.038	0.038	0.038	0.038	0.038	0.038	0.038	0.038

3-13. AXIOMS

For completeness we have borrowed the axioms section from Chapter 10 of my book *Fundamentals of Decision Making*. The reader might consult that book for a full description and results derived from the axioms, but the editors thought it would be useful to include them here for ready reference.

Let $\mathfrak{A}$ be a finite set of n elements called alternatives. Let $\mathfrak{C}$ be a set of properties or attributes with respect to which elements in $\mathfrak{A}$ are compared. A *property* is a feature that an object or individual possesses even if we are ignorant of this fact, whereas an *attribute* is a feature we assign to some object: it is a concept. Here we assume that properties and attributes are interchangeable, and we generally refer to them as criteria. A *criterion* is a primitive concept.

When two objects or elements in $\mathfrak{A}$ are compared according to a criterion C in $\mathfrak{C}$, we say that we are performing binary comparisons. Let $>_C$ be a binary relation on $\mathfrak{A}$ representing "more preferred than" or "dominates" with respect to a criterion C in $\mathfrak{C}$. Let $\sim_C$ be the binary relation "indifferent to" with respect to a criterion C in $\mathfrak{C}$. Hence, given two elements, $A_i, A_j \in \mathfrak{A}$, either $A_i >_C A_j$ or $A_j >_C A_i$ or $A_i \sim_C A_j$ for all $C \in \mathfrak{C}$. We use $A_i \gtrsim_C A_j$ to indicate more preferred or indifferent. A given *family of binary relations* $>_C$ with respect to a criterion C in $\mathfrak{C}$ is a primitive concept. We shall use this relation to derive the notion of priority or importance both with respect to one criterion and also with respect to several.

Let $\mathfrak{B}$ be the set of mappings from $\mathfrak{A} \times \mathfrak{A}$ to $\mathbb{R}^+$ (the set of positive reals). Let $f : \mathfrak{C} \to \mathfrak{B}$. Let $P_C \in f(C)$ for $C \in \mathfrak{C}$. P_C assigns a positive real number to every pair $(A_i, A_j) \in \mathfrak{A} \times \mathfrak{A}$. Let $P_C(A_i, A_j) \equiv a_{ij} \in \mathbb{R}^+$, $A_i, A_j \in \mathfrak{A}$. For each $C \in \mathfrak{C}$, the triple $(\mathfrak{A} \times \mathfrak{A}, \mathbb{R}^+, P_C)$ is a *fundamental* or *primitive scale*. A fundamental scale is a mapping of objects to a numerical system.

Definition: For all $A_i, A_j \in \mathfrak{A}$ and $C \in \mathfrak{C}$

$$A_i >_C A_j \qquad \text{if and only if } P_C(A_i, A_j) > 1,$$
$$A_i \sim_C A_j \qquad \text{if and only if } P_C(A_i, A_j) = 1.$$

If $A_i >_C A_j$, we say that A_i dominates A_j with respect to $C \in \mathfrak{C}$. Thus P_C represents the intensity or strength of preference for one alternative over another.

RECIPROCAL AXIOM

Axiom 1: For all A_i, $A_j \in \mathfrak{A}$ and $C \in \mathfrak{C}$

$$P_C(A_i, A_j) = 1/P_C(A_j, A_i)$$

Whenever we make paired comparisons, we need to consider both members of the pair to judge the relative value. The smaller or lesser one is first identified and used as the unit for the criterion in question. The other is then estimated as a not necessarily integer multiple of that unit. Thus, for example, if one stone is judged to be five times heavier than another, then the other is automatically one fifth as heavy as the first because it participated in making the first judgment. The comparison matrices that we consider are formed by making paired reciprocal comparisons. It is this simple yet powerful means of resolving multicriteria problems that is the basis of the AHP.

Let $A = (a_{ij}) \equiv (P_C(A_i, A_j))$ be the set of paired comparisons of the alternatives with respect to a criterion $C \in \mathfrak{C}$. By Axiom 1, A is a positive reciprocal matrix. The object is to obtain a *scale of relative dominance* (or *rank order*) of the alternatives from the paired comparisons given in A.

There is a natural way to derive the relative dominance of a set of alternatives from a pairwise comparison matrix A.

Definition: Let $R_{M(n)}$ be the set of $(n \times n)$ positive reciprocal matrices $A = (a_{ij}) \equiv (P_C(A_i,A_j))$ for all $C \in \mathfrak{C}$. Let $[0,1]^n$ be the n-fold cartesian product of $[0,1]$ and let $\psi(A) : R_{M(n)} \rightarrow [0,1]^n$ for $A \in R_{M(n)}$, $\psi(A)$ is an n-dimensional vector whose components lie in the interval $[0,1]$. The triple $(R_{M(n)}, [0,1]^n, \psi)$ is a *derived scale*. A derived scale is a mapping between two numerical relational systems.

It is important to point out that the rank order implied by the derived scale ψ may not coincide with the order represented by the pairwise comparisons. Let $\psi_i(A)$ be the ith component of $\psi(A)$. It denotes the relative dominance of the ith alternative. By definition, for $A_i, A_j \in \mathfrak{A}$, $A_i >_C A_j$ implies $P_C(A_i,A_j) > 1$. However, if $P_C(A_i,A_j) > 1$, the derived scale could imply that $\psi_j(A) > \psi_i(A)$. This occurs if row dominance does not hold, i.e., for $A_i, A_j \in \mathfrak{A}$, and $C \in \mathfrak{C}$, $P_C(A_i,A_j) \geq P_C(A_j,A_k)$ does not hold for all $A_k \in \mathfrak{A}$. In other words, it may happen that $P_C(A_i,A_j) > 1$, and for some $A_k \in \mathfrak{A}$ we have

$$P_C(A_i,A_k) < P_C(A_j,A_k)$$

A more restrictive condition is the following:

Definition: The mapping P_C is said to be *consistent* if and only if $P_c(A_i,A_j)P_c(A_j,A_k) = P_c(A_i,A_k)$ for all i, j, and k. Similarly the matrix A is consistent if and only if $a_{ij}a_{jk} = a_{ik}$ for all i, j, and k.

If P_C is consistent, then Axiom 1 automatically follows and the rank order induced by ψ coincides with pairwise comparisons.

Luis Vargas has proposed, through personal communication with the author, that the following "behavioral" independence axiom could be used instead of the more mathematical reciprocal axiom that would then follow as a theorem. However, the reciprocal relation does not imply independence as defined by him, and unless one wishes to assume independence, one should retain the reciprocal axiom.

Two alternatives A_i and A_j are said to be mutually independent with respect to a criterion $C \in \mathfrak{C}$ if and only if, for any A_k the paired comparison of the component $\{A_i, A_j\}$ with respect to A_k satisfies
$$P_C[\{A_i,A_j\},A_k] = P_C(A_i,A_k) \, P_C(A_j,A_k)$$

and

$$P_C [A_k, \{A_i, A_j\}] = P_C(A_k, A_i) \, P_C(A_k, A_j)$$

A set of alternatives is said to be independent if they are mutually independent.

Axiom 1: All the alternatives in $\mathfrak{A}$ are independent.

HIERARCHIC AXIOMS

Definition: A *partially ordered set* is a set S with a binary relation $\leq$ which satisfies the following conditions:

    a. *Reflexive*: For all $x \in S$, $x \leq x$,
    b. *Transitive*: For all $x, y, z \in S$, if $x \leq y$ and $y \leq z$ then $x \leq z$,
    c. *Antisymmetric*: For all $x, y \in S$, if $x \leq y$ and $y \leq x$ then $x = y$ (x and y coincide).

Definition: For any relation $x \leq y$ (read, y includes x) we define $x < y$ to mean that $x \leq y$ and $x \neq y$. y is said to *cover* (*dominate*) x if $x < y$ and if $x < t < y$ is possible for no t.

Partially ordered sets with a finite number of elements can be conveniently represented by a directed graph. Each element of the set is represented by a vertex so that an arc is directed from y to x if $x < y$.

Definition: A subset E of a partially ordered set S is said to be *bounded* from above (below) if there is an element $s \in S$ such that $x \leq s$ ($\geq s$) for every $x \in E$. The element s is called an upper (lower) bound of E. We say that E has a supremum (infimum) if it has upper (lower) bounds and if the set of upper (lower) bounds U (L) has an element $u_1(l_1)$ such that $u_1 \leq u$ for all $u \in U$ ($l_1 \geq l$ for all $l \in L$).

Definition: Let $\mathfrak{H}$ be a finite partially ordered set with largest element b. The set $\mathfrak{H}$ is a *hierarchy* if it satisfies the following conditions:

1. There is a partition of $\mathfrak{H}$ into sets called levels $\{L_k = 1, 2, ..., h\}$, where $L_1 = \{b\}$.

2. $x \in L_k$ implies $x^- \subseteq L_{k+1}$, where $x^- = \{y | x \text{ covers } y\}$, $k = 1, 2, \ldots, h\text{-}1$.

3. $x \in L_k$ implies $x^+ \subseteq L_{k\text{-}1}$, where $x^+ = \{y | y \text{ covers } x\}$, $k = 2, 3, \ldots, h$.

Definition: Given a positive real number $\rho \geq 1$, a nonempty set $x^- \subseteq L_{k+1}$ is said to be ρ-homogeneous with respect to $x \in L_k$ if for every pair of elements $y_1, y_2 \in x^-$, $1/\rho \leq P_C(y_1, y_2) \leq \rho$. In particular the reciprocal axiom implies that $P_C(y_i, y_i) = 1$.

Axiom 2: Given a hierarchy $\mathfrak{H}$, $x \in \mathfrak{H}$ and $x \in L_k$, $x^- \subseteq L_{k+1}$ is ρ-homogeneous for $k = 1, \ldots, h\text{-}1$.

Homogeneity is essential for comparing similar things, as the mind tends to make large errors in comparing widely disparate elements. For example, we cannot compare a grain of sand with an orange according to size. When the disparity is great, the elements are placed in separate components of comparable size, giving rise to the idea of levels and their decomposition. This axiom is closely related to the well-known Archimedean property which says that forming two real numbers x and y with $x < y$, there is an integer n such that $nx \geq y$, or $n \geq y/x$.

The notions of fundamental and derived scales can be extended to $x \in L_k$, $x^- \subseteq L_{k+1}$ replacing $\mathfrak{C}$ and $\mathfrak{A}$, respectively. The derived scale resulting from comparing the elements in x^- with respect to x is called a *local derived scale* or *local priorities*. Here no irrelevant alternative is included in the comparisons, and such alternatives are assumed to receive the value of zero in the derived scale.

Given L_k, $L_{k+1} \subseteq \mathfrak{H}$, let us denote the local derived scale for $y \in x^-$ and $x \in L_k$ by $\psi_{k+1}(y|x)$, $k = 2, 3, \ldots, h\text{-}1$. Without loss of generality we may assume that $\Sigma_{y \in x^-} \psi_{k+1}(y|x) = 1$. Consider the matrix $\psi_k(L_k|L_{k\text{-}1})$ whose columns are local derived scales of elements in L_k with respect to elements in $L_{k\text{-}1}$.

Definition: A set $\mathfrak{A}$ is said to be *outer dependent* on a set $\mathfrak{C}$ if a fundamental scale can be defined on $\mathfrak{A}$ with respect to every $c \in \mathfrak{C}$.

Decomposition implies containment of the small elements by the large components or levels. In turn, this means that the smaller elements depend on the outer parent elements to which they belong, which themselves fall in a large component of the hierarchy. The process of relating elements (e.g., alternatives) in one level of the hierarchy according to the elements of the next higher level (e.g., criteria) expresses the outer dependence of the lower elements on the higher elements. This way comparisons can be made between them. The steps are repeated upward in the hierarchy through each pair of adjacent levels to the top element, the focus or goal.

The elements in a level may depend on one another with respect to a property in another level. Input-output dependence of industries (e.g., manufacturing) demonstrates the idea of inner dependence. This may be formalized as follows:

Definition: Let $\mathfrak{A}$ be outer dependent on $\mathfrak{C}$. The elements in $\mathfrak{A}$ are said to be *inner dependent* with respect to $C \in \mathfrak{C}$ if for some $A \in \mathfrak{A}$, $\mathfrak{A}$ is outer dependent on A.

Axiom 3: Let $\mathfrak{H}$ be a hierarchy with levels $L_1, L_2, ..., L_h$. For each L_k, $k = 1, 2, ..., h\text{-}1$,

1. L_{k+1} is outer dependent on L_k

2. L_k is not outer dependent on L_{k+1}

3. L_{k+1} is not inner dependent with respect to any $x \in L_k$.

PRINCIPLE OF HIERARCHIC COMPOSITION

If Axiom 3 holds, the global derived scale (rank order) of any element in $\mathfrak{H}$ is obtained from its component in the corresponding vector of the following:

$$\psi_1(b) = 1$$
$$\psi_2(L_2) = \psi_2(b^-|b)$$
$$\vdots \qquad \vdots$$
$$\psi_k(L_k) = \psi_k(L_k|L_{k-1}), \psi_{k-1}(L_{k-1}), \qquad k=3,...,h$$

Were one to omit Axiom 3, the Principle of Hierarchic Composition would no longer apply because of outer and inner dependence among levels or components which need not form a hierarchy. The appropriate composition principle is derived from the supermatrix approach, of which the Principle of Hierarchic Composition is a special case.

A hierarchy is a special case of a system, defined as follows:

Definition: Let $\mathfrak{S}$ be a family of nonempty sets $\mathfrak{C}_1$, $\mathfrak{C}_2$, ..., $\mathfrak{C}_n$ where $\mathfrak{C}_i$ consists of the elements $\{e_{ij}, j = 1,..., m_i\}$, $i = 1,2,...,n$. $\mathfrak{S}$ is a system if it is a directed graph whose vertices are $\mathfrak{C}_i$ and whose arcs are defined through the concept of outer dependence; thus, given two components $\mathfrak{C}_i$ and $\mathfrak{C}_j \in \mathfrak{S}$, there is an arc from $\mathfrak{C}_i$ to $\mathfrak{C}_j$ if $\mathfrak{C}_j$ is outer dependent on $\mathfrak{C}_i$.

Axiom 3´: Let $\mathfrak{S}$ be a system consisting of the subsets C_1, $C_2,...C_n$. For each C_i there is some C_j so that either C_i is outer dependent on C_j or C_j is outer dependent on C_i, or both.

Note that C_i may be outer dependent on C_i , which is equivalent to inner dependence in a hierarchy. Actually Axiom 3´ would by itself be adequate without Axiom 3. We have separated them because of the importance of hierarchic structures, which are more widespread at the time of this writing than are systems with feedback.

Many of the concepts derived for hierarchies also relate to systems with feedback. Here one needs to characterize dependence among the elements. We now give a criterion for this purpose.

Let $D_A \subseteq \mathfrak{A}$ be the set of elements of $\mathfrak{A}$ outer dependent on $A \in \mathfrak{A}$. Let $\psi_{A_i,C}(A_j)$, $A_j \in \mathfrak{A}$ be the derived scale of the elements of $\mathfrak{A}$ with respect to

$A_i \in \mathfrak{A}$, for a criterion $C \in \mathfrak{C}$. Let $\psi_C(A_j)$, $A_j \in \mathfrak{A}$ be the derived scale of the elements of $\mathfrak{A}$ with respect to a criterion $C \in \mathfrak{C}$. We define the dependence weight

$$\phi_C(A_j) = \sum_{A_i \in D_{A_j}} \psi_{A_i,C}(A_j) \psi_C(A_i)$$

If the elements of $\mathfrak{A}$ are inner dependent with respect to $C \in \mathfrak{C}$, then $\psi_C(A_i) \neq \psi_C(A_j)$ for some $A_j \in \mathfrak{A}$.

EXPECTATIONS

Expectations are beliefs about the rank of alternatives derived from prior knowledge. Assume that a decision maker has a ranking, arrived at intuitively, of a finite set of alternatives $\mathfrak{A}$ with respect to prior knowledge of criteria $\mathfrak{C}$.

Axiom 4:

1. Completeness : $\mathfrak{C} \subset \mathfrak{H} - L_h$, $\mathfrak{A} = L_h$.
2. Rank: To preserve rank independently of what and how many other alternatives there may be. Alternatively, to allow rank to be influenced by the number and the measurements of alternatives that are added to or deleted from the set.

This axiom simply says that those thoughtful individuals who have reasons for their beliefs should make sure that their ideas are adequately represented for the outcome to match these expectations; i.e., all criteria are represented in the hierarchy. It assumes neither that the process is rational nor that it can accommodate only a rational outlook. People could have expectations that are branded irrational in someone else's framework. It also says that the rank of alternatives depends both on the expectations of the decision maker and on the nature of a decision problem.

REFERENCES

1. Dickson, L.E., 1939, *New First Course in the Theory of Equations*, John Wiley & Sons, Inc., New York.

2. Fraser, R.A., W.J. Duncan and A.R. Collar, 1955, *Elementary Matrices*, Cambridge University Press, London.

3. Horn, R.A. and C.R. Johnson, 1992, *Matrix Analysis*, Cambridge University Press.

4. Isaacson, D.L., and R.W. Madsen, 1976, *Markov Chains: Theory and Applications*, John Wiley & Sons, New York.

5. Harker, P.T., 1987, *Incomplete Pairwise Comparisons in the Analytic Hierarchy Process,* Mathematical Modeling 9/11, 837-848.

6. Harker, P.T., 1987, *Alternative Modes of Questioning in the Analytic Hierarchy Process*, Mathematical Modeling 9, 353-360.

Chapter 4

Elementary Examples

Homo Supermatricus - The humans of the future will make momentous decisions this way with the supermatrix.

4-1. INTRODUCTION

In this chapter we use the theory of the supermatrix to work out elementary examples. Our purpose here is two fold. The first is to show how to carry out the operations of forming the supermatrix and passing to the limit. The second is to demonstrate the validity of this approach to decision making with feedback; the widely used hierarchic composition is a special case of it and answers are obtained that are validated in practice to be realistic (correspond to actual dollar share of a market) as the hamburger model shows.

In each case we perform paired comparisons derive eigenvectors and form a supermatrix. If this supermatrix is column stochastic we raise it to powers to get our answer. Otherwise we weight the components according to their influence on each component, and then use the derived eigenvectors to weight the corresponding blocks of the supermatrix. We then raise this weighted supermatrix to powers to obtain the answer. If the stochastic supermatrix cycles, we can either take the average (Cesaro sum) over a cycle, or simply use the power that corresponds to the original setup (positioning of blocks) of the supermatrix. We then read off the limit priorities in the column next to the alternatives (or the criteria if we want their priorities).

There are two precautionary measures that we need to alert the reader about. If a block of the supermatrix consists entirely of zeros, in principle one does not compare the component whose influence gives rise to that block with the other components because if none of the elements has influence on the elements of a given component, then one may expect that the component itself has no influence. This is often but not always true. Sometimes some of the elements may have no influence and receive a zero entry in the eigenvector. In either case one must normalize the columns of the supermatrix after weighting the blocks with the priorities of the components to ensure its stochasticity. The reader may skip the next set of remarks and go directly to the examples.

When there is feedback in a network, it may only occur among other components than those of the alternatives. The alternatives would then form a component that is a sink, with flows into it but none out of it. In that case, one may include the alternatives in the supermatrix if one desires using the distributive mode of the AHP to synthesize the weights of the alternatives because of inner dependence among them with respect to their number and quality (dominance), or if one wishes to allocate resources among them. Otherwise, the alternatives may be excluded from the supermatrix and evaluated by the ideal mode of the AHP for performance. We do not consider the second case here because it involves no complications with respect to the supermatrix. In other words, for these examples, we keep the alternatives in the supermatrix.

The supermatrix takes into consideration both outer and inner dependence. Inner dependence leads to entries for block matrices on its main diagonal. The eigenvectors in each block are derived from paired comparisons. All paired comparisons are made to assess the influence of pairs of elements within a component on another element in that component with respect to a control criterion. In the same manner as with elements in one component, pairs of components in the network are compared with respect to a (control) criterion as to their influence on every other component.

We have used two kinds of loops at some nodes of the decision network. The first is the independence loop that we have at the bottom of a hierarchy or at a sink node. It represents the dependence of the elements in a component only on themselves. The submatrix corresponding to this simple type of dependence is the identity matrix. With this loop the synthesis of the alternatives under other elements of the hierarchy in any level appears in the supermatrix. The second kind of loop is the dependence loop that represents interdependence among the elements in a component. It is mandatory. Its matrix derives from paired comparisons of the impact of all the elements in the component on each of them with respect to a criterion of the control hierarchy (which for a hierarchy is the goal). We ask the question: Given an element, which of two elements influences that element more with respect to the control criterion? From comparisons, ratio scale eigenvectors are derived and become the columns of the block on the diagonal of the supermatrix corresponding to that particular complete loop.

First we illustrate with a familiar hierarchic example. Next we illustrate the irreducible imprimitive or cyclic case with two examples: a simple cycle for buying a car, and another for forecasting the date of a turn-around in the U.S. economy. Then we move to the irreducible primitive case with $\lambda_{max}=1$ a simple root, and there are no other roots of unity (no cycling), with a fast-food restaurant market share example. We then give an example of a reducible matrix for $\lambda_{max}=1$ a simple root (here we re-visit the fast-food example with a different (reducible) structure where $\lambda_{max}=1$ remains simple). In all these cases we raise the supermatrix to powers. The reader unfamiliar with matrix theory does not have to pay attention to our technical breakdown of the problems, just examine the applications.

4-2. ON THE DISTRIBUTION OF INFLUENCE

In a decision problem, the distribution of influence can be handled in two ways. One may determine, according to each of several criteria, the priorities of those elements that are influenced or impacted or favored more by another element (which may be one of them). One can also determine the influence or impact of elements on another element. In this case one asks the question: Given the criterion for the comparison, and given an element, which of a pair of elements is influenced more by the given element with respect to the criterion and how much more? The converse question would be: Which of the two elements influences or contributes more to the given element with respect to the criterion, and how much more? In a particular problem, the column eigenvectors that fill parts of the columns of the supermatrix must convey the same sense of direction. There is no reason why the same problem may not be worked out separately in both ways.

With regard to influence, one may think that an element can influence itself on all properties more than any other element. But this is not true. The coal industry influences the output of the electric industry and its profitability much more than does the output of the electric industry itself, because it uses very little electricity to do its job of generating electricity and must use coal (or oil). The study of influence relations requires not only knowledge of the real world but also analytical ability to identify relations and exercise imagination to pursue the analysis. The ANP generically asks questions that a thoughtful person would ask in making decisions.

Yet one more observation about the influence of components on other components and on elements in those components. A component is an abstract notion that represents a group of elements and more meaningfully the synergy of interaction of these elements. The elements and their interactions are the concrete representation of what is meant by a component. Thus when we speak of the influence of a component on another component, what we have in mind is its influence on each element of that component. But there may be elements that are not directly influenced by that component and their vector of priorities would be zero. Weighting them by the priority of the influencing component does not make the column of the supermatrix under that element sum to one. Thus, because that particular element is not influenced, we must normalize that particular column so that the matrix would be stochastic.

By making explicit the factors of a problem and describing their relations in a comprehensive framework, we can better communicate different perceptions of that problem. The ANP is a useful vehicle for the purpose.

4-3. A HIERARCHY IS A SPECIAL CASE OF A NETWORK - THE SCHOOL SELECTION EXAMPLE

First we show the classic AHP school selection example as a hierarchy, Figure 4-1, and then show its supermatrices from the equivalent ANP model.

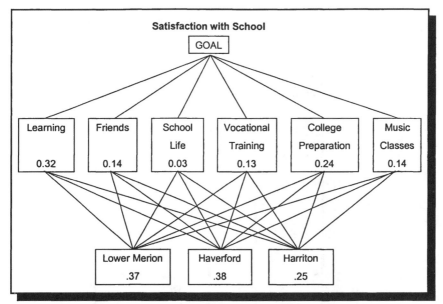

Figure 4-1 Hierarchical Model of School Selection Decision.

Three high schools, Lower Merion, Haverford and Harriton were analyzed from the standpoint of the author's son according to their desirability. Six independent characteristics were selected for the comparison – learning, friends, school life, vocational training, college preparation, and music classes. A hierarchy was constructed with the goal: satisfaction with the school. The criteria and schools were pairwise compared and their priorities derived. The resulting priority vectors were entered in the appropriate positions in the supermatrix of Table 4-1. Note that the supermatrix has been augmented with an identity submatrix for the alternatives vs. alternatives component. On squaring the matrix, we obtain, for this example and for any three level hierarchy (see Chapter 3), the limit supermatrix. The final answer for the alternatives is given by the bottom three numbers of the first column. It is precisely the same as we obtain through hierarchic synthesis in the AHP.

Table 4-1 The Unweighted and Limit Supermatrices for the School Selection Problem

Unweighted Supermatrix

Component	Nodes	1 GOAL	2 CRITERIA						3 ALTERNATIVES		
		GOAL	1 LEARN-ING	2 FRIENDS	3 SCHOOL LIFE	4 VOCAT TRNG	5 COLLEGE PREP	6 MUSIC CLASS	A LOWER	B HAVER-	C HARRI-
1 GOAL	GOAL NODE	0.000	0.000	0.000	0.000	0.000	0.000	0.000	0.000	0.000	0.000
2 CRITERIA	1 LEARNING	0.321	0.000	0.000	0.000	0.000	0.000	0.000	0.000	0.000	0.000
	2 FRIENDS	0.140	0.000	0.000	0.000	0.000	0.000	0.000	0.000	0.000	0.000
	3 SCHOOL LIF	0.035	0.000	0.000	0.000	0.000	0.000	0.000	0.000	0.000	0.000
	4 VOCATIONA	0.128	0.000	0.000	0.000	0.000	0.000	0.000	0.000	0.000	0.000
	5 COLLEGE PR.	0.237	0.000	0.000	0.000	0.000	0.000	0.000	0.000	0.000	0.000
	6 MUSIC CLA~	0.139	0.000	0.000	0.000	0.000	0.000	0.000	0.000	0.000	0.000
3 ALTERN.	A LOWER MER.	0.000	0.157	0.333	0.455	0.772	0.250	0.691	1.000	0.000	0.000
	B HAVERFORD~	0.000	0.594	0.333	0.091	0.055	0.500	0.091	0.000	1.000	0.000
	C HARRITON ~	0.000	0.249	0.333	0.455	0.173	0.250	0.218	0.000	0.000	1.000

Limiting Supermatrix

Component	Nodes	1 GOAL	2 CRITERIA						3 ALTERNATIVES		
		GOAL	1 LEARN	2 FRIEN	3 SCHOOL	4 VOCAT	5 COLLEGE	6 MUSIC	A	B	C
1 GOAL	GOAL NODE	0.000	0.000	0.000	0.000	0.000	0.000	0.000	0.000	0.000	0.000
2 CRITERIA	1 LEARNING	0.000	0.000	0.000	0.000	0.000	0.000	0.000	0.000	0.000	0.000
	2 FRIENDS	0.000	0.000	0.000	0.000	0.000	0.000	0.000	0.000	0.000	0.000
	3 SCHOOL LI~	0.000	0.000	0.000	0.000	0.000	0.000	0.000	0.000	0.000	0.000
	4 VOCATIONA~	0.000	0.000	0.000	0.000	0.000	0.000	0.000	0.000	0.000	0.000
	5 COLLEGE P~	0.000	0.000	0.000	0.000	0.000	0.000	0.000	0.000	0.000	0.000
	6 MUSIC CLA~	0.000	0.000	0.000	0.000	0.000	0.000	0.000	0.000	0.000	0.000
3 ALTERN.	A LOWER MER~	0.367	0.157	0.333	0.455	0.772	0.250	0.691	1.000	0.000	0.000
	B HAVERFORD~	0.378	0.594	0.333	0.091	0.055	0.500	0.091	0.000	1.000	0.000
	C HARRITON ~	0.254	0.249	0.333	0.455	0.173	0.250	0.218	0.000	0.000	1.000

4-4. TWO EXAMPLES: A SIMPLE CYCLE AND A HOLARCHY (BOTH IMPRIMITIVE MATRICES)

We use a car-buying example to illustrate the effect of feedback. It is the simplest illustration of how the process works.

A) Choosing a Car From Foreign and Domestic Types

The decision concerns which of three kinds of compact cars to buy: American (A), European (E), or Japanese (J), determined by three criteria: cost (C), repair (R), and durability (D) (see Figure 4-2).

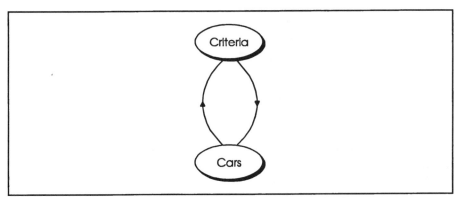

Figure 4-2 Car Modeled with Outer Dependence

First the three general types were compared in three separate matrices with respect to each criterion. Then the criteria were compared with respect to each type in three matrices. We asked: Which of two types of car satisfies a criterion more? We then asked: Which of two criteria is more characteristic of a given type of car? All six matrices are shown below.

For the first set of three matrices one answers the question: "For a given criterion, which of two cars is more desirable on that criterion and how much more?"

Cost	A	E	J	Eigenvector
A	1	5	3	.637
E	1/5	1	1/3	.105
J	1/3	3	1	.258

Consistency Ratio = .033

Repair Cost	A	E	J	Eigenvector
A	1	5	2	.582
E	1/5	1	1/3	.109
J	½	3	1	.003

Consistency Ratio = .003

Durability	A	E	J	Eigenvector
A	1	1/5	1/3	.105
E	5	1	3	.637
J	3	1/3	1	.258

Consistency Ratio = .033

For the second set of three matrices one answers the question: "For a given car, which of two criteria is more dominant (desirable) for that car and how much more?"

American	C	R	D	Eigenvector
C	1	3	4	.634
R	1/3	1	1	.192
D	1/4	1	1	.174

Consistency Ratio = .008

European	C	R	D	Eigenvector
C	1	1	½	.250
R	1	1	½	.250
D	2	2	1	.500

Consistency Ratio = .008

Japanese	C	R	D	Eigenvector
C	1	2	1	.400
R	½	1	½	.200
D	1	2	1	.400

Consistency Ratio = .000

The six eigenvectors were then introduced as columns of the following stochastic matrix:

$$
\begin{array}{c c c c c c c}
 & C & R & D & A & E & J \\
C & 0 & 0 & 0 & .634 & .250 & .400 \\
R & 0 & 0 & 0 & .192 & .250 & .200 \\
D & 0 & 0 & 0 & .174 & .500 & .400 \\
A & .637 & .582 & .105 & 0 & 0 & 0 \\
E & .105 & .109 & .637 & 0 & 0 & 0 \\
J & .259 & .309 & .258 & 0 & 0 & 0
\end{array}
$$

Here one must ensure that all columns sum to unity exactly. The final priorities for both types of car and for the criteria were obtained from the limiting power of this stochastic matrix.

Its powers stabilize after a few iterations. We have

$$
\begin{array}{c c c c c c c}
 & C & R & D & A & E & J \\
C & 0 & 0 & 0 & .464 & .464 & .464 \\
R & 0 & 0 & 0 & .210 & .210 & .210 \\
D & 0 & 0 & 0 & .326 & .326 & .326 \\
A & .452 & .452 & .452 & 0 & 0 & 0 \\
E & .279 & .279 & .279 & 0 & 0 & 0 \\
J & .269 & .269 & .269 & 0 & 0 & 0
\end{array}
$$

Decision Making with Dependence and Feedback

and

$$
\begin{array}{c c c c c c c}
 & C & R & D & A & E & J \\
C & .464 & .464 & .464 & 0 & 0 & 0 \\
R & .210 & .210 & .210 & 0 & 0 & 0 \\
D & .326 & .326 & .326 & 0 & 0 & 0 \\
A & 0 & 0 & 0 & .452 & .452 & .452 \\
E & 0 & 0 & 0 & .279 & .279 & .279 \\
J & 0 & 0 & 0 & .269 & .269 & .269
\end{array}
$$

for the limit priorities of the two cycles. The average of the values is obtained by adding the two matrices and dividing by two (which is unnecessary here because renormalization gives back the same results).

It is clear from this analysis that for the kind of judgments provided, an American compact car is preferred mainly because of the cheaper initial cost, even though it lags behind the other two in repair and durability.

The effect of adding two loops: Technical observations. If we introduce a loop for the criteria by simply connecting each criterion to itself, our entries would normally be equal to one. However, our supermatrix needs to be stochastic to ensure convergence. To do that in this case, we need to assign equal weights to the two components, and hence our entries become 0.5 for the elements in the loop, as in Figure 4-3. The limit outcome is half of what it was previously, but the ratios are the same as before. The matrix is primitive and does not cycle. All columns are identical, the top half yielding the weights of the criteria and the bottom half the weights of the alternatives. We have the supermatrix and its limit:

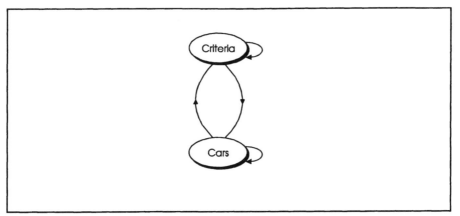

Figure 4-3 Car Model with Simple Inner Dependence

Unweighted Supermatrix for Figure 4-3.

	C	R	D	A	E	J
C	1	0	0	.634	.250	.400
R	0	1	0	.192	.250	.200
D	0	0	1	.174	.500	.400
A	.637	.582	.105	1	0	0
E	.105	.109	.637	0	1	0
J	.259	.309	.258	0	0	1

Weighted Supermatrix

	C	R	D	A	E	J
C	.5	0	0	.317	.125	.200
R	0	.5	0	.096	.125	.100
D	0	0	.5	.087	.250	.200
A	.319	.291	.053	.5	0	0
E	.053	.055	.319	0	.5	0
J	.129	.155	.129	0	0	.5

Limit Supermatrix

	C	R	D	A	E	J
C	.232	.232	.232	.232	.232	.232
R	.105	.105	.105	.105	.105	.105
D	.163	.163	.163	.163	.163	.163
A	.226	.226	.226	.226	.226	.226
E	.140	.140	.140	.140	.140	.140
J	.134	.134	.134	.134	.134	.134

Next, instead of simply connecting each criterion to itself with a loop and assigning it a value of one and then normalizing each column, we perform a pairwise comparison of the impact of the criteria on each criterion. This gives a complete loop of inner dependence. We create such a loop only for the criteria, as in Figure 4-4.

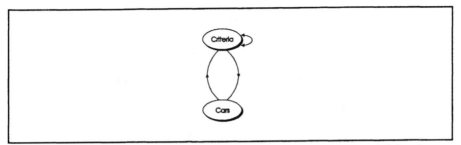

Figure 4-4 Car Model with Complete Inner Dependence of Criteria

The effect of adding one loop. Suppose that the corresponding eigenvectors are as shown in the block at the intersection of the first three columns and first three rows of the supermatrix below. If we artificially weight the elements in this block and those in the block below it by 0.5 as if the components were equally important and then raise the matrix to powers, we obtain the next supermatrix. Here, with inner dependence of the criteria, as would be expected, the ratios of the limit weights of the criteria are different than before. This is also true for the alternatives. Here, the best choice of car remains the same as before. This need not always be the case.

Weighted Supermatrix

	C	R	D	A	E	J
C	.150	.100	.300	.634	.250	.400
R	.200	.125	.150	.192	.250	.200
D	.150	.275	.050	.174	.500	.400
A	.319	.291	.053	0	0	0
E	.053	.055	.319	0	0	0
J	.219	.155	.129	0	0	0

Limit Supermatrix

	C	R	D	A	E	J
C	.278	.278	.278	.278	.278	.278
R	.179	.179	.179	.179	.179	.179
D	.210	.210	.210	.210	.210	.210
A	.152	.152	.152	.152	.152	.152
E	.091	.091	.091	.091	.091	.091
J	.091	.091	.091	.091	.091	.091

B) Forecasting the Date of a Turnaround in the U.S. Economy

The object of this exercise was to forecast the most likely date of a turnaround in the US economy in 1992. The top level of this hierarchy consists of the factors representing the forces or major influences driving the economy. These forces are grouped into two categories: "conventional adjustment" and "economic restructuring." Both of these categories are decomposed into subfactors represented in the second level. For the timing forecast, the third level consists of time periods in which the recovery can occur. Figure 4-5 provides a schematic layout used to forecast the timing of the economic turnaround. Example done with A. Blair and R. Nachtmann.

Because conventional adjustment and restructuring are both time-dependent factors, their relative importance had to be established in terms of each of the four contrasting time periods used to compose the forecast time frame. Thus, instead of establishing a single goal as one does for a conventional hierarchy, we used the bottom-level time periods to compare the two factors at the top. This entailed the creation of a feedback hierarchy known as a "holarchy," in which the priorities of the elements at the top level are determined in terms of the elements at the bottom level, thus creating an interactive loop.

With regard to forecasting the strength of the recovery, we used a standard format for the hierarchy, beginning with the primary factors of conventional adjustment and economic restructuring. Their importance for this part of the exercise was established over a six-month period after the turnaround.

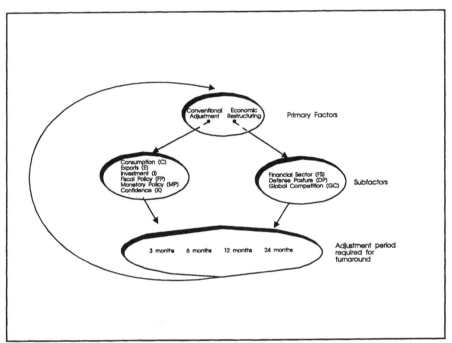

Figure 4-5 The U.S. Holarchy of Factors to Forecast a Turnaround in Economic Stagnation

Conventional adjustment assumes a status quo with regard to the system of causes and consequences in the economy. The presumption is that the underlying structure of the economy is stationary. Forecasting is possible within acceptable ranges of error. This is achieved by tracing the existing network of stimulus/response patterns initiated by a perturbation in a fundamental parameter of the economy. In our view, conventional adjustment can formally be divided into six macroeconomic subfactors that occupy the second level: consumer spending, investment spending, exports, indicators of confidence in the economy, fiscal policy, and monetary policy. We recognize that these subfactors are in some instances interdependent.

Viewed independently, for example, a lowering of interest rates by the Federal Reserve should induce portfolio rebalancing throughout the economy. In turn, this should reduce the cost of capital to firms and stimulate investment. Simultaneously, it should reduce financial costs to households and increase their disposable incomes. Any resulting increase in disposable income stimulates consumption and at the margin has a positive impact on employment and GNP. However, all of this assumes that the linkages of the economy are in place and are well understood.

Recent events in the global economy will exert fundamental changes in the way the U.S. economy will operate for the next several years and beyond by inducing an economic restructuring. The Gulf War, the demise of centrally planned economies in eastern Europe and the former Soviet Union, the integration of western Europe, the emergence of newly industrialized economies, and the quickening integration of financial sectors throughout the world are all events which suggest an economic structure that is not stationary but is undergoing dramatic change. Prudent recognition of these facts suggests that patience and monitoring of events are appropriate guidelines for public policy.

With regard to the nature of the current economic restructuring, we specifically recognized in this exercise the transformation of the financial sector, the reduction in the defense-based component of the economy, and the changing global competitiveness position of the U.S. economy as additional subfactors in the second level.

Changes in the domestic economic environment induced by these factors affect the economy in ways that are not well understood and are too complex to pursue here. We summarize these effects by estimating the impact of each subfactor on the expected length of time prior to a turnaround, as well as their impact on the relative strength of the ensuing expansion.

With respect to the timing of the turnaround, we considered four possible time periods of adjustment. They are located in the third level as a reasonable breakdown of time in periods long enough to discern change in making the comparisons, but short enough to consider all possible changes over the two-year horizon of the forecast. These periods were: 3 months, 6 months, 1 year, and 2 or more years, dated from late December 1991.

With regard to the strength of the expansion, our May 1992 exercise employed ranges of average real GNP growth. Specifically, we considered the following possible outcomes: very strong (5.5% to 6.5%), strong (4.5% to 5.5%), moderate (3.0% to 4.5%), and weak (2.0% to 3.0%). These ranges represent annualized measures of percentage change in real gross national product for the first two years of the recovery. While the ranges are somewhat arbitrary, they generally reflect actual experiences during various post World War II cyclical expansions.

The outcomes depend on the quality of judgments. As noted, the first exercise (timing of the turnaround) was conducted during the third week of December 1991 and refined during the first week of January 1992. Estimation of the strength of the recovery was conducted during the second week of May 1992.

Tables 4-2 through 4-5 provide the associated matrices of relative comparisons as well as a limit and completed supermatrix.

Table 4-2 Matrices for Subfactor Importance Relative to Primary Factors Influencing the Timing of Recovery

Panel A: Which subfactor has the greater potential to influence Conventional Adjustment and how strongly?

		C	E	I	K	F	M	Vector Weights
Consumption	(C)	1	7	5	1/5	½	1/5	0.118
Exports	(E)	1/7	1	1/5	1/5	1/5	1/7	0.029
Investment	(I)	1/5	5	1	1/5	1/3	1/5	0.058
Confidence	(K)	5	5	5	1	5	1	0.334
Fiscal Policy	(F)	2	5	3	1/5	1	1/5	0.118
Monetary Policy	(M)	5	7	5	1	5	1	0.343

Panel B: Which subfactor has the greater potential to influence Economic Restructuring and how strongly?

		FS	DP	GC	Vector Weights
Financial Sector	(FS)	1	3	3	0.584
Defense Posture	(DS)	1/3	1	3	0.281
Global Competition	(GC)	1/3	1/3	1	0.135

Table 4-3 Matrices for Relative Influence of Subfactors on Periods of Adjustment (Months) (Conventional Adjustment)

For each panel below, which time period is more likely to indicate a turnaround if the relevant factor is the sole driving force?

Panel A: Relative importance of targeted time periods for consumption to drive a turnaround

	3	6	12	24	Vec. Wts.
3 months	1	1/5	1/7	1/7	.043
6 months	5	1	1/5	1/5	.113
12 months		7	5	1	1/3 .310
24 months		7	5	3	1 .534

Panel B: Relative importance of targeted time periods for exports to drive a turnaround

	3	6	12	24	Vec. Wts.
3 months	1	1	1/5	1/5	.083
6 months	1	1	1/5	1/5	.083
12 months			5	5	1 1 .417
24 months			5	5	1 1 .417

Panel C: Relative importance of targeted time periods investment to drive a turnaround

	3	6	12	24	Vec. Wts.
3 months	1	1	1/5	1/5	.078
6 months	1	1	1/5	1/5	.078
12 months		5	5	1	1/3 .305
24 months		5	5	3	1 .538

Panel D: Relative importance of targeted time for periods for fiscal policy to drive a turnaround

	3	6	12	24	Vec. Wts.
3 months	1	1	1/3	1/5	.099
6 months		1	1	1/5	1/5 .087
12 months			3	5	1 1 .382
24 months			5	5	1 1 .432

Panel E: Relative importance of targeted time periods for monetary policy to drive a turnaround

	3	6	12	24	Vec. Wts.
3 months	1	5	7	7	.605
6 months	1/5	1	5	7	.262
12 months		1/7	1/5	1	1/5 .042
24 months		1/7	1/7	5	1 .091

Panel F: Expected time for a change of confidence indicators of consumer and investor activity to support a turnaround in the economy

	3	6	12	24	Vec. Wts.
3 months	1	3	5	5	.517
6 months	1/3	1	5	5	.305
12 months			1/5	1/5	1 5 .124
24 months			1/5	1/5	1/5 1 .054

Table 4-4 Matrices for Relative Influence of Subfactors on Periods of Adjustment (Months) (Economic Restructuring)

For each panel below, which time period is more likely to indicate a turnaround if the relevant factor is the sole driving force?

Panel A: Most likely length of time for restructuring of financial system to support a turnaround

Panel B: Most likely time required for defense readjustment to affect a turnaround in economy

	3	6	12	24	Vec. Wts.
3 months	1	1/3	1/5	1/7	.049
6 months	3	1	1/5	1/7	.085
12 months		5	5	1	1/5 .236
24 months		7	7	5	1 .630

	3	6	12	24	Vec. Wts.
3 months	1	1/3	1/5	1/7	.049
6 months	3	1	1/5	1/7	.085
12 months			5	5	1 1/5 .236
24 months			7	7	5 1 .630

Panel C: Most Likely time required for an adjustment to global competition can affect a turnaround in economy

	3	6	12	24	Vec. Wts.
3 months	1	1	1/3	1/5	.089
6 months	1	1	1/3	1/5	.089
12 months	3	3	1	1/5	.208
24 months	5	5	5	1	.613

Table 4-5 Most Likely Factor to Dominate During a Specified Time Period

For each panel below, which factor is more likely to produce a turnaround during the specified time period?

Conventional Adjustment --> CA

Restructuring --> R

Panel A: 3 Months

	CA	R	Vec. Wts.
CA	1	5	.833
R	1/5	1	.167

Panel B:: 6 Months

	CA	R	Vec. Wts.
CA	1	5	.833
R	1/5	1	.167

Panel C: 1 Year

	CA	R	Vec. Wts.
CA	1	1	.500
R	1	1	.500

Panel D: 2 Years

	CA	R	Vec. Wts.
CA	1	1/5	.167
R	5	1	.833

Now we group all the derived vector weights as columns in the appropriate positions of the supermatrix. For example, the first vector we derived from the matrix of subfactors of conventional adjustment is placed in the first column next to the six subfactors and under conventional adjustment. The factors are listed systematically so that the right vectors are listed to indicate the impact of the relevant factors on the left on the factors at the top. The supermatrix, being stochastic (with columns adding to one), is then raised to limiting powers. This is to capture all the interactions and obtain the steady-state outcome (Table 4-6) in which all columns within each block of factors are the same. We are particularly interested in the two identical columns at the bottom left corner of the matrix of Table 4-7a. Either one is given by (0.224, 0.151, 0.201, 0.424).

Synthesis/results. When the judgments were made, the software package known as Expert Choice[1], in which the AHP procedure is embedded, was used to perform a synthesis which produced the following results:

> A meaningful turnaround in the economy would likely require an additional ten to eleven months, occurring during the fourth quarter of 1992. This forecast was derived from weights generated in the normalized last four entries of the first column of the limit matrix in Table 4-9, coupled with the mid-points of the alternate time periods (so as to provide unbiased estimates):

.223 x 1.5 + .152 x 4.5 + .201 x 9 + .424 x 18 = 10.46 months.[*]

For completeness we give the limiting forms (Figures 4-7a, 4-7b, 4-7c) of all three phases of the holarchy, which is a cycle with c=3. We display the supermatrix for each phase: Tables 4-7a,b,c, with their sum in Table 4-8. Table 4-9 is derived from 4-8 by dividing by 3 to form the average and hence obtain the Cesaro sum.

---

[*] Number of months after late December 1991 or early January 1992.

Table 4-6 The Initial Completed Supermatrix W

	C.A.	E.R.	Con.	Exp.	Inv.	Con.	F.P.	M.P.	F.S.	D.P.	G.C.	3 mo.	6 mo.	1 yr.	≥2 years
Conven. Adjust	0.0	0.0	0.0	0.0	0.0	0.0	0.0	0.0	0.0	0.0	0.0	0.833	0.833	0.500	0.167
Econ. Restruct.	0.0	0.0	0.0	0.0	0.0	0.0	0.0	0.0	0.0	0.0	0.0	0.167	0.167	0.500	0.833
Consum.	0.118	0.0	0.0	0.0	0.0	0.0	0.0	0.0	0.0	0.0	0.0	0.0	0.0	0.0	0.0
Exports	0.029	0.0	0.0	0.0	0.0	0.0	0.0	0.0	0.0	0.0	0.0	0.0	0.0	0.0	0.0
Invest.	0.058	0.0	0.0	0.0	0.0	0.0	0.0	0.0	0.0	0.0	0.0	0.0	0.0	0.0	0.0
Confid.	0.334	0.0	0.0	0.0	0.0	0.0	0.0	0.0	0.0	0.0	0.0	0.0	0.0	0.0	0.0
Fiscal Policy	0.118	0.0	0.0	0.0	0.0	0.0	0.0	0.0	0.0	0.0	0.0	0.0	0.0	0.0	0.0
Monetary Policy	0.343	0.0	0.0	0.0	0.0	0.0	0.0	0.0	0.0	0.0	0.0	0.0	0.0	0.0	0.0
Financ. Sector	0.0	0.584	0.0	0.0	0.0	0.0	0.0	0.0	0.0	0.0	0.0	0.0	0.0	0.0	0.0
Defense Posture	0.0	0.281	0.0	0.0	0.0	0.0	0.0	0.0	0.0	0.0	0.0	0.0	0.0	0.0	0.0
Global Compet.	0.0	0.135	0.0	0.0	0.0	0.0	0.0	0.0	0.0	0.0	0.0	0.0	0.0	0.0	0.0
3 months	0.0	0.0	0.043	0.083	0.078	0.517	0.099	0.605	0.049	0.049	0.089	0.0	0.0	0.0	0.0
6 months	0.0	0.0	0.113	0.083	0.078	0.305	0.086	0.262	0.085	0.085	0.089	0.0	0.0	0.0	0.0
1 year	0.0	0.0	0.310	0.417	0.305	0.124	0.383	0.042	0.236	0.236	0.209	0.0	0.0	0.0	0.0
≥ 2 years	0.0	0.0	0.534	0.417	0.539	0.054	0.432	0.091	0.630	0.630	0.613	0.0	0.0	0.0	0.0

Table 4-7a Limit Supermatrix - Phase I

(W)	C.A.	E.R.	Con.	Exp.	Inv.	Con.	F.P.	M.P.	F.S.	D.P.	G.C.	3 mo.	6 mo.	1 yr.	≥ 2 years
Conven. Adjust	0	0	0	0	0	0	0	0	0	0	0	0.484	0.484	0.484	0.484
Econ. Restruct.	0	0	0	0	0	0	0	0	0	0	0	0.516	0.516	0.516	0.516
Consum.	0.057	0.057	0	0	0	0	0	0	0	0	0	0	0	0	0
Exports	0.014	0.014	0	0	0	0	0	0	0	0	0	0	0	0	0
Invest.	0.028	0.028	0	0	0	0	0	0	0	0	0	0	0	0	0
Confid.	0.162	0.162	0	0	0	0	0	0	0	0	0	0	0	0	0
Fiscal Policy	0.057	0.057	0	0	0	0	0	0	0	0	0	0	0	0	0
Monetary Policy	0.166	0.166	0	0	0	0	0	0	0	0	0	0	0	0	0
Financ. Sector	0.302	0.302	0	0	0	0	0	0	0	0	0	0	0	0	0
Defense Posture	0.145	0.145	0	0	0	0	0	0	0	0	0	0	0	0	0
Global Compet.	0.070	0.070	0	0	0	0	0	0	0	0	0	0	0	0	0
3 months	0	0	0.223	0.223	0.223	0.223	0.223	0.223	0.223	0.223	0.223	0	0	0	0
6 months	0	0	0.152	0.151	0.152	0.152	0.152	0.152	0.152	0.152	0.152	0	0	0	0
1 year	0	0	0.201	0.201	0.201	0.201	0.201	0.201	0.201	0.201	0.201	0	0	0	0
≥ 2 years	0	0	0.424	0.424	0.424	0.424	0.424	0.424	0.424	0.424	0.424	0	0	0	0

Table 4-7b The Limit Supermatrix - Phase II

	C.A.	E.R.	Con.	Exp.	Inv.	Con.	F.P.	M.P.	F.S.	D.P.	G.C.	3 mo.	6 mo.	1 yr.	≥ 2 years
Conven.-Adjust	0.0	0.0	0.484	0.484	0.484	0.484	0.484	0.484	0.484	0.484	0.484	0.0	0.0	0.0	0.0
Econ. Restruct.	0.0	0.0	0.516	0.516	0.516	0.516	0.516	0.516	0.516	0.516	0.516	0.0	0.0	0.0	0.0
Consum.	0.0	0.0	0.0	0.0	0.0	0.0	0.0	0.0	0.0	0.0	0.0	0.057	0.057	0.057	0.057
Exports	0.0	0.0	0.0	0.0	0.0	0.0	0.0	0.0	0.0	0.0	0.0	0.014	0.014	0.014	0.014
Invest.	0.0	0.0	0.0	0.0	0.0	0.0	0.0	0.0	0.0	0.0	0.0	0.028	0.028	0.028	0.028
Confid.	0.0	0.0	0.0	0.0	0.0	0.0	0.0	0.0	0.0	0.0	0.0	0.162	0.162	0.162	0.162
Fiscal Policy	0.0	0.0	0.0	0.0	0.0	0.0	0.0	0.0	0.0	0.0	0.0	0.057	0.057	0.057	0.057
Monetary Policy	0.0	0.0	0.0	0.0	0.0	0.0	0.0	0.0	0.0	0.0	0.0	0.166	0.166	0.166	0.166
Financ. Sector	0.0	0.0	0.0	0.0	0.0	0.0	0.0	0.0	0.0	0.0	0.0	0.301	0.301	0.301	0.301
Defense Posture	0.0	0.0	0.0	0.0	0.0	0.0	0.0	0.0	0.0	0.0	0.0	0.145	0.145	0.145	0.145
Global Compet.	0.0	0.0	0.0	0.0	0.0	0.0	0.0	0.0	0.0	0.0	0.0	0.070	0.070	0.070	0.070
3 months	0.224	0.224	0.0	0.0	0.0	0.0	0.0	0.0	0.0	0.0	0.0	0.0	0.0	0.0	0.0
6 months	0.151	0.151	0.0	0.0	0.0	0.0	0.0	0.0	0.0	0.0	0.0	0.0	0.0	0.0	0.0
1 year	0.201	0.201	0.0	0.0	0.0	0.0	0.0	0.0	0.0	0.0	0.0	0.0	0.0	0.0	0.0
≥ 2 years	0.424	0.424	0.0	0.0	0.0	0.0	0.0	0.0	0.0	0.0	0.0	0.0	0.0	0.0	0.0

Table 4-7c Limit Supermatrix   - Phase III

(W)	C.A.	E.R.	Con.	Exp.	Inv.	Con.	F.P.	M.P.	F.S.	D.P.	G.C.	3 mo.	6 mo.	1 yr.	≥ 2 yrs
Conven. Adjust	0.484	0.484	0	0	0	0	0	0	0	0	0	0	0	0	0
Econ. Restruct.	0.516	0.516	0	0	0	0	0	0	0	0	0	0	0	0	0
Consum.	0	0	0.057	0.057	0.057	0.057	0.057	0.057	0.057	0.057	0.057	0	0	0	0
Exports	0	0	0.014	0.014	0.014	0.014	0.014	0.014	0.014	0.014	0.014	0	0	0	0
Invest.	0	0	0.028	0.028	0.028	0.028	0.028	0.028	0.028	0.028	0.028	0	0	0	0
Confid.	0	0	0.162	0.162	0.162	0.162	0.162	0.162	0.162	0.162	0.162	0	0	0	0
Fiscal Policy	0	0	0.057	0.057	0.057	0.057	0.057	0.057	0.057	0.057	0.057	0	0	0	0
Monetary Policy	0	0	0.166	0.166	0.166	0.166	0.166	0.166	0.166	0.166	0.166	0	0	0	0
Financ. Sector	0	0	0.302	0.302	0.302	0.302	0.302	0.302	0.302	0.302	0.302	0	0	0	0
Defense Posture	0	0	0.145	0.145	0.145	0.145	0.145	0.145	0.145	0.145	0.145	0	0	0	0
Global Compet.	0	0	0.070	0.070	0.070	0.070	0.070	0.070	0.070	0.070	0.70	0	0	0	0
3 months	0	0	0	0	0	0	0	0	0	0	0	0.223	0.223	0.233	0.233
6 months	0	0	0	0	0	0	0	0	0	0	0	0.152	0.152	0.152	0.152
1 year	0	0	0	0	0	0	0	0	0	0	0	0.201	0.201	0.201	0.201
≥ 2 years	0	0	0	0	0	0	0	0	0	0	0	0.424	0.424	0.424	0.424

Table 4-8 Limit Supermatrix - Sum of Phases I, II and III.

	C.A.	E.R.	Con.	Exp.	Inv.	Con.	F.P.	M.P.	F.S.	D.P.	G.C.	3 mo.	6 mo.	1 yr.	≥ 2 years
Conven. Adjust	0.484	0.484	0.484	0.484	0.484	0.484	0.484	0.484	0.484	0.484	0.484	0.484	0.484	0.484	0.484
Econ. Restruct.	0.516	0.516	0.516	0.516	0.516	0.516	0.516	0.516	0.516	0.516	0.516	0.516	0.516	0.516	0.516
Consum.	0.057	0.057	0.057	0.057	0.057	0.057	0.057	0.057	0.057	0.057	0.057	0.057	0.057	0.057	0.057
Exports	0.014	0.014	0.014	0.014	0.014	0.014	0.014	0.014	0.014	0.014	0.014	0.014	0.014	0.014	0.014
Invest.	0.028	0.028	0.028	0.028	0.028	0.028	0.028	0.028	0.028	0.028	0.028	0.028	0.028	0.028	0.028
Confid.	0.162	0.162	0.162	0.162	0.162	0.162	0.162	0.162	0.162	0.162	0.162	0.162	0.162	0.162	0.162
Fiscal Policy	0.057	0.057	0.057	0.057	0.057	0.057	0.057	0.057	0.057	0.057	0.057	0.057	0.057	0.057	0.057
Monetary Policy	0.166	0.166	0.166	0.166	0.166	0.166	0.166	0.166	0.166	0.166	0.166	0.166	0.166	0.166	0.166
Finance. Sector	0.302	0.302	0.302	0.302	0.302	0.302	0.302	0.302	0.302	0.302	0.302	0.302	0.302	0.302	0.302
Defense Posture	0.145	0.145	0.145	0.145	0.145	0.145	0.145	0.145	0.145	0.145	0.145	0.145	0.145	0.145	0.145
Global Compet.	0.070	0.070	0.070	0.070	0.070	0.070	0.070	0.070	0.070	0.070	0.070	0.070	0.070	0.070	0.070
3 months	0.223	0.223	0.223	0.223	0.223	0.223	0.223	0.223	0.223	0.223	0.223	0.223	0.223	0.223	0.223
6 months	0.152	0.152	0.152	0.152	0.152	0.152	0.152	0.152	0.152	0.152	0.152	0.152	0.152	0.152	0.152
1 year	0.201	0.201	0.201	0.201	0.201	0.201	0.201	0.201	0.201	0.201	0.201	0.201	0.201	0.201	0.201
≥ 2 years	0.424	0.424	0.424	0.424	0.424	0.424	0.424	0.424	0.424	0.424	0.424	0.424	0.424	0.424	0.424

Table 4-9. Average Limit Supermatrix - Block Normalized

	C.A.	E.R.	Con.	Exp.	Inv.	Con.	F.P.	M.P.	F.S.	D.P.	G.C.	3 mo.	6 mo.	1 yr.	≥ 2 years
Conven. Adjust	0.161	0.161	0.161	0.161	0.161	0.161	0.161	0.161	0.161	0.161	0.161	0.161	0.161	0.161	0.161
Econ. Restruct.	0.172	0.172	0.172	0.172	0.172	0.172	0.172	0.172	0.172	0.172	0.172	0.172	0.172	0.172	0.172
Consum.	0.019	0.019	0.019	0.019	0.019	0.019	0.019	0.019	0.019	0.019	0.019	0.019	0.019	0.019	0.019
Exports	0.005	0.005	0.005	0.005	0.005	0.005	0.005	0.005	0.005	0.005	0.005	0.005	0.005	0.005	0.005
Invest.	0.009	0.009	0.009	0.009	0.009	0.009	0.009	0.009	0.009	0.009	0.009	0.009	0.009	0.009	0.009
Confid.	0.054	0.054	0.054	0.054	0.054	0.054	0.054	0.054	0.054	0.054	0.054	0.054	0.054	0.054	0.054
Fiscal Policy	0.019	0.019	0.019	0.019	0.019	0.019	0.019	0.019	0.019	0.019	0.019	0.019	0.019	0.019	0.019
Monetary Policy	0.055	0.055	0.055	0.055	0.055	0.055	0.055	0.055	0.055	0.055	0.055	0.055	0.055	0.055	0.055
Finance Sector	0.101	0.101	0.101	0.101	0.101	0.101	0.101	0.101	0.101	0.101	0.101	0.101	0.101	0.101	0.101
Defense Posture	0.048	0.048	0.048	0.048	0.048	0.048	0.048	0.048	0.048	0.048	0.048	0.048	0.048	0.048	0.048
Global Compet.	0.023	0.023	0.023	0.023	0.023	0.023	0.023	0.023	0.023	0.023	0.023	0.023	0.023	0.023	0.023
3 months	0.075	0.075	0.075	0.075	0.075	0.075	0.075	0.075	0.075	0.075	0.075	0.075	0.075	0.075	0.075
6 months	0.051	0.051	0.051	0.051	0.051	0.051	0.051	0.051	0.051	0.051	0.051	0.051	0.051	0.051	0.051
1 year	0.067	0.067	0.067	0.067	0.067	0.067	0.067	0.067	0.067	0.067	0.067	0.067	0.067	0.067	0.067
≥ 2 years	0.141	0.141	0.141	0.141	0.141	0.141	0.141	0.141	0.141	0.141	0.141	0.141	0.141	0.141	0.141

4-5A. A SINGLE CONTROL CRITERION: ECONOMIC BENEFITS OF FAST-FOOD RESTAURANTS (Irreducible Primitive Matrix)

Billions of dollars are spent each year on altering the perceptions of consumers in favor of a product, a service, a company or an idea. This notion, generally referred to as advertising, is often crucial in deciding the fate of a firm. McDonald's, Burger King, and Wendy's, for example, spend a major amount of their resources on attracting customers. Obviously these three companies are direct competitors. Advertising from indirect competitors, such as Pizza Hut, does in fact also alter the market-share game. The interactions through advertising between Coca-Cola and Pepsi-Cola are known to be intense. Each firm introduces new items such as Coke Classic or Clear-Pepsi, and each introduces a host of other tactics in order to increase market share. Nonetheless, the actions of one firm directly and indirectly influence the other firms. In turn, the reactions of the other firms have direct and indirect influences on the original firm. This ever continuing process is influenced by many actors (both direct players and indirect players) and by many factors (both internal and external).

Consider the well-known companies McDonald's, Burger King, Wendy's, and the other national fast food restaurant chains. Factors such as advertising, food quality, and health factors help determine the long-run market share of these companies. We want to model the fast-food operation (see Figure 4-6) that these firms are currently engaged in to determine their market share as it is now (February 1994) and perhaps also for the mid-term future. The objective of the decision is to invest in these companies in proportion to their priority ranking.

Despite a soft economy, Americans increasingly spend more of their food dollars on prepared foods. This trend reflects the larger presence of women in the work force, which means less time for food preparation at home, plus the easy access provided by a growing number of restaurant chains that offer take-out and delivery services. The components in the supermatrix represent four major factors that impact market share in the fast food industry.

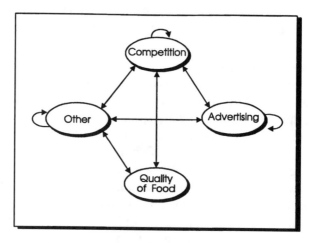

Figure 4-6 Components and Dependencies for the Hamburger Model

The Advertising component is the most important and consists of three elements (creativity, promotion, and frequency). Of these, the frequency of advertising was the most influential on market share. Promotion and creativity are equally influential, but are not as significant to the outcome as frequency. Differentiation among top fast-food chains is minimal. Hence billions of dollars are spent each year to influence consumer perceptions in favor of a particular restaurant or product.

Competition is the second most important component in the supermatrix model, consisting of three similar fast-food chains (McDonald's, Burger King, Wendy's). Not much differentiates one chain from another; therefore competition for market share is fierce. Unfortunately, because of time constraints indirect competitors could not be individually included in the model. However, one could easily incorporate such companies to more accurately predict market share using this model.

The component labeled Other includes elements such as price, location, customer service, speed, cleanliness, menu items, take-out, and reputation, all designed to attract a larger market share. Location and menu items are the most important determinants of market share in this component. Franchise chains now account for about 25% of U.S. restaurant outlets and roughly 43% of industry sales. With franchising, restaurant companies can rapidly expand brands without fully bearing the sizable costs of acquiring land, buildings, and equipment. In a franchising relationship, these costs are generally borne by the franchisee, who also pays a royalty (typically 3% to 5% of sales) to the parent company for the right to be part of the chain. Franchisees also generally contribute about 4% of sales toward advertising. In return, the franchisee receives brand-name recognition and often receives training and marketing support that would not otherwise be available. Some chains are heavily weighted toward franchised units, whereas others have a high proportion of company-owned outlets. While multiple-chain ownership offers economies of scale, purchasing power, and cross-promotional opportunities, a single-chain concept may allow top management to be more focused. Some restaurant companies, such as McDonald's and Wendy's, have largely made their mark through ownership of a single eating chain or concept. For example, about 70% of Wendy's units are franchised. However, the results of industry participants have been so diverse that it is not clear which approach is better.

Franchising has helped thousands of people to become entrepreneurs with less risk than they would face if heading into business completely on their own. Alternatively, independent restaurant operators, who avoid royalty fees, typically have more flexibility as to menus and operating procedures and are more likely to imprint their facilities with a distinctive style and ambiance. The reason for discussing ownership is that McDonald's remains the industry's sales leader by a wide margin. Unlike many other parent companies of restaurant chains, McDonald's is a substantial owner of the real estate on which franchisees operate under the golden arches. The company owns and develops many restaurant sites and then charges franchisees rent for the property. By doing so, McDonald's commits much more capital per unit to its franchise business than do other chains, but it receives a much greater revenue stream from its franchisees. This form of ownership enables McDonald's to have a large number of stores in a broader region. The more visible and accessible a restaurant is to consumers, the more convenient it is for them. Convenience usually translates into higher sales. Locations in airports and along highways are popular and provide the opportunity for impulse purchases. Some fast food chains have expanded into employee and school cafeterias, as well.

While all three restaurants in this model serve hamburgers, each differentiates itself by offering value-meals, which are combinations of a la carte items. Some have expanded their menu to include healthier items such as broiled versus breaded chicken sandwiches and salads. A variety of menu items seems to appeal to the customer. Reputation was the third most influential element in this particular component ("other") and relates to the concept of visibility and differentiation. Sponsorship of sports events enhances reputation. As purchases for off-premises consumption account for a growing share of the restaurant industry activity, take-out and price were equally influential following reputation. Take-out orders are particularly prevalent at fast-food chains, where features such as drive-through windows make transactions convenient and quick. The availability of take-out service furthers the objective of convenience and speed associated with fast-food chains.

During the past several years, restaurant earnings have been helped by generally favorable food costs. With food costs not a problem and consumers facing a soft economy, food prices at restaurants were raised only modestly in 1993. Quick-service restaurants in particular have been promoting a theme of good value to customers. Good value has included featuring low-cost menu items (e.g., less than $1) and offering consumers a combination of items for a lower price than they would cost individually. The combination approach helps restaurant to boost volumes, including sales of high-margin items such as french fries and soft drinks. Price is reflected in high sales of value-meals. By combining a la carte items, chains are able to offer more food for less money and even boost sales for some items that may have lower demand if not included in such packages. On average, about 33% of what consumers pay at restaurants (excluding tips) represents the cost of the food and beverage. Mark-ups tend to be greater on beverages than on food. When people pay $2 for a hamburger whose food content would cost about $0.75 at the supermarket, they are paying for the convenience of not having to prepare it themselves.

Cleanliness and speed are next in preference. Customers expect fast-food restaurants to be clean and to successfully pass inspection by the county health department. Speed is a concept incorporated into the name of the industry and generally taken for granted. Customer service has a minimal role in the outcome.

The component labeled Quality (of food) surprisingly ranked fourth in importance among the four components in the supermatrix and consists of nutrition, taste, and portion. Of these elements, portion is the most influential. This result likely reflects the fact that customers of fast-food chains are not necessarily eating at such restaurants for a tasty and nutritious meal, although nutrition is increasingly becoming a larger factor in the selection of menu items offered.

In sum, advertising definitely impacts consumer perceptions of fast-food chains. For instance, McDonald's (the market leader) sponsors many athletic events and has significantly more restaurant locations (more than 8,900 outlets in the U.S.) than its competitors. Although this study was limited to the domestic market share, it is interesting to note that McDonald's also has the largest presence in foreign markets, with more than 4,000 outlets in over 60 countries (including 1,000 in Japan, alone). Only three other U.S.-based chains have more than $500 million in foreign sales (KFC, Pizza Hut, and Burger King).

As the U.S. population ages, restaurant patrons are expected to increasingly move away from fast-food outlets toward mid-scale dining. The economics of choice largely depends on how people value their time. The generation born after World War II is entering its peak earning years and will likely put a higher value on the ambiance and menu features of sit-down, full-service restaurants. Meanwhile, fast-food restaurants should place further emphasis on convenient service, attractive prices, and healthier menu items to help stem potential future sales erosion. The paired comparison matrices have been left out, but the priority vectors derived from them as partial column entries are used in the supermatrix (Table 4-10), which also has some blocks of zeros (whose positions are designated with blanks indicating no interaction). The components were weighted in separate pairwise comparison matrices as to their impact on each component. The resulting priorities are shown in Table 4-11. These priorities are then used to weight the corresponding blocks of the supermatrix, yielding Table 4-12, which is raised to limiting powers as given in Table 4-13 and then normalized by blocks, yielding table 4-14. Since the limit matrix has no zeros, some power of the weighted supermatrix of Table 4-12 has no zeros, and thus the supermatrix in Table 4-12 itself is primitive.

Table 4-10 Supermatrix of Unweighted Priorities (in two parts)

		1 Alternatives			2 Advertising			3 Quality		
		1McD's	2BurgerK	3Wendy's	1Creativ~	2Promo	3Freq~	1Nutrit~	2Taste	3Portion
1Alterna	1 McD'ss	0.0000	0.8333	0.7500	0.6141	0.7174	0.7174	0.2488	0.2899	0.5989
	2 BurgerK	0.8000	0.0000	0.2500	0.2685	0.1942	0.1942	0.1561	0.1040	0.1262
	3 Wendy's	0.2000	0.1667	0.0000	0.1174	0.0884	0.0884	0.5951	0.6061	0.2749
2Adverti	1 Creativity	0.2074	0.1783	0.2810	0.0000	0.3333	0.5000	0.0000	0.0000	0.0000
	2Promo~	0.1298	0.1120	0.0720	0.1250	0.0000	0.5000	0.0000	0.0000	0.0000
	3Freq~	0.6628	0.7096	0.6470	0.8750	0.6667	0.0000	0.0000	0.0000	0.0000
3Quality	1Nutrition	0.3319	0.2810	0.6241	0.0000	0.0000	0.0000	0.0000	0.0000	0.0000
	2Taste	0.1388	0.0720	0.2823	0.0000	0.0000	0.0000	0.0000	0.0000	0.0000
	3Portion	0.5293	0.6470	0.0936	0.0000	0.0000	0.0000	0.0000	0.0000	0.0000
4 Other	1Price	0.0329	0.2408	0.0300	0.0000	0.8333	0.0000	0.0000	0.0000	0.8571
	2Location	0.1063	0.2231	0.1417	0.7095	0.0000	0.1958	0.0000	0.0000	0.0000
	3 Service	0.0237	0.1418	0.0648	0.0000	0.0000	0.0000	0.0000	0.0000	0.0000
	4 Speed	0.0483	0.1407	0.0641	0.0000	0.0000	0.0000	0.0000	0.0000	0.0000
	5Cleanli~	0.3328	0.1096	0.2756	0.0000	0.0000	0.0000	0.0000	0.0000	0.0000
	6 Menu	0.1593	0.0512	0.1571	0.1377	0.1667	0.3108	0.0000	0.0000	0.0000
	7 Take-out	0.0736	0.0506	0.0589	0.0000	0.0000	0.0000	0.0000	0.0000	0.1429
	8Reputa~	0.2232	0.0422	0.2078	0.1528	0.0000	0.4934	0.0000	0.0000	0.0000

		4 Other							
		1 Price	2 Location	3 Service	4 Speed	5 Cleanli~	6Menu	7Take-out	8Reputa~
1Alternat~	1 McD'ss	0.6531	0.6531	0.3319	0.5387	0.2500	0.4934	0.4837	0.6749
	2BurgerK	0.2507	0.2507	0.1388	0.3624	0.2500	0.1958	0.3133	0.2238
	3Wendy's	0.0962	0.0962	0.5293	0.0989	0.5000	0.3108	0.2029	0.1012
2Advertisi~	1Creativity	0.0000	0.0000	0.0000	0.0000	0.0000	0.0780	0.0000	0.0819
	2Promo~	0.8333	0.0000	0.0000	0.0000	0.0000	0.1711	0.0000	0.3678
	3Freq~	0.1667	0.0000	0.0000	0.0000	0.0000	0.7509	0.0000	0.5503
3Quality	1Nutrition	0.1667	0.0000	0.0000	0.0000	0.0000	0.0756	0.0000	0.0936
	2Taste	0.0000	0.0000	0.0000	0.0000	0.0000	0.6952	0.0000	0.6241
	3Portion	0.8333	0.0000	0.0000	0.0000	0.0000	0.2292	0.0000	0.2823
4 Other	1Price	0.0000	0.0000	0.0000	0.0000	0.0000	0.1153	0.0000	0.0627
	2Location	0.5000	0.0000	0.0981	0.0000	0.1711	0.0526	0.6572	0.2653
	3Service	0.0000	0.0000	0.0000	0.1873	0.0780	0.0000	0.0548	0.0444
	4Speed	0.0000	0.0000	0.2857	0.0000	0.7509	0.1946	0.2880	0.0835
	5Cleanli~	0.0000	0.0000	0.5181	0.0000	0.0000	0.6375	0.0000	0.2378
	6Menu	0.0000	0.0000	0.0000	0.0000	0.0000	0.0000	0.0000	0.1929
	7Take-out	0.5000	0.0000	0.0000	0.7313	0.0000	0.0000	0.0000	0.0567
	8Reputa~	0.0000	0.0000	0.0981	0.0814	0.0000	0.0000	0.0000	0.0567

Table 4-11 Component Influence Matrix

	1 Alternatives	2 Advertising	3 Quality of food	4 Other
1 Alternatives	0.2128	0.2956	0.5000	0.1304
2 Advertising	0.5319	0.2571	0.0000	0.6079
3 Quality of food	0.0659	0.0000	0.0000	0.0655
4 Other	0.1893	0.4473	0.5000	0.1961

Table 4-12 The Weighted Supermatrix (in two parts)

		1 Alternatives			2 Advertising			3 Quality		
		1McD's	2BurgerK	3Wendy's	1Creativ~	2Promo	3Freq~	1Nutrit~	2Taste	3Portion
1Alterna	1 McD'ss	0.0000	0.8333	0.7500	0.6141	0.7174	0.7174	0.2488	0.2899	0.5989
	2 BurgerK	0.8000	0.0000	0.2500	0.2685	0.1942	0.1942	0.1561	0.1040	0.1262
	3 Wendy's	0.2000	0.1667	0.0000	0.1174	0.0884	0.0884	0.5951	0.6061	0.2749
2Adverti	1 Creativity	0.2074	0.1783	0.2810	0.0000	0.3333	0.5000	0.0000	0.0000	0.0000
	2Promo~	0.1298	0.1120	0.0720	0.1250	0.0000	0.5000	0.0000	0.0000	0.0000
	3Freq~	0.6628	0.7096	0.6470	0.8750	0.6667	0.0000	0.0000	0.0000	0.0000
3Quality	1Nutrition	0.3319	0.2810	0.6241	0.0000	0.0000	0.0000	0.0000	0.0000	0.0000
	2Taste	0.1388	0.0720	0.2823	0.0000	0.0000	0.0000	0.0000	0.0000	0.0000
	3Portion	0.5293	0.6470	0.0936	0.0000	0.0000	0.0000	0.0000	0.0000	0.0000
4 Other	1Price	0.0329	0.2408	0.0300	0.0000	0.8333	0.0000	0.0000	0.0000	0.8571
	2Location	0.1063	0.2231	0.1417	0.7095	0.0000	0.1958	0.0000	0.0000	0.0000
	3 Service	0.0237	0.1418	0.0648	0.0000	0.0000	0.0000	0.0000	0.0000	0.0000
	4 Speed	0.0483	0.1407	0.0641	0.0000	0.0000	0.0000	0.0000	0.0000	0.0000
	5Cleanli~	0.3328	0.1096	0.2756	0.0000	0.0000	0.0000	0.0000	0.0000	0.0000
	6 Menu	0.1593	0.0512	0.1571	0.1377	0.1667	0.3108	0.0000	0.0000	0.0000
	7 Take-out	0.0736	0.0506	0.0589	0.0000	0.0000	0.0000	0.0000	0.0000	0.1429
	8Reputa~	0.2232	0.0422	0.2078	0.1528	0.0000	0.4934	0.0000	0.0000	0.0000

		4 Other							
		1 Price	2 Location	3 Service	4 Speed	5 Cleanli~	6Menu	7Take-out	8Reputa~
1Alternat~	1 McD'ss	0.6531	0.6531	0.3319	0.5387	0.2500	0.4934	0.4837	0.6749
	2BurgerK	0.2507	0.2507	0.1388	0.3624	0.2500	0.1958	0.3133	0.2238
	3Wendy's	0.0962	0.0962	0.5293	0.0989	0.5000	0.3108	0.2029	0.1012
2Advertisi~	1Creativity	0.0000	0.0000	0.0000	0.0000	0.0000	0.0780	0.0000	0.0819
	2Promo~	0.8333	0.0000	0.0000	0.0000	0.0000	0.1711	0.0000	0.3678
	3Freq~	0.1667	0.0000	0.0000	0.0000	0.0000	0.7509	0.0000	0.5503
3Quality	1Nutrition	0.1667	0.0000	0.0000	0.0000	0.0000	0.0756	0.0000	0.0936
	2Taste	0.0000	0.0000	0.0000	0.0000	0.0000	0.6952	0.0000	0.6241
	3Portion	0.8333	0.0000	0.0000	0.0000	0.0000	0.2292	0.0000	0.2823
4 Other	1Price	0.0000	0.0000	0.0000	0.0000	0.0000	0.1153	0.0000	0.0627
	2Location	0.5000	0.0000	0.0981	0.0000	0.1711	0.0526	0.6572	0.2653
	3Service	0.0000	0.0000	0.0000	0.1873	0.0780	0.0000	0.0548	0.0444
	4Speed	0.0000	0.0000	0.2857	0.0000	0.7509	0.1946	0.2880	0.0835
	5Cleanli~	0.0000	0.0000	0.5181	0.0000	0.0000	0.6375	0.0000	0.2378
	6Menu	0.0000	0.0000	0.0000	0.0000	0.0000	0.0000	0.0000	0.1929
	7Take-out	0.5000	0.0000	0.0000	0.7313	0.0000	0.0000	0.0000	0.0567
	8Reputa~	0.0000	0.0000	0.0981	0.0814	0.0000	0.0000	0.0000	0.0567

The Limit Supermatrix has the same form as the weighted supermatrix, but all the columns are the same. It is shown in the table below. To obtain the final priorities of all the elements in the matrix, normalize each block.

Decision Making with Dependence and Feedback

Table 4-13 The Limit Supermatrix (in two parts)

		1 Alternatives			2 Advertising			3 Quality of food		
		1McD's	2BurgerK	3Wendy's	1Creativit	2Promot~	3Freq~	1Nutrition	2Taste	3Portion
1Alternai~	1McD's	0.1749	0.1749	0.1749	0.1749	0.1749	0.1749	0.1749	0.1749	0.1749
	2BurgerK	0.0883	0.0883	0.0883	0.0883	0.0883	0.0883	0.0883	0.0883	0.0883
	3Wendy's	0.0520	0.0520	0.0520	0.0520	0.0520	0.0520	0.0520	0.0520	0.0520
2Adverti~	1Creativty	0.0727	0.0727	0.0727	0.0727	0.0727	0.0727	0.0727	0.0727	0.0727
	2Promot~	0.0878	0.0878	0.0878	0.0878	0.0878	0.0878	0.0878	0.0878	0.0878
	3Freque~	0.1905	0.1905	0.1905	0.1905	0.1905	0.1905	0.1905	0.1905	0.1905
3Quality	1 Nutrition	0.0087	0.0087	0.0087	0.0087	0.0087	0.0087	0.0087	0.0087	0.0087
	2 Taste	0.0076	0.0076	0.0076	0.0076	0.0076	0.0076	0.0076	0.0076	0.0076
	3Portion	0.0145	0.0145	0.0145	0.0145	0.0145	0.0145	0.0145	0.0145	0.0145
4 Other	1Price	0.0462	0.0462	0.0462	0.0462	0.0462	0.0462	0.0462	0.0462	0.0462
	2Location	0.0681	0.0681	0.0681	0.0681	0.0681	0.0681	0.0681	0.0681	0.0681
	3Service	0.0091	0.0091	0.0091	0.0091	0.0091	0.0091	0.0091	0.0091	0.0091
	4Speed	0.0248	0.0248	0.0248	0.0248	0.0248	0.0248	0.0248	0.0248	0.0248
	5Cleanli~	0.0271	0.0271	0.0271	0.0271	0.0271	0.0271	0.0271	0.0271	0.0271
	6 Menu	0.0474	0.0474	0.0474	0.0474	0.0474	0.0474	0.0474	0.0474	0.0474
	7 Takeout	0.0210	0.0210	0.0210	0.0210	0.0210	0.0210	0.0210	0.0210	0.0210
	8Reputa~	0.0596	0.0596	0.0596	0.0596	0.0596	0.0596	0.0596	0.0596	0.0596

		4 Other							
		1 Price	2 Location	3 Service	4 Speed	5Cleanl~	6Menu	7Take-out	8Reputa~
1Alternai~	1McD's	0.1749	0.1749	0.1749	0.1749	0.1749	0.1749	0.1749	0.1749
	2BurgerK	0.0883	0.0883	0.0883	0.0883	0.0883	0.0883	0.0883	0.0883
	3Wendy's	0.0520	0.0520	0.0520	0.0520	0.0520	0.0520	0.0520	0.0520
2Adverti~	1Creativ~	0.0727	0.0727	0.0727	0.0727	0.0727	0.0727	0.0727	0.0727
	2Promot~	0.0878	0.0878	0.0878	0.0878	0.0878	0.0878	0.0878	0.0878
	3Freque~	0.1905	0.1905	0.1905	0.1905	0.1905	0.1905	0.1905	0.1905
3Quality	1 Nutrition	0.0087	0.0087	0.0087	0.0087	0.0087	0.0087	0.0087	0.0087
	2 Taste	0.0076	0.0076	0.0076	0.0076	0.0076	0.0076	0.0076	0.0076
	3Portion	0.0145	0.0145	0.0145	0.0145	0.0145	0.0145	0.0145	0.0145
4 Other	1Price	0.0462	0.0462	0.0462	0.0462	0.0462	0.0462	0.0462	0.0462
	2Location	0.0681	0.0681	0.0681	0.0681	0.0681	0.0681	0.0681	0.0681
	3Service	0.0091	0.0091	0.0091	0.0091	0.0091	0.0091	0.0091	0.0091
	4Speed	0.0248	0.0248	0.0248	0.0248	0.0248	0.0248	0.0248	0.0248
	5Cleanli~	0.0271	0.0271	0.0271	0.0271	0.0271	0.0271	0.0271	0.0271
	6 Menu	0.0474	0.0474	0.0474	0.0474	0.0474	0.0474	0.0474	0.0474
	7Take-out	0.0210	0.0210	0.0210	0.0210	0.0210	0.0210	0.0210	0.0210
	8Reputa~	0.0596	0.0596	0.0596	0.0596	0.0596	0.0596	0.0596	0.0596

The table below shows the limit priorities of all the elements as they appear in the Limit Supermatrix (where the whole column sums to one) and the priorities normalized to one for each component.

Table 4-14 Priorities Obtained from Limit Supermatrix

		Priorities from Limit Matrix	Priorities Normalized by Cluster
1 Alternatives	1 McDonald's	0.1749	0.5549
	2 Burger King	0.0883	0.2801
	3 Wendy's	0.0520	0.1650
2 Advertising	1 Creativity	0.0727	0.2071
	2 Promotion	0.0878	0.2501
	3 Frequency	0.1905	0.5427
3 Quality of food	1 Nutrition	0.0087	0.2825
	2 Taste	0.0076	0.2468
	3 Portion	0.0145	0.4708
4 Other	1 Price	0.0462	0.1523
	2 Location	0.0681	0.2245
	3 Service	0.0091	0.0300
	4 Speed	0.0248	0.0818
	5 Cleanliness	0.0271	0.0894
	6 Menu Item	0.0474	0.1563
	7 Take-out	0.0210	0.0692
	8 Reputation	0.0596	0.1965

This limit supermatrix predicts the market share for three fast-food restaurant chains. Based on the outcome, competitors should be able to use the dominant factors in the model to their benefit and attempt to gain market share at the expense of the leaders. Sensitivity analysis can be performed to plan various strategies depending on market responses.

Market share for the fast food restaurants as determined by the supermatrix model is as follows:

McDonald's	55.9%
Burger King	28.4%
Wendy's	15.6%

Normalized industry statistics for these restaurant chains in terms of sales in dollars reported March 1993 (published in the Market Share Reporter 1994) reflect market share as follows:

McDonald's   61.4%
Burger King   25.1%
Wendy's   13.5%

For the market of the top 15 restaurant chain industries, early 1994 statistics reported the following:

McDonald's   32.3%
Burger King   13.2%
Wendy's   7.1%
Indirect   47.4%

These figures show that McDonald's has nearly one-third the share of the entire fast-food market.

4-5B. A SINGLE CONTROL CRITERION: ECONOMIC BENEFITS (Reducible Matrix with $\lambda_{MAX}=1$ Simple): FAST FOOD REVISITED

The following is an example of a reducible system with $\lambda_{max}=1$ that is acyclic. Consider the fast-food problem and attach to the competition component a small hierarchy above it. As in Figure 4-7, the goal is to decide whether McDonald's, Burger King, and Wendy's should expand abroad through competition with priorities (.657, 0.196, .147), or stay domestic with priorities (.540, .297, .163). Under the goal two criteria are included in the "Reach" component: internationalization with priority 0.2, and domestic with priority 0.8. Note that the outcome of the limit supermatrix is the same as the previous result when the "Reach" component has no feedback from competition, for then it would be a path from source to a cycle. The results are shown in Tables 4-15 to 4-19.

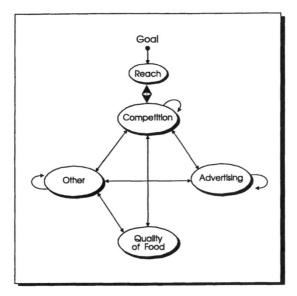

Figure 4-7 Reducible Supermatrix with $\lambda_{max} = 1$ a Simple Root

Table 4-15 Component Weights Matrix

	1	2	3	4
1. Quality	0.5171	0.0000	0.0657	0.0660
2. Advertising	0.3586	0.6223	0.5327	0.6066
3. Competition	0.1243	0.2470	0.2146	0.1290
4. Other	0.0000	0.1307	0.1869	0.1984

Table 4-16 Supermatrix of Unweighted Priorities

		GOAL	Reach		Competition			Advertising		
		1	1	2	1	2	3	1	2	3
	1. GOAL									
Reach	1. INTERNAT	0.2000								
	2. DOMESTIC	0.8000								
Competition	1. MCDON.		0.6571	0.5396		0.8333	0.7500	0.6144	0.7172	0.7172
	2. BURGER K.		0.1963	0.2970	0.8000	0.1667	0.2500	0.2684	0.1947	0.1947
	3. WENDY'S		0.1466	0.1634	0.2000			0.1172	0.0881	0.0881
Advertising	1. CREATIVITY				0.2081	0.1786	0.2790		0.3333	0.5000
	2. PROMOTION				0.1311	0.1125	0.0719	0.1250		0.5000
	3. FREQUENCY				0.6608	0.7089	0.6491	0.8750	0.6667	
Quality of Food	1. NUTRITION				0.3325	0.2790	0.6267			
	2. TASTE				0.1396	0.0719	0.2797			
	3. PORTION				0.5278	0.6491	0.0936			
Other	1. PRICE				0.0328	0.2394	0.0300		0.8333	
	2. LOCATION				0.1068	0.2236	0.1421	0.7096		0.1958
	3. SERVICE				0.0236	0.1428	0.0648			
	4. SPEED				0.0479	0.1399	0.0641			
	5. CLEAN.				0.3330	0.1101	0.2761			
	6. MENU ITEM				0.1586	0.0513	0.1570	0.1354	0.1667	0.3108
	7. TAKE-OUT				0.0737	0.0505	0.0590			
	8. REPUTATION				0.2235	0.0424	0.2070	0.1550		0.4934

Quality of Food			Other							
1	2	3	1	2	3	4	5	6	7	8
0.2493	0.2906	0.5954	0.6548	0.6548	0.3325	0.5368	0.2500	0.4934	0.4934	0.6738
0.1571	0.1048	0.1283	0.2499	0.2499	0.1396	0.3643	0.2500	0.1958	0.3108	0.2255
0.5936	0.6046	0.2764	0.0953	0.0953	0.5278	0.0989	0.5000	0.3108	0.1958	0.1007
			0.8333					0.0782		0.0821
			0.1667					0.1714		0.3680
								0.7504		0.5498
			0.1667					0.0754		0.0936
								0.6955		0.6267
			0.8333					0.2291		0.2797
		0.8571						0.1165		0.0661
			0.5000		0.0983		0.1713	0.0528	0.6554	0.2803
						0.1884	0.0782		0.0549	0.0475
					0.2847		0.7504	0.1937	0.2897	0.0880
					0.5187			0.6370		0.2534
						0.7306				0.2043
		0.1429	0.5000		0.0983	0.0810				0.0604

Table 4-17 Weighted Supermatrix

Left half of the supermatrix (source clusters: Goal, Reach, Competition, Advertising)

Cluster	Node	Goal 1	Reach 1	Reach 2	Competition 1	Competition 2	Competition 3	Advertising 1	Advertising 2	Advertising 3
	1. GOAL									
Reach	1. INTERNATIONAL	0.2000								
	2. DOMESTIC	0.8000								
Competition	1. MCDONALD'S		0.6571	0.5396		0.1788	0.1610	0.6144	0.7172	0.7172
	2. BURGER KING		0.1963	0.2970	0.1717		0.0537	0.2684	0.1947	0.1947
	3. WENDY'S		0.1466	0.1634	0.0429	0.0358		0.1172	0.0881	0.0881
Advertising	1. CREATIVITY				0.1109	0.0951	0.1486		0.3333	0.5000
	2. PROMOTION				0.0698	0.0599	0.0383	0.1250		0.5000
	3. FREQUENCY				0.3520	0.3776	0.1486	0.8750	0.6667	
Quality of Food	1. NUTRITION				0.0218	0.0183	0.0412			
	2. TASTE				0.0092	0.0047	0.0184			
	3. PORTION				0.0347	0.0426	0.0061			
Other	1. PRICE				0.0061	0.0238	0.0056		0.8333	
	2. LOCATION				0.0200	0.0492	0.0266	0.7096		0.1958
	3. SERVICE				0.0044	0.0063	0.0121			
	4. SPEED				0.0090	0.0313	0.0120			
	5. CLEANLINESS				0.0622	0.0250	0.0516			
	6. MENU ITEM				0.0296	0.0080	0.0293	0.1354	0.1667	0.3108
	7. TAKE-OUT				0.0138	0.0228	0.0110			
	8. REPUTATION				0.0418	0.0205	0.0387	0.1550		0.4934

• • •

Right half of the supermatrix (source clusters: Quality of Food, Other)

Node	Quality of Food 1	Quality of Food 2	Quality of Food 3	Other 1	Other 2	Other 3	Other 4	Other 5	Other 6	Other 7	Other 8
1. MCDONALD'S	0.1247	0.1453	0.2977	0.0845	0.0845	0.0429	0.0692	0.0323	0.0636	0.0636	0.0869
2. BURGER KING	0.0785	0.0524	0.0642	0.0322	0.0322	0.0180	0.0470	0.0323	0.0253	0.0401	0.0291
3. WENDY'S	0.2968	0.3023	0.1382	0.0123	0.0123	0.0681	0.0128	0.0645	0.0401	0.0253	0.0130
1. CREATIVITY									0.0474		0.0498
2. PROMOTION	0.5055								0.1040		0.2232
3. FREQUENCY	0.1011								0.4552		0.3335
1. NUTRITION				0.0110					0.0050		0.0062
2. TASTE				0.0550					0.0459		0.0414
3. PORTION									0.0151		0.0185
1. PRICE			0.4286						0.0231		0.0131
2. LOCATION	0.0992					0.0195		0.0340	0.0105	0.1300	0.0556
3. SERVICE						0.0374	0.0155		0.0109		0.0094
4. SPEED				0.0565				0.1489	0.0384	0.0575	0.0175
5. CLEANLINESS				0.1029					0.1264		0.0503
6. MENU ITEM	0.0715	0.0992					0.1450				0.0405
7. TAKE-OUT				0.0195	0.0161						0.0120
8. REPUTATION											

Table 4-18   Limit Supermatrix

		Competition			Advertising		
		1	2	3	1	2	3
	1. GOAL	0.0000	0.0000	0.0000	0.0000	0.0000	0.0000
Reach	1. INTERNATIONAL	0.0000	0.0000	0.0000	0.0000	0.0000	0.0000
	2. DOMESTIC	0.0000	0.0000	0.0000	0.0000	0.0000	0.0000
	1. MCDONALD'S	0.1557	0.1557	0.1557	0.1557	0.1557	0.1557
Competition	2. BURGER KING	0.0792	0.0792	0.0792	0.0792	0.0792	0.0792
	3. WENDY'S	0.0434	0.0434	0.0434	0.0434	0.0434	0.0434
	1. CREATIVITY	0.1410	0.1410	0.1410	0.1410	0.1410	0.1410
Advertising	2. PROMOTION	0.1288	0.1288	0.1288	0.1288	0.1288	0.1288
	3. FREQUENCY	0.2572	0.2572	0.2572	0.2572	0.2572	0.2572
Quality of	1. NUTRITION	0.0072	0.0072	0.0072	0.0072	0.0072	0.0072
Food	2. TASTE	0.0054	0.0054	0.0054	0.0054	0.0054	0.0054
	3. PORTION	0.0112	0.0112	0.0112	0.0112	0.0112	0.0112
	1. PRICE	0.0208	0.0208	0.0208	0.0208	0.0208	0.0208
	2. LOCATION	0.0368	0.0368	0.0368	0.0368	0.0368	0.0368
	3. SERVICE	0.0052	0.0052	0.0052	0.0052	0.0052	0.0052
Other	4. SPEED	0.0178	0.0178	0.0178	0.0178	0.0178	0.0178
	5. CLEANLINESS	0.0213	0.0213	0.0213	0.0213	0.0213	0.0213
	6. MENU ITEM	0.0338	0.0338	0.0338	0.0338	0.0338	0.0338
	7. TAKE-OUT	0.0060	0.0060	0.0060	0.0060	0.0060	0.0060
	8. REPUTATION	0.0292	0.0292	0.0292	0.0292	0.0292	0.0292

. . .

Quality of Food			Other							
1	2	3	1	2	3	4	5	6	7	8
0.0000	0.0000	0.0000	0.0000	0.0000	0.0000	0.0000	0.0000	0.0000	0.0000	0.0000
0.0000	0.0000	0.0000	0.0000	0.0000	0.0000	0.0000	0.0000	0.0000	0.0000	0.0000
0.0000	0.0000	0.0000	0.0000	0.0000	0.0000	0.0000	0.0000	0.0000	0.0000	0.0000
0.1557	0.1557	0.1557	0.1557	0.1557	0.1557	0.1557	0.1557	0.1557	0.1557	0.1557
0.0792	0.0792	0.0792	0.0792	0.0792	0.0792	0.0792	0.0792	0.0792	0.0792	0.0792
0.0434	0.0434	0.0434	0.0434	0.0434	0.0434	0.0434	0.0434	0.0434	0.0434	0.0434
0.1410	0.1410	0.1410	0.1410	0.1410	0.1410	0.1410	0.1410	0.1410	0.1410	0.1410
0.1288	0.1288	0.1288	0.1288	0.1288	0.1288	0.1288	0.1288	0.1288	0.1288	0.1288
0.2572	0.2572	0.2572	0.2572	0.2572	0.2572	0.2572	0.2572	0.2572	0.2572	0.2572
0.0072	0.0072	0.0072	0.0072	0.0072	0.0072	0.0072	0.0072	0.0072	0.0072	0.0072
0.0054	0.0054	0.0054	0.0054	0.0054	0.0054	0.0054	0.0054	0.0054	0.0054	0.0054
0.0112	0.0112	0.0112	0.0112	0.0112	0.0112	0.0112	0.0112	0.0112	0.0112	0.0112
0.0208	0.0208	0.0208	0.0208	0.0208	0.0208	0.0208	0.0208	0.0208	0.0208	0.0208
0.0368	0.0368	0.0368	0.0368	0.0368	0.0368	0.0368	0.0368	0.0368	0.0368	0.0368
0.0052	0.0052	0.0052	0.0052	0.0052	0.0052	0.0052	0.0052	0.0052	0.0052	0.0052
0.0178	0.0178	0.0178	0.0178	0.0178	0.0178	0.0178	0.0178	0.0178	0.0178	0.0178
0.0213	0.0213	0.0213	0.0213	0.0213	0.0213	0.0213	0.0213	0.0213	0.0213	0.0213
0.0338	0.0338	0.0338	0.0338	0.0338	0.0338	0.0338	0.0338	0.0338	0.0338	0.0338
0.0060	0.0060	0.0060	0.0060	0.0060	0.0060	0.0060	0.0060	0.0060	0.0060	0.0060
0.0292	0.0292	0.0292	0.0292	0.0292	0.0292	0.0292	0.0292	0.0292	0.0292	0.0292

. . .

Table 4-19 Limit Supermatrix - Normalized Column in Each Block

		Competition 1	2	3	Advertising 1	2	3
	1. GOAL	0.0000	0.0000	0.0000	0.0000	0.0000	0.0000
Reach	1. INTERNATIONAL	0.0000	0.0000	0.0000	0.0000	0.0000	0.0000
	2. GLOBAL	0.0000	0.0000	0.0000	0.0000	0.0000	0.0000
Competition	1. MCDONALD'S	0.5593	0.5593	0.5593	0.5593	0.5593	0.5593
	2. BURGER KING	0.2844	0.2844	0.2844	0.2844	0.2844	0.2844
	3. WENDY'S	0.1560	0.1560	0.1560	0.1560	0.1560	0.1560
Advertising	1. CREATIVITY	0.4880	0.4880	0.4880	0.4880	0.4880	0.4880
	2. PROMOTION	0.2444	0.2444	0.2444	0.2444	0.2444	0.2444
	3. FREQUENCY	0.2676	0.2676	0.2676	0.2676	0.2676	0.2676
Quality of Food	1. NUTRITION	0.3032	0.3032	0.3032	0.3032	0.3032	0.3032
	2. TASTE	0.2253	0.2253	0.2253	0.2253	0.2253	0.2253
	3. PORTION	0.4720	0.4720	0.4720	0.4720	0.4720	0.4720
Other	1. PRICE	0.1215	0.1215	0.1215	0.1215	0.1215	0.1215
	2. LOCATION	0.2150	0.2150	0.2150	0.2150	0.2150	0.2150
	3. SERVICE	0.0306	0.0306	0.0306	0.0306	0.0306	0.0306
	4. SPEED	0.1044	0.1044	0.1044	0.1044	0.1044	0.1044
	5. CLEANLINESS	0.1246	0.1246	0.1246	0.1246	0.1246	0.1246
	6. MENU ITEM	0.1979	0.1979	0.1979	0.1979	0.1979	0.1979
	7. TAKE-OUT	0.0349	0.0349	0.0349	0.0349	0.0349	0.0349
	8. REPUTATION	0.1711	0.1711	0.1711	0.1711	0.1711	0.1711

Quality of Food 1	2	3	Other 1	2	3	4	5	6	7	8
0.0000	0.0000	0.0000	0.0000	0.0000	0.0000	0.0000	0.0000	0.0000	0.0000	0.0000
0.0000	0.0000	0.0000	0.0000	0.0000	0.0000	0.0000	0.0000	0.0000	0.0000	0.0000
0.0000	0.0000	0.0000	0.0000	0.0000	0.0000	0.0000	0.0000	0.0000	0.0000	0.0000
0.5593	0.5593	0.5593	0.5593	0.5593	0.5593	0.5593	0.5593	0.5593	0.5593	0.5593
0.2844	0.2844	0.2844	0.2844	0.2844	0.2844	0.2844	0.2844	0.2844	0.2844	0.2844
0.1560	0.1560	0.1560	0.1560	0.1560	0.1560	0.1560	0.1560	0.1560	0.1560	0.1560
0.4880	0.4880	0.4880	0.4880	0.4880	0.4880	0.4880	0.4880	0.4880	0.4880	0.4880
0.2444	0.2444	0.2444	0.2444	0.2444	0.2444	0.2444	0.2444	0.2444	0.2444	0.2444
0.2676	0.2676	0.2676	0.2676	0.2676	0.2676	0.2676	0.2676	0.2676	0.2676	0.2676
0.3032	0.3032	0.3032	0.3032	0.3032	0.3032	0.3032	0.3032	0.3032	0.3032	0.3032
0.2253	0.2253	0.2253	0.2253	0.2253	0.2253	0.2253	0.2253	0.2253	0.2253	0.2253
0.4720	0.4720	0.4720	0.4720	0.4720	0.4720	0.4720	0.4720	0.4720	0.4720	0.4720
0.1215	0.1215	0.1215	0.1215	0.1215	0.1215	0.1215	0.1215	0.1215	0.1215	0.1215
0.2150	0.2150	0.2150	0.2150	0.2150	0.2150	0.2150	0.2150	0.2150	0.2150	0.2150
0.0306	0.0306	0.0306	0.0306	0.0306	0.0306	0.0306	0.0306	0.0306	0.0306	0.0306
0.1044	0.1044	0.1044	0.1044	0.1044	0.1044	0.1044	0.1044	0.1044	0.1044	0.1044
0.1246	0.1246	0.1246	0.1246	0.1246	0.1246	0.1246	0.1246	0.1246	0.1246	0.1246
0.1979	0.1979	0.1979	0.1979	0.1979	0.1979	0.1979	0.1979	0.1979	0.1979	0.1979
0.0349	0.0349	0.0349	0.0349	0.0349	0.0349	0.0349	0.0349	0.0349	0.0349	0.0349
0.1711	0.1711	0.1711	0.1711	0.1711	0.1711	0.1711	0.1711	0.1711	0.1711	0.1711

Chapter 5

Applications of the Analytic Network Process to Decision Making

5-1. INTRODUCTION

The ANP is a general theory of ratio scale measurement of influence with a methodology that deals with dependence and feedback. This chapter is concerned with applications of the ANP to complex decisions. Before we launch into these applications, we describe the framework we found to be essential for most such decisions, and the prioritization steps that accompany it. To be sure, as some of the applications show, not every step described here needs to be followed literally. We repeat some of the material of earlier chapters for people going directly to applications of the ANP.

The following observations are useful for understanding the framework described below. A decision appears to be objective in so far as we can all perceive it and understand it in the same way. Once we begin to interpret it, we link it to what we personally know or like, and that is no longer objective because knowledge, conditioning and awareness differ from person to person. The same objective facts have different significance to different people. In the end, it is not some hidden objectivity about a decision which when discovered makes it more desirable, but how we interpret the perceived objectivity within our own system of values and what significance we attach to these values. We can inflict our subjectivity on a decision early before we examine the facts, then use our vague impressions and select the alternative that appeals to us the most. It is far better to study the facts underlying the decision in detail to discover its positive and negative aspects, including the risks and opportunities that we would face in adopting it. This is a process of focusing on the merits of the decision before jumping to conclusions. In any case it is our system of values that determines the best answer for us. The objective facts of a decision are necessarily filtered through our subjectivity to serve our own purpose.

With the AHP/ANP one can do what one cannot with logic based on words alone without numbers. One can deal with numerical strengths of preference, whereas logic which uses words, deals with ordinal preference. Instead of "A is preferred to B five times more," with ordinary logic and the need to preserve the transitivity of preferences one can only say, "A is preferred to B," leaving out the very important magnitude of five times that indicates by how much A is preferred to B. The use of magnitudes enables us to perform arithmetic operations to synthesize the outcome of many preferences with greater precision, allowing for a degree of inconsistency. The rules of propositional logic have their counterparts in a hierarchy or a network. Both expressions "if then" and "and/or" occur in a network where the first represents transition from one node to an adjacent one and the second deals with alternative transitions to a given node. Because the AHP/ANP deals with intensities, feelings and emotions become important along-side rational thinking in acquiring understanding.

In making a decision, we need to distinguish between the hierarchic and the network structures that we use to represent its parts. In a hierarchy we have levels arranged in a descending order of importance. The elements in each level are compared according to dominance or influence with respect to the elements in the level immediately above that level. The arrows descend downwards from the goal even if influence, which is a kind of service, is sought for in elements in lower levels that contribute to the well-being and success of elements in higher levels. The arrows point downwards to stimulate the exertion of influence on higher levels.

In a network, the components (counterparts of levels in a hierarchy) are not arranged in any particular order, but are connected as appropriate in pairs with directed lines. Again an arrow points from one component to another to stimulate the influence of the elements of the second component on those in the first component. The pairwise comparisons of elements in a component are made according to the dominance of influence of each member of a pair on an element in the same or in another component. In addition, in a network, the system of components may be regarded as elements that interact and influence each other with respect to a criterion or property. That property itself must be of a higher order of complexity than the elements contained in the components. We call such a property a control criterion, and we have an entire system of such control criteria that belong to the domain of merits of a decision. The result is that such control criteria and their subcriteria serve as the basis for all comparisons made both for the components and for their elements. In a hierarchy one does not compare levels according to influence because they are already arranged in a predetermined order of importance from top to bottom. The criteria for comparisons are either included in a level, or more often implicitly replaced by using the idea of "importance, preference or likelihood" with respect to the goal, without being more finely detailed about what kind of importance it is. The control criteria for comparisons in a network are intended to be explicit about the importance of influence which they represent.

In a hierarchy, we ask the question for making a comparison, which of two elements is more dominant or has more influence (or is influenced more) with respect to a certain element in the level above? In a network we ask, which of two elements is more dominant in influencing another element with respect to a control criterion? **In both hierarchies and networks the sense of having influence or being influenced must be maintained in the entire analysis; the two should not be mixed together.** To repeat, an arrow in a diagram pointing into a component means that its elements influence the elements in the component from which the arrow emanates.

The ANP frees us from the burden of ordering the components in the form of a directed chain as in a hierarchy. We can represent any decision as a directed network. While the AHP has a visibly better structure that derives from a strict understanding of the flow of influence, the ANP allows the structure to develop more naturally, and therefore is a better way to describe faithfully what can happen in the real world. These observations lead us to conclude that hierarchic decisions, because of imposed structure are likely to be more subjective and predetermined. Further, by including dependence and feedback and by cycling their influence with the supermatrix, the ANP is more objective and more likely to capture what happens in the real world. It does things that the mind cannot do in a precise and thorough way. Putting the two observations together, the ANP should be a strongly better decision making tool than the AHP. But the ANP requires more work to capture the facts and interactions. For complex problems requiring thorough analysis we have no other alternative. For simpler decisions done hurriedly, the hard work detracts somewhat from its usefulness. For such ordinary decisions that people and small groups make often, the ANP is only moderately better than the AHP to capture real world outcomes. Major decisions need the ANP framework allowing a little longer time to do the analysis. Eventually, as its applications proliferate, the ANP will be the standard way to make serious decisions. It is interesting to note that both the AHP and the ANP had to wait for the computer age to find their use, but the ANP supermatrix needs the computer much more than does hierarchic composition. In other words, treating dependence and feedback faithfully have become possible only recently.

Structurally, a decision can be divided into three parts: *our value system, the merits* of the decision: *benefits, costs, opportunities* and *risks (BOCR)* to us in making that decision, and *the hierarchies or networks of influences* and "objective" facts that make one alternative of the decision more desirable than another. Figure 5-1a represents this structure. In each of these groups there are major concerns that are subdivided into less major ones and these in turn into still smaller ones. We call these criteria and subcriteria. They can form hierarchies or networks in each group. The entire set of three levels can sometimes be structured into a single network if that seems to make more sense. Knowledge about the top level of personal values where one must use the absolute mode of measurement of the AHP can be enriched by information from the lower levels, but does not depend on it for its priorities. It provides the intensities on which the BOCR merits are rated one at a time and then normalized. This level cannot be conveniently integrated into a single structure with the other two. In most decision problems, there may be three or four adjacent ranges of homogeneous elements to represent personal values (Maslow put them into seven groups). Roughly speaking, we have in decreasing order of importance: 1) Survival, health, security, family, friends and basic religious beliefs some people were known to die for; 2) Career, education, productivity and lifestyle; 3) Political and social beliefs and activities; 4) Philosophical thoughts and ideas and things that are changeable, and it does not matter exactly how one advocates or uses them. There are similar values for a group, a corporation, a country and for the entire world as represented for example by the United Nations. We will not itemize them here because they appear in other works on the AHP/ANP and are not difficult to itemize.

Figure 5-1b represents synthesis at the different parts of the structure shown in Figure 5-1a and also the overall synthesis. First we develop priorities for personal values. Next we rate each of the four BOCR merits on the personal values. Third, we create and prioritize the control criteria for each of the BOCR, and finally, we create and prioritize the decision networks for each of these control criteria. To obtain the answer we synthesize the priorities of the alternatives for benefits and then for opportunities and then for costs and then for risks, thus obtaining four different rankings for each alternative. We use the priorities of BOCR to weight and synthesize the overall weights of the alternatives obtained from the four merit structures. In this process we must use the reciprocals of the synthesized *final* priorities of the alternatives under costs and risks obtaining high priorities for the least costly and least risky alternatives instead of the original high priorities for the most costly, and most risky (see the China trade relations example below). Recall that paired comparisons enable us to ask for the dominance of the larger of two elements over the smaller because we need the smaller as the unit for the comparison. Thus we can only ask which is more costly or risky and then take the reciprocal at the end for the less costly and less risky.

Often, the analysis is performed backwards from the hierarchies and networks of influence at the bottom of the three stages, upwards to obtain deeper understanding and appreciation of the BOCR merits of that decision.

Why do we use the reciprocals of the synthesized results for the alternatives under costs and risks instead of some other way? A good and easy way to show that is to use the old classic example of choosing among several alternatives with costs under two criteria both measured in dollars. The example in the next section shows that to get the correct final values for the alternatives, one must first assign each criterion a priority consisting of the sum of the costs of all the alternatives under it to their sum under both criteria. Only then can one normalize the costs of the alternatives under each criterion, weight by the priority of the corresponding criterion and add to get the correct outcome. One can then take the reciprocals of the final outcomes and normalize them. One does not get a meaningful result by separately taking the reciprocals of the weighted values of the alternatives under each criterion and then add and normalize.

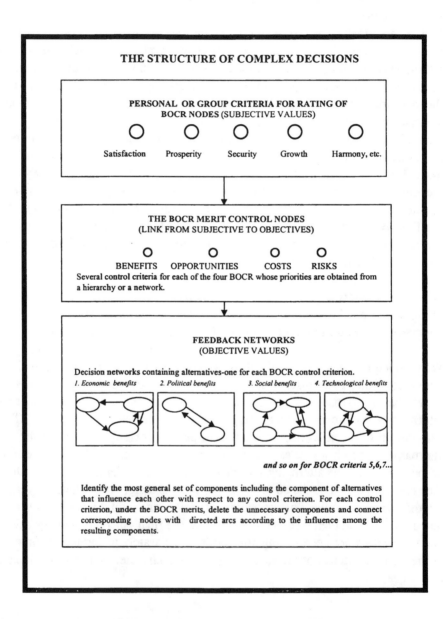

Figure 5-1a The Structure of Decisions

THE PRIORITIZATION OF COMPLEX DECISIONS

PERSONAL OR GROUP CRITERIA FOR RATING OF BOCR NODES (SUBJECTIVE VALUES)

1. Identify and prioritize personal or group criteria and subcriteria applied to all decisions you make.
2. Establish intensities and prioritize them for each lowest level criterion or subcriterion.
3. Rate the Benefits, Opportunities, Costs and the Risks one at a time on the intensities and then normalize.

THE BOCR MERIT CONTROL NODES
(LINK FROM SUBJECTIVE TO OBJECTIVES)

O   O   O   O

BENEFITS   OPPORTUNITIES   COSTS   RISKS

Identify and prioritize the control criteria and subcriteria for each of the four BOCR merits.

FEEDBACK NETWORKS
(OBJECTIVE VALUES)

Decision networks containing alternatives-one for each BOCR control criterion.

1. For each network corresponding to one of the several control criteria under benefits, derive priorities from paired comparison matrices and use them in a supermatrix. Do the same for the criteria under the other three BOCR merits.
2. Pairwise compare the impact of the components on each component of the network with respect to the control criterion, and use these priorities to weight the corresponding blocks of the super matrix. Obtain the limiting supermatrix by raising the weighted supermatrix to large powers.

SYNTHESIS

1. Obtain the priorities of the alternatives under each control criterion from the limiting supermatrix.
2. Synthesize these priorities with respect to all criteria under B, then under O, then etc..
3. Synthesize the resulting priorities with respect to the priorities of BOCR to obtain the final priorities.

Figure 5-1b The Prioritization of Decisions

Here is useful guidance for creating the network structures under each control criterion. We find it helpful to first brainstorm and identify exhaustively all the components and their elements that go into the decision problem. We then create the appropriate connections indicating influence within this structure for each control criterion separately leaving out those components that have no influence under a particular control criterion. This economizes on the number of times we look at the decision in terms of a particular control criterion.

The supermatrix takes into consideration both outer and inner dependence; inner dependence leads to entries for block matrices on the main diagonal of the supermatrix. The eigenvectors in each block are derived from paired comparisons. All paired comparisons are made to assess the influence of pairs of elements within a component on another element in that component with respect to a control criterion. In the same manner as with elements in a component, pairs of components in the network are compared with respect to a control criterion as to their influence on each other component.

We use two kinds of loops at some nodes of the decision network to indicate whether the elements depend on themselves alone or depend on each other. Both kinds of loops are represented by a block matrix of column eigenvectors that appear on the main diagonal of the supermatrix. The first is an **independence loop** as we have at the bottom of a hierarchy represented by an *identity matrix* in the (n, n) position of its supermatrix . A sink node would have this type of matrix unless there is inner dependence among its elements. The second kind of loop is the **dependence loop** that represents interdependence among the elements in a component. Its matrix derives from paired comparisons of the impact of all the elements in that component on each of its elements with respect to a criterion of the control hierarchy. We ask the question: Given an element, which of two elements influences that element more with respect to the control criterion? From comparisons, ratio scale eigenvectors are derived and become the columns of the block diagonal entry of the supermatrix corresponding to that particular loop.

When there is no feedback from the component of the alternatives in a network to other components in that network, the alternatives form a sink, with flows into the component, and none out of it. In that case, one may include the alternatives in the supermatrix (with an identity matrix on the main diagonal) if there is no dependence among them, or an inner dependence matrix on the main diagonal if there is dependence. Otherwise, the alternatives may be excluded from the supermatrix and evaluated by the ideal mode for performance. We need not consider the second case here because it involves no complications with respect to the supermatrix. If there is feedback from the alternatives to other components, they must be included in the supermatrix.

Because it is sometimes tedious to do the numerous comparisons through each of the control criteria hierarchy, in some applications of the ANP, for a speedy back-of-the-envelope analysis, one combines all the criteria of the control hierarchy into a single criterion designated as benefits and then makes the comparison judgments with respect to influence to produce benefits. One does this also for opportunities, for costs, and for risks. It is a compromise approach trading off some accuracy for speed and efficiency as in the drug marketing example shown below. Another way to shorten the analysis is to drop those control criteria whose priorities are very small and renormalize the priorities of the remaining ones, then developing decision networks only for them.

5-2. MULTIPLICATIVE AND ADDITIVE BOCR

Until recently, many examples of the ANP have used the BO/CR ratio to evaluate the alternatives in the final decision. This ratio assumes that all four merits are equally important which of course need not be the case. Now we have a way to develop priorities for each of the four merits B, O, C, R, and use them to compose the weights of the alternatives by multiplying and adding, remembering to use the reciprocals of the *final* priorities under costs and risks. This method of composition is in conformity with hierarchic and network composition. One multiplies and adds to synthesize. One does not raise the priorities of the alternatives to the power of their corresponding criteria and multiply to obtain the final synthesis for each alternative. Often the two outcomes are close, but not always. The examples below illustrate that. We caution the reader not to expect their final answers to coincide or even be close in every case. If we have the priorities p_i, $i=1,...,4$, for each of B, O, C, R, respectively, we have from the first term in the series expansion of the logarithmic function, valid for values of the variable lying between zero and two:

$$\log \frac{B^{P_1}O^{P_2}}{C^{P_3}R^{P_4}} \approx \frac{B^{P_1}O^{P_2}}{C^{P_3}R^{P_4}} - 1$$

$$p_1 \log B + p_2 \log O + p_3 \log(1/C) + p_4 \log(1/R) \approx$$

$$p_1 B + p_2 O + p_3 \frac{1}{C} + p_4 \frac{1}{R} - 1, \qquad \sum_{i=1}^{4} p_i = 1.$$

$$\frac{B^{P_1}O^{P_2}}{C^{P_3}R^{P_4}} \approx p_1 B + p_2 O + p_3 \frac{1}{C} + p_4 \frac{1}{R}$$

The additive approach on the right of the last relation finds its justification in the following example that favors it over the multiplicative approach on the left. Assume that a family is considering buying a house and there are three houses to consider A, B, and C. Four factors dominate their thinking: the price of the house, the remodeling costs, the size of the house as reflected by its footage and the style of the house which is an intangible. They have looked at three houses with numerical data shown below on the quantifiables (Figure 5-2a):

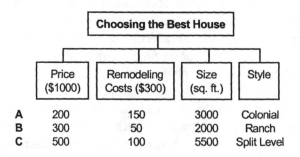

Figure 5-2a Ranking Houses on Four Criteria

If we add the costs for price and modeling and normalize we obtain respectively (A,B,C) = (.269,.269,.462). Now let us see what is needed for normalization to yield the same result.

First we normalize the alternatives for each of the quantifiable factors. Then we must normalize the priorities of the factors that are measured with respect to a single scale, here Price and Remodeling Costs (Figure 5-2b).

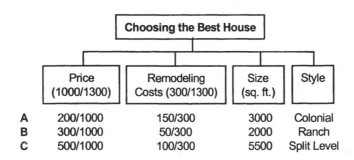

Figure 5-2b Normalization of the Measurements

We learn an important lesson to be used in the general approach of the AHP/ANP. Normalizing the alternatives for each of the two factors involving money leads us to *assign relative weights of importance to the criteria* so that synthesis of the normalized values of the alternatives leads to the same relative dollar values. Here for example, Price is in the ratio of about three to one when compared with Remodeling Cost. It is *reasonable to assign* Price the value of "moderate" or three times more, when compared with Remodeling Costs with respect to the goal of choosing the best house. The factors: Price and Remodeling Costs, when considering the economics of the problem alone, derive their priorities only from the alternatives because they are economically equally

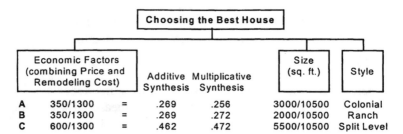

Figure 5-2c Combining the Two Costs through Additive and Multiplicative Syntheses

important factors, although they can also acquire priorities from higher level criteria as to their functional importance with respect to the ease and availability of different amounts of money. Figure 5-2c shows the outcome of combining the two economic factors. The left column and its decimal values in the second column give the exact value of the normalized dollars spent on each house obtained by additive synthesis (weighting and adding). By aggregating the two factors measured with dollars into a single factor, one then makes the decision as to which house to buy by comparing the aggregate economic factor with the other two as to their importance with respect to the goal. The third column shows that multiplicative synthesis gives the wrong results when compared with their relative dollar values. Houses A and B have different values despite the fact that they are the same.

5-3. DECISION BY THE US CONGRESS ON CHINA'S TRADE STATUS –A HIERARCHIC EXAMPLE TO ILLUSTRATE STRUCTURE

In this example, carried out with my student Yeonmin Cho and hand carried by a friend to several congressional leaders in Washington before that decision came before Congress for a vote, we analyzed the decision to select a trade status for China that is in the best interest of the United States. The analysis is conducted through four hierarchies: Benefits, opportunities, costs, and risks for each of which priorities are developed through the rating approach of the Analytic Hierarchy Process (AHP). In all, fifteen criteria are involved in the four hierarchies. Three options were prioritized with respect to the criteria.

Sensitivity analysis indicates that granting China the Permanent Normal Trade Relations status is the most desirable.

Since 1986, China has been trying to join the multilateral trade system, the General Agreement on Tariffs and Trade (GATT) and its successor, the World Trade Organization (WTO). According to the rules of the 135-member nation WTO, a candidate member must reach a trade agreement with any existing member country that wishes to trade with it. By the time this analysis was done, China signed bilateral agreements with 30 countries – including the US (November 1999)– out of 37 members that had requested a trade deal with it. As part of its negotiation deal with the US, China asked the US to remove its annual review of China's Normal Trade Relations (NTR) status, until 1998 called the Most Favored Nation (MFN) status.   In March 2000, President Clinton sent a bill to Congress requesting a Permanent Normal Trade Relations (PNTR) status for China. The decision by the US Congress on China's trade relations status will have an influence on US interests, in both direct and indirect ways, with China. The direct impact will include changes in economic, security and political relations between the US and China as the trade deal is actualized.   The indirect impact will occur when China becomes a WTO member nation and adheres to WTO rules and principles. China has said that it would join the WTO only if the US gives it permanent normal trade relations status.

We thought it likely that Congress would consider four options. The least likely option is that the US will deny China both PNTR and annual extension of NTR status. The other three options are:

Passage of a clean PNTR bill: Congress grants China permanent normal trade relations status with no conditions attached.   This option would allow implementation of the November 1999 WTO trade deal between China and the Clinton administration. China will also carry out other WTO principles and trade conditions.

Amendment of the current NTR status bill: This option would give China the same trade position as other countries and disassociate trade from other issues. As a supplement, a separate bill may be enacted and address other matters, such as human rights, labor rights, and environmental issues.

Annual Extension of NTR status: Congress extends China's normal trade relations status for one more year, and, thus, maintains the status quo.

There have been many debates as to whether Congress should grant China PNTR status. The debate has reflected the different attitudes about this subject. Proponents of the China trade bill emphasize only the benefits, and opportunities (mostly economic), to be derived from passage of the PNTR bill. Opponents are against the bill because of the costs and risks it involves, such as potential loss of jobs in the US. Moreover China's PNTR status eventually could increase its expenditures on military modernization and increase threats to Taiwan.

The following is a summary of the main criteria in the hierarchies of the benefits, costs, opportunities and risks to the US from acting on this decision.

BENEFITS TO US

A. Increase US Exports to China
China's PNTR will increase US exports by $3.1 billion per year in the short-term and could increase them by $12.7 billion to $13.9 billion a year by 2005. China promised to lower overall tariffs from an average of about 25% to 9%. US firms will have broader accessibility to the Chinese market, particularly in the agriculture, service and financial sectors. For example, there are currently only 25 foreign banks in China that are permitted to take deposits and lend money in China's currency, the renminbi, and there are only seven foreign insurers doing business in China. These foreign companies' operations are restricted to a few cities, such as Shanghai, Shenzen and Guangzhou. The geographical restrictions will be dropped in five years. Foreign banks are not allowed to take deposits from Chinese enterprises or individuals. However, once China joins the WTO, immense changes will come to the financial market. Foreign banks will be allowed to do business with Chinese enterprises in renminbi within two years of WTO accession, and with Chinese individuals within five years.

B. Improved Rule of Law
Improved Rule of Law will be guaranteed and could reduce China's infringement of intellectual property rights (IPR), which is a large source of profits. IPR has been a serious cause of trade dispute between the US and China, and has caused loss of US profits. One of the most important differences between

the WTO and its precursor, the GATT, is that the WTO not only deals with trade issues but also covers services and intellectual property rights, according to the Trade-Related Aspects of Intellectual Property rights (TRIPs). All WTO member nations are required to abide by TRIPs. Moreover, China agreed to US demands that upon its accession to the WTO it would implement TRIPs without a transition period. Accordingly, China's accession to the WTO should increase the profits of US businesses particularly in software, music recording, and other high-tech and cultural industries.

Once China joins the WTO, it must abide by the rule of law in accordance with WTO principles. As China becomes more law-abiding, the resulting transparency and predictability of China's actions would lead to an improved investment environment in China.

C. China's Promise to Respect US Provisions
China agreed to adhere to US demands to continue two powerful US provisions to protect its domestic industries. The first is that the US will maintain anti-dumping measures for 15 years after China joins the WTO. If the US International Trade Commission and the US Department of Commerce conclude that dumping is occurring, and if the dumping practice by foreign exporters injures the domestic industry, the government can impose an anti-dumping duty, an import tariff equal to the dumping margin. The US uses anti-dumping policies much more extensively than other countries.

The second is section 201 Law of the 1974 Trade Act, also called the escape clause or the safeguard, which stipulates that the president can impose severe restrictions for up to five years to reduce imports of a foreign product

D. Increased Employment
Increased exports can create more jobs, particularly in areas where the US is highly competitive such as in high-technology, telecommunication, and farm industries.

E. Benefits to Lower Income Consumers
If the US imposes higher tariffs on Chinese products, as a consequence of any trade dispute between the two countries, US consumers may pay higher prices for consumer goods, such as apparel, toys, and electronic appliances. This would become a burden for lower income households.

COSTS TO US

A. Loss of US Access to China's Market
Competition among nations over China's market is high. If China does not obtain Normal Trade Relations status, it is likely to blame the US. In that case, China would be less inclined to offer US businesses the opportunities given to other competitors in Chinese markets.

B. Possible Job Losses in the US
Labor unions have expressed their concern that jobs will be at risk if Congress passes the bill, because some US firms would move to China in pursuit of its low-wage labor.

OPPORTUNITIES FOR THE US

A. US–Sino Relations
Congress' decision could result in a breakthrough in US-Sino relations in the economic, political, social, cultural, and security arenas. Congress can help draw China, which was isolated until Deng Xiaoping began economic reform, closer to the rest of the world, and open wider arenas for US-China exchange.

B. Improve the Environment
China's large population and fast economic growth generate high-energy consumption and exhaust other natural resources, thus causing environmental concerns. There are two reasons why the US can expect better environmental policies in China with PNTR. First, many developing countries, such as China, cannot afford environment-friendly equipment. When China's economy develops further, it is more likely that China would take measures against environmental degradation. Second, as the US-China Forum on Environment and Development has demonstrated, close relations between China and the US can enhance US ability to influence China's behavior regarding environmental protection.

C. Promote Democracy
This aim is self-explanatory. The US believes it can influence human rights and other behavior.

D. Improve Human and Labor Rights
The more China is exposed to the rest of the world through the flow of goods, finance, technology and ideas, the more it is likely to become a democratic nation. Labor and human rights are also more likely to be improved through China's exposure to standards adhered to by developed nations.

RISKS FOR US

A. Loss of Trade as Leverage over Other Issues
Some believe that the annual review process of China's trade status gives the US an economic leverage over other issues such as human rights, labor rights, and security issues. Consequently, granting China Permanent Trade Relations is perceived by some as sacrificing US leverage over China.

B. US-China Conflict
Denying China PNTR can lead to conflicts between the US and China. Some analysts have suggested that China may become a major rival for the US, replacing the former Soviet Union. Thus, the potential friction with China could be a serious cause for risk.

C. China Violating Regional Stability
Failure of engagement with China can yield regional instability, particularly across the Taiwan Strait. Isolating China from the WTO may also lead to a withdrawal of China's commitment to alleviate potential conflict around the Korean Peninsula, and between Pakistan and India.

D. China's Reform Retreat
China's leaders, primarily Premier Zhu Rongji, are attempting to reform China's economic system and politics. If the US does not cooperate with this effort, China's reactionary forces, including officials of the Communist Party of China and other privileged groups, would try to pressure the current leaders to diminish their desire to reform China.

PULLING IT ALL TOGETHER
The two-sided debate and the imminent decision on China's trade status motivated us to use the Analytic Hierarchy Process, to examine the positives and negatives of the options. This approach will allow us to cull the most promising of the three positive alternatives.

This analysis brings two strengths to the debate. It is comprehensive by identifying all the issues bearing on the three factors of the decision: economic, security, and political. It is also an objective examination of the problem strictly based on criteria and priorities that anyone might consider in the decision.

Our analysis involves four steps. First, we prioritize the criteria in the benefits, costs, opportunities and risks hierarchies. Figure 5-3 shows the resulting prioritization of these criteria. The alternatives and their priorities are shown under each criterion. The syntheses of the priorities of the alternatives are shown beneath each hierarchy.

The priorities shown in Figure 5-3 were derived from judgments which compared the elements involved in pairs. It is easy to estimate our original pairwise judgments, which are not shown here, form the ratio of the corresponding two priorities shown and then take the closest whole number or its reciprocal if it is less than one.

Then we established priorities for the economic, security and political factors themselves as shown in Figure 5-4 and Table 5-1 and used them and their subfactors to rate the importance of the benefits, costs, opportunities and risks. Finally, we used the normalized priorities of the overall ratings of each to weight the priorities of the alternatives in the corresponding hierarchy and add to obtain their final priorities shown at the bottom of Table 5-1. We remembered to use the normalized reciprocal priorities of the synthesized priorities of the alternatives under costs and risks in this process. It turns out that PNTR is by far the preferred outcome. The assessment criteria we used to determine the priorities of the merits are shown in Figure 5-4.

The primary goal of any economic policy is to spur economic development. A trade policy always creates the inequity of "winners" and "losers," and this is why equity needs to be considered. Economic growth and equity should be used as the economic criteria. The security criterion has three sub-criteria. They are: regional security in Asia, particularly between China and Taiwan, non-proliferation efforts to diminish nuclear and conventional military competitions, and the direct threat to US security. Two sub-criteria are considered under the political criterion: the impact that the decision has on the American voters and the spread of American values such as democracy, human rights and labor rights.

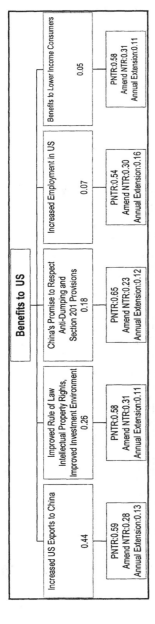

Benefits Synthesis: PNTR: 0.60   Amend NTR: 0.28   Annual Extension: 0.12

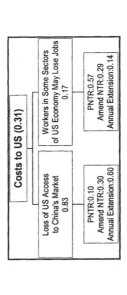

Costs Synthesis (which is more costly):   PNTR 0.18   Amend NTR: 0.30   Annual Extension: 0.52
Normalized Reciprocal form (which is less costly):   PNTR 0.51   Amend NTR: 0.31   Annual Extension: 0.18

Figure 5-3 The Four Decision Hierarchies for Benefits, Costs, Opportunities and Risks

Figure 5-3 (Cont'd)   The Four Decision Hierarchies for Benefits, Costs, Opportunities and Risks

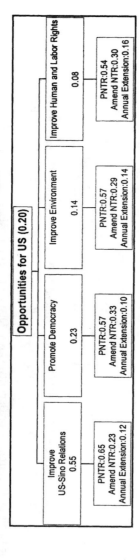

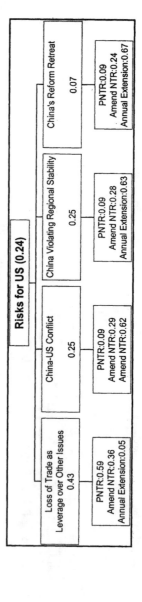

Opportunities Synthesis: PNTR: 0.61   Amend NTR: 0.27   Annual Extension: 0.12

Risks Synthesis (which is more risky):   PNTR 0.31   Amend NTR: 0.31   Annual Extension: 0.38

Normalized Reciprocal form (which is less risky):   PNTR: 0.36   Amend NTR: 0.36   Annual Extension: 0.28

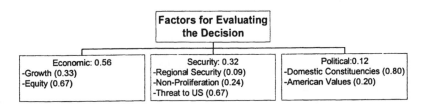

Figure 5-4 Hierarchy for Rating Benefits, Costs, Opportunities and Risks

Priorities for evaluating the significance of the criteria (see the four hierarchies in Figure 5-3) are given in Table 5-1. The results show that benefits and costs have larger significance than opportunities and risks, because by our definition, benefits and costs are more imminent and feasible criteria than opportunities and risks. We weighted costs and risks more heavily than benefits and opportunities, because negative impacts are more susceptible and vital.

Table 5-1 Rating Importance of Benefits, Costs, Opportunities and Risks

Rating Priorities: Very High (0.42), High (0.26), Medium (0.16), Low (0.1), Very Low (0.06)

Criteria	Sub-criteria	**Benefits**	Costs	**Oppor-tunities**	**Risks**
Econom-ic (0.56)	Growth (0.19)	High	Very Low	Medium	Very Low
	Equity (0.37)	Medium	High	Low	Low
Security (0.32)	Regional (0.03)	Low	Medium	Medium	High
	Non-Prolifer-ation(0.08)	Medium	Medium	High	High
	Threat to US (0.21)	High	Very High	High	Very High
Political (0.12)	Constituencies (0.1)	High	Very High	Medium	High
	American Values (0.02)	Very Low	Low	Low	Medium
Overall	*Priorities*	**0.25**	**0.31**	**0.20**	**0.24**

We are now able to obtain the overall priorities of the three decision alternatives as to what to do about China, and PNTR has the largest outcome priority of 0.51. We have:

Table 5-2 Final Synthesis of Priorities of Alternatives

	Benefits to US (0.25)	Opportun- ities to US (0. 20)	Costs to US (0. 31)	Risks to US (0.24)	Final Analysis (additive)	Multiplicative
PNTR	0.60	0.61	0.51	0.36	**0.51**	0.52
Amend NTR	0.28	0.27	0.31	0.36	**0.31**	0.31
Annual Extension	0.12	0.12	0.18	0.28	**0.18**	0.17

In additive synthesis, we have for example for PNTR: $.60x.25 + .51x.31 + .61x.20 + .36x.24 = .51$. In multiplicative synthesis, which we have generally argued against, but still would like to compare its outcome with that of additive synthesis, we have for PNTR: $.6^{.25}.51^{.31}.61^{.2}.36^{.24}$ which is then normalized by dividing by the sum of all three such expressions to obtain 0.52 for its priority.

STABILITY OF THE OUTCOME WITH CHANGING PRIORITIES

Our analysis indicates that granting China Permanent Normal Trade Relations status is the best alternative with a priority of (0.51), followed by Amend NTR by normalizing trade relations with China while enacting a separate bill (0.31). The status quo, extension of the NTR status with China, is the least favorable option (0.18).

Comprehensive sensitivity analysis would involve perturbing the priorities of the benefits, costs, opportunities, and risks and also jointly perturbing the priorities of the criteria and finally also perturbing the priorities of the alternatives. We would then note what happens to the rank order of the alternatives to determine if the most preferred one remains the same for all or at least for a preponderance of the perturbations. That would be a formidable task for anyone to do. There are two shortcuts in doing sensitivity. The first is to assume that the priorities of the alternatives with respect to the criteria are well understood and do not need to be perturbed. That leaves open the perturbations of the two higher level sets of criteria. Here we have one possible shortcut and that is to delimit the range of perturbation of the criteria with the assumption that very large perturbations would carry their priorities into unreasonable ranges no one would think is feasible. In that case, one would take the existing priorities and perturb them by small values up and down in combinations and note the resulting stability of the priorities of the alternatives. Even then, stability may not obtain in all the cases and one must decide on a way to justify adopting the leading alternative for the decision. The number of possibilities to try here can be very large. What we have done is to determine the stability of the outcome with respect to changes in the criteria with a fixed priority for the benefits, costs, opportunities, and risks. We, then performed sensitivity by not fixing the priorities of both the alternatives and criteria at their present values and perturbed the priorities of the benefits, costs, opportunities, and risks. This effort leads to the following abridged conclusions.

With the original priorities of the benefits, costs, opportunities, and risks, sensitivity analysis with the software Expert Choice shows that the best alternative is insensitive to thirteen out of the fifteen criteria in Figure 5-3. Only two criteria, "Workers in Some Sectors of US Economy May Lose Jobs," and "Loss of Trade as Leverage over Other Issues," change in whose priorities individually and together, can make the top alternative less desirable. That happens, if the importance of the first of the two criteria increases by more than twice its current value, or if the importance of the second increases several times more than its current value. In both cases, Annual Extension becomes the preferred alternative. There are numerous combinations of the priorities of the two criteria that can lead to rank reversal. Reversal begins to occur only when the priorities of both criteria are simultaneously increased twice their current value, which, given the present circumstances, is highly unlikely. Sensitivity analysis shows that the final outcome in Table 5-2 is very stable.

When we assumed that the priorities of the alternatives and of those of the criteria were fixed and varied the weights of the benefits, costs, opportunities and risks up and down by five percent in all possible combinations, we found that the priorities of the alternatives remained stable in all the cases.

Our sensitivity analysis indicates that overall it is in the best interests of the United States to grant China PNTR status.

5-4. DRUG -MARKETING DECISION. THREE MERITS: BENEFITS, COSTS, AND RISKS WITHOUT CONTROL CRITERIA

Here is a decision faced by a large pharmaceutical company. The problem was how should the company market a new drug, given the pending patent expiration of an already existing drug it had been marketing? The ANP model used to make the decision illustrates two important ideas. First, it uses a very simple control hierarchy involving the aggregate criteria of benefits, costs, and risks. (Figure 5-5) As we shall see later in the chapter, in many problems each of these control criteria is decomposed into subcriteria and even sub-subcriteria to produce and elaborate the control hierarchy. The control structure itself may even involve feedback among its parts, and after deriving the limiting priorities one would proceed to develop the submodels with respect to the driving criteria of the model using several submodels. Returning to our example, for each of these controlling considerations a separate network model of interactions was created. Thus there were three submodels, one for each control criterion.

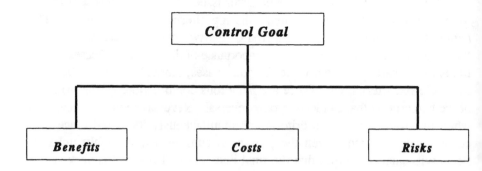

Figure 5-5 The Control Hierarchy

This ANP model was a live test case in that the company was actually in the process of making the decision when the study was conducted. With the pending expiration of the current market offering, their objective was clearly to launch the new drug successfully before the patent for the old drug expired. However, the company had to decide whether to market the new drug over the old. The questions were: Should the old drug be phased out slowly or entirely replaced by the new drug? How much of the marketing budget should be devoted to each strategy? Other important questions were also considered. Although the old drug would be facing stiffer competition, its brand recognition would continue to bring in revenue. The new drug was chemically improved over the old but needed greater promotion to be successful. There was also the risk that the new drug would be rejected by the HMOs and by customers. Moreover, with the added costs of promotion and the existing competition, the company could be facing slimmer profit margins, making these marketing decisions more critical.

The first step in building the model was to identify the stakeholders: HMO administrators, physicians, pharmacists, and nurses. Interviews with these stakeholders facilitated identifying the relevant components and the elements in each component and their interdependencies. The interviews also yielded invaluable information and knowledgeable judgments for the model.

The second step was to partition the decision by using the control model approach. This allowed the participants to focus on each aspect of the larger problem. When considering benefits alone for example, factors such as market share and profit margin were identified. Their importance may vary for the different stakeholders, and these are precisely the dependencies and priorities the model seeks and measures. For the costs side, the factors identified included marketing expenses, production costs and market share loss. Factors for the risks model included product acceptance, production backlog, patient expiration, and sales incentives. The last step was to synthesize the ANP submodels. The best outcome derived from the ANP was the decision to proceed to market the new drug but also continue to market the old one. The new drug would incur higher marketing expenses compared with the old, but the brand recognition of the old drug would continue to provide a healthy return even with a lower marketing effort.

The actual decision of the company was to proceed to market the new drug and continue to market the old drug. However, the company decided to eliminate the sales incentives and marketing expenses for the old drug and to increase the sales incentives and marketing expenses for the new drug. These decisions were consistent with the ANP model. To save space we illustrate in Table 5-3 with matrices of judgments only for the benefits network (Figure 5-6), but give all the supermatrices, the weighted supermatrices, and the limiting supermatrices for benefits, costs and risks (Tables 5-4 to 5-6). In Table 5-7 we evaluate the merits on the corporate criteria and in Table 5-8 we give the final answer for the alternatives.

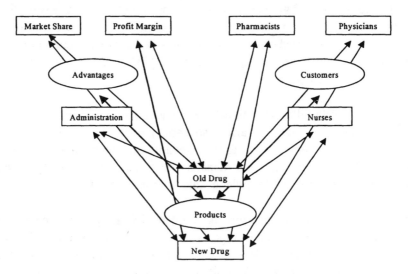

Figure 5-6 The Benefits Submodel

Here, we have used an oval to represent a component and a rectangle to represent an element belonging to a component. Table 5-3 below gives the component impacts on each other component.

Table 5-4 Supermatrices for Benefits

Local:	Old Drug	New Drug	Admin.	Market Share	Profit Margin	Nurses	Pharmacists	Physicians
Old Drug	0.0000	0.0000	0.5000	0.6667	0.7500	0.5000	0.3333	0.3333
New Drug	0.0000	0.0000	0.5000	0.3333	0.2500	0.5000	0.6667	0.6667
Administration	0.1396	0.2000	0.0000	0.0000	0.0000	0.0000	0.0000	0.0000
Market Share	0.3325	0.6001	0.0000	0.0000	0.0000	0.0000	0.0000	0.0000
Profit Margin	0.5278	0.1999	0.0000	0.0000	0.0000	0.0000	0.0000	0.0000
Nurses	0.1220	0.1172	0.0000	0.0000	0.0000	0.0000	0.0000	0.0000
Pharmacists	0.3196	0.2684	0.0000	0.0000	0.0000	0.0000	0.0000	0.0000
Physicians	0.5584	0.6144	0.0000	0.0000	0.0000	0.0000	0.0000	0.0000

Weighted Supermatrix	Old Drug	New Drug	Admin.	Market Share	Profit Margin	Nurses	Pharmacists	Physicians
Old Drug	0.0000	0.0000	0.5000	0.6667	0.7500	0.5000	0.3333	0.3333
New Drug	0.0000	0.0000	0.5000	0.3333	0.2500	0.5000	0.6667	0.6667
Administration	0.0349	0.0500	0.0000	0.0000	0.0000	0.0000	0.0000	0.0000
Market Share	0.0831	0.1500	0.0000	0.0000	0.0000	0.0000	0.0000	0.0000
Profit Margin	0.1320	0.0500	0.0000	0.0000	0.0000	0.0000	0.0000	0.0000
Nurses	0.0915	0.0879	0.0000	0.0000	0.0000	0.0000	0.0000	0.0000
Pharmacists	0.2397	0.2013	0.0000	0.0000	0.0000	0.0000	0.0000	0.0000
Physicians	0.4188	0.4608	0.0000	0.0000	0.0000	0.0000	0.0000	0.0000

Limiting Supermatrix	Old Drug	New Drug	Admin	Market Share	Profit Margin	Nurses	Pharmacists	Physicians
Old Drug	0.21575	0.21575	0.21575	0.21575	0.21575	0.21575	0.21575	0.21575
New Drug	0.28425	0.28425	0.28425	0.28425	0.28425	0.28425	0.28425	0.28425
Administration	0.02175	0.02175	0.02175	0.02175	0.02175	0.02175	0.02175	0.02175
Market Share	0.06055	0.06055	0.06055	0.06055	0.06055	0.06055	0.06055	0.06055
Profit Margin	0.04270	0.04270	0.04270	0.04270	0.04270	0.04270	0.04270	0.04270
Nurses	0.04475	0.04475	0.04475	0.04475	0.04475	0.04475	0.04475	0.04475
Pharmacists	0.10895	0.10895	0.10895	0.10895	0.10895	0.10895	0.10895	0.10895
Physicians	0.22135	0.22135	0.22135	0.22135	0.22135	0.22135	0.22135	0.22135

The final priorities for the alternatives appear in any column of the matrix. For example we have the priority for the old drugs 0.4315 and that for the new drug 0.5685.

Table 5-4 a Benefit Priorities of Alternatives

Old Drug	0.4315
New Drug	0.5685

Tables 5-5 Supermatrices for the Costs Analysis

Local:	Market Share Loss	Marketing Expenses	Production Costs	Old Drug	New Drug
Market Share Loss	0.0000	0.0000	0.0000	0.5815	0.3108
Marketing Expenses	0.0000	0.0000	0.0000	0.1094	0.4934
Production Costs	0.0000	0.0000	0.0000	0.3090	0.1958
Old Drug	0.8000	0.2500	0.8000	0.0000	0.0000
New Drug	0.2000	0.7500	0.2000	0.0000	0.0000

Weighted:	Market Share Loss	Marketing Expenses	Production Costs	Old Drug	New Drug
Market Share Loss	0.0000	0.0000	0.0000	0.5816	0.3108
Marketing Expenses	0.0000	0.0000	0.0000	0.1094	0.4934
Production Costs	0.0000	0.0000	0.0000	0.3090	0.1958
Old Drug	0.8000	0.2500	0.8000	0.0000	0.0000
New Drug	0.2000	0.7500	0.2000	0.0000	0.0000

Limiting Global	Market Share Loss	Marketing Expenses	Production Costs	Old Drug	New Drug
Market Share Loss	0.24615	0.24615	0.24615	0.24615	0.24615
Marketing Expenses	0.11805	0.11805	0.11805	0.11805	0.11805
Production Costs	0.13585	0.13585	0.13585	0.13585	0.13585
Old Drug	0.33510	0.33510	0.33510	0.33510	0.33510
New Drug	0.16490	0.16490	0.16490	0.16490	0.16490

Table 5-5 a Cost Priorities of Alternatives

Old Drug	0.6702
New Drug	0.3298

Tables 5-6 Supermatrices for the Risks Analysis.

Local:	New Drug	Old Drug	Sale Incentives	Patent Expiration	Production Backlog	Acceptance of Product
New Drug	0.0000	0.0000	0.8000	0.1667	0.8000	0.8333
Old Drug	0.0000	0.0000	0.2000	0.8333	0.2000	0.1667
Sales Incentives	0.1659	0.1318	0.0000	0.0000	0.5000	0.5000
Patent Expiration	0.0716	0.5897	0.0000	0.0000	0.0000	0.0000
Production Backlog	0.5186	0.1392	0.6667	0.0000	0.0000	0.5000
Acceptance of Product	0.2439	0.1392	0.3333	0.0000	0.5000	0.0000

Weighted	New Drug	Old Drug	Sale Incentives	Patent Expiration	Production Backlog	Acceptance of Product
New Drug	0.0000	0.0000	0.2000	0.1667	0.2000	0.2083
Old Drug	0.0000	0.0000	0.0500	0.8333	0.0500	0.0417
Sales Incentives	0.1659	0.1318	0.0000	0.0000	0.3750	0.3750
Patent Expiration	0.0716	0.5898	0.0000	0.0000	0.0000	0.0000
Production Backlog	0.5186	0.1392	0.5000	0.0000	0.0000	0.3750
Acceptance of Product	0.2439	0.1392	0.2500	0.0000	0.3750	0.0000

Synthesized Global	New Drug	Old Drug	Sales Incentives	Patent Expiration	Production Backlog	Acceptance of Product
New Drug	0.1525	0.1525	0.1525	0.1525	0.1525	0.1525
Old Drug	0.0837	0.0837	0.0837	0.0837	0.0837	0.0837
Sales Incentives	0.2183	0.2183	0.2183	0.2183	0.2183	0.2183
Patent Expiration	0.0603	0.0603	0.0603	0.0603	0.0603	0.0603
Production Backlog	0.2777	0.2777	0.2777	0.2777	0.2777	0.2777
Acceptance of Product	0.2075	0.2075	0.2075	0.2075	0.2075	0.2075

Table 5-6 a Risk Priorities of Alternatives

New Drug	0.6456
Old Drug	0.3542

Table 5-7 Evaluation of BCR on Corporate Criteria

High: 0.517 Medium: 0.359 Low:0.124

	Profits (0.419)	R & D (0.263)	FDA Rejec -tion (0.160)	Competit i-veness (0.097)	Psycho-logical effects (0.062)	Priorities
Benefits	High	Medium	Low	Medium	Low	**0.353**
Costs	Medium	High	High	Medium	High	**0.412**
Risks	Low	Medium	High	Low	Low	**0.235**

Table 5-8 Synthesis of Final Priorities of the Two
Alternatives

	Benefits (0.353)	Costs (less costly) (0.412)	Risks (less risky) (0.235)	Final Outcome: Additive	Multiplicative
Old Drug	0.4315	0.3298	0.6456	**0.4399**	0.438
New Drug	0.5685	0.6702	0.3544	**0.5601**	0.562

This example was worked out by my students, T. Benedict and F. Mubarak.

5-5. WHERE TO DISPOSE OF NUCLEAR WASTE

As of 1991, 123,400,000 cubic meters of radioactive waste had accumulated in the United States. While the generation of this waste has been decreasing, primarily because of the unforeseen costs of nuclear-generated electricity, the problem concerns what to do with the existing waste, which will remain dangerous for between 200,000 and 1,600,000 years. Where should the waste be stored?

Prior to the 1970s, the selection of disposal sites was haphazard due to lack of government regulations and adequate knowledge of the dangers of radiation. Following the 1970s, regulations began to appear. In 1982 the Nuclear Waste

Policy Act was passed, requiring the Department of Energy (DOE) to establish a system of permanent geologic facilities for the storage of high-level nuclear waste. The analysis focused on finding the best location in the U.S. for the storage of existing and future high-level waste (HLW) using the BOCR approach but using only BCR.

"Benefits" refers to the benefits of storing nuclear waste at a particular site. The benefits of the nuclear power or nuclear weapons that created the waste were not considered. The model assumes that the US has a significant amount of nuclear waste and must find a place to store it safely. The costs include the sure costs of storing nuclear wastes, such as transportation and the opportunity cost of the land. Risks in the model take the future into consideration.

The six alternative sites in this model are Hanford Nuclear Reservation, Washington; Mescalero Apache Tribe Reservation, New Mexico; seabed; space; Waste Isolation Pilot Project (WIPP), New Mexico; and Yucca Mountain, Nevada. Although Congress has designated Yucca Mountain as the official site, DOE tests remain unfinished; thus the suitability of the site is unclear. The other sites have been identified in the literature as possibilities.

The components and elements in each control hierarchy are listed in Table 5-9 and their connections are given in Table 5-10. All elements in the *alternative sites* component are included in all the networks. The *government* and the *other stakeholder* components are also common for all networks, but some elements are not part of certain networks. Some components and elements uniquely belong to certain networks only, such as *other benefits* for the economic and social benefit networks and *cost of resources* for the economic cost network.

Figure 5-10 shows the connection between elements indicating the flow of influence. To organize our thinking about the flows, we can either indicate connections to the set of elements that are influenced by each element or indicate connections from the other elements that transmit influence to each element. Connecting two components gives full connection among elements in these components. In this application we follow the first approach. and Table 5-10 indicates the elements that are influenced by each element in the left column.

Table 5-9 Component/Element Membership for Each Control Criterion

Component	Element	Benefits			Costs			Risks		
		Env	Ec	Soc	Env	Ec	Soc	S/E	Ec	Pol
Government (GO)	1. Congress	x	x	x	x	x	x	x	x	x
	2. State Government	x	x	x	x	x	x	x	x	x
	3. Local Government	x	x	x	x	x	x	x	x	x
	4. DOE	x	x	x	x	x	x	x	x	x
	5. NRC	x	x	x	x	x	x	x	x	x
	6. OSHA		x	x	x	x	x	x	x	x
	7. ICC				x	x	x	x		
	8. FPC	x			x	x	x			
	9. EPA	x	x	x	x	x	x	x	x	x
Regulations (RG)	1. Land	x								
	2. Water	x						x		
	3. Air	x								
	4. Radioact. emission							x	x	x
	5. Working conditions		x							
	6. Environmental		x						x	x
	7. Current				x	x	x			x
	8. Future						x			
Site characteristics (SC)	1. Prev. contamination	x						x	x	
	2. Accessibility	x			x				x	x
	3. Size/capacity				x				x	
	4. Habitat	x			x			x		
	5. Technology				x				x	
	6. Proximity to people							x		x
	7. Security							x		x
	8. Transport method									
	9. Land ownership							x	x	
	10. Time to get ready								x	x
Alternative sites (AS)	1. Hanford, WA	x	x	x	x	x	x	x	x	x
	2. Mescalero Apache tribe	x	x	x	x	x	x	x	x	x
	3. Seabed									
	4. Space	x	x	x	x	x	x	x	x	x
	5. WIPP, NM	x	x	x	x	x	x	x	x	x
	6. Yucca Mountain	x	x	x	x	x	x	x	x	x
		x	x	x	x	x	x	x	x	x

Component	Element	Benefits			Costs			Risks		
		Env	Ec	Soc	Env	Ec	Soc	S/E	Ec	Pol
Other stakeholders (OS)	1. Environmentalists	x	x	x	x	x	x	x	x	x
	2. Scientists	x	x	x				x	x	x
	3. Communities	x	x	x	x	x	x	x	x	x
	4. Nuclear waste disposal industry	x	x	x	x	x	x	x	x	x
	5. Waste producers	x	x	x	x	x	x	x	x	x
	6. Native Americans	x	x	x	x	x	x		x	x
	7. Workers	x	x	x		x		x		x
Other benefits (OB)	1. Income		x							
	2. Spin off industry		x							
	3. Reduced on site storage		x							
	4. Taxes									
	5. Central Management		x							
	6. Capacity		x							
	7. Nuclear nonproliferation		x	x						
	8. Controlled radiation exposure			x						
	9. Self-sufficiency			x						
	10. Level of technology									
	11. Future generations			x						
Cost of Resources (CR)	1. Time to become available				x					
	2. Legal				x					
	3. Operating				x					
	4. Land				x					
	5. Transport				x					
	6. Security				x					
Other costs (OC)	1. Public relations				x					
	2. Taxes				x					
Social costs (SC)	1. Stigma to the city						x			
	2. Lack of support						x			
	3. Loss of jobs						x			
	4. Radiation exposure						x			
	5. Future generations						x			
	6. Discouragement of new business						x			

Component	Element	Benefits			Costs			Risks		
		Env	Ec	Soc	Env	Ec	Soc	S/E	Ec	Pol
Other risks (OR)	1. Explosion							x		
	2. Ground water contamination							x		
	3. Radiation exposure							x		
	4. Seismic							x		
	5. Nuclear proliferation									x
	6. Reelection									x
	7. Sovereignty									x

Table 5-10 Flows of Influence from Each Component/Element

Influenced by	Components/Elements being influenced								
Components/Elements Transmit influence	Benefits Environmental			Costs Environmental			Risks Social/Environmental		
Government (GO)	RG	AS	OS	GO	RG	AS	GO	RG	SC
1. Congress	All	All	4,5	All but 1		All	All but 1	All	
2. State Government	All	All	4,5	All but 2		All	All but 2	All	
3. Local Government	All	All	4,5	All but 3		All	All but 3	All	
4. DOE	All	All	4,5	All but 4		All	All but 4	All	
5. NRC	All	All	4,5	All but 5		All	All but 5	All	
6. OSHA	All	All	4,5	All but 6		All	All but 6	All	
7. ICC	All	All	4,5	All but 7			All but 7	7	
8. FPC	All	All	4,5	All but 8		All	All but 8		All
9. EPA	All	All	4,5	All but 9		All	All but 9	All	
Regulation (RG)	SC			SC	OS		GO	SC	
1. Land	All								
2. Water	All						All	1,4,6	
3. Air	All								
4. Radioactive Emissions							All	1,4,6	
5. Working Conditions									
6. Environmental									
7. Current				All	3,4,5				
8. Future									
Site Charact. (SC)	AS	OS		AS			OS	AS	

Influenced by	Components/Elements being influenced								
Components/Elements Transmit influence	Benefits Environmental			Costs Environmental			Risks Social/Environmental		
1. Previous Contamination	All						7	All	
2. Accessibility	All			All					
3. Size/Capacity				All					
4. Habitat	All	All		All				All	
5. Technology				All					
6. Proximity to People								All	
7. Security								All	
8. Transport Method								All	
9. Land Ownership									
10. Time to get ready									
Alternative Sites (AS)	GO	AS	OS	SC			SC		
1. Hanford, WA				All			SC		
2. Mescalero Apache tribe				All			SC		
3. Seabed									
4. Space				All			SC		
5. WIPP, NM				All			SC		
6. Yucca Mountain				All			SC		
				All			SC		
Other Stakeholders (OS)	GO	RG	AS, OS	GO	AS		GO	SC	OS
1. Environmentalists	All	All	All	All			All		
2. Scientists	All		All				All		
3. Communities	All		All	All			All		
4. Nuclear waste disposal industry	All		All	All			All		3,7
5. Waste producers	All		All	All					
6. Native Americans	All		All	All	All				
7. Workers	All		All						
Other Benefits (OB)									
1. Income									
2. Spin off industries	(Applicable to economic or social benefits only)								
3. Reduced on site storage									
4. Taxes									
5. Central Management									
6. Capacity									
7. Nuclear Nonproliferation									
8. Controlled radiation exposure									
9. Self sufficiency									
10. Level of technology									
11. Future generations									
Cost of Resources (CR)									

Influenced by	Components/Elements being influenced							
Components/Elements Transmit influence	Benefits Environmental			Costs Environmental			Risks Social/Environmental	
1. Time to be available 2. Legal 3. Operating 4. Land 5. Transport 6. Security				(Applicable to economic costs only)				
Other Costs (OC)								
1. Public Relations 2. Taxes				(Applicable to economic costs only)				
Social Costs (SC)								
1. Stigma to the city 2. Lack of support 3. Loss of jobs 4. Radiation exposure 5. Future generations 6. Discouragement of new business				(Applicable to social costs only)				
Other Risks (OR)							OS	AS
1. Explosion 2. Ground water contamination 3. Radiation 4. Seismic 5. Nuclear proliferation 6. Reelection 7. Sovereignty							3,7 3,7 3,7 3,7	All All but 5 All All but 5

Figures 5-7 through 5-9 show the networks for the benefits, costs, and risks perspectives. The variety of structures for each control criterion indicates the importance of control hierarchies in the ANP. It makes sense to require that all networks contain all elements representing the alternative outcomes of the problem. However, there need not be a flow of influence from each and every element in the network to the alternatives.

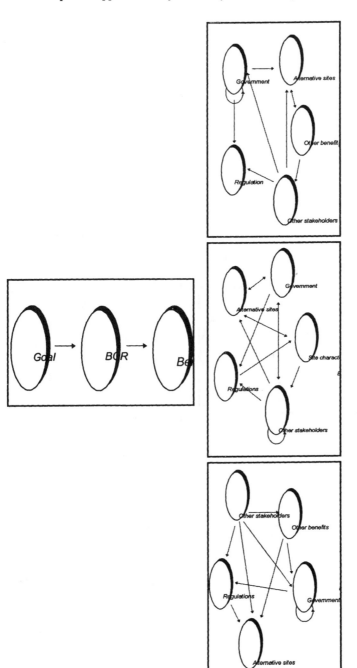

Figure 5-7 Benefits Control Hierarchy

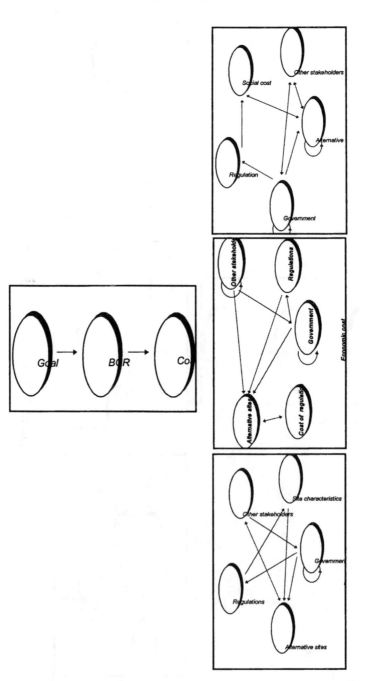

Figure 5-8 Costs Control Hierarchy

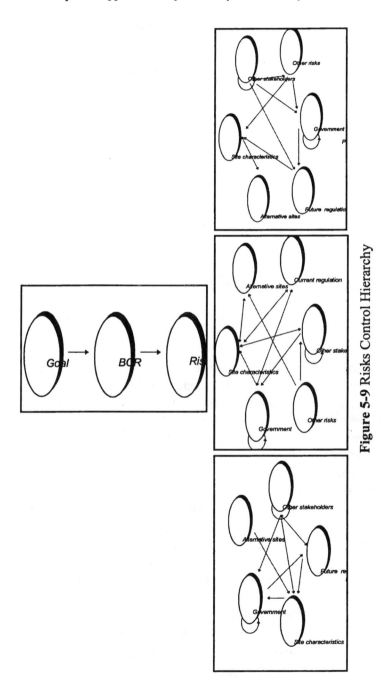

Figure 5-9 Risks Control Hierarchy

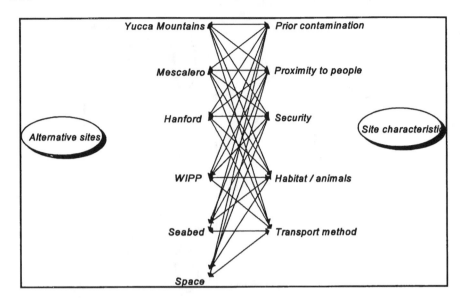

Figure 5-10   Flow of Influence for the Social-Environmental Criterion of
the Risks Control Hierarchy

A set of pairwise comparison matrices is constructed in response to the
questions formulated to elicit the judgments. Take Figure 5-10, for example,
which is part of the network under the social-environmental criterion for risks.
The relative influence from the elements in the site characteristics to those in
the alternative sites are elicited by questions such as: With respect to the social-
environmental criterion, which of a pair of alternative sites is made more risky
by prior contamination, and how much more?   Feedbacks from the alternative
sites to the site characteristics are elicited by questions such as: With respect
to the social-environmental criterion, does the Yucca Mountain site pose more
risk to prior contamination or to proximity to people, and by how much?
For the benefits control hierarchy, for example, the judgments are given in
response to the question: Which of a pair of control criteria is more important
in contributing to the benefits in selecting the best site, and how much more?

After the limiting priorities of the criteria are obtained from the supermatrix
and used to weight the alternatives (in case they are not in the supermatrix), the
weights of the alternatives for benefits, costs, and risks are each normalized

and weighted by the priorities of the criteria from the control hierarchy and synthesized for each of the three hierarchies.

Tables 5-11 give the necessary information to construct the overall synthesized results (Table 5-12) which shows that WIPP, New Mexico is the site chosen by the model primarily because the WIPP facility is currently ready to accept waste, pending only a few regulatory hurdles. The site, in the control networks, is rated as low in environmental cost and political risk. However, it is ranked in the middle for all of the benefits criteria. Selection based on benefit to cost ratio gives the same best location, with only slight differences in the overall ranking. This indicates that all sites are equally risky in such a way that risk does not significantly differentiate the alternatives.

Table 5-11 Priorities and Synthesized Results

Benefits	Economic 0.0719	Environmental 0.6491	Social 0.2790
Hanford, WA	0.1541	0.0734	0.1109
Mescalero Apache Tribe	0.0660	0.2020	0.1671
Seabed	0.0800	0.0642	0.0911
Space	0.0465	0.2610	0.3074
WIPP, NM	0.3528	0.1842	0.1511
Yucca Mountain	0.3006	0.2151	0.1726
Costs	Economic 0.1260	Environmental 0.4579	Social 0.4161
Hanford, WA	0.2048	0.1740	0.0523
Mescalero Apache Tribe	0.0656	0.0900	0.2691
Seabed	0.2791	0.3828	0.1119
Space	0.2846	0.1438	0.2483
WIPP, NM	0.1066	0.0734	0.0835
Yucca Mountain	0.0592	0.1360	0.2349
Risks	Economic 0.0643	Political 0.2370	Social/ Environmental 0.6986
Hanford, WA	0.3663	0.0738	0.0957
Mescalero Apache Tribe	0.1390	0.0695	0.1092
Seabed	0.0923	0.3373	0.2278
Space	0.1913	0.3155	0.1904
WIPP, NM	0.0875	0.1403	0.2065
Yucca Mountain	0.1235	0.0637	0.1804

High: 0.517   Medium: 0.359   Low:0.124

Overall Result	Safety (0.377)	Pollu -tion (0.062)	Longterm Effect (0.043)	Access ibility (0.252)	Politics (0.106)	Budget Constraints (0.160)	Priorities
Benefits	High	Low	Low	Low	Low	Low	0.259
Costs	High	High	Low	High	High	High	0.444
Risks	High	Medium	High	Low	Low	Low	0.298

	Benefits	Costs	Risks
Hanford, WA	0.0897	0.1272	0.1009
Mescalero Apache Tribe	0.1825	0.1615	0.1017
Seabed	0.0728	0.2570	0.2450
Space	0.2585	0.2050	0.2201
WIPP, NM	0.1871	0.0818	0.1832
Yucca Mountain	0.2094	0.1675	0.1491

Table 5-12 Final Synthesis of Alternatives

	Benefits 0.259	Costs 0.444 (less costly)	Risks 0.298 (less risky)	Final Outcome Additive	Multiplic -ative
Hanford, WA	0.0897	0.1917	0.2445	0.1812	0.176
Mescalero Apache Tribe	0.1825	0.1510	0.2426	0.1866	0.190
Seabed	0.0728	0.0949	0.1007	0.0910	0.094
Space	0.2585	0.1189	0.1121	0.1532	0.149
WIPP, NM	0.1871	0.2980	0.1347	0.2209	0.217
Yucca Mountain	0.2094	0.1456	0.1655	0.1682	0.173

There is a degree of uncertainty that is not captured in this model involving the reliability of the data obtained to make the judgments. While the techniques used to forecast future geologic conditions have improved over time, many experts argue about the methodology used to make such forecasts and assert the degree of certainty is low when extended out 10,000 years into the future. Therefore our confidence about the safety of a particular site is only as good as our confidence in the forecasts and the methodology used. This example was done by: C.Druehl, J. Flowers, S. Lynch, W. Marcenal, and V. Zyskowski of the University of Pittsburgh.

5-6. DECISION ON NATIONAL MISSILE DEFENSE PROGRAM-A COMPREHENSIVE EXAMPLE

INTRODUCTION

The United States government faces the crucial decision whether or not to commit itself to the deployment of a National Missile Defense (NMD) system. Many experts in politics, the military, and in academia have expressed different views regarding this decision. The most important rationale behind supporters of the NMD system is protecting the US from potential threats said to come from countries such as North Korea, Iran and Iraq. According to the Central Intelligence Agency, North Korea's Taepo Dong long-rage missile tests were successful and it is developing a second generation capable of reaching the US. Iran also tested its medium-range missile Shahab-3, in July 2000.

Opponents express doubts about the technical feasibility, high costs (estimated at $60 billion), political damage, possible arms race, and the exacerbation of foreign relations.

The current plan for the NMD originated from President Reagan's Strategic Defense Initiative (SDI) in the 1980s. SDI investigated technologies for destroying incoming missiles. There have been major changes every few years since the SDI was initiated. Beginning in 1993, the Clinton Administration put emphasis on NMD research and development. The strategy, called the "3 + 3" described a plan to spend three years in development and to be prepared to deploy it three years after that.

The controversies around the NMD project were intensified with the "National Missile Defense Act of 1996", introduced by Senator Sam Nunn (D-GA) in June 25, 1996. The bill required Congress to make a decision on whether the US should deploy the NMD system by 2000. The bill also targeted the United States to be capable of deploying NMD by the end of 2003.

The next year, the Senate Armed Services Committee approved the "National Missile Defense Act of 1997" by winning 10 votes out of 18, along party lines. This Act mandated deployment of an anti-missile system consisting of 100 ground-based interceptor missiles at a single site, plus ground-based radars and space-based sensors. The intelligence community estimated shortened warning time for the US against intercontinental ballistic missiles (ICBMs) deployment. However, deployment of NMD by 2003, analyzed by an independent "Commission to Assess the Ballistic Missile Threat to the United States" concluded that it would generate high risks and possible failure. Accordingly, the Administration adjusted its plan to deploy NMD in 2005.

However, deployment of NMD is not solely based on technological development. The next president of the US has to deal with international politics. The Anti-Ballistic Missile (ABM) treaty signed by the US and the former Soviet Union in 1972 would ban NMD, and the next president should be able to persuade or renegotiate the ABM treaty with Russia's president, Vladimir Putin who strongly opposes the plan. How to deal with the reactions of China and NATO is another issue for the president after Mr. Clinton to consider. My students Yeonmin Cho, Youxu Tjader, and Rina Wikandari did the analysis summarized in this section. They borrowed the foregoing material in the introduction from various expert sources.

THE ANP MODEL

Under the current situation in October 2000, what is the best direction for the NMD to take? Through intense reading and online research, the following alternatives and criteria for evaluating the decision were identified.

Alternatives:

1. Termination of the NMD program. Disregarding any further research and development plan and deployment.

2. Global Defense. Amending the ABM treaty to be more restrictive by using any economic, political, and diplomatic means as well as implementing joint-development of a worldwide defense system.

3. Deploy NMD. This alternative refers to the full deployment of the program.

4. R & D. This alternative is not concerned with deployment, but proceeds with Research and Development of the missile defense technology.

The evaluation criteria are categorized into benefits, costs, opportunities, and risks. A three level decision-making network model was developed using the ANP software. It consists of a control submodel (the top level) with four nodes: Benefits, Costs, Opportunities, and Risks. Each of these nodes has a decision subnet under it. They are called the Benefits subnet, the Costs subnet, the Opportunities subnet, and the Risks subnet.

BOCR WEIGHT DEVELOPMENT

The assessment criteria used to determine the priorities of the BOCR merits are shown in Figure 5-11.

The decision on the NMD project is reviewed in the context of the three criteria that are used to evaluate the merits. These are World Peace, Human Well-being, and International Politics. The three sub-criteria, Adversary Countries, Security Dilemma, and Terrorism cover all the causes disturbing or stabilizing peace in the world. The first sub-criterion, "Adversary Countries" concerns the potential threats by adversary countries. The second criterion "Security" Dilemma means that increasing one country's security inevitably decreases other countries' security. The very point that developing NMD enhances US security implies that the security of other countries is decreased. "Terrorism" indicates any possibility of the rise or decline of terrorism in the world.

Human Well-being includes "Technological Advancement" and "Market Creation." Technological Advancement driven by the NMD research and development process can ultimately benefit all people particularly, in providing possible space exploration which can lead to the creation of new markets. The 21st century is characterized as a post-industrialization era. Service industries in communication and transportation will benefit not only businesses associated with these industries, but also consumers who can enjoy the products. The last criterion is International Politics. It is composed of two sub-criteria, "Military Relations" and "Diplomatic Relations." "Military Relations" refer to the impact of NMD on relations with US allies for better or for worse. Also, the impact of NMD on diplomatic relations among all countries should be considered.

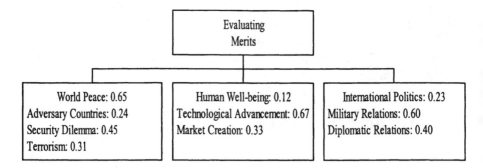

Figure 5-11 Hierarchy for Rating Benefits, Costs, Opportunities and Risks

The four merits of the benefits, costs, opportunities, and risks were rated according to five intensities listed below along with their priorities. The outcome is summarized in Table 5-13.

Table 5-13 Priority Ratings for the Merits: Benefits, Costs, Opportunities and Risks

Very High (0.42), High (0.26), Medium (0.16), Low (0.1), Very Low (0.06)

		Benefits	Costs	Opportunities	Risks
World Peace	Adversary Countries	Very High	High	Medium	Very Low
	Security Dilemma	Very Low	Very High	Very Low	Very Low
	Terrorism	Medium	High	Very Low	High
Human Well-Being	Technological	High	Low	High	Very Low
	Market Creation	Medium	Very Low	High	Very Low
International Politics	Military Relations	High	Medium	High	Very Low
	Diplomatic Relations	Low	Low	Low	Very High
Priorities		0.264	0.361	0.186	0.190

Table 5-14 shows the 23 criteria under the benefits, opportunities costs and risks and their priorities.

Table 5-14 Criteria and Their Priorities

Merits	Components	Elements	Local Priorities	Global Priorities
Benefits (0.267)	Economic (0.157)	Local Economy	0.141	0.006
		Defense Industry	0.859	0.036
	Political (0.074)	Bargaining Power	0.859	0.017
		U.S. Military Leadership	0.141	0.003
	Security (0.481)	Deterrence	0.267	0.034
		Military Capability	0.590	**0.076**
		Anti-terrorism	0.143	0.018
	Technology (0.288)	Tech. Advancement	0.834	**0.064**
		Tech. Leadership	0.166	0.013
Opportunities (0.182)		Arms Sales	0.520	**0.094**
		Spin- off	0.326	**0.059**
		Space Development	0.051	0.009
		Protection of Allies	0.103	0.019
Costs (0.361)	Security (0.687)	Security Threat (vulnerability to the security threat)	1.000	**0.248**
	Economic (0.228)	Sunk Cost	0.539	**0.044**
		Further Investment	0.461	**0.038**
	Political (0.085)	ABN Treaty	0.589	0.018
		Foreign Relations	0.411	0.013
Risks (0.190)		Technical Failure	0.430	**0.082**
		Arms Race	0.268	**0.051**
		Increased Terrorism	0.052	0.010
		Environmental Damage	0.080	0.015
		U.S. Reputation	0.170	0.032

The 23 criteria were prioritized by pairwise comparisons. Among these 23 criteria, the sum of the priorities of nine of them, security threat, arms sales, technical failure, military capability, technological advancement, sunk cost, spin off, arms race, and further investment account for over 0.77 of the total. To economize effort, we used nine to do the analysis. We renormalize their priorities within their respective merits and continue. The network for each criterion and its connections are shown in Figures 5-12 to 5-20.

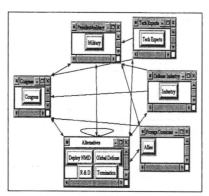

Figure 5-12 Military Capability
Subnetwork under Benefits

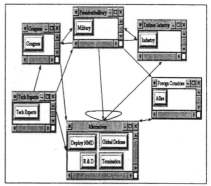

Figure 5-13 Technological Advancement
Subnetwork under Benefits

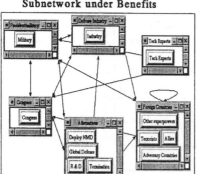

Figure 5-14 Arms Sales Subnetwork
under Opportunities

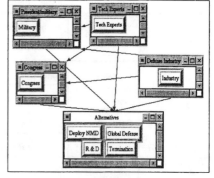

Figure 5-15 Spin-off Subnetwork
under Opportunities

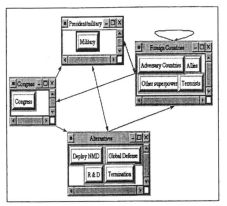

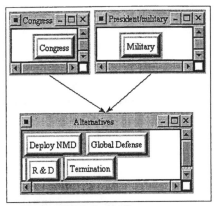

Figure 5-16 Security Threat
Subnetwork under Costs

Figure 5-17 Sunk Cost
Subnetwork under Costs

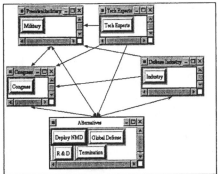

Figure 5-18 Further Investment Subnetwork under Costs

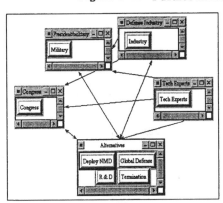

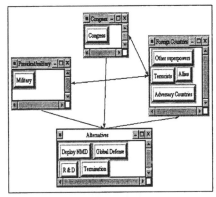

Figure 5-19 Technical Failure
Subnetwork under Risks

Figure 5-20 Arms Race
Subnetwork under Risks

The Networks

We explain in outline form our thinking about the network under one of the criteria. Figure 5-12, shows the "Military Capability" control criterion with two decision makers, Congress and the executive branch consisting of the President and the Department of Defense (the node name is military). Technical experts, and the defense industry influence Congress and the executive branch by providing their professional expertise and technical information.

Congress, Military, (Defense) Industry, and Technical Experts all have a say as to what extent the decision contributes to the Military Capability of the U.S. All think that Deploy N.D. will increase military capability followed by Global Defense, R&D and Termination but to very different degrees. The first table under Table 5-15, the unweighted Supermatrix, summarizes the different views on the contribution of each of the four alternatives to U.S. military capability. Defense industry gives the highest priority to Deploy N.D. (0.56), followed by the President/military (0.52) and Congress (0.51). The low priority given by Technical experts (0.29) reflects the opinion of some scientists who think Deploy N.D. will not contribute to the enhancement of U.S. military capability because it is technically infeasible. The next set of tables under Table 5-15 show the pairwise comparisons of the components. The eigenvectors of the pairwise comparisons of the components are summarized in the eighth table (Clusters). The weighted supermatrix illustrates the weighting of the blocks of the supermatrix by the corresponding priority from the corresponding eigenvector of comparisons of the components. The last table, limit matrix shows the stable priorities of all the elements. From it the priorities of the four alternatives are extracted and normalized.

Apart from Military Capability, we do not give all the details for the other control criteria. It is easy to determine the appropriate judgments and priorities from the data given. Tables 5-15, to 5- 20 include all the unweighted supermatrices, eigenvectors for comparisons of the components, weighted supermatrices and limit supermatrices of the nine control criteria. The two tables corresponding to the Figures for Spin-Off and Sunk Cost are not available in usable form to include in this chapter. Table 5-21 shows the final synthesis of the alternatives for each of the BOCR merits and the overall result, using the reciprocals of the synthesized priorities of costs and risks.

Table 5-15 Military Capability Control Criterion under Benefits

MilCap Unweighted		Alternatives				Cong~	Pre/Mil~	Defense Ind~	For~	Tech~
		NMD	Glob~	R & D	Term~	Cong~	Military	Industry	Allies	Tech~
Alternatives	NMD	0.0000	0.5760	1.0000	0.0000	0 5060	0.5158	0.5587	0 0000	0 2878
	Glob~	0.0000	0.0000	0.0000	0.0000	0 2890	0.2929	0.2574	1.0000	0.2623
	R & D	0.0000	0.4240	0.0000	0.0000	0.1307	0.1367	0.1382	0.0000	0 2369
	Term~	0.0000	0 0000	0.0000	0 0000	0 0744	0.0546	0 0457	0.0000	0.2130
Cong~	Cong~	1.0000	1.0000	1.0000	0 0000	0.0000	1 0000	1 0000	1 0000	1.0000
Pre/Mil~	Military	1.0000	1.0000	1 0000	0 0000	1.0000	0 0000	1 0000	1.0000	1.0000
Defense Ind~	Industry	1.0000	1.0000	1 0000	0 0000	0.0000	0 0000	0.0000	0 0000	0.0000
For~	Allies	1 0000	1.0000	1 0000	0 0000	0 0000	1.0000	0.0000	0 0000	0.0000
Tech~	Tech~	1 0000	1.0000	1 0000	0 0000	0 0000	0.0000	0.0000	0 0000	0.0000

Pairwise Comparing Components with Respect to Alternatives' Component

	Altern~	Cong~	Def~	For~	Pres~	Tech~	Prior.
Altern~	1.0000	0.1667	0.2500	1.3300	0 1429	0 5556	0.0486
Congr~	5.9999	1 0000	2 2000	6.2000	0.7407	3.2000	0.2889
Def~	4 0000	0 4546	1.0000	4.0000	0.4115	2.2600	0.1653
For~	0.7519	0 1613	0.2500	1 0000	0 1250	0.5263	0.0425
Pres~	7.0000	1 3500	2 4300	8 0000	1 0000	5.1000	0.3742
Tech~	1.8000	0.3125	0 4425	1 9000	0 1961	1.0000	0.0805

Pairwise Comparing Components with Respect to Congress

	Altern~	Pres~	Prior.
Altern~	1 0000	0.5638	0.3605
Pres~	1 7736	1.0000	0.6395

Pairwise Comparing Components with Respect to Defense Industry

	Altern~	Cong~	Pres~	Prior.
Altern~	1.0000	0.6769	0 5388	0.2292
Congr~	1.4773	1 0000	0 6600	0.3181
Pres~	1.8561	1.5152	1 0000	0.4528

Pairwise Comparing Components with Respect to Foreign Countries

	Altern~	Cong~	Pres~	Prior.
Altern~	1 0000	0.5556	0 3259	0.1671
Congr~	1.8000	1.0000	0 4632	0.2781
Pres~	3 0682	2.1591	1.0000	0.5548

Pairwise Comparing Components with Respect to President/Military

	Altern~	Cong~	For~	Prior.
Altern~	1 0000	2.1887	3 6604	0.5735
Congr~	0 4569	1 0000	2 0377	0.2799
For~	0.2732	0 4907	1 0000	0.1467

Pairwise Comparing Components with Respect to Technical Expertise

	Altern~	Cong~	Pres~	Prior.
Altern~	1.0000	2.5379	2.5379	0.5593
Congr~	0 3940	1.0000	1.0000	0.2204
Pres~	0 3940	1.0000	1.0000	0.2204

Clusters	Alternatives	Cong~	Pre/Mil~	Defense Ind~	For~	Tech~
Alternatives	0.0486	0 3605	0.5735	0.2292	0 1671	0.5593
Cong~	0.2889	0.0000	0.2799	0.3181	0 2780	0.2204
Pre/Mil~	0.3742	0.6395	0.0000	0.4528	0 5548	0 2204
Defense Ind~	0.1653	0.0000	0.0000	0 0000	0.0000	0.0000
For~	0.0425	0.0000	0.1467	0.0000	0 0000	0.0000
Tech~	0.0805	0.0000	0 0000	0.0000	0 0000	0.0000

MilCap Weighted		Alternatives				Cong~	Pre/Mil~	Defense Ind~	For~	Tech~
		NMD	Glob~	R & D	Term~	Cong~	Military	Industry	Allies	Tech~
Alternatives	NMD	0.0000	0.0280	0.0485	0.0000	0.1824	0.2958	0.1280	0.0000	0.1610
	Glob~	0.0000	0.0000	0.0000	0.0000	0.1042	0.1680	0.0590	0.1671	0.1467
	R & D	0 0000	0.0206	0.0000	0.0000	0.0471	0.0784	0.0317	0 0000	0.1325
	Term~	0 0000	0.0000	0.0000	0 0000	0.0268	0 0313	0.0105	0 0000	0.1191
Cong~	Cong~	0 3037	0.2889	0.2889	0.0000	0 0000	0 2799	0.3181	0.2780	0.2204
Pre/Mil~	Military	0.3933	0.3742	0 3742	0.0000	0 6395	0 0000	0.4528	0.5548	0.2204
Defense Ind~	Industry	0 1737	0.1653	0.1653	0.0000	0.0000	0 0000	0.0000	0.0000	0.0000
For~	Allies	0 0446	0.0425	0.0425	0.0000	0.0000	0.1467	0 0000	0.0000	0.0000
Tech~	Tech~	0.0846	0.0805	0 0805	0.0000	0 0000	0 0000	0.0000	0 0000	0.0000

MilCap Limit		Alternatives				Cong~	Pre/Mil~			
		NMD	Glob~	R & D	Term~	Cong~	Military	Industry	Allies	Tech~
Alternatives	NMD	0.1543	0.1543	0.1543	0.0000	0.1543	0.1543	0 1543	0.1543	0.1543
	Glob~	0.0962	0.0962	0.0962	0.0000	0.0962	0.0962	0.0962	0.0962	0.0962
	R & D	0.0435	0 0435	0.0435	0.0000	0.0435	0 0435	0.0435	0.0435	0.0435
	Term~	0.0199	0 0199	0.0199	0.0000	0.0199	0.0199	0.0199	0.0199	0.0199
Cong~	Cong~	0.2222	0.2222	0.2222	0.0000	0.2222	0.2222	0.2222	0.2222	0.2222
Pre/Mil~	Military	0.3253	0 3253	0.3253	0.0000	0 3253	0.3253	0.3253	0.3253	0.3253
Defense Ind~	Industry	0.0518	0.0518	0.0518	0 0000	0.0518	0.0518	0 0518	0.0518	0.0518
For~	Allies	0.0617	0.0617	0.0617	0 0000	0 0617	0 0617	0 0617	0.0617	0.0617
Tech~	Tech~	0.0252	0.0252	0.0252	0.0000	0 0252	0 0252	0 0252	0.0252	0.0252

Table 5-16 Technological Advancement Control Criterion under Benefits

TechAdv Unweighted	Alternatives	NMD	Glob~	R&D	Term~	Cong~ Cong~	PreMil~ Military	Defense Ind~ Industry	For~ Allies	Tech~ Tech~
Alternatives	NMD	0.0000	0.5691	0.0000	0.0000	0.4263	0.4944	0.5132	0.0000	0.3402
	Glob~	0.0000	0.0000	0.0000	0.0000	0.2843	0.2792	0.2903	1.0000	0.2995
	R&D	0.0000	0.4309	0.0000	0.0000	0.1739	0.1616	0.1464	0.0000	0.2104
	Term~	0.0000	0.0000	0.0000	0.0000	0.1155	0.0648	0.0501	0.0000	0.1499
Cong~	Cong~	0.0000	0.0000	0.0000	0.0000	0.0000	0.0000	1.0000	0.0000	1.0000
PreMil~	Military	0.0000	0.0000	0.0000	0.0000	1.0000	0.0000	1.0000	0.0000	1.0000
Defense Ind~	Industry	1.0000	0.0000	1.0000	0.0000	0.0000	1.0000	0.0000	0.0000	0.0000
For~	Allies	0.0000	1.0000	0.0000	0.0000	0.0000	1.0000	0.0000	0.0000	0.0000
Tech~	Tech~	0.0000	0.0000	0.0000	0.0000	0.0000	0.0000	0.0000	0.0000	0.0000

Clusters	Alternatives	Cong~	PreMil~	Defense Ind~	For~	Tech~
Alternatives	0.3285	0.3697	0.3708	0.2173	1.0000	0.5180
Cong~	0.0000	0.0000	0.0000	0.3500	0.0000	0.2384
PreMil~	0.0000	0.6403	0.0000	0.4327	0.0000	0.2436
Defense Ind~	0.4396	0.0000	0.4618	0.0000	0.0000	0.0000
For~	0.2319	0.0000	0.1675	0.0000	0.0000	0.0000
Tech~	0.0000	0.0000	0.0000	0.0000	0.0000	0.0000

TechAdv Weighted	Alternatives	NMD	Glob~	R&D	Term~	Cong~ Cong~	PreMil~ Military	Defense Ind~ Industry	For~ Allies	Tech~ Tech~
Alternatives	NMD	0.0000	0.3336	0.0000	0.0000	0.1533	0.1833	0.1115	0.0000	0.1762
	Glob~	0.0000	0.0000	0.0000	0.0000	0.1022	0.1035	0.0631	1.0000	0.1552
	R&D	0.0000	0.2526	0.0000	0.0000	0.0625	0.0599	0.0318	0.0000	0.1090
	Term~	0.0000	0.0000	0.0000	0.0000	0.0415	0.0240	0.0109	0.0000	0.0776
Cong~	Cong~	0.0000	0.0000	0.0000	0.0000	0.0000	0.0000	0.3500	0.0000	0.2384
PreMil~	Military	0.0000	0.0000	0.0000	0.0000	0.6403	0.0000	0.4327	0.0000	0.2436
Defense Ind~	Industry	1.0000	0.0000	1.0000	0.0000	0.0000	0.4618	0.0000	0.0000	0.0000
For~	Allies	0.0000	0.4138	0.0000	0.0000	0.0000	0.1675	0.0000	0.0000	0.0000
Tech~	Tech~	0.0000	0.0000	0.0000	0.0000	0.0000	0.0000	0.0000	0.0000	0.0000

TechAdv Limit	Alternatives	NMD	Glob~	R&D	Term~	Cong~ Cong~	PreMil~ Military	Defense Ind~ Industry	For~ Allies	Tech~ Tech~
Alternatives	NMD	0.1290	0.1290	0.1290	0.0000	0.1290	0.1290	0.1290	0.1290	0.1290
	Glob~	0.1384	0.1384	0.1384	0.0000	0.1384	0.1384	0.1384	0.1384	0.1384
	R&D	0.0622	0.0622	0.0622	0.0000	0.0622	0.0622	0.0622	0.0622	0.0622
	Term~	0.0119	0.0119	0.0119	0.0000	0.0119	0.0119	0.0119	0.0119	0.0119
Cong~	Cong~	0.0992	0.0992	0.0992	0.0000	0.0992	0.0992	0.0992	0.0992	0.0992
PreMil~	Military	0.1874	0.1874	0.1874	0.0000	0.1874	0.1874	0.1874	0.1874	0.1874
Defense Ind~	Industry	0.2817	0.2817	0.2817	0.0000	0.2817	0.2817	0.2817	0.2817	0.2817
For~	Allies	0.0901	0.0901	0.0901	0.0000	0.0901	0.0901	0.0901	0.0901	0.0901
Tech~	Tech~	0.0000	0.0000	0.0000	0.0000	0.0000	0.0000	0.0000	0.0000	0.0000

Table 5-17 Arms Sales Control Criterion under Opportunities

ArmsSales Unweighted	Alternatives	NWD	Glob~	R&D	Term~	Org~ Org~	PreMil~ Miltary	Defense Ind~ Industry	For~ Adversary C~	Allies	Other super~	Terrorists	Tech~ Tech~
Alternatives	NWD	0.0000	0.0000	0.0000	0.0000	0.5100	0.0000	0.0000	0.0000	0.0000	0.0000	0.0000	0.0000
	Glob~	0.0000	0.0000	0.0000	0.0000	0.3163	0.2965	0.0000	0.0000	0.0000	0.0000	0.0000	0.0000
	R&D	0.0000	0.0000	0.0000	0.0000	0.1787	0.1362	0.0000	0.0000	0.0000	0.0000	0.0000	0.0000
	Term~	0.0000	0.0000	0.0000	0.0000	0.1222	0.0583	0.0000	0.0000	0.0000	0.0000	0.0000	0.0000
Org~	Org~	1.0000	1.0000	1.0000	0.0000	0.0000	1.0000	1.0000	0.0000	1.0000	0.0000	0.0000	1.0000
PreMil~	Miltary	1.0000	1.0000	1.0000	0.0000	1.0000	0.0000	1.0000	0.0000	1.0000	0.0000	0.0000	1.0000
Defense Ind~	Industry	1.0000	1.0000	1.0000	0.0000	1.0000	1.0000	0.0000	0.0000	0.0000	0.0000	0.0000	0.0000
For~	Adversary C~	0.0000	0.0000	0.0000	0.0000	0.0000	0.0000	0.0000	0.0000	0.0000	0.0000	0.0000	0.0000
	Allies	1.0000	1.0000	1.0000	0.0000	0.0000	1.0000	1.0000	1.0000	0.0000	1.0000	1.0000	0.0000
	Other super~	0.0000	0.0000	0.0000	0.0000	0.0000	0.0000	0.0000	0.0000	0.0000	0.0000	0.0000	0.0000
	Terrorists	0.0000	0.0000	0.0000	0.0000	0.0000	0.0000	0.0000	0.0000	0.0000	0.0000	0.0000	0.0000
Tech~	Tech~	0.0000	0.0000	0.0000	0.0000	0.0000	0.0000	0.0000	0.0000	0.0000	0.0000	0.0000	0.0000

Clusters	Alternatives	Org~	PreMil~	Defense Ind~	For~	Tech~
Alternatives	0.0000	0.2248	0.1805	0.1443	0.0000	0.0000
Org~	0.2309	0.0000	0.0930	0.1639	0.3381	0.4944
PreMil~	0.4658	0.4553	0.0000	0.2415	0.4008	0.5056
Defense Ind~	0.1467	0.3199	0.2365	0.2086	0.0000	0.0000
For~	0.0067	0.0000	0.4898	0.2418	0.2561	0.0000
Tech~	0.0000	0.0000	0.0000	0.0000	0.0000	0.0000

ArmsSales Weighted	Alternatives	NWD	Glob~	R&D	Term~	Org~ Org~	PreMil~ Miltary	Defense Ind~ Industry	For~ Adversary C~	Allies	Other super~	Terrorists	Tech~ Tech~
Alternatives	NWD	0.0000	0.0000	0.0000	0.0000	0.0956	0.0921	0.0000	0.0000	0.0000	0.0000	0.0000	0.0000
	Glob~	0.0000	0.0000	0.0000	0.0000	0.0716	0.0534	0.0000	0.0000	0.0000	0.0000	0.0000	0.0000
	R&D	0.0000	0.0000	0.0000	0.0000	0.0402	0.0246	0.0000	0.0000	0.0000	0.0000	0.0000	0.0000
	Term~	0.0000	0.0000	0.0000	0.0000	0.0275	0.0105	0.0000	0.0000	0.0000	0.0000	0.0000	0.0000
Org~	Org~	0.2309	0.2309	0.2309	0.0000	0.0000	0.0930	0.2533	0.0000	0.4557	0.0000	0.0000	0.4944
PreMil~	Miltary	0.4658	0.4658	0.4658	0.0000	0.4553	0.0000	0.3731	0.0000	0.5543	0.0000	0.0000	0.5056
Defense Ind~	Industry	0.1467	0.1467	0.1467	0.0000	0.3199	0.2365	0.0000	0.0000	0.0000	0.0000	0.0000	0.0000
For~	Adversary C~	0.0000	0.0000	0.0000	0.0000	0.0000	0.0000	0.0000	0.0000	0.0000	0.0000	0.0000	0.0000
	Allies	0.0067	0.0067	0.0067	0.0000	0.0000	0.4898	0.3736	1.0000	0.0000	1.0000	1.0000	0.0000
	Other super~	0.0000	0.0000	0.0000	0.0000	0.0000	0.0000	0.0000	0.0000	0.0000	0.0000	0.0000	0.0000
	Terrorists	0.0000	0.0000	0.0000	0.0000	0.0000	0.0000	0.0000	0.0000	0.0000	0.0000	0.0000	0.0000
Tech~	Tech~	0.0000	0.0000	0.0000	0.0000	0.0000	0.0000	0.0000	0.0000	0.0000	0.0000	0.0000	0.0000

ArmsSales Limit	Alternatives	NWD	Glob~	R&D	Term~	Org~ Org~	PreMil~ Miltary	Defense Ind~ Industry	For~ Adversary C~	Allies	Other super~	Terrorists	Tech~ Tech~
Alternatives	NWD	0.0467	0.0467	0.0467	0.0000	0.0467	0.0467	0.0467	0.0467	0.0467	0.0467	0.0467	0.0467
	Glob~	0.0315	0.0315	0.0315	0.0000	0.0315	0.0315	0.0315	0.0315	0.0315	0.0315	0.0315	0.0315
	R&D	0.0180	0.0180	0.0180	0.0000	0.0180	0.0180	0.0180	0.0180	0.0180	0.0180	0.0180	0.0180
	Term~	0.0089	0.0089	0.0089	0.0000	0.0089	0.0089	0.0089	0.0089	0.0089	0.0089	0.0089	0.0089
Org~	Org~	0.2204	0.2204	0.2204	0.0000	0.2204	0.2204	0.2204	0.2204	0.2204	0.2204	0.2204	0.2204
PreMil~	Miltary	0.3175	0.3175	0.3175	0.0000	0.3175	0.3175	0.3175	0.3175	0.3175	0.3175	0.3175	0.3175
Defense Ind~	Industry	0.1542	0.1542	0.1542	0.0000	0.1542	0.1542	0.1542	0.1542	0.1542	0.1542	0.1542	0.1542
For~	Adversary C~	0.0000	0.0000	0.0000	0.0000	0.0000	0.0000	0.0000	0.0000	0.0000	0.0000	0.0000	0.0000
	Allies	0.2249	0.2249	0.2249	0.0000	0.2249	0.2249	0.2249	0.2249	0.2249	0.2249	0.2249	0.2249
	Other super~	0.0000	0.0000	0.0000	0.0000	0.0000	0.0000	0.0000	0.0000	0.0000	0.0000	0.0000	0.0000
	Terrorists	0.0000	0.0000	0.0000	0.0000	0.0000	0.0000	0.0000	0.0000	0.0000	0.0000	0.0000	0.0000
Tech~	Tech~	0.0000	0.0000	0.0000	0.0000	0.0000	0.0000	0.0000	0.0000	0.0000	0.0000	0.0000	0.0000

Table 5-18 Security Threat Control Criterion under Costs

SecThreat Unweighted	Alternatives				Cong~	PreMi~	For~			
Alternatives		NMD	Glob~	R&D	Term~	Cong~	Military	Adversary C~	Allies	Other super~	Terrorists
Alternatives	NMD	0.0000	0.0000	0.0000	0.0000	0.1397	0.0780	0.0000	0.0000	0.0000	0.0000
	Glob~	0.0000	0.0000	0.0000	0.0000	0.2039	0.1554	0.0000	0.0000	0.0000	0.0000
	R&D	0.0000	0.0000	0.0000	0.0000	0.2610	0.2779	0.0000	0.0000	0.0000	0.0000
	Term~	0.0000	0.0000	0.0000	0.0000	0.3954	0.4908	0.0000	0.0000	0.0000	0.0000
Cong~	Cong~	0.0000	0.0000	0.0000	0.0000	0.0000	0.0000	1.0000	1.0000	1.0000	1.0000
PreMi~	Military	1.0000	1.0000	1.0000	1.0000	1.0000	0.0000	1.0000	1.0000	1.0000	1.0000
For~	Adversary C~	0.4625	0.4552	0.4552	0.4552	0.0000	0.0000	0.0000	0.0000	0.0000	0.0000
	Allies	0.0829	0.0696	0.0696	0.0696	0.0000	1.0000	1.0000	0.0000	1.0000	1.0000
	Other super~	0.2994	0.3124	0.3124	0.3124	0.0000	0.0000	0.0000	0.0000	0.0000	0.0000
	Terrorists	0.1552	0.1628	0.1628	0.1628	0.0000	0.0000	0.0000	0.0000	0.0000	0.0000

Clusters	Alternatives	Cong~	PreMi~	For~
Alternatives	0.0000	0.3750	0.4037	0.0000
Cong~	0.0000	0.0000	0.0000	0.1229
PreMi~	0.4099	0.6250	0.0000	0.3766
For~	0.5901	0.0000	0.5963	0.5005

SecThreat Weighted	Alternatives				Cong~	PreMi~	For~			
Alternatives		NMD	Glob~	R&D	Term~	Cong~	Military	Adversary C~	Allies	Other super~	Terrorists
Alternatives	NMD	0.0000	0.0000	0.0000	0.0000	0.0524	0.0307	0.0000	0.0000	0.0000	0.0000
	Glob~	0.0000	0.0000	0.0000	0.0000	0.0764	0.0627	0.0000	0.0000	0.0000	0.0000
	R&D	0.0000	0.0000	0.0000	0.0000	0.0979	0.1122	0.0000	0.0000	0.0000	0.0000
	Term~	0.0000	0.0000	0.0000	0.0000	0.1483	0.1981	0.0000	0.0000	0.0000	0.0000
Cong~	Cong~	0.0000	0.0000	0.0000	0.0000	0.0000	0.0000	0.1229	0.2460	0.1229	0.1229
PreMi~	Military	0.4099	0.4099	0.4099	0.4099	0.6250	0.0000	0.3766	0.7540	0.3766	0.3766
For~	Adversary C~	0.2729	0.2686	0.2686	0.2686	0.0000	0.0000	0.0000	0.0000	0.0000	0.0000
	Allies	0.0489	0.0411	0.0411	0.0411	0.0000	0.5963	0.5005	0.0000	0.5005	0.5005
	Other super~	0.1767	0.1843	0.1843	0.1843	0.0000	0.0000	0.0000	0.0000	0.0000	0.0000
	Terrorists	0.0916	0.0960	0.0960	0.0960	0.0000	0.0000	0.0000	0.0000	0.0000	0.0000

SecThreat Limit	Alternatives				Cong~	PreMi~	For~			
Alternatives		NMD	Glob~	R&D	Term~	Cong~	Military	Adversary C~	Allies	Other super~	Terrorists
Alternatives	NMD	0.0155	0.0155	0.0155	0.0155	0.0155	0.0155	0.0155	0.0155	0.0155	0.0155
	Glob~	0.0292	0.0292	0.0292	0.0292	0.0292	0.0292	0.0292	0.0292	0.0292	0.0292
	R&D	0.0491	0.0491	0.0491	0.0491	0.0491	0.0491	0.0491	0.0491	0.0491	0.0491
	Term~	0.0847	0.0847	0.0847	0.0847	0.0847	0.0847	0.0847	0.0847	0.0847	0.0847
Cong~	Cong~	0.0799	0.0799	0.0799	0.0799	0.0799	0.0799	0.0799	0.0799	0.0799	0.0799
PreMi~	Military	0.3679	0.3679	0.3679	0.3679	0.3679	0.3679	0.3679	0.3679	0.3679	0.3679
For~	Adversary C~	0.0480	0.0480	0.0480	0.0480	0.0480	0.0480	0.0480	0.0480	0.0480	0.0480
	Allies	0.2758	0.2758	0.2758	0.2758	0.2758	0.2758	0.2758	0.2758	0.2758	0.2758
	Other super~	0.0328	0.0328	0.0328	0.0328	0.0328	0.0328	0.0328	0.0328	0.0328	0.0328
	Terrorists	0.0171	0.0171	0.0171	0.0171	0.0171	0.0171	0.0171	0.0171	0.0171	0.0171

Table 5-19 Further Investment Control Criteria under Costs

FurInv Unweighted		Alternatives				Cong~	Pre/Mil~	Defense Ind~	Tech~
		NMD	Glob~	R & D	Term~	Cong~	Military	Industry	Tech~
Alternatives	NMD	0.0000	0 0000	0.0000	0.0000	0.5316	0.5195	0 4888	0.5603
	Glob~	0.0000	0.0000	0.0000	0.0000	0.2752	0 2282	0.3163	0.2581
	R & D	0.0000	0.0000	0 0000	0.0000	0 1303	0 1603	0.1336	0.1264
	Term~	0.0000	0.0000	0 0000	0 0000	0 0629	0.0920	0.0613	0.0553
Cong~	Cong~	1.0000	1 0000	1.0000	0.0000	0.0000	1 0000	1.0000	1 0000
Pre/Mil~	Military	1 0000	1.0000	1.0000	0 0000	1 0000	0 0000	1.0000	1.0000
Defense Ind~	Industry	1 0000	1.0000	1 0000	0.0000	0 0000	0.0000	0 0000	0.0000
Tech~	Tech~	0 0000	0.0000	0 0000	0.0000	0 0000	0 0000	0 0000	0.0000

Clusters	Alternatives	Cong~	Pre/Mil~	Defense Ind~	Tech~
Alternatives	0.0000	0 5147	0.5629	0.5564	0.7143
Cong~	0.3511	0.0000	0.4371	0.2048	0.1429
Pre/Mil~	0.4181	0.4853	0.0000	0 2387	0 1429
Defense Ind~	0 2307	0 0000	0.0000	0.0000	0.0000
Tech~	0.0000	0 0000	0 0000	0 0000	0.0000

FurInvWeighted		Alternatives				Cong~	Pre/Mil~	Defense Ind~	Tech~
		NMD	Glob~	R & D	Term~	Cong~	Military	Industry	Tech~
Alternatives	NMD	0 0000	0.0000	0.0000	0.0000	0.2736	0.2924	0.2720	0.4002
	Glob~	0.0000	0.0000	0.0000	0.0000	0.1417	0.1285	0.1760	0.1843
	R & D	0.0000	0.0000	0 0000	0.0000	0.0671	0.0902	0.0743	0.0903
	Term~	0.0000	0.0000	0.0000	0.0000	0.0324	0.0518	0.0341	0.0395
Cong~	Cong~	0.3511	0 3511	0.3511	0.0000	0 0000	0.4371	0.2048	0 1429
Pre/Mil~	Military	0.4181	0.4181	0.4181	0 0000	0.4853	0 0000	0.2387	0.1429
Defense Ind~	Industry	0 2307	0.2307	0 2307	0 0000	0.0000	0.0000	0.0000	0.0000
Tech~	Tech~	0 0000	0.0000	0.0000	0.0000	0.0000	0.0000	0 0000	0 0000

FurInvLimit		Alternatives				Cong~	Pre/Mil~	Defense Ind~	Tech~
		NMD	Glob~	R & D	Term~	Cong~	Military	Industry	Tech~
Alternatives	NMD	0.1844	0.1844	0 1844	0.0000	0.1844	0.1844	0 1844	0.1844
	Glob~	0.0913	0.0913	0.0913	0.0000	0 0913	0.0913	0.0913	0.0913
	R & D	0.0514	0.0514	0.0514	0.0000	0.0514	0.0514	0.0514	0.0514
	Term~	0.0271	0.0271	0.0271	0 0000	0.0271	0 0271	0.0271	0.0271
Cong~	Cong~	0.2685	0.2685	0 2685	0.0000	0 2685	0.2685	0.2685	0.2685
Pre/Mil~	Military	0 2974	0.2974	0.2974	0.0000	0.2974	0.2974	0.2974	0 2974
Defense Ind~	Industry	0.0799	0.0799	0.0799	0.0000	0.0799	0 0799	0 0799	0.0799
Tech~	Tech~	0.0000	0 0000	0.0000	0 0000	0.0000	0.0000	0.0000	0.0000

Table 5-20 Technical Failure and Arms Race Control Criteria under Risks

TechFailure Unweighted	Alternatives					Cong~	Pre/Mil~	Defense Ind~	Tech~
		NMD	Glob~	R & D	Term~	Cong~	Military	Industry	Tech~
Alternatives	NMD	0 0000	0 0000	0.0000	0.0000	0.5179	0 4653	0 3590	0.5899
	Glob~	0 0000	0 0000	0.0000	0 0000	0.2661	0 2869	0 2665	0.2454
	R & D	0.0000	0 0000	0 0000	0 0000	0.1396	0.1536	0.2020	0 1077
	Term~	0 0000	0 0000	0 0000	0.0000	0.0764	0.0942	0.1725	0 0570
Cong~	Cong~	1.0000	1 0000	1.0000	0 0000	0 0000	0.0000	1.0000	1 0000
Pre/Mil~	Military	1.0000	1 0000	1.0000	0.0000	0 0000	0.0000	1.0000	1 0000
Defense Ind~	Industry	1.0000	1.0000	1 0000	0.0000	0 0000	0 0000	0 0000	0 0000
Tech~	Tech~	0.0000	0.0000	0 0000	0 0000	0 0000	0 0000	0 0000	0 0000

Clusters	Alternatives	Cong~	Pre/Mil~	Defense Ind~	Tech~
Alternatives	0 0000	1 0000	1 0000	0 6638	0 7180
Cong~	0 1654	0.0000	0 0000	0.1622	0 1364
Pre/Mil~	0 3254	0.0000	0.0000	0 1741	0.1456
Defense Ind~	0 5093	0.0000	0.0000	0.0000	0.0000
Tech~	0 0000	0.0000	0.0000	0 0000	0.0000

TechFailure Weighted	Alternatives					Cong~	Pre/Mil~	Defense Ind~	Tech~
		NMD	Glob~	R & D	Term~	Cong~	Military	Industry	Tech~
Alternatives	NMD	0.0000	0.0000	0.0000	0 0000	0.5179	0 4653	0 2383	0 4235
	Glob~	0.0000	0.0000	0.0000	0 0000	0.2661	0.2869	0 1769	0.1762
	R & D	0 0000	0 0000	0 0000	0 0000	0.1396	0.1536	0.1341	0.0774
	Term~	0.0000	0.0000	0.0000	0 0000	0 0764	0.0942	0 1145	0.0409
Cong~	Cong~	0 1654	0.1654	0.1654	0.0000	0.0000	0 0000	0.1622	0.1364
Pre/Mil~	Military	0.3254	0.3254	0.3254	0 0000	0.0000	0 0000	0 1741	0.1456
Defense Ind~	Industry	0 5093	0.5093	0.5093	0 0000	0 0000	0 0000	0 0000	0 0000
Tech~	Tech~	0.0000	0 0000	0.0000	0 0000	0.0000	0 0000	0 0000	0 0000

TechFailure Limit	Alternatives					Cong~	Pre/Mil~	Defense Ind~	Tech~
		NMD	Glob~	R & D	Term~	Cong~	Military	Industry	Tech~
Alternatives	NMD	0 2024	0 2024	0 2024	0.0000	0.2024	0.2024	0.2024	0.2024
	Glob~	0.1252	0 1252	0.1252	0.0000	0 1252	0.1252	0.1252	0 1252
	R & D	0 0755	0 0755	0 0755	0.0000	0 0755	0.0755	0 0755	0 0755
	Term~	0.0524	0 0524	0.0524	0.0000	0 0524	0 0524	0 0524	0.0524
Cong~	Cong~	0.1138	0 1138	0 1138	0.0000	0 1138	0 1138	0 1138	0 1138
Pre/Mil~	Military	0 1916	0.1916	0 1916	0 0000	0.1916	0.1916	0.1916	0.1916
Defense Ind~	Industry	0.2391	0 2391	0.2391	0.0000	0.2391	0 2391	0.2391	0.2391
Tech~	Tech~	0.0000	0 0000	0.0000	0 0000	0.0000	0.0000	0.0000	0 0000

ArmsRace Unweighted	Alternatives					Cong~	Pre/Mil~	For~			
		NMD	Glob	R & D	Term~	Cong~	Military	Adversary C~	Allies	Other super~	Terrorists
Alternatives	NMD	0.0000	0 0000	0 0000	0.0000	0 4365	0.3928	0 0000	0 0000	0.0000	0 0000
	Glob	0.0000	0.0000	0.0000	0.0000	0 2696	0.2945	0.0000	0 0000	0.0000	0 0000
	R & D	0.0000	0.0000	0 0000	0 0000	0 1727	0.1867	0.0000	0 0000	0 0000	0 0000
	Term~	0.0000	0.0000	0 0000	0 0000	0 1212	0 1261	0.0000	0 0000	0 0000	0 0000
Cong~	Cong~	0.0000	0.0000	0 0000	0.0000	0.0000	0 0000	1.0000	1 0000	1.0000	1.0000
Pre/Mil~	Military	0.0000	0.0000	0 0000	0.0000	0.0000	0 0000	1.0000	1 0000	1.0000	1 0000
For~	Adversary C~	0 4300	0 4704	0.4300	0.4300	0.4323	0.4362	0.0000	0.0000	0.0000	0.0000
	Allies	0 0887	0.0782	0 0887	0 0887	0.0874	0.0891	0.0000	0.0000	0.0000	0.0000
	Other super~	0 3282	0.2764	0.3282	0 3282	0.3316	0.3296	0.0000	0.0000	0 0000	0.0000
	Terrorists	0 1530	0.1750	0.1530	0.1530	0.1487	0.1451	0.0000	0 0000	0 0000	0.0000

Clusters	Alternatives	Cong~	Pre/Mil~	For~
Alternatives	0.0000	0.4099	0 2953	0 0000
Cong~	0.0000	0.0000	0 0000	0 3284
Pre/Mil~	0 0000	0 0000	0.0000	0 6716
For~	1.0000	0.5901	0 7046	0 0000

ArmsRace Weighted	Alternatives					Cong~	Pre/Mil~	For~			
		NMD	Glob	R & D	Term~	Cong~	Military	Adversary C~	Allies	Other super~	Terrorists
Alternatives	NMD	0.0000	0.0000	0 0000	0 0000	0.1789	0 1160	0.0000	0 0000	0 0000	0.0000
	Glob	0.0000	0.0000	0 0000	0 0000	0.1105	0 0870	0.0000	0 0000	0 0000	0.0000
	R & D	0.0000	0.0000	0 0000	0.0000	0.0708	0 0551	0.0000	0 0000	0 0000	0.0000
	Term~	0.0000	0.0000	0 0000	0 0000	0.0497	0 0372	0.0000	0 0000	0 0000	0.0000
Cong~	Cong~	0.0000	0.0000	0 0000	0 0000	0.0000	0 0000	0 3284	0 3284	0.3284	0 3284
Pre/Mil~	Military	0.0000	0.0000	0 0000	0.0000	0.0000	0 0000	0.6716	0.6716	0.6716	0.6716
For~	Adversary C~	0.4300	0 4704	0.4300	0.4300	0.2551	0 3074	0.0000	0 0000	0.0000	0.0000
	Allies	0.0887	0.0782	0.0887	0.0887	0.0516	0 0628	0.0000	0.0000	0 0000	0.0000
	Other super~	0.3282	0.2764	0.3282	0.3282	0.1957	0.2323	0.0000	0 0000	0 0000	0.0000
	Terrorists	0 1530	0 1750	0 1530	0.1530	0 0877	0.1022	0.0000	0 0000	0 0000	0.0000

ArmsRace Limit	Alternatives					Cong~	Pre/Mil~	For~			
		NMD	Glob	R & D	Term~	Cong~	Military	Adversary C~	Allies	Other super~	Terrorists
Alternatives	NMD	0.0586	0.0586	0 0586	0 0586	0.0586	0.0586	0 0586	0.0586	0.0586	0.0586
	Glob	0.0406	0.0406	0.0406	0 0406	0.0406	0 0406	0.0406	0.0406	0.0406	0.0406
	R & D	0.0258	0.0258	0 0258	0.0258	0.0258	0 0258	0.0258	0.0258	0 0258	0.0258
	Term~	0.0177	0 0177	0 0177	0.0177	0.0177	0.0177	0.0177	0 0177	0.0177	0.0177
Cong~	Cong~	0.1407	0 1407	0 1407	0 1407	0.1407	0.1407	0.1407	0 1407	0 1407	0.1407
Pre/Mil~	Military	0.2879	0.2879	0 2879	0 2879	0.2879	0.2879	0.2879	0 2879	0 2879	0.2879
For~	Adversary C~	0 1874	0.1874	0 1874	0.1874	0.1874	0 1874	0.1874	0 1874	0.1874	0.1874
	Allies	0 0376	0.0376	0 0376	0.0376	0.0376	0 0376	0.0376	0 0376	0.0376	0.0376
	Other super~	0.1391	0.1391	0 1391	0.1391	0 1391	0 1391	0 1391	0.1391	0.1391	0.1391
	Terrorists	0 0645	0.0645	0 0645	0 0645	0 0645	0 0645	0.0645	0.0645	0 0645	0 0645

Table 5-21   Final Table

	Benefits (0.267)	Opportu-nities (0.182)	Costs (0.361)	Risks (0.190)	Final Outcome Additive	Multiplicat ive
Deploy NMD	0.439	0.474	0.306	0.122	**0.337**	0.334
Global Defense	0.352	0.289	0.305	0.180	**0.291**	0.310
R & D	0.158	0.151	0.236	0.284	**0.209**	0.221
Termination	0.050	0.086	0.153	0.414	**0.163**	0.135

Overall Outcome and Conclusion

Deploy NMD (0.337) scores the highest. It is a comprehensive result that takes into consideration all benefits, costs, opportunities, and risks. The conclusion of this analysis is that pursuing the deployment of NMD is the best alternative. It is because, as it is shown in the Table 5-21, the Deploy NMD had the highest priorities for three criteria out of four criteria under Benefits and Opportunities and had the smallest priority for the Security Threat (the vulnerability to the security threat) which means that the least costly. I am grateful to Yeonmin Cho, Youxu Cai Tjader, and Rina Wikandari for their diligent help in preparing this application both in hierarchic and then also in network form.

5-7.   DECISION TO DEVELOP A 22 UNIT CONDOMINIUM

The author of this monumental study, Marcel Minutolo, treated this decision, in which he was personally involved, as both an intellectual and an economic (several million dollar) challenge.   He needed to decide whether or not to purchase a building and convert it into condominiums.   He included all the relevant factors that one might consider in such a decision. There were 58 control criteria in all, and for each he created and evaluated a decision network containing the alternatives of the decision.   He said it took him 60 hours to complete the analysis which he showed to the Mayor's office. A government or a corporation with a complex decision can perhaps invest a week or two of its experts' time to do the same.

Background of the Problem

When a property developer considers a location for development there are many factors to be taken into account. Often these factors may be broken down into tangible elements. However, there are other factors that are more important but can not easily be considered in tangible form. The building in this case is a large multi-story schoolhouse built around the turn of the century that is located in the downtown area of a large American city. It is on the National Historic Register. It currently has tenants in it but is in a decayed state. It is up for sale and might be a good investment for the developer, but before he can put together a package to take to investors and bankers he needs a complete picture of the situation

There are three alternatives as to how he might proceed: 1) Do not purchase; 2) Purchase and do staged development; or, 3) Purchase and do complete development.

Several tangible and intangible factors that must be considered.

Tangibles

There are several non-profit organizations that are the current tenants, but more than half of the building is unoccupied. It has a new roof and it has a sprinkler and fire alarm systems. However, it contains asbestos in various forms and the boiler is almost one hundred years old. Along with these and other structural issues the developer must weigh the purchase price, interest rates, loan terms, and tax rates, as well as the cost to renovate the building and build the condominium units.

Intangibles

The political climate: the developer must consider ward, local and other governmental agencies in various phases of the proposed project. The local ward wants to improve the area so tax advantages are being offered to attract developers. The ward authorities will also assist developers in obtaining the necessary code and zone variances. The current Mayor has a track record of leveling historic landmarks in the area to make room for new projects in business. Many of the residents of the city disapprove of this and are searching for a way to preserve the city's past as it moves into the future. Most of the money that was once available for reclamation of the State's historic monuments has long dried-up. So there is little that the state or federal government can do to help. However, both of these agencies may be willing to help with the removal of hazardous waste.

Local considerations: the city has recently gone through some economic troubles but now is recovering from them. The people that are moving back into the city are young professionals with relatively large disposable incomes. There are several universities and the city has a thriving nightlife. The downtown area where the building is located is experiencing renewal.

Personal concerns: these are image, the developer's financial and personal outlook, loan institutions, various governmental agencies and local businesses. In the final analysis it is up to the developer to decide whether or not to purchase the building.

Recognizing that in most decision problems the *merits*, the benefits, opportunities, costs and risks, (the BOCR), are not equally important, the top level uses a ratings approach to evaluate them in this decision in light of the decision maker's personal criteria. See Figure 5-21. The second level consists of the four merit nodes: *Benefits, Opportunities, Costs* and *Risks*. Because we have assumed that the control criteria are interdependent, instead of itemizing them in a hierarchy, we have created four feedback networks of control criteria, one for each of the BOCR. For an example, see Figure 5-22, the feedback network for *Benefits*. All four networks have Economic, Social and Political components, but the nodes in the components are different. For example, the *Benefits'* Economic component contains the control criteria nodes Revitalization, Tax Base, Jobs and ROI, while the *Costs'* Economic component contains the control criteria nodes Purchase, Build-out, Legal Fees, Brokerage Fees, Contracting Costs and Architect Costs.

Finally, in the fourth level, there are the 58 decision networks containing the alternatives of choice, Do Not Buy, Staged Development or Complete Development, for each of the control criteria. The decision networks all have the same structure in this model. See Figure 5-23. But the judgments are different in each. It is not necessary that the bottom level networks containing the alternatives have the same structure. In fact, usually they do not. This model is unusual in that respect. The only requirement is that all bottom level networks have a component containing the node of the alternatives of the decision.

There are certain personal satisfaction criteria that the developer must consider in order to evaluate the project. A hierarchy for 'rating' the overall significance of the *Benefits, Opportunities, Costs* and *Risks*, the merits of the decision, was developed. In it the personal satisfaction criteria themselves are prioritized by pairwise comparing them with respect to the overall goal of satisfaction as shown in Figure 5-21 . The Ratings: *Very High, High, Medium, Low* and *Very Low* are prioritized in the same way, yielding the priorities shown in Figure 5-21.

The ratings of B, O, C and R are shown in Table 5-22. The results for each cell are computed by multiplying the weight of the personal satisfaction criteria at the top of the column by the priority of the rating selected and adding across each row. For example, the (Benefits, Economic Growth) cell in Table 5-22 is assigned a rating of *High*. So the value for *High*, 0.26, is multiplied by the value for Economic Growth, 0.16, to give the value for that cell. The total score is the sum of the numbers in the row. The totals thus obtained are normalized to yield the numbers in bold in Table 5-22. These numbers will be used to weight the results for *Benefits, Opportunities, Costs* and *Risks* that arise from the feedback networks.

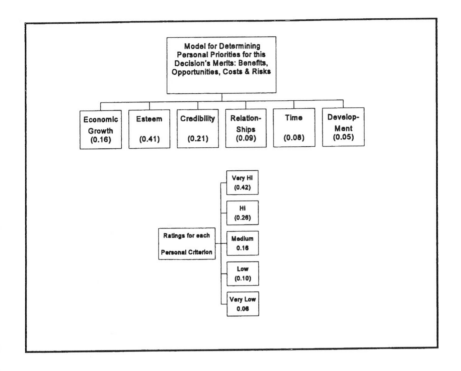

Figure 5-21 Personal Criteria for Rating *Merits* of BOCR

Table 5-22 Rating the BOCR using Personal Criteria.

Merits	Econ. Growth (0.16)	Esteem (0.41)	Credib- ility (0.21)	Relation- ships (0.09)	Time (0.08)	Develop- ment (0.05)	TOTAL (Norm- alized)
Benefits	High	Medium	Low	Low	Low	Medium	.184
Opportun	Very Hi	Medium	High	Medium	Very Lo	High	.263
Costs	Very Hi	Low	Low	Medium	Very Hi	High	.228
Risks	Very Hi	Medium	Very Hi	Low	High	Very Hi	.326

The merit priorities show that *Risks* are the greatest concern for the development project. The result of this concern is that the risk associated with the development of the project will influence the final decision the most.

We now turn to the control criteria networks in level three of Figure 5-21. There are four such networks and we show an example of one of them, for *Benefits*, in Figure 5-22 below.

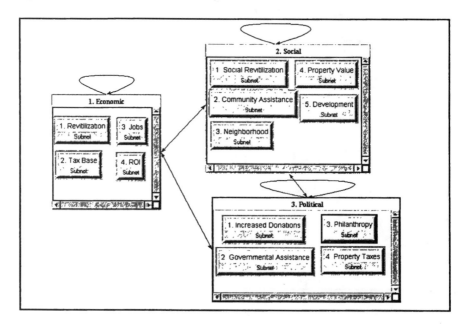

Figure 5-22   The Network of Control Criteria under *Benefits*.

DEVELOPING THE CONTROL CRITERIA

The control criteria in the feedback networks were developed by considering the effects described below:

Benefits

Economic Benefits: The economic benefits are expected to come in four areas: revitalization, tax base, jobs and ROI. The project is intended to restore a piece of the city's history. The movement of additional young professionals in the area will provide a larger tax base for the city. Furthermore, the project itself will provide construction jobs immediately and later more jobs will come into the area in the form of service industries to support the increased population base. Based on the projected figures, the ROI is anticipated to be "moderate".

Social Benefits: We expect to see an increase in 'social revitalization'. By social revitalization, we mean the degree to which the project helps generate an increase in organizations focused on improving the living conditions in the area. Additionally, outside sources to community assistance come in the form of government grants to assist the revitalization, of mayoral support and donations. *Political Benefits*: Political benefits are in the form of increased donations, governmental assistance, increased philanthropy and increase in property taxes.

Opportunities

Economic opportunities: These are reflected by the increase in the potential ROI, associated condo fees, future projects and increased retail sales in the area.
Social opportunities: These are: growth in the community, more residential dwellings and a general clean-up of an otherwise depressed area.
Political opportunities: Political effects are anticipated as a result of an improved local image, community support, donations, zoning reclassification, code development and historic reclamation.

Costs

Economic costs: First, there is the purchase price of the building ($575,000). The build-out cost of creating the condominium units is projected to be $3 million. Legal fees are estimated to be approximately $36,000; brokerage fees $12,000; contractor fees $35,000; and, architect fees $35,000.
Social costs: The social costs are inconvenience, noise and displacement and the developer's funds being diverted from other uses.
Political costs: Political costs include the way resources are allocated, time of construction, dislocation of people, zoning and codes.

Risks

Economic risks: Loans, interest rates, local threats, systems synthesis (the ability to pull the whole project together).
Social risks: The effects on the social life in the community include the effects from federal and local government assistance becoming involved, and health and physical effects.
Political risks: Negative effects on federal, local and ward images; and on poll returns and zoning reclassification.

Interpreting the Priorities of the Control Criteria

There are component interactions involving both inner and outer dependence in the control criteria networks. The economy has elements that influence each other , ROI and Future Development, for example, which is inner dependence as well influencing elements in the social and political components which is outer dependence. Social and political elements often are influenced by various aspects of the economy. Additionally, social influences put pressures on government agencies thus driving the economy.

In the opportunities control criteria network, the control criteria with the highest priorities are ROI (0.147) and community (0.130). This indicates that an economic aspect is most important; but that a social aspect, community, is a close runner-up. The priorities for the network also provide information on what is of little concern overall. For instance, code development (0.023) is of little importance as far as opportunities are concerned.

In the control criteria networks the pairwise comparisons are made with respect to the *Merit* node to which the network belongs. For instance, if we compare the Health Effects node with the Physical Effects node with respect to the Supply Requirements node in the *Risk* network, we ask the question "What is riskier for Supply Requirements, Health Effects or Physical Effects?" They are judged to be the same and a value of 1 is assigned in the pairwise comparison process. A table of all 58 control criteria and their derived weights under *Benefits*, *Opportunities*, *Costs* and *Risks*, are given in Tables 5-23 and 5-24. These numbers were obtained from the limiting supermatrices of the four networks.

Table 5-23 Weights of Control Criteria in the Benefits and Opportunities Control Networks.

	BENEFITS	Local Wts.	Global Wts.	OPPORTUN-ITIES	Local Wts.	Global Wts.
Economic	Revitalization	.145	.287	ROI	.364	.147
	Tax Base	.109	.217	Condo Fees	.152	.061
	Jobs	.160	.318	Future Develop	.291	.117
	ROI	.089	.178	Retail Sales	.193	.078
Social	Social Revital.	.041	.155	Community	.349	.130
	Commun. Ass't	.026	.097	Res. Dwellings	.306	.114
	Neighborhood	.047	.176	Clean-up	.346	.129
	Property Values	.072	.267			
	Development	.082	.304			
Political	Incr. Donations	.040	.177	Local Image	.352	.078
	Gov't. Assist.	.074	.326	Com. Support	.174	.039
	Philanthropy	.040	.178	Donations	.108	.024
	Property Taxes	.072	.319	Zoning Class.	.098	.022
				Code Develop.	.103	.023
				Historic Recl.	.165	.037

Table 5-24 Weights of Control Criteria in Costs and Risks Control Networks.

	COSTS	Local Wts.	Global Wts.	RISKS	Local Wts.	Global Wts.
Economic	Purchase Price	.217	.052	Loan	.158	.083
	Buildout Exp.	.489	.118	Interest	.102	.053
	Legal Fees	.082	.020	Local	.095	.050
	Brokers Fees	.045	.011	Systems Synthesis	.237	.125
	Contractor	.089	.022	Demand	.189	.099
	Architect	.078	.019	Suppliers	.219	.115
Social	Diverted Funds	.313	.158	Community	.145	.038
	Inconveniences	.286	.144	Fed. Gov't.	.293	.078
	Noise	.176	.089	Local Gov't.	.181	.048
	Displacement	.225	.114	Health Effects	.187	.050
				Physic'l Effect	.193	.051
Political	Allocations	.203	.052	Federal Image	.165	.035
	Time	.118	.030	Local Image	.185	.039
	People	.371	.095	Ward Image	.141	.030
	Zoning	.155	.039	Polls	.134	.028
	Codes	.154	.039	Zoning	.183	.038
				Codes	.193	.040

The decision networks in level four of Figure 5-21 are all the same and are shown in detail in Figure 5-23. Every sub-model needs to contain the alternatives of choice. Here there are three components: 1) Personal; 2) Alternatives; and 3) Other. The elements in the components are listed in Table 5-25. Recall that the influence in each depends on its control criterion. The pairwise comparison questions in the sub-models are much more complex than those for the control criteria.

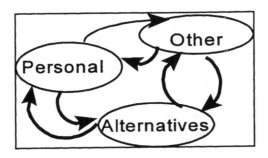

Figure 5-23 Structure of the 58 Decision Networks - One for each Control Criterion .

Table 5-25 The Nodes in the Decision Network Components.

Components	Elements in Components
1. Personal	1. Economic 2. Esteem 3. Credibility 4. Relationships 5. Time 6. Develop
2.Alternatives	1. Do Not Develop 2. Staged Development 3. Complete Development
3. Other Actors	1. Lessor 2. Union 3. URA 4. Bank 5. CDC 6. HLF

RESULTS

The results are obtained by multiplying the synthesized values for the alternatives in each of the 58 decision sub-models by the priorities of their controlling criterion in the control criteria network, then summing for the alternatives for Benefits, Opportunities, Costs and Risks control criterion networks. The synthesized results for the Alternatives are shown in Table 5-26 below.

Table 5-26 Synthesized Results for the Alternatives in the Control Criteria Networks under the BOCR.

Alternatives	Benefits	Opportunities	Costs	Risks
Do Not Purchase	0.097	.112	.191	0.167
Staged Development	0.461	.356	.391	0.374
Complete Development	0.442	.532	.418	0.459

The alternatives that have the highest priority under Costs and Risks are *more* costly or risky, and hence less preferred. To convert the priorities so that less preferred alternatives have lower values than more preferred ones, take the reciprocal of each alternative's priority, as shown in Table 5-27 below, then normalize these reciprocals.

Table 5-27 Inverting Costs and Risks Priorities for use in an Additive Formula

Alternatives	Costs	1/Costs	*1/Costs Normalized*	Risks	1/Risks	*1/Risks Normalized*
Do Not Purchase	0.191	5.236	*.514*	0.167	5.988	*0.552*
Staged Development	0.391	2.558	*.251*	0.374	2.674	*0.247*
Complete Development	0.418	2.392	*.235*	0.459	2.179	*0.201*
Sum	1.000	10.185	1.000	1.000	10.840	1.000

Apply the formula B + O + 1/C + 1/R to obtain the overall priorities for each alternative shown in the right hand column of Table 5-28. The BOCR in this formula are weighted by their personal value priorities as in Table 5-22.

Table 5-28 Final Synthesis of Alternatives using BOCR Weighted by Personal Value Priorities

	Benefits 0.184	Opportunit ies 0.263	Costs(least costly) 0.228	Risks (least risky) 0.326	**Final Outcome Additive**	Final Outcome Multiplicat ive
Do Not Purchase	0.097	0.112	0.514	0.552	**0.344**	0.296
Staged Development	0.461	0.356	0.251	0.247	**0.316**	0.349
Complete Development	0.442	0.532	0.235	0.201	**0.340**	0.355

The results here show that the best option is not to purchase the building. But the option of Complete Development is very close behind, so if the building were to be purchased the best plan would be to develop completely and not in stages. The multiplicative outcome gives credence to this conclusion.

Chapter 6

Probability, Bayes Theory and the Analytic Network Process

6-1. INTRODUCTION - DIAGNOSES WITH DEPENDENT SYMPTOMS, BAYES THEOREM

In this chapter we commit the great heresy of demonstrating that probability theory is a way of conjecturing influences with uncertainty and hence its methods and computations can be done within the framework of the ANP. We were compelled to look at this interpretation because we were approached by doctors at a well-known hospital who felt that they needed to change their approach to diagnoses using Bayes theory because they were taken to court following the death of a patient resulting from their actions which had been guided by Bayes theory without regard to the history of the unfortunate patient. As the saying goes, the proof of the pudding is in the eating, and the reader should judge for him/herself what one internationally known Bayes theory expert said, "If you can show that Bayes theorem is part of the ANP, then probability theory is indeed also part of the ANP." I have revised the arrangement of an important section (Section 5) of an otherwise identical paper I co-authored with L. Vargas and published in the July-August, 1998, issue of *Operations Research* after several years of passing through the hands of numerous referees.

Judgments are needed in medical diagnosis to determine what tests to perform given certain symptoms. For many diseases, what information to gather on symptoms and what combination of symptoms lead to a given disease are not well known. Even when the number of symptoms is small, the required number of experiments to generate adequate statistical data can be unmanageably large. There is need in diagnosis for an integrative model that incorporates both statistical data and expert judgment. When statistical data are present but no expert judgment is available, one property of this model should be to reproduce results obtained through time honored procedures such as Bayes theorem. When expert judgment is also present, it should be possible to combine judgment with statistical data to identify the disease that best describes the observed symptoms. Here we are interested in the Analytic Hierarchy Process (AHP) framework that deals with dependence among the elements or clusters of a decision structure to combine statistical and judgmental information. It is shown that the posterior probabilities derived from Bayes theorem are part of this framework and hence that Bayes theorem is a sufficient condition of a solution in the sense of the AHP. An illustration is given as to how a purely judgment based model in the AHP can be used in medical diagnosis. The application of the model to a case study demonstrates that both, statistics and judgment, can be combined to provide diagnostic support to medical practitioner colleagues with whom we have interacted in doing this work. In medical diagnoses the symptoms (effects) and the probable diseases (causes) can be many and not always independent. The real situation is that there are multiple symptoms that depend on each other, making it difficult to determine the disease from which they originate. In many cases, the symptoms are produced by several diseases at once, complicating the treatment process. The treatment is based on the diagnosis (or diagnoses) which in turn depend on how well physicians can isolate the relationships between symptoms and diseases. Consider the following case of a patient treated at a local hospital.

HISTORY:

"A woman in her second trimester was admitted with symptoms involving abnormalities in her blood (anemia, low platelet counts, blood clots, elevated PTT reflecting clotting abnormalities), liver (abnormal liver tests reflecting inflammation) and immunologic system (elevated ANA and ACA titers reflecting the presence of abnormal antibodies against the patient's own cellular components). At this point the physicians considered four diagnoses (SLE, TTP, HELLP, ACA) suggested by the symptoms. The physicians needed to decide whether or not to terminate the pregnancy as part of the therapy for the patient's condition."

The information obtained from these tests revealed that a complicated and hard decision (strategy) had to be made within the next few weeks depending on the diagnosis reached. Thus, different diagnoses can lead to different strategies and one can think of strategies as being paired with diagnoses and hence we shall speak of disease-strategy pairs. The terms used in this case will be more fully described in Section 6 (see p. 19).

Despite the development of alternative approaches to medical diagnostics based on artificial intelligence and artificial neural networks, Bayes theorem remains a popular statistical approach (See for example Bouros et al., 1995; Deval et al., 1995; Prince, 1996; Skates et al., 1995). A search using BRS/Search at the University of Pittsburgh restricted to 1995 and 1996 in the area of clinical medicine yielded 14 citations of publications using Bayes theorem, 44 artificial intelligence based publications, and 29 publications using artificial neural networks. Bayes theory (Berger, 1985; Howson and Urbach, 1989) provides a paradigm for updating diagnostic information encoded in the form of probabilities. It assumes that decisions with uncertainty can only be made with the aid of information about the environment in which the decision is made. By environment is meant the knowledge of the doctor and the medical community and the practices they believe have worked in the past to successfully diagnose and treat patients by reasoning from observed symptoms of known diseases. Bayes theory updates information by using Bayes theorem, a statement in conditional probabilities relating causes (states of nature) to outcomes. Outcomes are results of experiments used to uncover the causes. The use of conditional probabilities makes it possible to revise initial or prior probabilities of causes known from a large sample of a population, into posterior probabilities by using the outcome of an experiment or test with a certain probability of success performed on a particular individual. Prior probabilities are obtained either subjectively or empirically by sampling the frequency of occurrence of a cause in a population. Posterior probabilities are those based on the prior probabilities, and on both the outcome of the experiment and on the observed reliability of that experiment.

A simplifying assumption seldom satisfied in real life is that the symptoms are independent of each other. Some authors believe that assuming the independence of symptoms does not decrease the quality of the diagnosis (DeDombal, 1972; Adams, 1986; Spiegelhalter and Knill-Jones, 1984; Lauritzen and Spiegelhalter, 1988). Other authors such as Jonson (1991) question the use of Bayes formula. He writes:

> *"Do the fundamental conditions for Bayesian calculus really exist in the reality of everyday diagnostics? Can one recommend using the utilities of decision analysis for selecting tests during diagnostic management of a particular patient? ... The distance between model and reality, caused by the haphazardness of the clinical settings motivates the question if the diagnostic hypotheses really possess any credibility comparable to probability in the mathematical sense. There is an additional circumstance which raises doubt about this ... According to the prevalent frequency interpretation of probability, the probability that a patient with certain test results has a certain disease, depends on the relative frequency of patients with this collection of test results and the distribution of diseases among them ... The combinations of test results alone will not permit us to estimate the probability of the diagnostic hypothesis."*

The reason why independence is assumed is to make it possible to estimate the probabilities that the patient has a disease or diseases given several symptoms, because information on symptoms and combinations of symptoms is not well known and easily recognized for many diseases. To apply Bayes theorem in this context in a meaningful way, one needs statistical data from experiments or expert knowledge relating the symptoms to the diseases. Even when the number of symptoms is small, the required number of experiments to generate adequate statistical data can be unmanageably large. The experiments should consider patients with and without each of the diseases, and the fact that a person could have more than one disease. The number of experiments needed to gather these data can be astronomical. This way of addressing the diagnostic problem with combinatorics reminds one of computer chess programs which search large portions of the space of possible chess moves and assign to each of the moves values according to some expert judgment. Judgments are needed in medical diagnosis to determine what test to perform given certain symptoms and once the results of the tests are available, to estimate how much more likely one disease is than another for given sets of symptoms. Without this information, Bayes theorem cannot be applied in a scientifically defensible way.

The simplified version of Bayes theorem would be to estimate posterior probabilities under the assumption that the symptoms are statistically independent because data may be available for some combinations of symptoms. Note that the assumption of independence does not necessarily make diagnosis with Bayes theorem more inaccurate. Gammerman and Thatcher (1991) compared the diagnostic accuracy of using Bayes Theorem with and without independence in a sample of 6000 patients with acute abdominal pain. They estimated from past data the probabilities that these patients have certain disease, given their symptoms, with the following accuracy:

Diagnosis by:	*Accuracy*
Physician (preliminary diagnosis) -	76%
Simple Bayes (with independence assumption) -	74%
Proper Bayes (without independence assumption) -	65%

This seems to indicate that increasing the mathematical formalism in diagnosis does not produce more accurate results. There is a need in diagnosis for a model that incorporates both statistical data and expert (physician) judgment about the particular patient based on his or her history. When statistical data are present but no expert judgment is available, one property of this model should be to reproduce results obtained through time honored procedures such as Bayes theorem. When expert judgment is present, it should be possible to combine judgment with statistical data to identify the disease that best describes the observed symptoms. The desired model should be a generalization that can account for the workings of both the statistical model and the judgment model. This implies that the model must be based on a unifying theory of measurement that can equally deal with and combine statistical and judgmental data. In principle, the ratio scales resulting from comparisons of statistical data could be taken as fine structured judgments applied to the underlying information. Thus statistics and judgments can be combined through a common ratio scale. That is what the judgment and data based multicriteria decision theory, the Analytic Hierarchy Process (AHP) does.

We are interested in the AHP framework that deals with dependence among the elements or clusters of a decision structure to combine statistical and judgmental evidence. Before we use the AHP to provide a decision in the case mentioned above, we need to discuss some theoretical foundations of the relationship between Bayes theorem and an AHP model with dependence. We then illustrate with the case introduced above, how a purely judgment based model in the AHP can be used in medical diagnosis. The application of the model to the case study illustrates that both, statistics and judgment, can be combined to provide diagnostic support to the medical practitioner. Our goal is to estimate priorities, which correspond to probabilities in Bayes theorem, to be coupled with a relative preference matrix for the disease-strategy pairs.

6-2. THE ANALYTIC HIERARCHY PROCESS

The Analytic Hierarchy Process (AHP) (Saaty, 1996; Saaty, 1991; Saaty, 1986) is used to derive priorities in multicriteria decision making. It is based on three principles: *Decomposition, Measurement of preferences* and *Synthesis*. *Decomposition* breaks a problem down into manageable elements that are treated individually. It begins with implicit descriptors of the problem (the goal) and proceeds logically to criteria (or states of nature) in terms of which outcomes are evaluated. The result of this phase is a hierarchic structure consisting of levels for grouping issues together as to importance or influence with respect to the elements in the adjacent level above. A relative ratio scale of *measurement* is derived from paired comparisons of the elements in a level of the hierarchy with respect to the influence of an element in the level above. Pairwise comparisons are made, with judgments provided as verbal statements about the strength of dominance (importance or likelihood) of one element over another represented numerically on an absolute scale. These judgments are made in the framework of a matrix used to derive a local priority vector as an estimate of relative magnitudes associated with the elements being compared. When priority vectors are derived for all comparisons in the hierarchy, one proceeds to *synthesize* the local priorities to derive a global measure of priority used in making the final decision. These global priorities are obtained by successively weighting and adding from the top level to the bottom level of the hierarchy. The outcome of the synthesis is a multilinear (and hence nonlinear) form whose complexity depends on the number of elements in each level and on the number of levels in the hierarchy.

The AHP can be used, in the context of Bayes theorem, to link prior probabilities and the probabilities of the outcomes from an experiment. Consider a hierarchy consisting of three levels: the goal, the states of nature (Θ) and the outcomes of the experiment (X). Let $P(\Theta)$ be the column vector of prior probabilities and let P(Θ) coincide with the priorities of the states of nature under the goal in the hierarchy. Let P(X|Θ) be the matrix of likelihoods, and let it coincide with the priorities of the outcomes according to the states of nature. Hierarchic composition yields priorities of the outcomes in the form:

$$P(X) = P(X|Θ)\ P(Θ).$$

This form coincides with the probabilities of the outcomes as obtained under probability rules. What we need in this framework is a way to represent the dependence of causes on outcomes generalized to the case of dependence of outcomes on other outcomes. In its simplest form, this type of dependence involves inversion of a hierarchy (turning it upside-down) and evaluating states of nature in terms of outcomes, precisely the reverse of what we have just done in synthesizing the impact of outcomes in terms of states of nature.

6-3. BACKGROUND - THE SUPERMATRIX

To derive priorities in a system with interdependent influences, the feedback approach, a generalization of the idea of a hierarchy, is used (Saaty, 1996). In this framework the elements of a system are represented as nodes of a network. Two nodes are connected by an arc if there is interaction between them. To obtain global priorities, the local priority vectors are entered in the appropriate columns of a matrix of influence among the elements, known as a supermatrix. *Raising this matrix to limiting powers yields the cumulative (nonlinear) influence of each element on every other element with which it interacts.* The matrix representation of a hierarchy with three levels is given by:

$$W = \begin{array}{c} Goal\ (G) \\ Criteria\ (C) \\ Alternatives\ (A) \end{array} \begin{array}{ccc} G & C & A \end{array} \left(\begin{array}{ccc} 0 & 0 & 0 \\ W_{21} & 0 & 0 \\ 0 & W_{32} & I \end{array} \right)$$

where W_{21} and W_{32} are matrices. W_{21} is actually a vector that represents the impact of the Goal on the criteria, and W_{32} represents the impact of the criteria on each of the alternatives. W is referred to as a supermatrix because its entries are matrices. By impact we mean the potential of for example the alternatives to satisfy the requirements implicit in each of the criteria and similarly for the criteria in terms of the goal. If the criteria are dependent among themselves, then the (2,2) entry of W given by W_{22} would be non-zero and we would have:

$$
W = \begin{pmatrix} 0 & 0 & 0 \\ W_{21} & W_{22} & 0 \\ 0 & W_{32} & I \end{pmatrix}
$$

This system can be represented by the network of Figure 6-1, in which the arrows represent the "impact" of the elements in a cluster (e.g., criteria) on elements in the same or another cluster (e.g., alternatives). Impact or influence with respect to a property is a primitive notion. In a given supermatrix all the comparisons are made with respect to what element has more influence or impact. Alternatively, one can ask which element is influenced more. In a typical dependence problem between two clusters, one identifies the elements one at a time in one cluster and pairwise compares the impact of the elements in the other cluster on that element. For example, if one cluster includes diseases and the other symptoms, one selects a disease and a pair of symptoms and asks: of the pair, which symptom is more characteristic of that disease and how strongly more when compared with the other? One goes through the comparisons of all pairs. This process is repeated in a separate matrix for all of the other diseases. Similarly, one takes a symptom and a pair of diseases and responds to the question: which disease is more likely to exhibit the symptom? The matrices lead to priority vectors that are arranged in appropriate blocks of the supermatrix. One advantage of the AHP is that pairwise comparison questions are more readily interpreted by interviewees.

Since W is a column stochastic matrix, it is known that the synthesis of all the interactions among the elements of this system is given by: W^{∞}. If the matrix is irreducible and primitive, the limiting value is obtained by raising W to

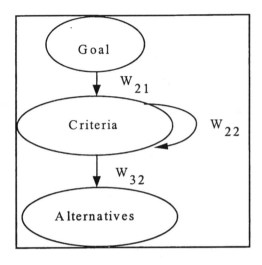

Figure 6-1. Network Represented by Matrix W

powers, i.e., $W^\infty = \lim_{k \to \infty} W^k$. The limit is unique and there is a column

vector w^∞ for which $W^\infty = w^\infty e^T$ where $e^T = (1, ..., 1)$. However, if W is

reducible, then one needs to consider the multiplicity n_1 of the principal eigenvalue 1. As an illustration, when $n_1 = 1$, W^∞ is given by:

$$W^\infty = (I - W)^{-1} \psi(1)/\psi'(1)$$

where $\Psi(\lambda)$ is the minimum polynomial of W and $\Psi'(\lambda)$ is its first derivative with respect to λ. (For $n_1 > 1$ see Gantmacher, 1959, 2nd vol., p.90; Saaty, 1996). If for the example given in Figure 6-1, n_1 were to turn out to have the value $n_1 = 1$, we would have:

$$W^\infty = \lim_{k \to \infty} \begin{pmatrix} 0 & 0 & 0 \\ W_{22}^k W_{21} & W_{22}^k & 0 \\ W_{32}\left(\sum_{h=0}^{k-2} W_{22}^h\right)W_{21} & W_{32}\left(\sum_{h=0}^{k-1} W_{22}^h\right) & I \end{pmatrix}$$

Now $|W_{22}| < 1$ implies that $(W_{22})^k$ tends to zero as k tends to infinity, and we have:

$$W^\infty = \begin{pmatrix} 0 & 0 & 0 \\ 0 & 0 & 0 \\ W_{32}\left(I-W_{22}\right)^{-1}W_{21} & W_{32}\left(I-W_{22}\right)^{-1} & I \end{pmatrix}$$

Thus, the impact of the goal on the ranking of the alternatives (their potential to satisfy the goal) is given by the (3,1) entry of W^∞. We should note here that the problem addressed in this paper is a particular case of the Analytic Network Process (ANP) which has already been applied to more complex situations with interdependence (Saaty, 1996; Blair, Nachtmann, and Saaty, 1993; Saaty and Turner, 1996).

6-4. BAYES THEOREM AND THE SUPERMATRIX

Consider the network of Figure 6-2 consisting of three nodes. Let $P_1 = P(L_1)$ be the column vector of impact or influence of G_1 on the node L_1, let $P_{21} = P(L_2|L_1)$ be the column stochastic matrix of impact of the node L_1 on the node L_2, and let $P_{12} = P(L_1|L_2)$ be the column stochastic matrix of impact of the elements of L_2 on the elements of L_1. In the context of Bayes theorem, P_{21} corresponds to the likelihoods and P_1 to the prior probabilities. Bayes theorem requires finding the matrix P_{12} as a function of P_1 and P_{21}. We use P_1, P_{12} and P_{21} to find the vector of limiting priorities of the network. This vector can be put together by adjoining the limiting priorities of the network components. Thus, we must ensure that the vector of limiting priorities corresponding to the level L_1 is given by the vector P_1 or a constant multiple of it.

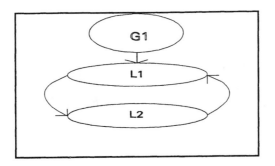

Figure 6-2. Bayes Theorem Network.

The supermatrix corresponding to this feedback network is given by:

$$W = \begin{array}{c} \\ G_1 \\ L_1 \\ L_2 \end{array} \begin{array}{c} G_1 \;\; L_1 \;\; L_2 \\ \begin{pmatrix} 0 & 0 & 0 \\ P_1 & 0 & P_{12} \\ 0 & P_{21} & 0 \end{pmatrix} \end{array} \tag{1}$$

Theorem 6-1 *Given the stochastic matrix W in (1), there exist two vectors* $\overline{a}$ *and* $\overline{b}$ *, unique to within a multiplicative constant, that satisfy:*

$$P_{12}\, \overline{b} = \overline{a} \qquad and \qquad P_{21}\, \overline{a} = \overline{b} \tag{2}$$

and they are the principal right eigenvectors of

$$(P_{12}P_{21}) \qquad and \qquad (P_{21}P_{12}) \; ,$$

respectively.

<u>Proof</u>: For a periodic stochastic matrix *W*, with period 2, the limiting impact priorities are given by:

$$W^\infty = \frac{1}{2}(I + W)(W^2)^\infty.$$ (3)

We have

$$(W^2)^k = \begin{pmatrix} 0 & 0 & 0 \\ 0 & [P_{12}P_{21}]^k & 0 \\ [P_{21}P_{12}]^{k-1}P_{21}P_1 & 0 & [P_{21}P_{12}]^k \end{pmatrix}$$

and hence:

$$W^\infty = \frac{1}{2}\begin{pmatrix} 0 & 0 & 0 \\ P_{12}BP_{21}P_1 & A & P_{12}B \\ BP_{21}P_1 & P_{21}A & B \end{pmatrix}$$ (4)

where $\quad A = \lim_{k\to\infty}[P_{12}P_{21}]^k \quad and \quad B = \lim_{k\to\infty}[P_{21}P_{12}]^k.$

Because $(P_{12}P_{21})$ and $(P_{21}P_{12})$ are irreducible and primitive by the traditional AHP construction, it follows that all columns of A, and of B are identical. This implies that if $e_n^T = (1,...,1)$ and $e_m^T = (1,...,1)$ are row vectors of dimension n and m, respectively, then:

$$A = \overline{a}e_n^T, \qquad and \qquad B = \overline{b}e_m^T$$

where $\quad \overline{a} = (a_1,...,a_n)^T$ and $\overline{b} = (b_1,...,b_n)^T$. It follows from

$$A = \lim_{k\to\infty}[P_{12}P_{21}]^k \quad and \quad B = \lim_{k\to\infty}[P_{21}P_{12}]^k$$

that $\bar{a}$ and $\bar{b}$ are the principal right eigenvectors of $(P_{12}P_{21})$ and

$(P_{21}P_{12})$, respectively. By construction, both vectors are unique to within

a multiplicative constant. To show that $\bar{a}$ and $\bar{b}$ satisfy (2), we note

that by multiplying both sides of $(P_{12}P_{21})\bar{a} = \bar{a}$ on the left by P_{21} we have

$(P_{21}P_{12})P_{21}\bar{a} = P_{21}\bar{a}$. In $(P_{21}P_{12})\bar{b} = \bar{b}$, $\bar{b}$ is unique to

within a multiplicative constant, and because it is normalized to unity by
construction, we have $P_{21}\,\bar{a} = \bar{b}$. Similarly, for the other eigenvalue

problem, $(P_{12}P_{21})P_{12}\bar{b} = P_{12}\bar{b}$ and from the uniqueness of $\bar{a}$ the

result follows.

Note that the system of equations (2), can be represented as an eigenvalue
problem in the following form:

$$\begin{pmatrix} 0 & P_{12} \\ P_{21} & 0 \end{pmatrix} \begin{pmatrix} \bar{a} \\ \bar{b} \end{pmatrix} = \begin{pmatrix} \bar{a} \\ \bar{b} \end{pmatrix}. \tag{5}$$

Let $P_2 \equiv P_{21}P_1$ be the probabilities of the outcomes of the experiment in Bayes
theorem. P_2 must be the limiting priority of level L_2. We want P_1 and P_2 to
be part of the limiting probabilities resulting from the network in Figure 6-2,

and thus we must equate $\bar{a}$ and $\bar{b}$ to P_1 and P_2 , respectively.

Theorem 6-2 (Existence) *Given the network of Figure 6-2 represented by the
stochastic matrix*

$$W = \begin{array}{c} \\ G_1 \\ L_1 \\ L_2 \end{array} \begin{array}{c} G_1 \ \ L_1 \ \ L_2 \\ \begin{pmatrix} 0 & 0 & 0 \\ P_1 & 0 & P_{12} \\ 0 & P_{21} & 0 \end{pmatrix} \end{array}$$

and the matrices P_1 and P_{21} , there exists a matrix P_{12} that satisfies the conditions:

$$(P_{12}P_{21})P_1 = P_1$$

$$(P_{21}P_{12})P_2 = P_2 \tag{6}$$

where $P_2 \equiv P_{21}P_1$.

Proof: If $P_{12} = (\Delta P_1)P_{21}^T(\Delta P_2)^{-1}$, where $\Delta P_1 = \begin{pmatrix} p_{11} & \cdots & 0 \\ & \ddots & \\ 0 & \cdots & p_{1n} \end{pmatrix}$ and

$$\Delta P_2 = \begin{pmatrix} p_{21} & \cdots & 0 \\ & \ddots & \\ 0 & \cdots & p_{2m} \end{pmatrix},$$

then on multiplying both sides on the right by $(\Delta P_2)e_m$ we obtain:

$$P_{12}P_2 = (\Delta P_1)P_{21}^T e_m$$

or

$$P_{12}(\Delta P_2)e_m = (\Delta P_1)P_{21}^T e_m.$$

Similarly, transposing P_{12} and multiplying both sides on the left by ΔP_2, and on the right by e_n we obtain:

$$(\Delta P_2)P_{12}^T e_n = P_{21}(\Delta P_1)e_n$$

From
$$\begin{pmatrix} 0 & P_{21}^T \\ P_{12}^T & 0 \end{pmatrix}\begin{pmatrix} e_n \\ e_m \end{pmatrix} = \begin{pmatrix} e_n \\ e_m \end{pmatrix}$$

we have:

$$P_{12}P_2 = (\Delta P_1)e_n = P_1$$

$$P_{21}P_1 = (\Delta P_2)e_m = P_2$$

and (6) follows.

The matrix P_{12} need not be unique. Thus, for some Q we also have:

$$\begin{pmatrix} 0 & Q \\ P_{21} & 0 \end{pmatrix}\begin{pmatrix} P_1 \\ P_2 \end{pmatrix} = \begin{pmatrix} P_1 \\ P_2 \end{pmatrix}$$

but $Q \ne (\Delta P_1)P_{21}^T(\Delta P_2)^{-1}$. From $QP_2 = P_1$, $P_{12}P_2 = P_1$ and $P_{21}P_1 = P_2$ we have

$$(P_{21}Q)P_2 = (P_{21}P_{12})P_2 \quad \text{or} \quad P_{21}(Q-P_{12})P_2 = 0,$$

and any matrix Q that satisfies the condition:

$$P_{21}(Q-P_{12})P_2 = 0 \tag{7}$$

yields limiting priorities for the corresponding network given by the vector $(0, P_1, P_2)^T$.

Note that $Q = P_{12}$ corresponds to the solution of Bayes theorem. In other words, Bayes theorem is a special case of dependence and feedback represented in the supermatrix. This points to the existence of other interactions between L_2 and L_1 different than those represented by Bayes theorem, as one would expect from a theory that deals with the synthesis of judgments not always concerned with probabilities in every situation and involving dominance expressed through: importance, preference and likelihood (probabilities). For example, if $P_1 = (.1, .9)^T$ and $P_{21} = \begin{pmatrix} .99 & .05 \\ .01 & .95 \end{pmatrix}$ then $P_2 = (.144, .856)^T$

and

$P_{12} = \begin{pmatrix} .6875 & .0012 \\ .3125 & .9988 \end{pmatrix}$. However, any matrix Q that satisfies (7) would

yield the same limit priorities as P_{12} for the network of Figure 6-2. Thus, for

example, for $Q = \begin{pmatrix} .01 & .1151 \\ .99 & .8849 \end{pmatrix}$ the principal right eigenvectors of

(QP_{21}) and $(P_{21}Q)$ are also given by $P_1 = (.1, .9)^T$ and $P_2 = (.144, .856)^T$,

respectively. Note that the first column of Q and the first column of

P_{12} would lead to *totally different conclusions*. Hence, there is more than

one matrix, and they are all different from the matrix P_{12} of posterior

probabilities. The probabilities of the outcomes of the experiment P_2 can be obtained as the limit priorities of all these matrices. If there is more than one such matrix which in the limit leads to the same mix of outcomes, how do we know that the Bayes posteriors matrix is the one we should use to make the decision, since it can imply different actions? We answer this question in Section 6 after we show that within the dependence network of the AHP, Bayes theorem is one of many possible conditions that are satisfied by the limit priority supermatrix.

6-5. RELATIONSHIP BETWEEN BAYES THEOREM AND THE ANALYTIC HIERARCHY PROCESS

Assume that $L_1 \equiv \theta = \{\theta_1, \theta_2, ..., \theta_n\}$ is the space of states of nature (e.g., consequences of actions), and let $L_2 \equiv X = \{x_1, x_2, ..., x_m\}$ be the sample space from which observations are drawn at random. Let $P_{12} \equiv P(\theta|X) = P(\theta_i|X=x_j)$ be the $n \times m$ column stochastic matrix of posterior probabilities, let $P_{21} \equiv P(X|\theta) = P(X=x_j|\theta_i)$ be the $m \times n$ column stochastic matrix of likelihoods, and let $P_1 \equiv P(\theta)$ be the $n \times 1$ vector of prior probabilities.

Let $P_1 = P(\theta)$, $P_2 = P(X)$, and $P_2 = P_{21}P_1$. If

$$P_{12} \equiv P(\theta|X) = \Delta P(\theta)P(X|\theta)^T \Delta P(X)^{-1} \qquad (8)$$

where

$$\Delta P(\theta) = \begin{pmatrix} P(\theta_1) & 0 & \cdots & 0 \\ \vdots & \vdots & \ddots & \vdots \\ 0 & 0 & \cdots & P(\theta_n) \end{pmatrix} and \ \Delta P(X) = \begin{pmatrix} P(X=x_1) & 0 & \cdots & 0 \\ \vdots & \vdots & \ddots & \vdots \\ 0 & 0 & \cdots & P(X=x_n) \end{pmatrix}$$

then by Theorem 6-1, $(0,P(\theta),P(X))^T$ is the vector of limiting priorities corresponding to the network of Figure 6-2. Bayes theorem is a sufficient, but not a necessary condition for the network of Figure 6-2 to have the entries of the vector $(0,P(\theta),P(X))^T$ as limiting priorities.

Expression (8) is the matrix form of Bayes theorem:

$$P(\theta_i|X=x_j) = \frac{P(X=x_j|\theta_i)P(\theta_i)}{P(X=x_j)} = \frac{P(X=x_j|\theta_i)P(\theta_i)}{\displaystyle\sum_{j=1}^{m} P(X=x_j|\theta_i)P(\theta_i)}.$$

As with Bayes theorem, the foregoing easily generalizes to the case of hierarchical priors.

Note that the assumption $P(X) = P(X|\theta)P(\theta)$ is a consequence of the definition of conditional probability:

$$P(X|\theta) \equiv \frac{P(X \cap \theta)}{P(\theta)}$$

on which Bayes theorem is based, in contrast to Theorem 6-1 which follows from the network model used to represent interactions (flow of influence) among nodes, and hence, *is independent of the idea of conditional probability*. The following example illustrates the aforementioned relationship.

An Elementary Example

Consider the following problem which appeared in the Economist, July 4, 1992, p. 74: If a test to detect a disease, whose prevalence is 1/1,000, has a false-positive (false-negative) rate of 5%, what is the chance that a person found to have a positive result actually has the disease, assuming that one knows nothing about the person's symptoms? The AHP supermatrix of this problem is given by:

$$
W = \begin{array}{c} \\ G_1 \\ Disease\ (D) \\ NoDisease\ (NoD) \\ Positive\ (+) \\ Negative\ (-) \end{array}
\begin{array}{ccccc} G_1 & D & NoD & + & - \\ \end{array}
\left(\begin{array}{ccccc}
0 & 0 & 0 & 0 & 0 \\
0.001 & 0 & 0 & P(\theta_1|x_1) & P(\theta_1|x_2) \\
0.999 & 0 & 0 & P(\theta_2|x_1) & P(\theta_2|x_2) \\
0 & 0.95 & .05 & 0 & 0 \\
0 & .05 & .95 & 0 & 0
\end{array}\right)
$$

Here $\quad P(X|\theta)P(\theta) = \begin{pmatrix} .95 & .05 \\ .05 & .95 \end{pmatrix} \begin{pmatrix} .001 \\ .999 \end{pmatrix} = \begin{pmatrix} .0509 \\ .9491 \end{pmatrix}$

are the probabilities of the test results, i.e., $P(+) = 0.0509$ and $P(-) = 0.9491$.

To compute the probability that a person with a positive test actually has the disease we must determine the entries of the matrix

$$P(\theta|X) = \begin{pmatrix} P(\theta_1|x_1) & P(\theta_1|x_2) \\ P(\theta_2|x_1) & P(\theta_2|x_2) \end{pmatrix}.$$ Thus, our problem is to find the

limiting outcome of W which we know. We have

$$
W^k = \begin{pmatrix}
0 & 0 & 0 & 0 & 0 \\
0.001 & 0 & 0 & P(\theta_1|x_1) & P(\theta_1|x_2) \\
0.999 & 0 & 0 & P(\theta_2|x_1) & P(\theta_2|x_2) \\
0 & 0.95 & .05 & 0 & 0 \\
0 & .05 & .95 & 0 & 0
\end{pmatrix}^k
$$

$$
\rightarrow \frac{1}{2} \begin{pmatrix}
0 & 0 & 0 & 0 & 0 \\
0.001 & 0.001 & 0.001 & 0.001 & 0.001 \\
0.999 & 0.999 & 0.999 & 0.999 & 0.999 \\
0.0509 & 0.0509 & 0.0509 & 0.0509 & 0.0509 \\
0.9491 & 0.9491 & 0.9491 & 0.9491 & 0.9491
\end{pmatrix}
$$

The powers of the supermatrix W with the (1,2) block $P(\theta|X)$ converge to the limiting probabilities given by the prior probability vector augmented with the probability vector of outcomes from the experiment. This combined vector is normalized to unity so that the matrix is column stochastic.

Component1: Diseases

Component 2: Symptoms

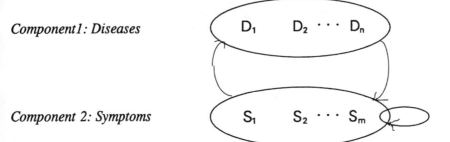

Figure 6-3. Diseases/Symptoms Network

From Theorem 6-2 we have:

$$P(\theta|X) = \overset{\Delta P(\theta)}{\begin{pmatrix} .001 & 0 \\ 0 & .999 \end{pmatrix}} \overset{P(X|\theta)^T}{\begin{pmatrix} .95 & .05 \\ .05 & .95 \end{pmatrix}} \overset{\Delta P(X)^{-1}}{\begin{pmatrix} 1/.0509 & 0 \\ 0 & 1/.9491 \end{pmatrix}}$$

$$= \begin{pmatrix} .01866 & .00005 \\ .98134 & .99995 \end{pmatrix}$$

The $(1,1)$ entry of $P(\theta|X)$ is the desired probability which is equal to 0.01866. To this point the only conceivable advantage we have gained is to obtain a known result from a more general approach based on ratio scales used in decision making. Ratio scales and probabilities both satisfy certain arithmetic operations. In addition, probabilities and Bayes theorem can be derived in the form of priorities.

The example illustrates that a network model can reproduce Bayes results in the simplest case in which only one symptom or piece of evidence exists. This example suggests extending the approach to the case of many symptoms. When formulated in this way there are two problems with this simple approach. The first is combinatorial and requires statistical data about the likelihood of occurrences of combinations of symptoms, which are difficult to obtain. The second has to do with the accuracy and reliability of these data.

6-6. BEYOND BAYES THEOREM

A model designed to represent dependencies among symptoms that incorporates both statistical data together with cause and effect relationships is likely to give a better outcome than a model based solely on statistical data because one has greater choice in using a diversity of information. The reliability of such information depends on the expert knowledge of experienced physicians, for example, whom one seeks when a diagnosis seems difficult and beyond easy reach. How to capture the details and accuracy of the judgments of experts and represent them in a reliable mathematical framework is one of the objectives of the AHP. A very simple network model such as that shown in Figure 6-3 can be used to diagnose the most likely disease given the set of symptoms of the patient at a local hospital described earlier.

The following supermatrix would be used to compute limiting priorities:

$$
W \equiv \begin{array}{c} \\ \textit{Diseases} \\ \textit{Symptoms} \end{array} \begin{array}{cc} \textit{Diseases} & \textit{Symptoms} \\ \left(\begin{array}{cc} 0 & W_{12} \\ W_{21} & W_{22} \end{array} \right) \end{array} \tag{9}
$$

At the level of diseases, the priorities in W_{12} indicate which disease is more likely to cause the observed symptoms. At the level of symptoms, W_{21}, the priorities indicate which symptom is more prevalent for a given disease. Thus, W_{12} represents the probabilities of the diseases causing a given set of symptoms and W_{21} represents the matrix of relative importance, salience or presence of the symptoms (or set of symptoms) given a disease. Both W_{12} and W_{21} may be estimated either through statistics or through judgment (see Tables 6-1 and 6-2). If statistics are used, then W_{12} corresponds to the posteriors of W_{21}. Finally, W_{22} represents the matrix of interrelations among the symptoms estimated through judgments. Probabilistically, W_{22} gives the likelihood that given a symptom the other symptoms are also present. The symptoms we consider are not all those that are possible for a disease but those observed in a given patient. It is from the matrix W that one can derive the priorities or likelihoods of the diseases given the symptoms. The blocks W_{12} and W_{22} are column stochastic, and hence the resulting supermatrix is not column stochastic. To transform it to such a form we must weigh the impacts of the clusters on each cluster. In general one needs to compare the impact of the collection of clusters or categories of elements (e.g., diseases and symptoms) on each of these clusters in a pairwise comparison matrix (obtaining a vector of weights for that column of blocks) by answering the question: Which of two clusters has greater influence on a given cluster? Let α_1 and α_2 be the weights of the clusters of diseases and symptoms, respectively, with respect to the cluster of symptoms. The ratio $\dfrac{\alpha_1}{\alpha_2}$ represents how strongly the cluster of diseases influences the cluster of symptoms as compared with that same cluster of symptoms itself . These weights are estimated by asking the question: Is knowledge of a symptom and its intensity to identify a disease a direct result of knowing about the disease or of knowing about the other symptoms? If the answer is that both contribute equally, then $\alpha_1 = \alpha_2 = \frac{1}{2}$. Note that in input-output analysis one asks, for example, how much more does the electric industry influence the electric output of the electric industry itself than another resource, e.g., oil. The answer is: little, because the electric industry mostly uses resources such as coal, oil, or steel, to produce electricity.

Because the matrix W is irreducible, the resulting weighted supermatrix is also irreducible, and the limiting priorities are obtained by solving the following eigenvalue problem:

$$\begin{pmatrix} 0 & \alpha_1 W_{12} \\ W_{21} & \alpha_2 W_{22} \end{pmatrix} \begin{pmatrix} w_1 \\ w_2 \end{pmatrix} = \begin{pmatrix} w_1 \\ w_2 \end{pmatrix}$$ .The solution of this problem is given by:

$$(10) \quad w_2 = \left[\lim_{k \to \infty} (\alpha_1 W_{21} W_{12} + \alpha_2 W_{22})^k \right] e, \quad e = (1,...,1)^T$$

and $w_1 = \alpha_1 W_{12} w_2$.

Note that if $W_{22} = 0$ and hence there are no dependencies among the symptoms, then w_1 is the vector of prior probabilities of the diseases in Bayes theorem, and w_2 is the vector of likelihoods of the symptoms.

The outcome of this model is the set of priorities or likelihoods of all the components of the problem. In our case this outcome is the vector of priorities $\begin{pmatrix} w_1 \\ w_2 \end{pmatrix}$. These priorities can now be used to choose among alternative courses of action to deal with the most likely disease(s) with the symptoms observed.

To determine which of the methods of treatment $A_1, A_2, ..., A_k$ is best for the symptoms observed we can proceed in two equivalent ways. The first, and for our purpose less interesting way, assumes that the likelihood of the diseases are already known. It can be represented by a hierarchy as in Figure 6- 4:

GOAL

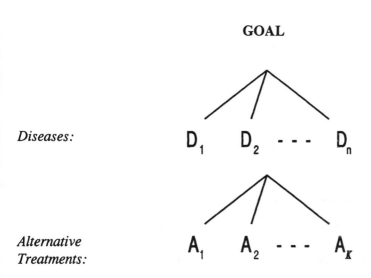

Diseases:

Alternative Treatments:

Figure 6-4. Hierarchy of Treatments

Here, if $w(A|D)$ is the matrix of relative importance of the alternative treatments with respect to each disease, then the priorities of the treatments are given by:

$$w(A|D)\frac{w_1}{\|w_1\|}$$

where $\|w_1\| = e^T w_1$, and $e^T = (1,1,\cdots,1)$. Each column of $w(A|D)$ can be obtained by constructing a hierarchy of criteria and alternatives with the purpose of finding the best treatment for the given disease. The physician has in his mind a set of criteria according to which he compares the alternative treatments.

The second way is more general and involves the symptoms themselves along with the diseases and their alternative treatments. It can be represented by a network as in Figure 6-5:

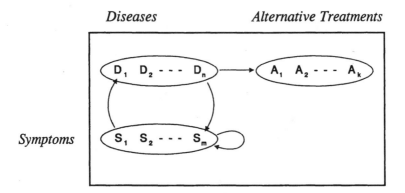

Figure 6-5. Diseases/Treatments Network.

The supermatrix corresponding to this network is given by:

$$W = \begin{array}{c} \\ Diseases \\ Symptoms \\ Alternatives \end{array} \begin{array}{ccc} D & S & A \end{array} \\ \begin{pmatrix} 0 & \alpha_1 W_{12} & 0 \\ \beta_1 W_{21} & \alpha_2 W_{22} & 0 \\ \beta_2 W_{31} & 0 & I \end{pmatrix}$$

Let us write the matrix, $Q = \begin{pmatrix} 0 & \alpha_1 W_{12} \\ W_{21} & \alpha_2 W_{22} \end{pmatrix}$. The limiting priorities of the

non-zero components of the system in the steady state are given by

$$[W_{31}, \ 0] \ Q^\infty.$$

They are also the priorities of the alternatives, and coincide with the result obtained previously for a hierarchy because

$$W_{31} = w(A|D)$$

and the columns of Q^∞ are all identical and equal to the vector $\begin{pmatrix} w_1 \\ w_2 \end{pmatrix}$ whose components are given by (10).

Let us apply our ANP model to the medical case described in the introduction. To do that, we asked the attending physician to provide us with his expert opinion about the relative importance or the relative likelihood of the various elements involved in the details of the model. Given the condition of the patient, a decision had to be made (i.e., selection among alternative treatments) to either terminate (T) the pregnancy, or to treat the patient and let her proceed with it (NT). The tests at the local hospital revealed the following symptoms:

- Anemia (An),
- Low Platelets (LP),
- Abnormal Liver (ABL),
- Blood Clotting (BC),
- High Activated Partial ThromboPlastin Time (APTT-H),
- High AntiNuclear Antibody (ANA-H),
- High AntiCardiolipin Antibody (ACA-H),

and the diseases that could be the cause of these symptoms were:

- Lupus,
- Thrombotic Thrombocytopenic Purpura (TTP),
- Hemolysis, Elevated Liver function, and Low Platelets (HELLP), and
- AntiCardiolipin Antibody Syndrome (ACA Syn).

For definitions and explanations of the symptoms and diseases in this example see the classical book by Colman et al. (1994).

The physician who performed some of the tests on this patient provided the judgments given in Comparison Matrices 1 to 3. We have included one paired comparison matrix before each table to illustrate how the judgments are made in response to an appropriate question, and how a column of weights is derived from each. The vector of priorities derived from a judgment matrix is shown on the right of that matrix and becomes a column under the appropriate element of the corresponding table. Comparison Matrix 1 yields the weights for the Lupus column in Table 6-1, augmented by a zero for Abnormal Liver (see later), Comparison Matrix 2 yields the weights for the Anemia column in Table 6-2, and Comparison Matrix 3 yields the weights for the High ANA column in Table 6-3.

The judgments in the comparison matrices can be substituted for statistical frequencies obtained by observing the symptoms more prevalent for each disease when compared with every other symptom. Since statistical data do not characterize individuals, it is essential to adjust such data to specific situations by taking into account patient specific data. The judgments can take into account the physician's perception of how statistical data change from patient to patient.

Table 6-1 provides the weights to obtain the columns of W_{21} in the supermatrix, the likelihoods of the symptoms associated with a given disease. Tables 6-2 and 6-3 are W_{12} and W_{22}, respectively. W_{12} corresponds to the likelihoods of the diseases producing the symptom observed, and W_{22} corresponds to the strengths of the relationships among symptoms, i.e., given a symptom and all other symptoms related to it, it gives the likelihood of other symptoms appearing at the same time. Their columns are the eigenvectors of pairwise comparison matrices. In principle there is a comparison judgment matrix for each column of Tables 6-1, 6-2, and 6-3. In fact, some of them are not needed because one already knows the answer, as in the first column of Table 6-3 which has a 1.000 for Anemia and 0's for the remaining entries. The reader would have no trouble constructing a consistent approximation to the original pairwise comparison matrices. A matrix is constructed by forming the ratios from the entries of the appropriate corresponding column in any of these three tables. Thus there would be nothing missing in our presentation.

The question that the physician answered to obtain these priorities was:

For a given a disease and for two symptoms, which symptom is more characteristic of the disease, and how strongly is it?

The judgments are expressed verbally as: equal, moderate, strong, very strong and extreme. With these judgments are associated the absolute numbers (how many times more): 1, 3, 5, 7, 9. The numbers: 2, 4, 6, 8, are used for compromise between the verbal judgments. In addition, reciprocals are used to represent the inverse comparison. This scale is used to compare any homogeneous set. For example, with respect to Lupus, which symptom is more characteristic, Anemia or Low Platelets? The answer was: Anemia is strongly (5) more characteristic of Lupus than Low Platelets. Comparing all the symptoms yielded the following matrix of paired comparisons whose principal right eigenvector is given in the first column of Table 6-1. Note that the symptom "Abnormal Liver" was not included in the comparison set because it is not characteristic of Lupus. Instead of including it along with zeros in its row and column, it is simply assigned the value zero in the augmented vector of weights shown in the first column of Table 6-1. Note that one could include an infinite number of irrelevant factors to which one could then assign zeros for their paired comparison rows and columns. One avoids doing that in the AHP. When a factor does play a role in some, but not all, of the matrices, one avoids these rows and columns of zeros by assigning it a zero in the appropriate position in the derived vector without including it in the comparison matrix.

Back to our matrix of judgments, we only need its upper triangular part. The elements of the main diagonal are equal to one and the elements in the lower triangular part of the matrix are each the reciprocal of the transpose element in the upper triangular part. It is important to note that when the judgments are ratios of statistical frequencies, the resulting weights are these frequencies given in normalized form.

Comparison Matrix 1. Priorities of Symptoms with respect to Diseases (in this case Lupus)

Lupus	Ane-mia	LP	BC	APTT-H	ANA-H	*ACA-H*	WTS
Anemia	1	5	4	4	1/9	2	0.156
LP	1/5	1	1	1	1/9	1	0.050
BC	1/4	1	1	1	1/9	1/2	0.046
APTT-H	1/4	1	1	1	1/9	1/2	0.046
ANA-H	9	9	9	9	1	9	0.630
ACA-H	½	1	2	2	1/9	1	0.072

TABLE 6-1: Priorities of Symptoms with respect to the Diseases

	LUPUS	TTP	HELLP	ACASyn
Anemia	0.156	0.133	0.313	0.053
LP	0.050	0.789	0.313	0.158
AB Liver	0.000	0.000	0.313	0.000
BC	0.046	0.026	0.000	0.263
APTT-H	0.046	0.026	0.061	0.263
ANA-H	0.630	0.000	0.000	0.000
ACA-H	0.072	0.026	0.000	0.263

To obtain the Comparison Matrix 2, the physician answered the question:

Given a symptom and two diseases, which disease is more likely to exhibit this symptom, and how much more likely is it?

For example, with respect to Anemia, which of the two diseases, Lupus or TTP, is more likely to exhibit Anemia as a symptom? The answer to this question was: TTP is strongly (5) more likely than Lupus of exhibiting Anemia as a symptom. The same as with Table 6-1, the matrix of paired comparisons of all the diseases considered with respect the symptoms is given in Comparison Matrix 2 below.

Comparison Matrix 2. Priorities of Diseases with respect to Symptoms (in this case Anemia)

Anemia	Lupus	TTP	HELLP	ACA Syn	Weights
Lupus	1	1/5	1/9	1/5	0.052
TTP	5	1	1	1	0.299
HELLP	9	1	1	1	0.350
ACA Syn	5	1	1	1	0.299

TABLE 6-2. Priorities of Diseases with respect to the Symptoms

	Ane-mia	LP	AB Liver	BC	APTT-H	ANA-H	ACA-H
Lupus	0.052	0.231	0.000	0.279	0.222	0.706	0.119
TTP	0.299	0.461	0.000	0.070	0.056	0.088	0.030
HELLP	0.350	0.231	1.000	0.093	0.056	0.088	0.020
ACA Syn	0.299	0.077	0.000	0.558	0.666	0.118	0.831

The judgments in Comparison Matrix 3 were obtained by asking the physician to answer the question: *Given a symptom, e.g., High ANA, and given two other symptoms that may be related to it, e.g., Anemia and Low Platelets, which of the symptoms is more likely to be associated with or occur jointly with the given symptom and how much more likely is it?*

The answer to the question in the example was: Anemia is equally (1) likely to be associated with or occur jointly with Low Platelets. The matrix of all the paired comparisons of all the symptoms related to High ANA is given by:

Comparison Matrix 3. Priorities of Symptoms with respect to Symptoms (in this case High ANA)

High ANA	Anemia	LP	BC	ACA-C	Weights
Anemia	1	1	4	4	0.455
LP	1	1	1	1	0.235
BC	1/4	1	1	1	0.155
ACA-H	1/4	1	1	1	0.155

TABLE 6-3. Priorities of Symptoms with respect to the Symptoms

	Ane-mia	LP	AB Liver	BC	APTT-H	ANA-H	ACA-H
Anemia	1.000	0.000	0.25	0.000	0.000	0.455	0.095
LP	0.000	0.000	0.75	0.105	0.106	0.235	0.048
AB Liver	0.000	0.500	0.000	0.000	0.000	0.000	0.000
BC	0.000	0.000	0.000	0.000	0.429	0.155	0.381
APTT-H	0.000	0.000	0.000	0.421	0.000	0.000	0.381
ANA-H	0.000	0.500	0.000	0.053	0.036	0.000	0.095
ACA-H	0.000	0.000	0.000	0.421	0.429	0.155	0.000

Table 5-4 gives the transpose of the matrix W_{3I}, the priorities of the alternatives for each of the diseases obtained from pairwise comparison matrices whose data were provided by the physician who based his answers on his experience with the diseases. These priorities suggest which alternative treatment would be most appropriate given the disease in question.

TABLE 6-4: Priorities of Alternative Treatments with respect to Diseases

Diseases	Alternatives	
	T	NT
Lupus	0.20	0.80
TTP	0.80	0.20
HELLP	0.80	0.20
ACA Syn	0.83	0.17

Table 6-5 is the Q block of the supermatrix corresponding to Figure 6-5 with $\alpha_1 = \alpha_2 = \frac{1}{2}$.

TABLE 6-5. Q block of the supermatrix

$Q=$

	Lupus	TTP	HELLP	ACASynd	Anemia	LowPlt	ABLiver	BloodClot	APTT-H	ANA-H	ACA-H
Lupus	0	0	0	0	0.025	0.115	0	0.140	0.111	0.353	0.059
TTP	0	0	0	0	0.150	0.231	0	0.035	0.028	0.044	0.015
HELLP	0	0	0	0	0.175	0.115	0.500	0.047	0.028	0.044	0.010
ACASynd	0	0	0	0	0.150	0.038	0	0.279	0.333	0.059	0.416
Anemia	0.156	0.133	0.313	0.053	0.500	0	0.125	0	0	0.227	0.048
LowPlt	0.050	0.789	0.313	0.158	0	0	0.375	0.053	0.053	0.117	0.024
ABLiver	0	0	0.313	0	0	0.250	0	0	0	0	0
BloodClot	0.046	0.026	0	0.263	0	0	0	0	0.214	0.078	0.190
APTT-H	0.046	0.026	0.061	0.263	0	0	0	0.211	0	0	0.190
ANA-H	0.630	0	0	0	0	0.250	0	0.026	0.018	0	0.048
ACA-H	0.072	0.026	0	0.263	0	0	0	0.211	0.214	0.078	0

Raising the matrix in Table 6-5 to powers we obtain the limiting priority vector w:

$$
w = \begin{pmatrix} 0.073 \\ 0.068 \\ 0.087 \\ 0.106 \\ 0.169 \\ 0.144 \\ 0.063 \\ 0.067 \\ 0.066 \\ 0.088 \\ 0.070 \end{pmatrix} \begin{array}{l} \left.\begin{array}{c} \\ \\ \\ \end{array}\right\} w_1 \\ \\ \\ \left.\begin{array}{c} \\ \\ \\ \\ \end{array}\right\} w_2 \end{array}
$$

from which we obtain the relative likelihood of the diseases by normalizing the first four components of w. We have

$$
\frac{w_1}{e^T w_1} = \begin{pmatrix} 0.218 \\ 0.203 \\ 0.262 \\ 0.317 \end{pmatrix} \begin{array}{l} Lupus \\ TTP \\ HELLP \\ ACASyn \end{array}
$$

The composite priorities of the alternatives are obtained using the priorities of the diseases and those in Table 6-4. We have

$$
\begin{pmatrix} 0.2 & 0.8 & 0.8 & 0.833 \\ 0.8 & 0.2 & 0.2 & 0.167 \end{pmatrix} \begin{pmatrix} 0.218 \\ 0.203 \\ 0.262 \\ 0.317 \end{pmatrix} = \begin{pmatrix} 0.68 \\ 0.32 \end{pmatrix} \begin{array}{l} T \\ NT \end{array}
$$

The pregnancy was terminated (w(T) = 0.68) two weeks after the discharge date. The doctor who made the decision then tested his judgments within the framework of the model and found that it validated his recommendation. In this case, no statistics were available that could be used as input to Bayes theorem (blocks W_{12} and W_{21}) in this diagnosis. To make a decision using Bayes theorem would have required unavailable statistical information about the likelihood that patients who have had the diseases in question would exhibit the same symptoms as presented by the patient.

Recall that the weight of the dependencies among the symptoms, i.e., α_1 and α_2, were obtained by asking the question: Is knowledge of a symptom a direct result of knowing about the disease or of knowing about the other symptoms? If the answer is that both contribute equally, then $\alpha_1 = \alpha_2 = \frac{1}{2}$. As we vary the weight of the dependencies among the symptoms from more dependency (for example, 50 percent in Table 6-5 corresponding to $\alpha_1 = \alpha_2 = \frac{1}{2}$) to less dependency (for example, 1 percent, i.e., the vectors in Tables 6-2 and 6-3 are multiplied by $\alpha_1 = 0.99$ and $\alpha_2 = 0.01$, respectively, yielding Table 6-6), the model decreases (slightly) the intensity with which it recommends the termination of the pregnancy from 0.68 to 0.658.

TABLE 6-6. The Q block of the supermatrix corresponding to the network in Figure 6-5 with $\alpha_1 = 0.99$ and $\alpha_2 = 0.01$

	Lupus	TTP	HELLP	ACASynd	Anemia	LowPlt	ABLiver	BloodClot	APTT-H	ANA-H	ACA-H
Lupus	0	0	0	0	0.051	0.229	0	0.276	0.220	0.699	0.118
TTP	0	0	0	0	0.296	0.456	0	0.069	0.055	0.087	0.029
HELLP	0	0	0	0	0.347	0.229	0.99	0.092	0.055	0.087	0.019
ACASynd	0	0	0	0	0.296	0.076	0	0.552	0.660	0.117	0.824
Anemia	0.156	0.133	0.313	0.053	0.010	0	0.003	0	0	0.004	0.001
LowPlt	0.050	0.789	0.313	0.158	0	0	0.007	0.001	0.001	0.002	0.000
ABLiver	0	0	0.313	0	0	0.005	0	0	0	0	0
BloodClot	0.046	0.026	0	0.263	0	0	0	0	0.004	0.0002	0.004
APTT-H	0.046	0.026	0.061	0.263	0	0	0	0.004	0	0	0.004
ANA-H	0.630	0	0	0	0	0.005	0	0.001	0.001	0	0.001
ACA-H	0.072	0.026	0	0.263	0	0	0	0.004	0.004	0.002	0

Q= (matrix label at left of the matrix)

Thus, the dependence of the symptoms among themselves is not an important contributor to the final decision. This need not always be the case. In some cases what we know about the diseases exceeds the importance of the symptoms observed in the patient in the early stages of the disease, so depending on who the patient is, the weight of the cluster of diseases may not be 50/50 when compared with the symptoms.

6-7. CONCLUSIONS

The foregoing shows that if we were to use the same information as in Bayes theorem, the limiting priorities obtained through the supermatrix yield the same information we started with: the priors and the probabilities of the outcomes (the symptoms given the diseases) of the experiment, i.e., the likelihoods. Thus, if one estimates the matrix of likelihoods W_{21} in (9) and the posteriors W_{12}, the priors can be obtained as the principal right eigenvector of the stochastic matrix $W_{12} W_{21}$. If in addition to this information, one includes dependencies among clusters, i.e., dependencies of symptoms on symptoms, the limiting result obtained is different and more general than what one would obtain by using Bayes theorem. We have shown that:

1) There are other plausible ways of combining prior information and past knowledge to model uncertain situations. Some of these ways may account for the accuracy of the predictions made with the AHP and ANP. In Bayes theorem this leads to posteriors. In our case, it leads to an outcome with a general necessary condition that is satisfied by Bayes theorem, but is not identical with it. The residual part in our approach involves an infinite set of ways of combining priors and likelihoods of which Bayes theorem is only one. It is worthwhile to continue this research to understand both the philosophical and operational implications of alternative ways for combining such information.

2) Diagnosis with dependent symptoms needs expert judgments along with statistical information to provide knowledge from experience on the relationships of symptoms and combinations of symptoms and diseases. Bayes theorem with dependence does not appear to be the final arbiter in medical diagnosis.

The supermatrix approach provides a rationale for associating symptoms with other known symptoms of a disease, using the experience of an expert rather using statistical data which may not be available and bypassing the combinatorial problem posed by the astronomical number of ways in which symptoms may be combined. The judgments allow the physician to focus on the specific situation rather than on the broad occurrences of a disease. Many decision problems require interpretations that allow for dependence of the kind described in this paper. By starting with the framework of the AHP/ANP one could have arrived at Bayes relation without assuming conditional probabilities on which Bayes theory is based. In the AHP, where the comparisons of pairs of elements are made with respect to an element in the level above, judgments replace conditional probabilities. If these probabilities are available they can replace the pairwise comparison judgments or at least can be used to support making them.

The AHP/ANP is a theory that makes it possible to use both, the physician's judgments based on all kinds of subjective information together with the statistics of test results. The outcome is a compromise between the Bayesian approach which requires empirical evidence to make a diagnosis, and the more subjective clinical approach in which physicians use experience, evidence and environmental variables to diagnose patients.

The reader may inquire about the general validity of the AHP of which numerous applications have been made. Predictions made by a theory serve as indicators of the validity of that theory. Here are some references to examples of successful predictions made with the AHP (Saaty and Vargas, 1991) and the Analytic Network Process (ANP), the generalization of the AHP to dependence and feedback (Saaty, 1996). We have predictions of the stock market (Saaty, Rogers, and Pell, 1980), political candidacy (Saaty and Bennett, 1977), oil prices (Gholam-Nezhad, 1985; Gholam-Nezhad, 1977; Saaty and Gholamnezhad, 1981), energy rationing (Saaty and Mariano, 1979), international chess competition (Saaty and Vargas, 1980, 1985), family size in rural India (Saaty and Wong, 1983), foreign exchange rates for the US dollar versus the Japanese yen (Blair, Nachtmann and Saaty, 1987), the turn around of the US economy and the strength of its recovery (Blair, Nachtmann, 1993), and the outcomes of the playoff games and Superbowl in the 1995-1996 football season (Saaty and Turner, 1996).

References

Adams, I.D., 1986, "Computer-Aided Diagnosis of Acute Abdominal Pain: A Multicentre Study," *British Medical Journal* 293, 800-804.

Berger, J.O., 1985, *Statistical Decision Theory and Bayesian Analysis*, Springer-Verlag.

Blair, A., R. Nachtmann, J. Olson, and T. Saaty, 1987, "Forecasting Foreign Exchange Rates: An Expert Judgment Approach," *Socio-Economic Planning Sciences* 21, 6, 363-369.

Blair, A., R. Nachtmann, and T.L. Saaty, 1993, "Incorporating Expert Judgment in Economic Forecasts: The Case of the U.S. Economy in 1992", in *Fundamentals of Decision Making and Priority Theory with The Analytic Hierarchy Process*, Saaty, Thomas L., 1994 RWS Publications, Pittsburgh, PA.

Bouros, D., Panagou, P., Tzanakis, N., and N. Siafakas, 1995, "Probability And Characteristics Of Human-Immunodeficiency-Virus Infection In Male Greek Military Personnel With Tuberculosis," *Respiration* 62, 5, 280-285.

Brown, G.W., 1981, "Bayes' Formula: Conditional Probability and Clinical Medicine", *Am. J. Dis. Child* 135, 1125-1129.

Charniak, E. and D. McDermott, 1985, *Introduction to Artificial Intelligence*, Addison-Wesley.

Colman, R.W., J. Hirsh, V.J. Marder, E.W. Salzman (eds.), 1994, *Homeostasis and Thrombosis*, J.B. Lippincott Company, Philadelphia, PA 19106.

DeDombal, F.T., 1972, "Computer-Aided Diagnosis of Acute Abdominal Pain," *British Medical Journal* 2, 9-13.

Feinstein, A.R., 1977, "The Haze of Bayes, the Serial Places of Decision Analysis, and the Computerized Ouija Board," *Clin. Pharmacol. Therap.* 21, 482-496.

Gammerman, A. and A.R. Thatcher, 1991, "Bayesian Diagnostic Probabilities without Assuming Independence of Symptoms", *Methods of Information in Medicine* 30, 15-22.

Gantmacher, F.R., 1959, *Matrix Theory*, John Wiley, New York.

Gholam-Nezhad, H. "1995: The Turning Point in Oil Prices," The Global Economy: Today, Tomorrow, and the Transition. Edited by H.F. Didsbury, Jr., World Future Society, Washington, DC, 1985.

Gholam-Nezhad, H., 1987, "Oil Price Scenarios: 1989 and 1995," *Strategic Planning and Energy Management* 7, 1, 19-31.

Howson C. and P. Urbach, 1989, *Scientific Reasoning: The Bayesian Approach*, Open Court, La Salle, Illinois.

Jonson, N.E.G., 1991,"Everyday Diagnostics -- A Critique of the Bayesian Model," *Medical Hypotheses* 34, 289-295.

Lauritzen, S.L. and D.J. Spiegelhalter, 1988, "Local Computations with Probabilities on Graphical Structures and Their Application to Expert Systems," *Journal of the Royal Statistical Society*, Series B, 50, 157-224.

Miller, G.A., 1956, "The Magical Number Seven Plus or Minus Two: Some Limits on Our Capacity for Processing Information," *Psychological Review* 63, 81-97.

Prince, M.J., 1996, "Predicting The Onset Of Alzheimers-Disease Using Bayes theorem," *American Journal Of Epidemiology* 143, 3, 301-308.

Saaty, T.L., 1981, "Priorities in Systems with Feedback," *The International Journal of Systems, Measurement and Decisions* 1, 24-38.

Saaty, T.L., 1986, "Axiomatic Foundation of the Analytic Hierarchy Process," *Management Science* 32/7, 841-855.

Saaty, T.L., 1991, *Multicriteria Decision Making: The Analytic Hierarchy Process*, RWS Publications, 4922 Ellsworth Ave., Pittsburgh, PA 15213.

Saaty T.L., 1996, *The Analytic Network Process* - Decision Making With Dependence And Feedback, RWS Publications, 5001 Baum Blvd., Pittsburgh, PA 15213.

Saaty, T.L. and J.M. Alexander, 1989, *Conflict Resolution: The Analytic Hierarchy Approach*, Praeger, New York.

Saaty, T.L. and J.P. Bennett, 1977, "A Theory of Analytical Hierarchies Applied to Political Candidacy", *Behavioral Science* 22, 237-245.

Saaty, T.L. and H. Gholamnezhad, 1981, "Oil Prices: 1985 and 1990," *Energy Systems and Policy* 5, 4, 303-318.

Saaty, T.L. and K.P. Kearns, 1985, *Analytical Planning: The Organization of Systems*, Pergamon Press, New York.

Saaty, T.L. and R.S. Mariano, 1979, "Rationing Energy to Industries: Priorities and Input-Output Dependence," *Energy Systems and Policy* 8, 85-111.

Saaty, T.L. and M. Takizawa, 1986, "Dependence and Independence : From Linear Hierarchies to Nonlinear Networks," *European Journal of Operational Research* 26/2, 229-237.

Saaty, T.L., D.S. Turner, 1996, "Prediction of the 1996 Superbowl: An Application of the AHP with Feedback (the Supermatrix Approach)," *Proceedings of the 4th International Symposium on the Analytic Hierarchy Process*, Vancouver , Canada. Expert Choice Inc., 5001 Baum Boulevard, Pittsburgh, PA 15213.

Saaty, T.L. and L.G. Vargas, 1980, "Hierarchical Analysis of Behavior in competition: Prediction in Chess," *Behavioral Science* 25, 180-191.

Saaty, T.L. and L.G. Vargas, 1985, "Modeling Behavior in Competition: The Analytic Hierarchy Process," *Applied Mathematics and Computation* 16, 49-92.

Saaty, T.L. and L.G. Vargas, 1991, *Prediction, Projection and Forecasting*, Kluwer Academic Publishers, Boston.

Saaty, T.L. and L.G. Vargas, 1998, "Diagnosis with Dependent Symptoms: Bayes Theorem and the Analytic Hierarchy Process," *Operations Research* 46, No. 4, July-August 1998, 491-502.

Saaty, T.L. and M. Wong, 1983, "The Average Family Size in Rural India," *Journal of Mathematical Sociology* 9, 181-209.

Saaty, T.L., P.C. Rogers, and R. Pell, 1980, "Portfolio Selection Through Hierarchies," *Journal of Portfolio Management* 3, 16-21.

Skates S.J., Xu F.J., Yu Y.H., Sjovall K., Einhorn N., Chang Y.C, Bast , R.C., and R.C. Knapp, 1995, "Toward An Optimal Algorithm For Ovarian-Cancer Screening With Longitudinal Tumor-Markers," *Cancer* 76, 10, 2004-2010.

Chapter 7

The Allocation of Intangible Resources: The Analytic Hierarchy Process and Linear Programming

7-1. INTRODUCTION

An intangible is an attribute that has no scale of measurement. Intangibles such as effort and skill arise in conjunction with resource allocation but are not usually included directly in a mathematical allocation model because of the absence of a unit of measurement to attach numbers to them. But there is a nontrivial way to quantify intangibles through relative measurement and derive priorities for them. It then becomes possible to combine these priorities with normalized measures of tangibles to allocate resources. To perform such allocation, a linear programming model is transformed to an equivalent model with coefficients and variables measured in relative terms. The priorities derived include among them relative values of the tangible resources as given on measurement scales. The optimum solution gives the relative amount of each resource. The presence of tangible resources makes it possible to estimate the cost or value of the intangibles for that particular problem in proportion to their priorities. A detailed example is given to illustrate the ideas. (This chapter is a selection from a paper co-authored with my colleagues Klaus Dellmann and Luis Vargas.)

Intangible resources such as quality, care, attention, and intelligence are often needed to develop a plan, design a system or solve a problem. So far, resource allocation models have not dealt with intangibles directly, but only by assigning them worth usually measured in time and money. Our goal here is to show that although there is no scale of measurement for an intangible, it can be measured in relative terms side by side with tangibles and thus a ratio scale of priorities is derived for them. These priorities serve as coefficients in an optimization framework to derive relative amounts of resources to be allocated. For the intangible resources, because there is no unit of measurement, no absolute amount of a resource can be specified, but in the presence of tangibles, it becomes possible to compute their absolute equivalents because of the proportionality inherent in their priorities.

Our concern with the measurement of intangibles relates to the value of assets owned by corporations. While one may argue that the market value of a company including its intangible resources is concretely calculated from its tangible assets, intangibles become particularly significant when, for example, two companies merge, and synergy gives rise to new intangibles with potential positive and negative impact on the value of the combined company. Measuring such intangibles could help assess the wisdom of a merger. An example given later on illustrates this point.

7-2. ON THE MEASUREMENT OF INTANGIBLES

Webster's unabridged dictionary defines a tangible as something "conceived or thought of as definable or measurable," and an intangible as something "incapable of being defined or determined with certainty or precision." Thus measurement is central in transforming an intangible to become a tangible. A scale of measurement requires a unit. A unit is the single most important building block on which a scale is founded A measurement on a scale involves the numerical assignment of multiples and fractions of the unit of that scale. A scale is a set of objects, a numerical space and a mapping from the objects to the numbers invariant under some transformation. To construct the mapping *consistently* so that for example objects having more of the attribute being measured are assigned larger values, one must compare that measurement with all other measurements on *that scale that have been experienced. Thus it appears that comparison and* experience are an integral part of measurement.

To measure intangibles we need comparisons made by someone – an expert – who has experienced different amounts of the quality that characterizes the intangible. Because there is no scale, these comparisons must be made in relative terms. To see how this can be done and that its results are credible and valid, we first illustrate the approach with a tangible attribute, the area of several geometric figures. Figure 7-1 gives five geometric figures that we wish to compare according to area.

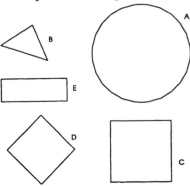

Figure 7-1. Five Geometric Figures

To compare two figures according to the relative sizes of their corresponding areas, one determines which of the two is the smaller, and then estimates how many multiples of it is the larger area. The result of these comparisons is arranged in a matrix $A = \{a_{ij}\}$. If the area of figure i is a_{ij} times larger than the area of figure j, then the area of figure j is $a_{ji} = 1/a_{ij}$ times larger than the area of figure i, a reciprocal relationship. The matrix for these comparisons, the derived scale of relative values (priorities), and the relative values obtained from actual measurement are shown in Table 7-1. Later we show how the priorities are derived from the comparisons. Each area represented on the left of the matrix is compared with each area at the top of the matrix to determine how many times it is larger or smaller than that area.

Table 7-1. Relative Areas of Five Geometric Figures

	A	B	C	D	E	Estimated Relative Areas	Actual Relative Areas
FIVE FIGURES							
A	1	9	2.5	3.5	5	0.490	0.471
B	1/9	1	1/5	1/2.5	1/2	0.050	0.050
C	1/2.5	5	1	2	2.5	0.235	0.234
D	1/3.5	2.5	1/2	1	1.5	0.131	0149
E	1/5	2	1/2.5	1/1.5	1	0.094	0.096

A more abstract form of comparisons would involve elements with tangible properties that one must think about but cannot be perceived through the senses. Here is another example. See the pairwise comparison judgment matrix below in Table 7-2 for estimating the relative amount of protein in seven food items compared in pairs.

Table 7-2. Relative Amount of Protein in Seven Foods

Which Food has more Protein?

Protein in Food	A	B	C	D	E	F	G
A: Steak	1	9	9	6	4	5	1
B: Potatoes		1	1	1/2	1/4	1/3	1/4
C: Apples			1	1/3	1/3	1/5	1/9
D: Soybean				1	1/2	1	1/6
E: Whole Wheat Bread					1	3	1/3
F: Tasty Cake						1	1/5
G: Fish							1

The values are:

	Steak	Potatoes	Apples	Soybean	W. Bread	T. Cake	Fish
Derived	.345	.031	.030	.065	.124	.078	.328
Actual	.370	.040	.000	.070	.110	.090	.320

with a consistency ratio of .028.

Both examples show that an experienced person can provide informed numerical judgments from which relatively good estimates are derived. Before we proceed to deal with intangibles we give a sketch of the theoretical concepts underlying the way scales are derived from paired comparisons.

We use this approach to deal with the measurement and optimal allocation of intangible resources as shown in the example given in Section 7-4. Because our allocation model in this case involves linear programming (LP) we first transform the LP model from its traditional setting with real number coefficients taken from ratio measurement scales to one in which the coefficients are relative in the sense of the estimates given in the examples above.

7-3. ON ESTIMATING LP COEFFICIENTS

A linear programming (LP) model can be represented with relative measurement and hence, when measurement scales exist, the relative linear programming (RLP) model with measurements prescribed in relative terms, and the absolute linear programming (LP) model (the usual model with measurements on physical scales which Roberts [1] showed must belong to ratio scales) are the same to within a multiplicative constant. It is then possible to construct LP models using solely relative measurement to optimize the allocation of intangible resources.

Traditional LP $\Leftrightarrow$ Relative LP

Decision Variables: $\overline{x} = (\overline{x}_1, \cdots, \overline{x}_n)^T$ $\overline{w} = (w_1, \cdots, w_n)^T$

Objective Function: $\sum_j c_j x_j \;\rightarrow\; {}_R c_j = \dfrac{c_j}{\sum_k |c_k|} \;\rightarrow\; \sum_j {}_R c_j w_j$

Constraints: $\displaystyle\sum_j a_{ij}x_j \le b_i \;\rightarrow\; \left\{\begin{array}{l} {}_R a_{ij} = \dfrac{a_{ij}}{\displaystyle\sum_k |a_{ik}|} \\[6mm] {}_R b_i = \dfrac{\dfrac{b_i}{\sum_k |a_{ik}|}}{\displaystyle\sum_h \dfrac{|b_h|}{\sum_k |a_{hk}|}} \\[8mm] w_j = \dfrac{x_j}{\displaystyle\sum_h \dfrac{|b_h|}{\sum_k |a_{hk}|}} \end{array}\right\} \;\rightarrow\; \sum_j {}_R a_{ij} w_j \le {}_R b_i$

Primal:
$$Max \sum_j c_j x_j$$
$$s.t.: \sum_j a_{ij} x_j \le b_i$$
$$x_j \ge 0$$

$\Leftrightarrow$

$$Max \sum_j {}_R c_j w_j$$
$$s.t.: \sum_j {}_R a_{ij} w_j \le {}_R b_i$$
$$w_j \ge 0$$

(note that *s.t.* stands for *subject to*)

Dual:
$$Min \sum_i b_i y_i$$
$$s.t.: \sum_i a_{ij} y_i \ge c_j$$
$$y_i \ge 0$$

$\Leftrightarrow$

$$Min \sum_i {}_R b_i v_i$$
$$s.t.: \sum_i {}_R a_{ij} v_i \ge {}_R c_j$$
$$v_j \ge 0$$

It is significant to note that all the coefficients in the relative formulation are unit free, although their relative magnitudes are preserved. Thus the underlying magnitudes they represent can be compared in pairs.

There are three places where intangibles can arise in an LP problem. The most common is in the objective function in which the coefficients can be estimated as priorities, and the rest of the problem is formulated in the usual way. This problem presents no practical complications because the solution is the same if the objective function coefficients are given in relative terms tantamount to dividing by a constant (see [4]).

If the problem already has tangible constraints, it is transformed into an RLP model. A new intangible constraint can be added by first deriving the coefficients, $_Ra_{ij}, j = 1,...,n$ through paired comparisons, according to the relative use of that resource by the activities represented with the decision variables. Then one determines $_Rb_i, i = 1,...,n$ by making paired comparisons as to the availability (or need) of the resources. If the problem has no tangible constraints, we simply compare the availability (or need) of the intangible resources involved to determine the $_Rb_i$.

Incorporating a decision variable corresponding to an activity or resource for which there is no scale requires two steps: prioritizing the contribution of the variable to the objective and prioritizing the contribution of the activity or resource in the constraints. Intangibles in the decision variables are more difficult to treat because implementing a decision prescribed by the LP solution requires a unit. When tangibles are included, the unit may be applied through the priorities of the variables to the intangibles. Without a unit, we cannot interpret the absolute meaning of each component of the solution as we only have their relative values in the form of priorities.

7-4. EXAMPLE

Two companies, A and B, entertain the possibility of merging because their management believes that their integration would create positive synergistic effects giving them increased competitive advantage in:

- Markets: with positive impacts on image as a function of brand and quality.

- Innovation, and

- Cost Reduction: as a consequence of the integration of human resources from technical and managerial areas.

The areas in which management can concentrate its efforts, i.e., Markets, Innovation and Cost Reduction, use resources such as brand image (BIM), product quality (PQ), technical human resources (THR) and managerial human resources (MHR). When the merger takes place, each company would contribute differently to Markets, Innovation and Cost Reduction.

The companies have budgets allocated to technical (THR) and managerial (MHR) resources as shown in Table 7-3. The areas considered here, Markets, Innovation and Cost Reduction, use these resources at rates also given in Table 7-3. For example, Firm A uses 10, 70 and 20 percent, of the budget allocated to THR per unit effort allocated to Markets, Innovation and Cost Reduction, respectively. Similarly, Firm B uses 10, 80 and 20 percent of THR for every unit of effort allocated to Markets, Innovation and Cost Reduction, respectively.

Table 7-3. Budgets & Use of Resources Per Unit of Effort Allocated

	Markets	Innovation	Cost Reduction	THR($M)
FIRM A	0.1	0.7	0.2	182
FIRM B	0.1	0.8	0.1	455
				MHR($M)
FIRM A	0.3	0.1	0.6	435
FIRM B	0.4	0	0.6	155

Let w_{ij} be the amount of effort in area j (i.e., Markets, Innovation or Cost Reduction) contributed by company i. Let s_{ij} be the relative contribution of area j to the total worth of company i. We would like to determine w_{ij}, how much each company should contribute in each area so that the total worth of the company is maximized, i.e., $Z = Max \sum_{i,j} s_{ij} w_{ij}$.

To estimate the coefficients s_{ij}, we ask the question: Which area contributes more to the total worth of the company? The pairwise comparisons and the corresponding priorities are given in Table 7-4.

Table 7-4. Relative Contribution of Areas to the Total Worth of the Company

$$
\begin{array}{c}
\textit{FirmA} \\
\textit{Markets} \\
\textit{Innovation} \\
\textit{Costs}
\end{array}
\begin{array}{ccc}
MKTS & I & C \\
\begin{bmatrix} 1 & 2 & 2 \\ 1/2 & 1 & 1/2 \\ 1/2 & 2 & 1 \end{bmatrix}
\end{array} \Rightarrow
\begin{array}{c}
\text{Priorities} \\
\begin{bmatrix} 0.49 \\ 0.20 \\ 0.31 \end{bmatrix}
\end{array}
$$

$$
\begin{array}{c}
\textit{FirmB} \\
\textit{Markets} \\
\textit{Innovation} \\
\textit{Costs}
\end{array}
\begin{array}{ccc}
MKTS & I & C \\
\begin{bmatrix} 1 & 1 & 2 \\ 1 & 1 & 2 \\ 1/2 & 1/2 & 1 \end{bmatrix}
\end{array} \Rightarrow
\begin{array}{c}
\text{Priorities} \\
\begin{bmatrix} 0.40 \\ 0.40 \\ 0.20 \end{bmatrix}
\end{array}
$$

The companies then allocate effort expressed in monetary units according to the solution of the following LP models:

FIRM A	FIRM B
$Max \quad 0.49w_{11} + 0.20w_{12} + 0.31w_{13}$ s.t. $0.10w_{11} + 0.70w_{12} + 0.20w_{13} \leq 182$ $0.30w_{11} + 0.10w_{12} + 0.60w_{13} \leq 435$ $\qquad\qquad\qquad\qquad w_{ij} \geq 0;$	$Max \quad 0.40w_{21} + 0.40w_{22} + 0.20w_{23}$ s.t. $0.10w_{21} + 0.80w_{22} + 0.10w_{23} \leq 455$ $\qquad 0.40w_{21} + 0.60w_{23} \leq 155$ $\qquad\qquad\qquad\qquad w_{ij} \geq 0;$

The constraints are specified in Table 7-3. The solutions of these models are given by:

FIRM A

$$w_{11} = 1431.5$$
$$w_{12} = 55.5$$
$$w_{13} = 0$$
$$Z_A = 711.98$$

FIRM B

$$w_{21} = 387.5$$
$$w_{22} = 520.3125$$
$$w_{23} = 0$$
$$Z_B = 363.125$$

If the companies merge, the resources merge and the efforts are now allocated by using the solution of the following LP model:

Max: $0.49w_{11} + 0.20w_{12} + 0.31w_{13} + 0.40w_{21} + 0.40w_{22} + 0.20w_{23}$

s.t.:

$$0.10w_{11} + 0.70w_{12} + 0.20w_{13} + 0.10w_{21} + 0.80w_{22} + 0.10w_{23} \leq 637$$
$$0.30w_{11} + 0.10w_{12} + 0.60w_{13} + 0.40w_{21} + 0.60w_{23} \leq 590$$
$$w_{ij} \geq 0.$$

given by:

$$w_{11} = 1966.667$$
$$w_{12} = w_{13} = w_{21} = w_{23} = 0$$
$$w_{22} = 550.4167$$
$$Z_{A+B} = 1183.833$$

Note that the merger produces an objective function value that is greater than the sum of the individual objective functions:

$Z_A + Z_B = 711.98 + 363.125 = 1075.105$

vs.

$Z_A = 1183.833$

or an increase of 10.11 percent.

Assume now that we wish to allocate resources by considering two new resources, Brand Image and Product Quality. Because these resources are qualitative, we first prioritize the relative use of resources. Let R a_{ijk} be the relative amount of resource k used if a unit of effort is allocated to the jth area by the ith company. The question we need to ask here to estimate the relative amount of a resource k used is: Given a company and a resource, for example, Brand Image (BIM) and two areas (e.g., Markets and Innovation) which one uses that resource more and how much more?

$$
\begin{array}{c}
\begin{array}{cccc} BIM & MKTS & I & C \end{array} \\
\begin{array}{c} Markets \\ Innovation \\ Costs \end{array}
\begin{bmatrix} 1 & 8 & 2 \\ 1/8 & 1 & 2 \\ 1/2 & 1/2 & 1 \end{bmatrix}
\Rightarrow
\begin{bmatrix} 0.666 \\ 0.167 \\ 0.167 \end{bmatrix}
\end{array}
\qquad (Firm \quad A)
$$

$$
\begin{array}{c}
\begin{array}{cccc} BIM & MKTS & I & C \end{array} \\
\begin{array}{c} Markets \\ Innovation \\ Costs \end{array}
\begin{bmatrix} 1 & 1 & 9 \\ 1 & 1 & 1/3 \\ 1/9 & 3 & 1 \end{bmatrix}
\Rightarrow
\begin{bmatrix} 0.60 \\ 0.20 \\ 0.20 \end{bmatrix}
\end{array}
\qquad (Firm \quad B)
$$

The relative amounts for all the resources are given in Table 7-5.

Table 7-5. Matrix $_R A$ of Relative Use of Resources to Attain Objectives

	Firm A			Firm B		
	Markets	Innovation	Cost Red.	Markets	Innovation	Cost Red.
BIM	0.667	0.167	0.166	0.6	0.2	0.2
PQ	0.7	0.2	0.1	0.6	0.3	0.1
THR	0.1	0.7	0.2	0.1	0.8	0.1
MHR	0.3	0.1	0.6	0.4	0.0	0.6

Finally, we prioritize the relative importance of the resources. Let $_Rb_{ik}$ be the relative amount of resource k available to company i. The question asked here is: Given a company and two resources (e.g., Brand Image and Product quality), which one is more abundant for that company, or is more important, and by how much? The following matrices of paired comparisons yield the priorities given in Table 7-6:

FIRM A   FIRM B

	BIM	PQ	THR	MHR
BIM	1	3	2	1/2
PQ	1/3	1	1/2	1/4
THR	1/2	2	1	1/2
MHR	2	4	2	1

	BIM	PQ	THR	MHR
BIM	1	1/2	1/3	1
PQ	2	1	1/2	2
THR	3	2	1	3
MHR	1	1/2	1/3	1

The priorities of the resources for each company and for the newly formed one are given in Table 7-6.

Table 7-6. RHS Coefficients $_R\overline{b}$. Relative Importance of the Resources

FIRM A	BIM	PQ	THR	MHR
BIM	1	3	2	1/2
PQ	1/3	1	1/2	0.25
THR	1/2	2	1	1/2
MHR	2	4	2	1

FIRM B	BIM	PQ	THR	MHR
BIM	1	1/2	1/3	1
PQ	2	1	1/2	2
THR	3	2	1	3
MHR	1	1/2	1/3	1

RESOURCES	Firm A	Firm B	Firms A+B
Brand image (BIM)	0.286	0.141	0.2135
Product Quality (PQ)	0.097	0.263	0.18
Technical Human Resources (THR)	0.186	0.455	0.3185
Managerial Human Resources (MHR)	0.431	0.141	0.288

Thus, the LP model for company A is given by:

$$Max \quad 0.49w_{11} + 0.20w_{12} + 0.31w_{13}$$

s.t.:

$$0.80w_{11} + 0.10w_{12} + 0.10w_{13} \le 0.286$$
$$0.70w_{11} + 0.20w_{12} + 0.10w_{13} \le 0.097$$
$$0.10w_{11} + 0.70w_{12} + 0.20w_{13} \le 0.182$$
$$0.30w_{11} + 0.10w_{12} + 0.60w_{13} \le 0.435$$
$$w_{ij} \ge 0;$$

and for company B is given by:

$$Max \quad 0.40w_{21} + 0.40w_{22} + 0.20w_{23}$$

s.t.:

$$0.60w_{21} + 0.20w_{22} + 0.20w_{23} \leq 0.141$$
$$0.60w_{21} + 0.30w_{22} + 0.10w_{23} \leq 0.263$$
$$0.10w_{21} + 0.80w_{22} + 0.10w_{23} \leq 0.455$$
$$0.40w_{21} + 0.60w_{23} \leq 0.155$$
$$w_{ij} \geq 0;$$

and for the combined company is given by:

$$Max: \quad 0.49w_{11} + 0.20w_{12} + 0.31w_{13} + 0.40w_{21} + 0.40w_{22} + 0.20w_{23}$$
s.t.:

$$0.3335w_{11} + 0.0835w_{12} + 0.083w_{13} + 0.30w_{21} + 0.10w_{22} + 0.10w_{23} \leq 0.2135$$
$$0.35w_{11} + 0.10w_{12} + 0.05w_{13} + 0.30w_{21} + 0.15w_{22} + 0.05w_{23} \leq 0.18$$
$$0.05w_{11} + 0.35w_{12} + 0.10w_{13} + 0.05w_{21} + 0.40w_{22} + 0.05w_{23} \leq 0.3185$$
$$0.15w_{11} + 0.05w_{12} + 0.30w_{13} + 0.20w_{21} + 0.30w_{23} \leq 0.288$$
$$w_{ij} \geq 0.$$

The solutions of these three LP models are given in Table 7-7 below. It is worth pointing out that with the merger, the objective function increased from $0.24686 + 0.25086 = 0.49772$ to 0.57901 or 16.33 percent. The efforts are now shared by the two firms, with Firm A contributing to Markets and Cost Reduction and Firm B contributing to Innovation. In relative terms, Firm A will allocate

$$\frac{0.149423}{0.149423 + 0.885288} = 14.44\% \quad \text{of its efforts to Markets and}$$

$$\frac{0.885288}{0.149423 + 0.885288} = 85.56\%$$

to Cost Reduction, and Firm B will dedicate all its efforts to Innovation; and the resulting company should allocate, in relative terms: 9.4% to Markets, 34.96% to Innovation, and 55.64% to Cost Reduction.

Table 7-7. Solutions of the LP Models

FIRM A

0.667	0.167	0.166
0.7	0.2	0.1
0.1	0.7	0.2
0.3	0.1	0.6

0.140953461	0.286
0.097	0.097
0.182	0.182
0.435	0.435

0.49	0.19	0.32

0.246857692

Solution: 0.022038   0.0555   0.704731

FIRM B

0.6	0.2	0.2
0.6	0.3	0.1
0.1	0.8	0.1
0.4	0	0.6

0.141	0.141
0.180357	0.263
0.455	0.455
0.093429	0.141

0.4	0.4	0.2

0.250857

Solution: 0   0.549286   0.155714

FIRMS A+B   RHS

0.3335	0.0835	0.083	0.3	0.1	0.1
0.35	0.1	0.05	0.3	0.15	0.05
0.05	0.35	0.1	0.05	0.4	0.05
0.15	0.05	0.3	0.2	0	0.3

0.178937	0.2135
0.18	0.18
0.3185	0.3185
0.288	0.288

OBJCOEF

0.49	0.19	0.32	0.4	0.4	0.2

Z=| 0.57901 |

Solution: 0.149423   0   0.885288   0   0.55625   0

Alternatively, it is possible to translate these priorities into monetary values if there are some resources that are tangible and measured on a monetary scale. One must be careful and not assume that this translation can be done for all priorities in all circumstances. First, we convert the priorities of the intangible resources into monetary units by using one of the priorities of the tangible resources as the unit. For example, the priority of the tangible resource THR (0.3185) corresponds to the value $\dfrac{b_3}{\sum_j a_{3j}} = \dfrac{637}{1} = 637$.

Hence, the monetary equivalent of the priority of the intangible resource Brand Image is given by: (0.2135/0.3185)*637 = 427, and similarly, for Product Quality we have (0.180/0.3185)*637 = 360. Had we used the tangible resource MHR, the monetary equivalents would have been 437 and 369, respectively. This happens when more than one tangible resource is involved in the prioritization of the intangible resources. To preserve the proportionality among the tangible resources one could have included for comparison just one of the tangible resources with the intangibles, and then adjusted the priorities of the remaining tangible resources accordingly. Alternatively, we could average over the monetary equivalents obtaining 432 and 364, respectively. Finally, the solution can be expressed in monetary values by applying the transformation $x_{ij} = w_{ij} \sum_i \dfrac{b_i}{\sum_{j,k} a_{ijk}}$. We have:

$$x_{11} = 0.149423(432 + 364 + 637 + 590) \approx 302$$

$$x_{13} = 0.885288(432 + 364 + 637 + 590) \approx 1{,}791$$

$$x_{22} = 0.55625(432 + 364 + 637 + 590) \approx 1{,}125.$$

$$x_{12} = x_{21} = x_{23} = 0$$

It is now possible to express the variables in terms of dollars and interpret this solution in terms of budgetary amounts allocated to different areas to fulfill a mission.

7-5. CONCLUSION

Priorities are ratio scale utilities. By deriving priorities on a ratio scale, it is possible to include intangibles with tangibles in the effort to optimize the allocation of scarce resources. In another example we have considered only intangibles, but the solution of the RLP formulation must be normalized to unity to give one a meaningful estimate of the relative magnitude of the resources to be allocated. We then transformed these relative magnitudes into a tangible resource through cross modality matching.

References

1. Roberts, F.S. (1991): "Limitations on Conclusions Using Scales of Measurement, " *RUTCOR Research Report* #48-91, Rutgers University, New Brunswick, NJ 08903-5062, 1991.

2. Saaty, T.L., "A Scaling Method for Priorities in Hierarchical Structures," *Journal of Mathematical Psychology* 15, 3 (1977) 234-281.

3. Saaty, T.L., "Axiomatic Foundations of the Analytic Hierarchy Process," *Management Science* 21, 1986.

4. Saaty, T.L. and K. Peniwati, "The Analytic Hierarchy Process and Linear Programming in Human Resource Allocation," *Proceedings of the Fourth International Symposium on the Analytic Hierarchy Process*, Simon Fraser University, Burnaby, B.C., Canada, July 12-15, 1996, pp. 492-504.

5. Saaty, T.L., "Seven Pillars of the Analytic Hierarchy Process," in *Proceedings of the 5th International Symposium on the AHP*, Kobe, Japan, August 12-14, 1999.

6. Saaty, T.L., *Fundamental of Decision Making and Priority Theory*, RWS Publications, Pittsburgh, PA, 2000.

Chapter 8

Summary of the Analytic Hierarchy Process

8-1. INTRODUCTION

The Analytic Hierarchy Process (AHP) provides the objective mathematics to process the inescapably subjective and personal preferences of an individual or a group in making a decision. With the AHP and its generalization, the Analytic Network Process (ANP), one constructs hierarchies or feedback networks, then makes judgments or performs measurements on pairs of elements with respect to a controlling element to derive ratio scales that are then synthesized throughout the structure to select the best alternative.

Fundamentally, the AHP works by developing priorities for alternatives and the criteria used to judge the alternatives. Usually the criteria, whose choice is at the mercy of the understanding of the decision-maker (irrelevant criteria are those that are not included in the hierarchy), are measured on different scales, such as weight and length, or are even intangible for which no scales yet exist. Measurements on different scales, of course, cannot be directly combined. First, priorities are derived for the criteria in terms of their importance to achieve the goal, then priorities are derived for the performance of the alternatives on each criterion. These priorities are derived based on pairwise assessments using judgment, or ratios of measurements from a scale if one exists. The process of prioritization solves the problem of having to deal with different types of scales, by interpreting their significance to the values of the user or users. Finally, a weighting and adding process is used to obtain overall priorities for the alternatives as to how they contribute to the goal. This weighting and adding parallels what one would have done arithmetically prior to the

AHP to combine alternatives measured under several criteria having the *same* scale (a scale that is often common to several criteria is money) to obtain an overall result. With the AHP a multidimensional scaling problem is thus transformed to a uni-dimensional scaling problem.

The seven principles of the AHP are:

1) **Ratio scales, proportionality, and normalized ratio scales** are central to the generation and synthesis of priorities, whether in the AHP or in any multicriteria method that needs to integrate existing ratio scale measurements with its own derived scales; in addition, ratio scales are the only way to generalize a decision theory to the case of dependence and feedback because ratio scales can be both multiplied, and added when they belong to the same scale such as a priority scale; when two judges arrive at two different ratio scales for the same problem one needs to test the compatibility of their answers and accept or reject their closeness. The AHP has a non-statistical index for doing this. Ratio scales can also be used to make decisions within an even more general framework involving several hierarchies for benefits, costs, opportunities and risks, and using a common criterion such as *economic* to ensure commensurability; ratio scales are essential in proportionate resource allocation as in linear programming, recently generalized to deal with relative measurement for both the objective function and the constraints obtaining a ratio scale solution vector from which it is possible to decide on the relative values of the allocated resources; one can associate with each alternative a vector of benefits, costs, time of completion, etc., to determine the best alternative subject to all these general concerns;

2) **Reciprocal paired comparisons** are used to express judgments semantically automatically linking them to a numerical fundamental scale of absolute numbers (derived from stimulus-response relations) from which the principal eigenvector of priorities is then derived; the eigenvector shows the dominance of each element with respect to the other elements; an element that does not have a particular property is automatically assigned the value zero in the eigenvector without including it in the comparisons; dominance along all possible paths is obtained by raising the matrix to powers and normalizing the sum of

the rows; inconsistency in judgment is allowed and a measure for it is provided which can direct the decision maker in both improving judgment and arriving at a better understanding of the problem; scientific procedures for giving less than the full set of $n(n-1)/2$ judgments in a matrix have been developed; using interval judgments eventually leading to the use of optimization and statistical procedures is a complex process which is often replaced by comparing ranges of values of the criteria, performing sensitivity analysis, and relying on conditions for the insensitivity of the eigenvector to perturbations in the judgments; the judgments may be considered as random variables with probability distributions; the AHP has at least three modes for arriving at a ranking of the alternatives:

a) *Relative*, which *ranks* a few alternatives by comparing them in pairs and is particularly useful in new and exploratory decisions,

b) *Absolute*, which *rates* an unlimited number of alternatives one at a time on intensity scales constructed separately for each covering criterion and is particularly useful in decisions where there is considerable knowledge to judge the relative importance of the intensities and develop priorities for them; if desired, a few of the top rated alternatives can then be compared against each other using the relative mode to obtain further refinement of the priorities;

c) *Benchmarking*, which ranks alternatives by including a known alternative in the group and comparing the other against it;

3) **Sensitivity of the principal right eigenvector** to perturbation in judgments limits the number of elements in each set of comparisons to a few and requires that they be homogeneous; the left eigenvector is only meaningful as reciprocal; due to the choice of a unit as one of the two elements in each paired comparison to determine the relative dominance of the second element, it is not possible to derive the principal left eigenvector directly from paired comparisons as the dominant element cannot be decomposed a priori ; as a result, to ask for how much less one element is than another we must take the

reciprocal of what we get by asking how much more the larger element is;

4) **Homogeneity and clustering** are used to extend the fundamental scale gradually from cluster to adjacent cluster, eventually enlarging the scale from 1-9 to 1-∞;

5) **Synthesis that can be extended to dependence and feedback** is applied to the derived ratio scales to create a uni-dimensional ratio scale for representing the overall outcome. Synthesis of the scales derived in the decision structure can only be made to yield correct outcomes on known scales by additive weighting. It should be carefully noted that additive weighting in a hierarchical structure leads to a multilinear form and hence is nonlinear. It is known that under very general conditions such multilinear forms are dense in general function spaces (discrete or continuous), and thus linear combinations of them can be used to approximate arbitrarily close to any nonlinear element in that space. Multiplicative weighting, by raising the priorities of the alternatives to the power of the priorities of the criteria (which it determines through additive weighting!) then multiplying the results, has four major flaws: a) It does not give back weights of existing same ratio scale measurements on several criteria as it should; b) It assumes that the matrix of judgments is always consistent, thus sacrificing the idea of inconsistency and how to deal with it, and not allowing redundancy of judgments to improve validity about the real world; c) Most critically, it does not generalize to the case of interdependence and feedback, as the AHP generalizes to the Analytic Network Process (ANP), so essential for the many decision problems in which the criteria and alternatives depend on each other; d) It always preserves rank which leads to unreasonable outcomes and contradicts the many counterexamples that show rank reversals should be allowed;

6) **Rank preservation and reversal** can be shown to occur without adding or deleting criteria, such as by simply introducing enough copies of an alternative or for numerous other reasons; this leaves no doubt that rank reversal is as intrinsic to decision making as rank preservation also is; it follows that any decision theory must have at least two modes of synthesis; in the AHP they are called the distributive and ideal modes,

with guidelines for which mode to use; rank can always be preserved by using the ideal mode in both absolute measurement and relative measurement;

7) **Group judgments** must be integrated one at a time carefully and mathematically, taking into consideration when desired the experience, knowledge, and power of each person involved in the decision, without the need to force consensus, or to use majority or other ordinal ways of voting; the theorem regarding the *impossibility* of constructing a social utility function from individual utilities that satisfies four reasonable conditions which found their validity with *ordinal* preferences is *no longer true* when *cardinal* ratio scale preferences are used as in the AHP. Instead, one has the *possibility* of constructing such a function. To deal with a large group requires the use of questionnaires and statistical procedures for large samples.

8-2. RATIO SCALES

A *ratio* is the relative value or quotient a/b of two quantities a and b *of the same kind*; it is called commensurate if it is a rational number, otherwise it is incommensurate. A statement of the equality of two ratios a/b and c/d is called *proportionality*. A ratio scale is a set of numbers that is invariant under a similarity transformation (multiplication by a positive constant). The constant cancels when the ratio of any two numbers is formed. Either pounds or kilograms can be used to measure weight, but the ratio of the weight of two objects is the same for both scales. An extension of this idea is that the weights of an entire set of objects whether in pounds or in kilograms can be standardized to read the same by normalizing. In general if the readings from a ratio scale are aw_i^*, $i=1,...,n$, the standard form is given by $w_i = aw_i^*/aw_i^* = w_i^*/w_i^*$ as a result of which we have $w_i = 1$, and the w_i, $i=1,...,n$, are said to be normalized. We no longer need to specify whether weight for example is given in pounds or in kilograms or in another kind of unit. The weights (2.21, 4.42) in pounds and (1, 2) in kilograms, are both given by (1/3, 2/3) in the standard ratio scale form.

The relative ratio scale derived from a pairwise comparison reciprocal matrix of judgments is derived by solving:

$$\sum_{j=1}^{n} a_{ij}\, w_j = \lambda_{max}\, w_i \tag{1}$$

$$\sum_{i=1}^{n} w_i = 1 \tag{2}$$

with $a_{ji} = 1/a_{ij}$ or $a_{ij}\, a_{ji} = 1$ (the reciprocal property), $a_{ij} > 0$ (thus A is known as a positive matrix) whose solution, known as the principal right eigenvector, is normalized as in (2). A relative ratio scale does not need a unit of measurement.

When $a_{ij}\, a_{jk} = a_{ik}$, the matrix $A = (a_{ij})$ is said to be consistent and its principal eigenvalue is equal to n. Otherwise, it is simply reciprocal. The general eigenvalue formulation given in (1) is obtained by perturbation of the following consistent formulation:

$$Aw = \begin{array}{c} \\ A_1 \\ \vdots \\ A_n \end{array} \begin{array}{cc} A_1 & \cdots & A_n \end{array} \left[\begin{array}{ccc} \dfrac{w_1}{w_1} & \cdots & \dfrac{w_1}{w_n} \\ \vdots & & \vdots \\ \dfrac{w_n}{w_1} & \cdots & \dfrac{w_n}{w_n} \end{array} \right] \left[\begin{array}{c} w_1 \\ \vdots \\ w_n \end{array} \right] = n \left[\begin{array}{c} w_1 \\ \vdots \\ w_n \end{array} \right] = nw$$

where A has been multiplied on the right by the transpose of the vector of weights $w = (w_1,...,w_n)$. The result of this multiplication is nw. Thus, to recover the scale from the matrix of ratios, one must solve the problem $Aw = nw$ or $(A - nI)w = 0$. This is a system of homogeneous linear equations. It has a nontrivial solution if and only if the determinant of $A-nI$ vanishes, that is, n is an eigenvalue of A. Now A has unit rank since every row is a constant multiple of the first row. Thus all its eigenvalues except one are zero. The sum of the eigenvalues of a matrix is equal to its trace, that is, the sum of its diagonal elements. In this case the trace of A is equal to n. Thus n is an eigenvalue of A, and one has a nontrivial solution. The solution consists of positive entries and is unique to within a multiplicative constant.

The discrete formulation given in (1) and (2) above generalizes to the continuous case through Fredholm's integral equation of the second kind and is given by:

$$\int_a^b K(s,t)\, w(t)\, dt \;=\; \lambda_{\max}\, w(s) \tag{3}$$

$$\lambda \int_a^b K(s,t) w(t) dt \;=\; w(s) \tag{4}$$

$$\int_a^b w(s) ds \;=\; 1 \tag{5}$$

where instead of the matrix A we have as a positive kernel, $K(s,t) > 0$. Note that the entries in a matrix depend on the two variables i and j which assume discrete values. Thus the matrix itself depends on these discrete variables, and its generalization, the kernel function also depends on two (continuous) variables. The reason for calling it kernel is the role it plays in the integral, where without knowing it we cannot determine the exact form of the solution. The standard way in which (3) is written is to move the eigenvalue to the left hand side which gives it the reciprocal form. In general, by abuse of notation, one continues to use the symbol λ to represent the reciprocal value. Our equation for response to a stimulus is now written in the standard form (4) with the normalization condition (5). Here also, we have the reciprocal property (6) and as in the finite case, the kernel $K(s,t)$ is consistent if it satisfies the relation (7):

$$K(s,t)\, K(t,s) = 1 \qquad\qquad (6)$$

$$K(s,t)\, K(t,u) = K(s,u), \text{ for all } s,\, t,\, \text{and } u \qquad\qquad (7)$$

An example of this type of kernel is $K(s,t) = e^{s-t} = e^s / e^t$. It follows by putting $s = t = u$, that $K(s,s) = 1$ for all s which is analogous to having ones down the diagonal of the matrix in the discrete case. A value of λ for which Fredholm's equation has a nonzero solution $w(t)$ is called a characteristic value (or its reciprocal is called an eigenvalue) and the corresponding solution is called an eigenfunction. An eigenfunction is determined to within a multiplicative constant. If $w(t)$ is an eigenfunction corresponding to the characteristic value λ and if C is an arbitrary constant, we can easily see by substituting in the equation that $Cw(t)$ is also an eigenfunction corresponding to the same λ. The value $\lambda = 0$ is not a characteristic value because we have the corresponding solution $w(t) = 0$ for every value of t, which is the trivial case, excluded in our discussion.

It may be useful to recount a little of the history of how Fredholm's equation came about in the ratio scale formulation of the AHP. My student Hasan Ait-Kaci and I first recognized the connection between Fredholm's equation and the AHP in a paper we wrote in the late 1970's. In the early 1980's, I and my friend and colleague, Professor Luis Vargas, used this formulation in the framework of neural firing and published several papers on the subject. In December of 1996, I had the nagging idea that the ratio scale relation for electrical firing was not reflected in our solution, and that periodicity had to be involved in the solution with which I began. Many researchers on the brain had considered neural firing in the framework of a damped periodic oscillator. It was my friend Janos Aczel, the leading functional equation mathematician in the world, who provided me with a variety of solutions for the functional equation $(w(as) = bw(s))$. I had proved in the theorem given below that this equation characterizes the solution of Fredholm's equation and its solution is an eigenfunction of that equation. My work is an extension of the work I had done earlier with Vargas. The solution has the form of a damped periodic oscillator of period one. It has an additional logarithmic property that corresponds to Fechner's law discussed later in this paper.

A matrix is consistent if and only if it has the form $A = (w_i / w_j)$ which is equivalent to multiplying a column vector that is the transpose of $(w_1, ..., w_n)$ by the row vector $(1/w_1, ..., 1/w_n)$. As we see below, the kernel $K(s,t)$ is separable and can be written as

$$K(s,t) = k_1(s) k_2(t)$$

Theorem 8-1 $K(s,t)$ *is consistent if and only if it is separable of the form:*

$$K(s,t) = k(s)/k(t) \tag{8}$$

Theorem 8-2 *If $K(s,t)$ is consistent, the solution of (4) is given by*

$$w(s) = \frac{k(s)}{\int_s k(s)ds} \tag{9}$$

In the discrete case, the normalized eigenvector was independent of whether all the elements of the pairwise comparison matrix A are multiplied by the same constant a or not, and thus we can replace A by aA and obtain the same eigenvector. Generalizing this result we have:

$$K(as, at) = aK(s,t) = k(as)/k(at) = a\, k(s)/k(t)$$

which means that K is a homogeneous function of order one. In general, when $f(ax_1, ..., ax_n) = a^n f(x_1, ..., x_n)$ holds, f is said to be homogeneous of order n. Because K is a degenerate kernel, we can replace $k(s)$ above by $k(as)$ and obtain $w(as)$. We have now derived from considerations of ratio scales the following condition to be satisfied by a ratio scale:

Theorem 8-3 A necessary and sufficient condition for $w(s)$ to be an eigenfunction solution of Fredholm's equation of the second kind, with a consistent kernel that is homogeneous of order one, is that it satisfy the functional equation

$$w(as) = bw(s)$$

where $b = \alpha a$.

We have for the general damped periodic response function $w(s)$,

$$w(s) = C e^{\log b \frac{\log s}{\log a}} P\left(\frac{\log s}{\log a}\right)$$

where P is periodic of period 1 and $P(0)=1$.

We can write this solution as

$$v(u)=C_1 e^{-\beta u} P(u) \approx C_2 \log s + C_3$$

where $P(u)$ is periodic of period 1, $u=\log s/\log a$ and $\log ab \equiv -\beta$, $\beta>0$. It is interesting to observe the logarithmic function appear as part of the solution and its series expansion approximation. It gives greater confirmation to the Weber-Fechner law developed in the next section.

8-3. PAIRED COMPARISONS AND THE FUNDAMENTAL SCALE

Instead of assigning two numbers w_i and w_j and forming the ratio w_i/w_j we assign a single number drawn from the fundamental 1-9 scale of absolute numbers to represent the ratio $(w_i/w_j)/1$. It is a nearest integer approximation to the ratio w_i/w_j. The derived scale will reveal what the w_i and w_j are. This is a central fact about the relative measurement approach of the AHP and the need for a fundamental scale.

In 1846 Weber found, for example, that people while holding in their hand different weights, could distinguish between a weight of 20 g and a weight of 21 g, but could not if the second weight is only 20.5 g. On the other hand, while they could not distinguish between 40 g and 41 g, they could between 40g and 42g, and so on at higher levels. We need to increase a stimulus s by a minimum amount Δs to reach a point where our senses can first discriminate between s and $s + \Delta s$. Δs is called the just noticeable difference (jnd). The ratio $r = \Delta s/s$ does not depend on s. Weber's law states that change in sensation is noticed when the stimulus is increased by a constant percentage of the stimulus itself. This law holds in ranges where

Δs is small when compared with s, and hence in practice it fails to hold when s is either too small or too large. Aggregating or decomposing stimuli as needed into clusters or hierarchy levels is an effective way for extending the uses of this law.

In 1860 Fechner considered a sequence of just noticeable increasing stimuli. He denotes the first one by s_0. The next just noticeable stimulus is given by

$$s_1 = s_0 + \Delta s_0 = s_0 + \frac{\Delta s_0}{s_0} s_0 = s_0 (1 + r)$$

based on Weber's law.

Similarly

$$s_2 = s_1 + \Delta s_1 = s_1 (1 + r) = s_0 (1 + r)^2 \equiv s_0 \alpha^2 .$$

In general

$$s_n = s_{n-1} \alpha = s_0 \alpha^n \quad (n = 0, 1, 2, ...) .$$

Thus stimuli of noticeable differences follow sequentially in a geometric progression. Fechner noted that the corresponding sensations should follow each other in an arithmetic sequence at the discrete points at which just noticeable differences occur. But the latter are obtained when we solve for n. We have $n = \dfrac{(\log s_n - \log s_0)}{\log \alpha}$ and sensation is a linear function of the logarithm of the stimulus. Thus if M denotes the sensation and s the stimulus, the psychophysical law of Weber-Fechner is given by

$$M = a \log s + b, \quad a \neq 0$$

We assume that the stimuli arise in making pairwise comparisons of relatively comparable activities. We are interested in responses whose numerical values are in the form of ratios. Thus $b = 0$, from which we must have $\log s_0 = 0$ or $s_0 = 1$, which is possible by calibrating a unit stimulus. Here the unit stimulus is s_0. The next noticeable stimulus is $s_1 = s_0 \alpha = \alpha$ which yields the second noticeable response $a \log \alpha$. The third noticeable stimulus is $s_2 = s_0 \alpha^2$ which yields a response of $2a \log \alpha$. Thus we have for the different responses:

$$M_0 = a \log s_0, \ M_1 = a \log \alpha, \ M_2 = 2a \log \alpha, \dots , \ M_n = na \log \alpha.$$

While the noticeable ratio stimulus increases geometrically, the response to that stimulus increases arithmetically. Note that $M_0 = 0$ and there is no response. By dividing each M_i by M_1 we obtain the sequence of absolute numbers 1, 2, 3, ... of the fundamental 1-9 scale. Paired comparisons are made by identifying the less dominant of two elements and using it as the unit of measurement. One then determines, using the scale 1-9 or its verbal equivalent, how many times more the dominant member of the pair is than this unit. In making paired comparisons, we use the nearest integer approximation from the scale, relying on the insensitivity of the eigenvector to small perturbations (discussed below). The reciprocal value is then automatically used for the comparison of the less dominant element with the more dominant one. Despite the foregoing derivation of the scale in the form of integers, someone might think that other scale values would be better, for example using 1.3 in the place of 2. Imagine comparing the magnitude of two people with respect to the magnitude of one person and using 1.3 for how many there are instead of 2.

We note that there may be elements that are closer than 2 on the 1-9 scale, and we need a variant of the foregoing. Among the elements that are close, we select the smallest. Observe the incremental increases between that smallest one and the rest of the elements in the close group. We now consider these increments to be new elements and pairwise compare them on the scale 1-9. If two of the increments are themselves closer than 2 we treat them as identical, assigning a 1 (we could carry this on ad infinitum – but we will not). In the end each component of the eigenvector of comparisons of the increments is added to unity to yield the un-normalized priorities of the close elements for that criterion. Note that only the least of these close elements is used in comparisons with the other elements that can be compared directly using the normal 1-9 scale. Its priority is used to multiply the priorities of these close elements and finally the priorities of all the elements are re-normalized.

How large should the upper value of the scale be? Qualitatively, people have a capacity to divide their response to stimuli into three categories: high, medium and low. They also have the capacity to refine this division by further subdividing each of these intensities of responses into high, medium and low, thus yielding in all nine subdivisions. It turns out, from the requirement of homogeneity developed below, that to maintain stability, our minds work with a few elements at a time. Using a large number of elements in one matrix leads to greater inconsistency.

8-4. SENSITIVITY OF THE PRINCIPAL EIGENVECTOR PLACES A LIMIT ON THE NUMBER OF ELEMENTS AND THEIR HOMOGENEITY

To a first order approximation, perturbation Δw_1 in the principal eigenvector w_1 due to a perturbation ΔA in the matrix A where A is consistent is given by:

$$\Delta w_1 = \sum_{j=2}^{n} (v_j^T \Delta A \, w_1 / (\lambda_1 - \lambda_j) v_j^T w_j) w_j$$

The eigenvector w_1 is insensitive to perturbation in A, if the principal eigenvalue λ_1 is separated from the other eigenvalues λ_j, here assumed to be distinct, and none of the products $v_j^T w_j$ of left and right eigenvectors is small. We should recall that the nonprincipal eigenvectors need not be positive in all components, and they may be complex. One can show that all the $v_j^T w_j$ are of the same order, and that $v_1^T w_1$, the product of the normalized left and right principal eigenvectors is equal to n. If n is relatively small and the elements being compared are homogeneous, none of the components of w_1 is arbitrarily small and correspondingly, none of the components of v_1^T is arbitrarily small. Their product cannot be arbitrarily small, and thus w is insensitive to small perturbations of the consistent matrix A. The conclusion is that n must be small, and one must compare homogeneous elements. Later we discuss placing a limit on the value of n.

8-5. CLUSTERING AND USING PIVOTS TO EXTEND THE SCALE FROM 1-9 TO 1- ∞

In Figure 8-1, an unripe cherry tomato is eventually and indirectly compared with a large watermelon by first comparing it with a small tomato and a lime, the lime is then used again in a second cluster with a grapefruit and a honey dew where we then divide by the weight of the lime and then multiply by its weight in the first cluster, and then use the honey dew again in a third cluster and so on. In the end we have a comparison of the unripe cherry tomato with the large watermelon and would accordingly extended the scale from 1– 9 to 1–721.

Such clustering is essential, and must be done separately for each criterion. We should note that in most decision problems, there may be one or two levels of clusters and conceivably it may go up to three or four adjacent ranges of homogeneous elements (Maslow put them in seven groupings). Very roughly we have in decreasing order of importance: 1) Survival, health, family, friends and basic religious beliefs some people were known to die for; 2) Career, education, productivity and lifestyle; 3) Political and social beliefs and contributions; 4) Beliefs, ideas, and things that are flexible and it does not matter exactly how one advocates or uses them. Nevertheless one needs them, such as learning to eat with a fork or a chopstick or with the fingers as many people do interchangeably. These categories can be generalized to a group, a corporation, or a government. For very important decisions, two categories may need to be considered. Note that the priorities in two adjacent categories would be sufficiently different, one being an order of magnitude smaller than the other, that in the synthesis, the priorities of the elements in the smaller set have little effect on the decision. We do not have space to show how some *undesirable* elements can be compared among themselves and gradually extended to compare them with *desirable* ones as above. Thus one can go from negatives to positives but keep the measurement of the two types positive, by eventually clustering them separately.

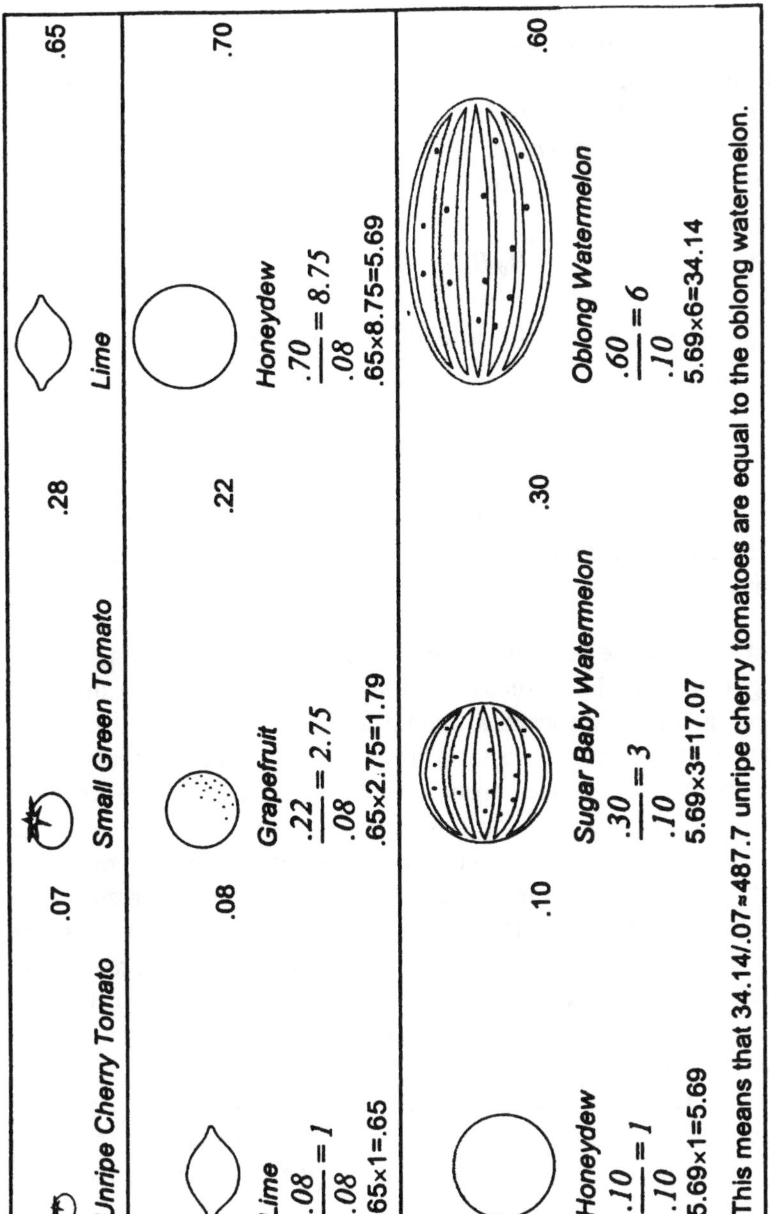

Unripe Cherry Tomato	Small Green Tomato	Lime
.07	.28	.65

	Grapefruit	Honeydew
.08	.22	.70
Lime	$\dfrac{.22}{.08} = 2.75$	$\dfrac{.70}{.08} = 8.75$
$\dfrac{.08}{.08} = 1$	$.65 \times 2.75 = 1.79$	$.65 \times 8.75 = 5.69$
$.65 \times 1 = .65$		

	Sugar Baby Watermelon	Oblong Watermelon
.10	.30	.60
Honeydew	$\dfrac{.30}{.10} = 3$	$\dfrac{.60}{.10} = 6$
$\dfrac{.10}{.10} = 1$	$5.69 \times 3 = 17.07$	$5.69 \times 6 = 34.14$
$5.69 \times 1 = 5.69$		

This means that 34.14/.07≈487.7 unripe cherry tomatoes are equal to the oblong watermelon.

Figure 8-1 Comparisons According to Volume

8-6. SYNTHESIS: HOW TO COMBINE TANGIBLES WITH INTANGIBLES – ADDITIVE VS MULTIPLICATIVE

Let H be a complete hierarchy with h levels. Let B_k be the priority matrix of the kth level, $k = 2, ..., h$. If W' is the global priority vector of the pth level with respect to some element z in the (p-1)st level, then the priority vector W of the qth level ($p < q$) with respect to z is given by the multilinear (and thus nonlinear) form,

$$W = B_q B_{q-1} \cdots B_{p+1} W'.$$

The global priority vector of the lowest level with respect to the goal is given by

$$W = B_h B_{h-1} \cdots B_2 W'.$$

In general, $W' = 1$. The sensitivity of the bottom level alternatives with respect to changes in the weights of elements in any level can be studied by means of this multilinear form.

The fact that the additive but not the multiplicative method of composition gives the right outcome has already been shown in the House example in Chapter 5. In addition, we learn a second lesson from that example. The second lesson is that when the criteria have different measurements, their importance cannot be determined from the bottom up through measurement of the alternatives, but from the top down, in terms of the goal. The same process of comparison of the criteria with respect to the goal is applied to all criteria if, despite the presence of a physical scale, they are assumed to be measurable on different scales as they might when actual values are unavailable or when it is thought that such measurement does not reflect the relative importance of the alternatives with respect to the given criterion. Imagine that no physical scale of any kind is known! We might note in passing that the outcome of this process of comparison with respect to higher level criteria yields meaningful (not arbitrary) results as noted by two distinguished proponents of multi-attribute value theory (MAVT) Buede and Maxwell (1995), who wrote about their own experiments in decision making:

These experiments demonstrated that the MAVT and AHP techniques, when provided with the same decision outcome data, very often identify the same alternatives as 'best'. The other techniques are noticeably less consistent with MAVT, the Fuzzy algorithm being the least consistent.

Multiplicative synthesis, as in the third column of numbers above, done by raising each number in the two columns in the previous table to the power of its criterion measured in the relative total dollars under it, multiplying the two outcomes for each alternative and normalizing, *does not* yield the *exact answer* obtained by adding dollars! In addition, A and B should have the same value, but they do not with multiplicative synthesis. The multiplicative "solution" devised for the fallacy of always preserving rank and avoiding inconsistency fails, because it violates the most basic of several requirements mentioned in the introduction to this paper.

Multiplicative and additive syntheses are related analytically through approximation. If we denote by a_i the priority of the ith criterion, i = 1,...,n, and by x_i , the priority of alternative x with respect to the ith criterion, then

$$\prod x_i{}^{a_i} = \exp \log \prod x_i{}^{a_i} = \exp \left(\Sigma \log x_i{}^{a_i}\right) = \exp \left(\Sigma a_i \log x_i\right) \approx 1 + \Sigma a_i \log x_i$$
$$\approx 1 + \Sigma (a_i x_i - a_i) = \Sigma a_i x_i$$

If desired, one can include a remainder term to estimate the error. With regard to additive and multiplicative syntheses being close, one may think that in the end it does not matter which one is used, but it does. Saaty and Hu (1998) have shown that despite such closeness on every matrix of consistent judgments in a decision, the synthesized outcomes by the two methods not only lead to different final priorities (which can cause a faulty allocation of resources) but more significantly to *different rankings* of the alternatives. For all these problems, but more significantly because it does not generalize to dependence and feedback even with consistency guaranteed, and because of the additive nature of matrix multiplication needed to compute feedback in network circuits to extend the AHP to the ANP, I do not recommend ever using multiplicative synthesis. It can lead to an undesirable ranking of the alternatives of a decision.

8-7. RANK PRESERVATION AND REVERSAL

Given the assumption that the alternatives of a decision are completely independent of one another, can and should the introduction (deletion) of new (old) alternatives change the rank of some alternatives without introducing new (deleting old) criteria, so that a less preferred alternative becomes most preferred? Incidentally, how one prioritizes the criteria and subcriteria is even more important than how one does the alternatives which are themselves composites of criteria. Can rank reverse among the criteria themselves if new criteria are introduced? Why should that not be as critical a concern? The answer is simple. In its original form utility theory assumed that criteria could not be weighted and the only important elements in a decision were the alternatives and their utilities under the various criteria. Today utility theorists imitate the AHP by rating, and some even by comparing the criteria, somehow. There was no concern then about what would happen to the ranks of the alternatives should the criteria weights themselves change as there were none. The tendency, even today, is to be unconcerned about the theory of rank preservation and reversal among the criteria themselves.

The house example of Chapter 5 teaches us an important lesson. If we add a fourth house to the collection, the priority weights of the criteria Price and Remodeling Cost would change accordingly. Thus the measurements of the alternatives and their number which we call structural factors, always affect the importance of the criteria. When the criteria are incommensurate and their functional priorities are determined in terms of yet higher level criteria or goals, one must still weight such functional importance of the criteria by the structural effect of the alternatives. What is significant in all this is that the importance of the criteria always depends on the measurements of the alternatives. If we assume that the alternatives are measured on a different scale for each criterion, it becomes obvious that normalization is the instrument that provides the structural effect to update the importance of the criteria in terms of what alternatives there are. Finally, the priorities of the alternatives are weighted by the priorities of the criteria that depend on the measurements of the alternatives. This implies that the overall ranking of any alternative depends on the measurement and number of all the alternatives. To always preserve rank means that the priorities of the criteria should not depend on the measurements of the alternatives but should only derive from their own functional importance with respect to higher goals. This implies that the alternatives should not depend on the measurements of other alternatives. Thus one way to always preserve rank is to rate the alternatives one at a time. In the AHP this is done through absolute measurement with respect to a complete set of intensity ranges with the largest value intensity value equal to one. It is also possible to preserve rank in relative measurement by using an ideal alternative with full value of one for each criterion.

The logic about what can or should happen to rank when the alternatives *depend* on each other has always been that *anything* can happen. Thus, when the criteria functionally depend on the alternatives, which implies that the alternatives, which of course depend on the criteria, would then depend on the alternatives themselves, rank may be allowed to reverse. The Analytic Network Process (ANP) is the generalization of the AHP to deal with ranking alternatives when there is functional dependence and feedback of any kind. Even here, one can have a decision problem with dependence among the criteria, but with no dependence of criteria on alternatives and rank may still need to be preserved. The ANP takes care of functional dependence, but if the criteria do not depend on the alternatives, the latter are kept out of the supermatrix and ranked precisely as they are dealt with in a hierarchy (Saaty, 1996).

Examples of rank reversal abound in practice, and they do not occur because new criteria are introduced. The requirement that rank always be preserved or that it should be preserved with respect to irrelevant alternatives. To every rule or generalization that one may wish to set down about rank, it is possible to find a counterexample that violates that rule. Here is the last and most extreme form of four variants of an attempt to qualify what should happen to rank given by Luce and Raiffa, each of which is followed by a counterexample. They state it but and then reject it. *The addition of new acts to a decision problem under uncertainty never changes old, originally non-optimal acts into optimal ones. The all-or-none feature of the last form may seem a bit too stringent ... a severe criticism is that it yields unreasonable results.* The AHP has a theory and implementation procedures and guidelines for when to preserve rank and when to allow it to reverse. One mode of the AHP allows an irrelevant alternative to cause reversal among the ranks of the original alternatives.

Guidelines for Selecting the Distributive or Ideal Mode

The distributive mode of the AHP produces preference scores by normalizing the performance scores; it takes the performance score received by each alternative and divides it by the sum of performance scores of all alternatives under that criterion. This means that with the Distributive mode the preference for any given alternative would go up if we reduce the performance score of another alternative or remove some alternatives.

The Ideal mode compares each performance score to a fixed benchmark such as the performance of the best alternative under that criterion. This means that with the Ideal mode the preference for any given alternative is independent of the performance of other alternatives, except for the alternative selected as a benchmark. Saaty and Vargas (1993) have shown by using simulation, that there are only minor differences produced by the two synthesis modes. This means that the decision should select one or the other if the results diverge beyond a given set of acceptable data.

The following guidelines were developed by Millet and Saaty (1999) to reflect the core differences in translating performance measures to preference measures of alternatives. *The Distributive (dominance) synthesis mode should be used when the decision maker is concerned with the extent to which each alternative dominates all other alternatives under the criterion. The Ideal (performance) synthesis mode should be used when the decision maker is concerned with how well each alternative performs relative to a fixed benchmark.* In order for dominance to be an issue the decision-maker should regard inferior alternatives as relevant even after the ranking process is completed. This suggests a simple test for the use of the Distributive mode: *if the decision maker indicates that the preference for a top ranked alternative under a given criterion would improve if the performance of any lower ranked alternative was adjusted downward, then one should use the Distributive synthesis mode.* To make this test more actionable we can ask the decision-maker to imagine the amount of money he or she would be willing to pay for the top ranked alternative. If the decision maker would be willing to pay more for a top ranked alternative after learning that the performance of one of the lower-ranked alternatives was adjusted downward, then the Distributive mode should be used.

Consider selecting a car: Two different decision makers may approach the same problem from two different points of views even if the criteria and standards are the same. The one who is interested in "getting a well performing car" should use the Ideal mode. The one who is interested in "getting a car that stands out" among the alternatives purchased by co-workers or neighbors, should use the Distributive mode.

8-8. GROUP DECISION MAKING

Here we consider two issues in group decision making. The first is how to aggregate individual judgments, and the second is how to construct a group choice from individual choices.

How to Aggregate Individual Judgments

Let the function $f(x_1, x_2, ..., x_n)$ for synthesizing the judgments given by n judges, satisfy the:

(i) Separability condition (S): $\quad f(x_1, x_2,...,x_n) = g(x_1)g(x_2)... g(x_n)$
for all $x_1, x_2,...,x_n$ in an interval P of positive numbers, where g is a function mapping P onto a proper interval J and is a continuous, associative and cancellative operation.[(S) means that the influences of the individual judgments can be separated as above.]

(ii) *Unanimity condition* (U): $\quad f(x, x,...,x) = x$ for all x in P. [(U) means that if all individuals give the same judgment x, that judgment should also be the synthesized judgment.]

(iii) *Homogeneity condition* (H): $\quad f(ux_1, ux_2,...,ux_n) = uf(x_1, x_2,...,x_n)$ where $u > 0$ and x_k, ux_k (k=1,2,...,n) are all in P. [For ratio judgments (H) means that if all individuals judge a ratio u times as large as another ratio, then the synthesized judgment should also be u times as large.]

(iv) *Power conditions* (P_p) : $f(x_1^p, x_2^p, ..., x_n^p) = f^p(x_1, x_2, ..., x_n)$. $[(P_2)$ for example means that if the kth individual judges the length of a side of a square to be x_k, the synthesized judgment on the area of that square will be given by the square of the synthesized judgment on the length of its side.]

Special case $(R = P_{-1})$: $f(1/x_1, 1/x_2, ..., 1/x_n) = 1/f(x_1, x_2, ..., x_n)$. $[(R)$ is of particular importance in ratio judgments. It means that the synthesized value of the reciprocal of the individual judgments should be the reciprocal of the synthesized value of the original judgments.]

Aczel and Saaty (see Saaty 1990 and 1994) proved the following theorem:

Theorem 8-4 *The general separable (S) synthesizing functions satisfying the unanimity (U) and homogeneity (H) conditions are the geometric mean and the root-mean-power.* If moreover the reciprocal property (R) is assumed even for a single n-tuple $(x_1, x_2, ..., x_n)$ of the judgments of n individuals, where not all x_k are equal, then only the geometric mean satisfies all the above conditions.

In any rational consensus, those who know more should, accordingly, influence the consensus more strongly than those who are less knowledgeable. Some people are clearly wiser and more sensible in such matters than others, others may be more powerful and their opinions should be given appropriately greater weight. For such unequal importance of voters not all g's in (S) are the same function. In place of (S), the weighted separability property (WS) is now: $f(x_1, x_2, ..., x_n) = g_1(x_1)g_2(x_2)... g_n(x_n)$. [(WS) implies that not all judging individuals have the same weight when the judgments are synthesized and the different influences are reflected in the different functions $(g_1, g_2, ..., g_n)$.]

In this situation, Aczel and Alsina (see Saaty 1994) proved the following theorem:

Theorem 8-5 *The general weighted-separable (WS) synthesizing functions with the unanimity (U) and homogeneity (H) properties are the weighted geometric mean* $f(x_1, x_2, ..., x_n) = x_1^{q_1} x_2^{q_2} ... x_n^{q_n}$ *and the weighted root-*

mean-powers $f(x_1, x_2, ..., x_n) = \sqrt[\gamma]{q_1 x_1^\gamma + q_2 x_2^\gamma ... + q_n x_n^\gamma}$,   *where*

$q_1 + q_2 + ... + q_n = 1$, $q_k > 0$ $(k = 1, 2, ..., n)$, $\gamma > 0$, *but otherwise* $q_1, q_2, ..., q_n, \gamma$ *are arbitrary constants.*

If f also has the reciprocal property (R) and for a single set of entries $(x_1, x_2, ..., x_n)$ of judgments of n individuals, where not all x_k are equal, then *only the weighted geometric mean* applies. We give the following theorem which is an explicit statement of the synthesis problem that follows from the previous results, and applies to the second and third cases of the deterministic approach:

Theorem 8-6 *If* $x_1^{(i)}, ..., x_n^{(i)}$ $i = 1, ..., m$ *are rankings of n alternatives by m independent judges and if* a_i *is the importance of judge i developed from a hierarchy for evaluating the judges, and hence* $\sum_{i=1}^{m} a_i = 1$, *then*

$$\left(\prod_{i=1}^{m} x_1^{a_i} \right), ..., \left(\prod_{i=1}^{m} x_n^{a_i} \right)$$ *are the combined ranks of the alternatives for the m judges.*

The power or priority of judge i is simply a replication of the judgment of that judge (as if there are as many other judges as indicated by his/her power a_i), which implies multiplying his/her ratio by itself a_i times, and the result follows.

The first requires knowledge of the functions which the particular alternative performs and how well it compares with a standard or benchmark. The second requires comparison with the other alternatives to determine its importance.

On the Construction of Group Choice from Individual Choices

Given a group of individuals, a set of alternatives (with cardinality greater than 2), and individual ordinal preferences for the alternatives, Arrow proved with his Impossibility Theorem that it is impossible to derive a rational group choice (construct a social choice function that aggregates individual preferences) from ordinal preferences of the individuals that satisfy the following four conditions, i.e., at least one of them is violated:

Decisiveness: the aggregation procedure must generally produce a group order.

Unanimity: if all individuals prefer alternative A to alternative B, then the aggregation procedure must produce a group order indicating that the group prefers A to B.

Independence of irrelevant alternatives: given two sets of alternatives which both include A and B, if all individuals prefer A to B in both sets, then the aggregation procedure must produce a group order indicating that the group, given any of the two sets of alternatives, prefers A to B.

No dictator: no single individual preferences determine the group order.

Using the ratio scale approach of the AHP, it can be shown that because now the individual preferences are cardinal rather than ordinal, it is possible to derive a rational group choice satisfying the above four conditions. It is possible because: a) Individual priority scales can always be derived from a set of pairwise cardinal preference judgments as long as they form at least a minimal spanning tree in the completely connected graph of the elements being compared; and b) The cardinal preference judgments associated with group choice belong to a ratio scale that represents the relative intensity of the group preferences.

References

Buede, D. and D.T. Maxwell, (1995),"Rank Disagreement: A Comparison of Multi-criteria Methodologies", *Journal of Multi-Criteria Decision Analysis*, Vol. 4, 1-21.

Luce, R. D. and H. Raiffa, (1957), *Games and Decisions*, Wiley, New York.

Millet,I. And T.L. Saaty, (1999), "On the Relativity of Relative Measures- -Accommodating Both Rank Preservation and Rank Reversal in the AHP". *European Journal of Operational Research.*

Peniwati, K., (1996), "The Analytic Hierarchy Process: The Possibility for Group Decision Making", pp. 202-214, *Proceedings of the Fourth International Symposium on the Analytic Hierarchy Process*, Vancouver, Canada. (Obtainable from RWS Publications, 4922 Ellsworth Avenue, Pittsburgh, PA 15213.)

Saaty, T. L., (1999-2000 ed.), *Decision Making For Leaders.* RWS Publications, 4922 Ellsworth Avenue, Pittsburgh, PA 15213.

Saaty, T. L., (2000), *The Brain, Unraveling the Mystery of How It Works: The Neural Network Process*, RWS Publications, 4922 Ellsworth Avenue, Pittsburgh, PA 15213.

Saaty, T. L. and G. Hu, (1998), "Ranking by Eigenvector Versus Other Methods in the Analytic Hierarchy Process", *Appl. Math. Letters*,Vol. 11, No. 4, pp. 121-125.

Saaty, T. L., (1996), *Decision Making with Dependence and Feedback: The Analytic Network Process*, RWS Publications, 4922 Ellsworth Avenue, Pittsburgh, PA 15213.

Saaty, T. L., (1994), *Fundamentals of Decision Making and Priority Theory*, RWS Publications, 4922 Ellsworth Avenue, Pittsburgh, PA 15213.

Saaty, T. L., (1990), *Multicriteria Decision Making: The Analytic Hierarchy Process*, RWS Publications, 4922 Ellsworth Avenue, Pittsburgh, PA.

Saaty, T.L. and L. G. Vargas, (1993), "Experiments on Rank Preservation and Reversal in Relative Measurement," *Mathematical and Computer Modeling*, 17, No. 4/5, pp. 13-18.

Vargas, L. G., (1994), "Reply to Schenkerman's Avoiding Rank Reversal in AHP Decision Support Models", *European Journal of Operational Research*, 74, pp. 420-425.

Appendix 1

Facts from Matrix and Graph Theory

In this appendix we have included some facts about matrix theory and graph theory that relate to the material of the book. We hope the reader will find them useful.

1. MATRICES[1,2,3,4,5,6]

A matrix is a rectangular array of mn numbers arranged in m rows and n columns. The number, element, or entry of the matrix A in the ith row and jth column is denoted by a_{ij}. Thus we have for the m by n matrix A:

$$A = \begin{bmatrix} a_{11} & a_{12} & \cdots & a_{1n} \\ a_{21} & a_{22} & \cdots & a_{2n} \\ \vdots & & & \vdots \\ a_{m1} & a_{m2} & \cdots & a_{mn} \end{bmatrix}$$

Generally we denote the matrix A by (a_{ij}) and specify the number of its rows and columns. The subscripts i and j refer to the row and column, respectively, in which the entry is located. A is called a square matrix of order n if $m = n$. We shall be mostly interested in square $n \times n$ (n by n) matrices.

The rows and columns of A are called vectors. The matrix A may consist of a single row vector or a single column vector. In that case, a single subscript on this entry suffices. For example, $A \equiv (a_1, ..., a_n)$ is a row vector. The diagonal elements of a square matrix A of order n are a_{ii}, $i = 1, ..., n$. A *diagonal* matrix A has the property that $a_{ij} = 0$, for all i and j with $i \neq j$. If also all $a_{ii} = 0$ for all i, A is called the *zero* or *null* matrix and is denoted by boldface zero or by boldface capital O. The unit or *identity* matrix I is a diagonal matrix with $a_{ij} = 1$ for $i = j$; and $a_{ij} = 0$ for $i \neq j$. The *transpose* of $A = (a_{ij})$, denoted by $A^T = (a_{ji})$, is defined by replacing the element in the i,j position of A by the element in the j,i position; that is, we interchange the rows and columns of A by reflecting around the main diagonal to obtain A^T. Since two matrices are equal if their corresponding elements are equal, we can define a *symmetric* matrix by $A = A^T$; that is $a_{ij} = a_{ji}$ for all i and j. A scalar multiple kA of a matrix $A = (a_{ij})$ is a matrix each of whose coefficients is equal to the product of each coefficient of A by a constant k. Thus we have $kA = (ka_{ij})$.

Let $A = (a_{ij})$ be an $n \times n$ matrix. Then A is nonnegative ($A \geq 0$) if $a_{ij} \geq 0$ for all i and j. A matrix A is positive ($A > 0$) if $a_{ij} > 0$ for all i and j. A matrix A is cogradient to a matrix B if there is a permutation matrix P such that $A = P^T B P$. A is reducible or decomposable if it is cogradient to a matrix of the form

$$\begin{bmatrix} B_1 & 0 \\ B_2 & B_3 \end{bmatrix}$$

where B_1 and B_3 are square submatrices. Otherwise A is irreducible or non-decomposable. By definition, a 1×1 matrix is irreducible. $A \geq 0$ is primitive if and only if there is an integer $m > 0$ such that $A^m > 0$. Otherwise it is imprimitive. A is column stochastic if $a_{ij} \geq 0$ and $\sum_{i=1}^{n} a_{ij} = 1$ for $j = 1, \ldots, n$. It is row stochastic if $\sum_{j=1}^{n} a_{ij} = 1$ for $i = 1, \ldots, n$. A is doubly stochastic if it is both column and row stochastic.

There are rules by which matrices A and B can be added, subtracted, multiplied, and "divided." These operations constitute an algebra of matrices, somewhat similar to the algebra of ordinary numbers, but care must be taken, as all the rules that work with ordinary numbers do not work with matrices, which have a more general algebra. Indeed, a matrix of order one by one is a single number, called a scalar, and all laws which apply to matrices in general must also apply to that special kind of matrix and hence to ordinary numbers. However, unlike multiplying numbers, matrix multiplication is non-commutative, and not every nonzero matrix has an inverse.

Historically, matrices arose as a shorthand method of listing coefficients of a system of equations, and the origins of matrix addition and multiplication may be related to operations on systems of equations. A general set of m equations in n unknowns is given by

$$a_{11}x_1 + a_{12}x_2 + \cdots + a_{1n}x_n = y_1$$
$$a_{21}x_1 + a_{22}x_2 + \cdots + a_{2n}x_n = y_2$$
$$\vdots \qquad\qquad \vdots \qquad \vdots$$
$$a_{m1}x_1 + a_{m2}x_2 + \cdots + a_{mn}x_n = y_m$$

The writing of such a system can be made simple if the coefficients, the elements of the array (a_{ij}), are separated from the variables, the x_j. Then the x_j, which are repeated in each row, need be written only once; thus

$$\begin{bmatrix} a_{11} & a_{12} & \cdots & a_{1n} \\ a_{21} & a_{22} & \cdots & a_{2n} \\ \vdots & & & \\ a_{m1} & a_{m2} & \cdots & a_{mn} \end{bmatrix} \begin{bmatrix} x_1 \\ x_2 \\ \vdots \\ x_n \end{bmatrix} = \begin{bmatrix} y_1 \\ y_2 \\ \vdots \\ y_m \end{bmatrix}$$

If we write the x_j as a column, then the rule to reassemble the original system is: with every a_{ij} associate the corresponding x_j, i.e., a_{32} and x_2 yield $a_{32}x_2$. That is, as you move across the rows of coefficients, move *down* the column of x's for the proper association. This simple operation is the basis for the general matrix multiplication rule.

We may refer to $(x_1, x_2, ..., x_n)$ as the vector x and $(y_1, y_2, ..., y_m)$ as the vector y. Notice that in general the number of elements in x is not the same as that in y. The product of an m by n matrix and a p by q matrix is only possible when $p = n$ and results in a matrix of size m by q. Thus if $q = 1$, that is, the second matrix is a vector, the product is also a vector. To prevent confusion, keep in mind that subscripted letters refer to elements of matrices or vectors and unsubscripted letters refer to a whole matrix or vector.

The system of linear equations given above, known as an inhomogeneous system, may be simply represented as $Ax = y$. To solve this system, one can use the method of Gaussian elimination. By analogy with the solution of $ax = y$ whose solution is $x = y/a$ or $x = a^{-1}y$ for scalars, we find the inverse A^{-1} of the matrix A, that is, a matrix A^{-1} such that $AA^{-1} = A^{-1}A = I$. We then have $x = A^{-1}y$. An inefficient but time-honored procedure in computing the inverse of a matrix is to obtain its determinant and its adjoint. If $y = 0$, then a nonzero solution of the homogeneous equation $Ax = 0$ exists if and only if A^{-1} does not exist; otherwise $x = A^{-1}0 = 0$ and $x=0$ would be the only solution. It will be seen below that A^{-1} does not exist when the determinant of A is equal to zero. A final comment here is that in the Analytic Hierarchy Process we encounter a homogeneous equation of the form $(\lambda_{max}I-A)w=0$. This equation has a nonzero solution w because λ_{max} is a root of the characteristic polynomial of A which is the determinant of $(\lambda I-A)$.

DETERMINANT OF A

To compute the determinant of a matrix, we need the recursive definitions of a minor and of a cofactor. The minor M_{ij} of a_{ij} is the determinant of the submatrix obtained by striking out the row and column of a_{ij}. The cofactor A_{ij} of a_{ij} is given by $A_{ij} = (-1)^{i+j}M_{ij}$. The determinant of A, often written as $|A|$, for a given i is:

$$|A| = \sum_{j=1}^{n} a_{ij}A_{ij}$$

or for a given j is:

$$|A| = \sum_{i=1}^{n} a_{ij} A_{ij}$$

Consider the matrix:

$$A = \begin{pmatrix} 2 & 0 & 1 & 4 \\ 3 & 1 & 5 & 2 \\ 6 & 4 & 1 & 0 \\ 4 & 2 & 2 & 1 \end{pmatrix}$$

Then

$$|A| = 2 \begin{vmatrix} 1 & 5 & 2 \\ 4 & 1 & 0 \\ 2 & 2 & 1 \end{vmatrix} - 0 \begin{vmatrix} 3 & 5 & 2 \\ 6 & 1 & 0 \\ 4 & 2 & 1 \end{vmatrix}$$

$$+ 1 \begin{vmatrix} 3 & 1 & 2 \\ 6 & 4 & 0 \\ 4 & 2 & 1 \end{vmatrix} - 4 \begin{vmatrix} 3 & 1 & 5 \\ 6 & 4 & 1 \\ 4 & 2 & 2 \end{vmatrix}$$

$$= 2(-7) - 0(-11) + 1(-2) - 4(-10) = 24$$

To show how the process is extended to submatrices, we have, for example:

$$2 \begin{vmatrix} 1 & 5 & 2 \\ 4 & 1 & 0 \\ 2 & 2 & 1 \end{vmatrix} = 2 \left(1 \begin{vmatrix} 1 & 0 \\ 2 & 1 \end{vmatrix} - 5 \begin{vmatrix} 4 & 0 \\ 2 & 1 \end{vmatrix} + 2 \begin{vmatrix} 4 & 1 \\ 2 & 2 \end{vmatrix} \right)$$

A matrix whose determinant is zero is called singular.

ADJOINT OF A

Adjoint of $A = (A_{ij}) = (-1)^{i+j}$ cofactor of a_{ji} of A.

This gives

$$\begin{pmatrix} -7 & -20 & -29 & 68 \\ 11 & 28 & 49 & -100 \\ -2 & 8 & 2 & -8 \\ 10 & 8 & 14 & -32 \end{pmatrix}$$

for the adjoint of A. Finally the inverse of A is given by:

$$A^{-1} = \frac{Adjoint\ A}{|A|}$$

This approach is not to be used computationally, because it is inefficient. Its number of operations is of the order of one-third the fifth power of n, $0(\frac{n^5}{3})$. It can be shown that $|AB| = |A||B|$, from which we can deduce that $|Adjoint\ A| = |A|^{n-1}$.

As noted above, determinants arise from the solution of equations by elimination. Thus in

$$a_{11}x_1 = y_1 \qquad \text{we have} \qquad x_1 = \frac{y_1}{a_{11}}$$

and in the system of two equations

$$a_{11}x_1 + a_{12}x_2 = y_1$$

$$a_{21}x_1 + a_{22}x_2 = y_2$$

by elimination in the first equation,

$$x_2 = \frac{y_1 - a_{11}x_1}{a_{12}}$$

and substitution in the second,

$$a_{21}x_1 + \frac{a_{22}}{a_{12}}(y_1 - a_{11}x_1) = y_2$$

followed by simplification,

$$\left(a_{21} - \frac{a_{11}a_{22}}{a_{12}}\right)x_1 = y_2 - \frac{a_{22}}{a_{12}}y_1$$

and solution

$$x_1 = \frac{a_{12}y_2 - a_{22}y_1}{a_{12}a_{21} - a_{11}a_{22}} = \frac{a_{22}}{a_{11}}\frac{y_1 - a_{12}y_2}{a_{22} - a_{12}a_{21}}$$

$$= \frac{\begin{vmatrix} y_1 & a_{12} \\ y_2 & a_{22} \end{vmatrix}}{\begin{vmatrix} a_{11} & a_{12} \\ a_{21} & a_{22} \end{vmatrix}}$$

Here the determinant of $A = \begin{pmatrix} a_{11} & a_{12} \\ a_{21} & a_{22} \end{pmatrix}$ appears in the denominator.
Similarly we have:

$$x_2 = \frac{\begin{vmatrix} a_{11} & y_1 \\ a_{21} & y_2 \end{vmatrix}}{\begin{vmatrix} a_{11} & a_{12} \\ a_{21} & a_{22} \end{vmatrix}}$$

This is a solution of the system by Cramer's rule, which again is computationally very inefficient. It replaces the coefficient of x_i by the vector of y's in the determinant of the numerator and calculates the determinant of the coefficient matrix in the denominator. The same approach can be generalized for the solution of an n by n system.

THE CHARACTERISTIC EQUATION: EIGENVALUES AND EIGENVECTORS

A proper vector (characteristic vector or eigenvector) of A is a nonnull vector $w = (w_1, ..., w_n)$ such that $Aw = \lambda w$ or $(1/\lambda)A$ transforms w to w, i.e., leaves w fixed. The values of λ corresponding to such a w are called the proper values (characteristic values or eigenvalues) of A. Thus w would be a proper vector or eigenvector if it is a nontrivial (nonzero) solution of $(\lambda I - A)w = 0$ for some number λ. The components of w constitute a solution(s) of a homogeneous linear system with matrix $\lambda I - A$. In fact, this system has the trivial solution $w_1 = \cdots = w_n = 0$. But in order that there be a nontrivial solution, the matrix $\lambda I - A$ must be singular, i.e., its determinant, $\det(\lambda I - A) = 0$, or simply $|\lambda I - A| = 0$. This determinant is an nth degree polynomial in λ. It has the form $\lambda^n - a_1 \lambda^{n-1} + \cdots + (-1)^n |A|$ and is called the degree equation called the characteristic equation of A. The roots λ_i,

$i = 1, \ldots, n$, of the characteristic equation $|\lambda I - A| = 0$ are the desired eigenvalues. The fundamental theorem of algebra assures the existence of n roots (not necessarily all distinct) for a polynomial equation of degree n. The eigenvectors are obtained by solving the corresponding systems of equations for each λ_i, $i = 1, \ldots, n$. Care must be taken in getting all the eigenvectors when there are multiple roots.

Note that in the characteristic polynomial the coefficient of λ^{n-1} is the sum of the diagonal elements of A. Thus

$$a_1 = \sum_{i=1}^{n} a_{ii} \equiv trace(A)$$

It is also true that the roots of the characteristic equation as roots of an nth degree equation satisfy

$$\sum_{i=1}^{n} \lambda_i = a_1 = trace(A)$$

and the last term in that equation is the product of the roots:

$$\prod_{i=1}^{n} \lambda_i = |A|$$

We can see this by expanding the factorization $(\lambda - \lambda_1)(\lambda - \lambda_2) \cdots (\lambda - \lambda_n)$ of the characteristic polynomial. We note that the characteristic equation may have multiple roots, and hence the total number of distinct roots may be less than n. A multiple root λ_i of multiplicity k would appear in the factorization in the form $(\lambda - \lambda_i)^k$. For a simple root we have $k = 1$.

From $Aw = \lambda w$ and $A\lambda = \lambda A$, since λ is a constant, we have $A^2 w = A(Aw) = A(\lambda w) = \lambda Aw = \lambda(\lambda w) = \lambda^2 w$. Thus, λ^2 is an eigenvalue of A^2 and similarly λ^k is an eigenvalue of A^k.

Consider the matrix

$$A = \begin{bmatrix} 1 & 2 \\ 3 & 4 \end{bmatrix}, \quad I = \begin{bmatrix} 1 & 0 \\ 0 & 1 \end{bmatrix}, \quad \lambda I = \begin{bmatrix} \lambda & 0 \\ 0 & \lambda \end{bmatrix}$$

$$(\lambda I - A) = \begin{bmatrix} 1-\lambda & 2 \\ 3 & 4-\lambda \end{bmatrix}$$

$$|\lambda I - A| = (1-\lambda)(4-\lambda) - 6 = \lambda^2 - 5\lambda - 2 = 0$$

Since the characteristic equation is a quadratic, we solve it by using the well-known quadratic formula for the roots of such an equation. We have for the eigenvalues

$$\lambda_1 = \frac{5+\sqrt{33}}{2} \qquad\qquad \lambda_2 = \frac{5-\sqrt{33}}{2}$$

and to obtain the eigenvector corresponding to λ_1, we write $Aw = \lambda_1 w$, that is,

$$\begin{bmatrix} 1 & 2 \\ 3 & 4 \end{bmatrix} \begin{bmatrix} w_1 \\ w_2 \end{bmatrix} = \lambda_1 \begin{bmatrix} w_1 \\ w_2 \end{bmatrix}$$

or

$$w_1 + 2w_2 = \lambda_1 w_1$$

that is,

$$w_1 = -\frac{2}{1-\lambda_1} w_2$$

We also have

$$3w_1 + 4w_2 = \lambda_1 w_2$$

Since the matrix $\lambda_1 I$-A is singular (its determinant is zero because its characteristic equation is evaluated at λ_1, one of the two roots), there is dependence between its rows, and hence the second equation yields no new information. Thus the eigenvector w is obtained by assigning an arbitrary value to w_2 and calculating w_1 from the above relation. Assigning w_2 the value 1, we have

$$w = \left[\frac{2}{\lambda_1 - 1}, \ 1\right]$$

We can normalize w by making its coefficients sum to unity. We do this by dividing each coefficient by the sum $w_1 + w_2$, which is $(\lambda + 1)/(\lambda - 1)$. The resulting normalized vector is

$$\left[\frac{2}{\lambda_1 + 1}, \ \frac{\lambda_1 - 1}{\lambda_1 + 1}\right]$$

Since multiplying by a constant does not affect the solution of $Aw = \lambda w$, we shall think of the eigenvectors w to be always given in normalized form. We may similarly obtain the eigenvector corresponding to λ_2.

Recall that a complex number is of the form $a + ib$ where $i = \sqrt{-1}$ and a and b are real. The modulus of such a number is denoted by $|a + ib|$ and is equal to $(a^2 + b^2)^{1/2}$. The complex conjugate of $a + ib$ is $a - ib$ and $(a + ib)(a - ib) = a^2 + b^2$. The eigenvalues of a real matrix, as the roots of any equation, may be complex numbers and occur in pairs as complex conjugates. If a matrix has real entries and is symmetric, all its eigenvalues are real and the eigenvectors corresponding to different eigenvalues are orthogonal in pairs. Thus, for example, if u and v are two such eigenvectors, then $uv^T = vu^T = 0$. The same is also true of a Hermitian matrix, which is a matrix of complex numbers in which a_{ji} is the complex conjugate of a_{ij}.

A theorem in matrix theory asserts that the eigenvalues of a matrix depend continuously on its entries (the same as proving that the roots of a polynomial depend continuously on its coefficients).

The eigenvalues, as the roots of any polynomial equation, are obtained by standard numerical methods, of which there are several. There are nowadays canned computer programs like MATHEMATICA, MAPLE, EISPACK, MATLAB, and LAPACK for getting these roots. When the equation is the characteristic equation of a matrix, these computer programs also find the eigenvectors.

Two well-known methods in the literature for obtaining the characteristic polynomial of a matrix, which is simply the determinant of $(\lambda I - A)$, are those of U.J.J. Leverrier[7] and of D.K. Faddeev.[8] There is a more efficient way to obtain the roots $\lambda_1, ..., \lambda_n$ directly and use them to derive the characteristic polynomial $(\lambda - \lambda_1) \cdots (\lambda - \lambda_n)$.

A matrix $A = (a_{ij})$ is upper triangular if $a_{ij} = 0$ for $i > j$. A is orthogonal if $A^T A = I$. Any matrix with real entries can be written as a product $A = QR$ where Q is orthogonal and R is upper triangular. An efficient way (not fully free of problems) for deriving the eigenvalues and eigenvectors of a matrix A is the QR algorithm developed in 1961 by J.G. Francis. The basic algorithm described in Cullen[9] is as follows:

1. INPUT: an n by n matrix A and allow m iterations.

2. Take $A_1 = A$

3. For $i = 1, 2, ..., m$, factor $A_i = Q_i R_i$ where $Q_i^T A_i = R_i$, Q_i is orthogonal and R_i is upper triangular.

4. Compute $A_{i+1} = R_i Q_i$.

5. OUTPUT: A_m orthogonally similar to A ($A_m = Q_m^t \cdots Q_1^T A Q_1 \cdots Q_m$) and close to upper triangular (the elements below the diagonal are close to zero).

The diagonal entries of A_m converge to the eigenvalues of A. The programs MATLAB and MATALG use EISPACK subroutines to compute the eigenvalues and eigenvectors.

ON IRREDUCIBILITY, PRIMITIVITY, CYCLICITY, AND STOCHASTICITY [9,10]

Why do we need the irreducibility, primitivity, and cyclicity of matrices? Before the days of the computer it was necessary to work out the details of a mathematical theory in such a way as to make certain types of computations possible to obtain a limiting answer with a finite number of calculations when one could. *Thus irreducibility, needed in Frobenius' theorem, has to do with the fact that the principal eigenvalue λ_{max} of a nonnegative matrix is simple and therefore occurs only once. Primitivity ensures that there are no other roots whose moduli are equal to one. Imprimitivity deals with roots of unity and accounts for cycling.* Note that λ_{max} can be a simple root and a multiple root of a reducible matrix. In either case, there may be additional nth roots of unity. When the root is simple, the case of additional nth roots of unity is dealt with precisely as in the case of an irreducible matrix.

Irreducibility and Graphs: $W \geq 0$ is irreducible if and only if its directed graph is strongly connected. A connected graph is strongly connected if and only if every arc belongs to at least one cycle. The greatest common divisor (g.c.d.) c of the lengths of all cycles in a strongly connected graph is called the *index of imprimitivity* of that graph. The g.c.d. of the lengths of all cycles through any vertex is equal to c. The index of imprimitivity of an irreducible matrix is equal to the index of imprimitivity of its associated directed graph. Adding loops to the vertices of the graph does not affect its connectedness.

Lemma: W is irreducible if and only if $I + W$ is irreducible.

Proof: Adding loops to the vertices of the graph does not affect its connectedness.

Theorem: A necessary and sufficient condition for an $n \times n$ nonnegative matrix W to be irreducible is that $(I + W)^{n-1} > 0$.

Proof: The condition is necessary, for if $(I + W)^{n-1} > 0$, then every vertex in $I + W$ can be reached by a path of length n-1 from every other vertex and thus $I + W$

is irreducible. By the lemma, if $I+W$ is irreducible, then W is also irreducible. Conversely, by the lemma, $I+W$ is irreducible. Now $(I+W)^{n-1} \geq I+W^{n-1} > 0$, since in W every vertex can be reached by a path of at most length n-1 from any other vertex. Hence, except possibly for the diagonal elements, the entries of W^{n-1} are all positive. Adding I ensures that the diagonal is also positive.

The sum and product of two irreducible matrices and any power of an irreducible matrix are irreducible. If an integer power of a matrix is irreducible, then that matrix is irreducible.

Irreducibility and the Principal Eigenvalue: If W is an irreducible nonnegative matrix, its principal eigenvalue is a simple root of its characteristic equation.

The principal eigenvalue of an irreducible matrix dominates in modulus the principal eigenvalue of any of its submatrices (which lie on the main diagonal, called principal submatrices). For a nonnegative matrix, dominance or equality can hold. A nonnegative matrix W with principal eigenvalue λ_{max} is reducible if and only if λ_{max} is an eigenvalue of a principal submatrix of W. A nonnegative matrix W with a simple eigenvalue λ_{max} is irreducible if and only if both W and W^T have corresponding positive principal eigenvectors.

Irreducibility and the Principal Eigenvector: If W is an irreducible nonnegative matrix with principal eigenvalue λ_{max}, and $Aw = \lambda_{max} w$, then w is a scalar multiple of a positive vector. An irreducible nonnegative matrix has just one eigenvector w whose components satisfy $\sum_{i=1}^{n} w_i = 1$. Its only eigenvalue with a positive eigenvector is λ_{max}.

Irreducibility and Primitivity: If W is primitive of order n, then $m \leq n^2-2n+2$ where m is the first value for which $W^m > 0$. A primitive matrix is irreducible. The product of primitive matrices may not be irreducible, and the product of reducible matrices may be positive and hence primitive. A positive power of a primitive matrix is primitive. An irreducible matrix is primitive if (1) it has a positive trace, or (2) it has a nonzero main diagonal. If the Hadamard (elementwise) product $W*W^2$ of an irreducible matrix W is nonzero, then W is primitive.

A matrix A is reducible if and only if at least one of the principal minors of order $n\text{-}1$ of the matrix $(\lambda_{max}I\text{-}A)$ is zero. A nonnegative matrix is reducible if and only if one entry on the main diagonal of its adjoint is equal to zero.

PERRON-FROBENIUS

Let W be an irreducible nonnegative matrix. Then W has an eigenvalue λ_{max} (called the principal eigenvalue) which is real, positive, and simple. For any other eigenvalue λ of W, we have $|\lambda| \le \lambda_{max}$. To this principal eigenvalue λ_{max} there corresponds a nonnegative eigenvector (called the principal eigenvector) which is unique to within multiplication by a positive constant.

If W is primitive, then for any other eigenvalue λ of A we actually have $|\lambda| < \lambda_{max}$, and the eigenvector is strictly positive. If A is imprimitive (cyclic) with index (cycle) c, then there are exactly c eigenvalues $\lambda_1, ..., \lambda_c$ with moduli equal to λ_{max}. These eigenvalues are all distinct and are given by

$$\lambda_1 = \lambda_{max}, \quad \lambda_2 = \lambda_{max}z, \quad \lambda_3 = \lambda_{max}z^2, \quad ..., \quad \lambda_c = \lambda_{max}z^{c-1},$$

where z is the complex number $z = e^{2\pi i/c}$, $i = \sqrt{-1}$.

For example, the following graph (strictly speaking, the matrix of the graph) is irreducible because one can reach either of the two nodes from the other.

It also gives rise to cycling, as is obvious from the diagram. To see this algebraically, consider its matrix:

$$A \;=\; \begin{bmatrix} 0 & 1 \\ 1 & 0 \end{bmatrix}$$

We have

$$A^2 = \begin{bmatrix} 1 & 0 \\ 0 & 1 \end{bmatrix}, \qquad A^3 = \begin{bmatrix} 0 & 1 \\ 1 & 0 \end{bmatrix}$$

In general

$$A^{2k} = \begin{bmatrix} 1 & 0 \\ 0 & 1 \end{bmatrix}, \quad A^{2k+1} = \begin{bmatrix} 0 & 1 \\ 1 & 0 \end{bmatrix}$$

and we have no unique limit result because the matrix is imprimitive (no power of it can be positive). If, on the other hand, we add a loop at X as shown in the graph below, we obtain a primitive matrix.

Here we have

$$A = \begin{bmatrix} 1 & 1 \\ 1 & 0 \end{bmatrix}, \quad A^2 = \begin{bmatrix} 2 & 1 \\ 1 & 1 \end{bmatrix}, \quad A^3 = \begin{bmatrix} 3 & 2 \\ 2 & 1 \end{bmatrix},$$

and A^k tends to a unique limit because it is primitive. The graph is reducible. Its matrix A and powers of A are as follows:

$$A = \begin{bmatrix} 1 & 0 \\ 1 & 1 \end{bmatrix}, \; A^2 = \begin{bmatrix} 1 & 0 \\ 2 & 1 \end{bmatrix}, \; A^3 = \begin{bmatrix} 1 & 0 \\ 3 & 1 \end{bmatrix}, \; ..., A^k = \begin{bmatrix} 1 & 0 \\ k & 1 \end{bmatrix}$$

which does not cycle. But the matrix of the following graph is reducible and cyclic:

Remark: Occasionally, one can simplify much of the analysis of supermatrices by assuming that for some component there are influence priorities within the elements of that component, defined by an identity matrix, as we have just done by adding a loop at a vertex.

Irreducibility and Block Submatrices: The general normal form for an irreducible (in particular column stochastic) matrix is given by the following theorem.

Theorem: A square matrix A is either irreducible or can be reduced by a permutation of indices to a block diagonal matrix of irreducible matrices and other block matrices having the normal form

$$\begin{bmatrix} A_1 & 0 & 0 & A_{1,k+1} & \cdots & A_{1m} \\ 0 & A_2 & 0 & A_{2,k+1} & \cdots & A_{2m} \\ \vdots & \vdots & \vdots & \vdots & & \vdots \\ 0 & 0 & A_k & A_{k,k+1} & \cdots & A_{k+1,m} \\ \vdots & \vdots & \vdots & \vdots & \ddots & \vdots \\ 0 & 0 & 0 & 0 & \cdots & A_m \end{bmatrix}$$

At least one of the matrices with double subscripts in each column in which they appear is nonzero.

Among irreducible matrices W we need to distinguish two types: those that are primitive and thus $W^m > 0$ for some m (and therefore for all m sufficiently large), and those for which there is no such m. In the case of a column stochastic matrix W, these are, respectively, the acyclic and cyclic ones. Accordingly, an irreducible nonnegative matrix W is called *acyclic* if $W^m > 0$ for some m. Otherwise it is called *cyclic* with cycle $c \geq 2$ if there exists a permutation which puts it in the form:

$$W' = \begin{bmatrix} 0 & 0 & \cdots & 0 & W_c \\ W_1 & 0 & \cdots & 0 & 0 \\ 0 & W_2 & \cdots & 0 & 0 \\ \vdots & \vdots & \ddots & \vdots & \vdots \\ 0 & 0 & \cdots & W_{c-1} & 0 \end{bmatrix}$$

where the diagonal blocks are square, but $W_1, ..., W_c$ may not be square. Then the powers of W have the form

$$W^c = \begin{bmatrix} V_1 & & & 0 \\ & V_2 & & \\ & & \ddots & \\ 0 & & & V_c \end{bmatrix}$$

where the matrices $V_1, \ldots, V_c$ are all irreducible and acyclic and

$$V_1 = W_c W_{c-1} \cdots W_2 W_1; \quad V_2 = W_1 W_c \cdots W_3 W_2; \quad \cdots; \quad V_c = W_{c-1} W_{c-2} \cdots W_1 W_c$$

STOCHASTIC MATRICES

$W \geq 0$ is stochastic if and only if $WE = E$ where E is the $n \times n$ matrix of 1's. Because of this it follows that if W and X are stochastic, then so is WX. $W \geq 0$ is stochastic if and only if $e = (1, 1, \ldots, 1)$ is its principal eigenvector corresponding to the principal eigenvalue 1. The moduli of the eigenvalues of a stochastic matrix cannot exceed 1.

If W is an irreducible stochastic matrix, then the matrix $W^\infty = \lim_{k \to \infty} W^k$ exists if and only if W is primitive.

To summarize, if W be an irreducible stochastic matrix, then the number 1 is a simple eigenvalue of A. For any other eigenvalue λ of W, we have $|\lambda| \leq 1$. If W is also primitive, then $|\lambda| < 1$ for all other eigenvalues λ of W. If W is imprimitive with index (period) length c, then there are c eigenvalues with absolute value one.

STOCHASTICITY AND PERRON-FROBENIUS

Let W be an irreducible acyclic stochastic matrix. Then for all i, j,

$$\lim_{k \to \infty} W^k = we > 0, Ww = w, eW = e, e = (1,1,\ldots,1)$$

The row vector w is the unique solution of

$$Ww = w, \quad \sum w_i = 1$$

Moreover, the convergence is geometric[6]: there exist constants $\alpha > 0$ and $0 \le \beta < 1$ such that

$$|W^k - we| \le \alpha \beta^k, \quad k = 1, 2, \ldots$$

for all i, j. The constant β can be taken to be the largest modulus of the eigenvalues other than $\lambda_{max} = 1$.

If W is irreducible but imprimitive (cyclic) with cycle length c, then the foregoing holds for each one of the irreducible acyclic matrices $V_1, \ldots, V_c$ on the diagonal of W^c. If W is reducible, then again the result applies to each irreducible block separately.

2. GRAPHS[10]

There are at least two reasons why we need some knowledge of graphs for our analysis of priorities of influence. The first is obvious. Graphs are a geometric framework to structure a decision problem based on priorities. We need to identify and draw a diagram of the components, their elements, and the connections between them to represent their interactions. The second has to do with a characterization of irreducible matrices in terms of their associated graphs. A graph is a set of points V called *vertices* or *nodes* and a set of simple curves E called *edges* with a rule (of incidence) which associates each edge with vertices which are called its end points. The vertices are said to be incident with the edge. An *open* edge is incident with precisely two distinct vertices. A *closed* edge (called a loop) is incident with precisely one vertex and hence its end points coincide. No edges have points in common other than vertices.

In Figure 1 v_1 and v_2 are examples of vertices; e_1 is a loop whose end point is v_5; e_2 is an open edge whose end points are v_2 and v_3.

Two edges with a common vertex or two vertices that are the end points of an edge are said to be *adjacent*. A vertex is *isolated* if it is not incident with any edge. We denote a graph by $G = (V, E)$.

A *subgraph* of a graph G is a subset V_I of the set of vertices V and a subset E_I of the set of edges E with the same incidence between vertices and edges as in G.

A graph is called *simple* if it has neither loops nor parallel edges, i.e., multiple edges between pairs of vertices. Most of the time we shall be concerned with simple graphs, but since we have allowed for loops and parallel edges in our definition of graphs, we will usually make it clear when we are considering nonsimple graphs.

With each edge, one may associate a direction or orientation indicated by an arrow. The resulting graph is then called a *directed graph* and its edges are called arcs (see Figure 2). A directed graph is denoted by $D = (V, A)$.

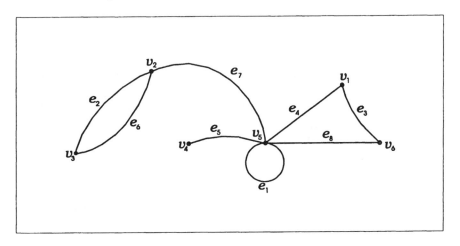

Figure 1 A Graph with Vertices, Loops and Open Edges.

The number of edges incident with a vertex $v \in V$ is called the degree of the vertex and is denoted by $d(v)$. We denote by $d^-(v)$ the number of arcs directed toward v, and by $d^+(v)$ the number of arcs directed away from v. A loop incident with a vertex is counted twice in determining the degree. For an isolated vertex we have $d(v) = 0$.

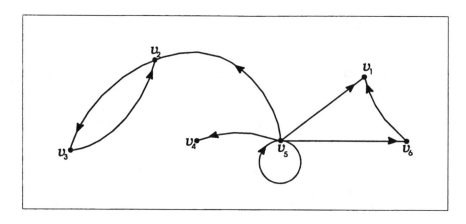

Figure 2 A Directed Graph

For a graph $G = (V,E)$ we denote the number of vertices and the number of edges by $|V|$ and $|E|$, respectively, and $|V|$ is called the order of the graph. The graph in Figure 3 has $|V| = 7$ and $|E| = 10$. A graph is called finite if both $|V|$ and $|E|$ are finite, and infinite if either is infinite. We shall be concerned exclusively with finite graphs. In the graph of Figure 3, the degree of v_1 is 5; v_7 is isolated.

A sequence of k edges $e_1, ..., e_k$ in a graph G is called a *walk* or *edge progression* if there exists an appropriate sequence of $k+1$ (not necessarily distinct) vertices $v_0, v_1, ..., v_n$ such that e_i is incident with v_i and v_j, $i,j = 1, ..., n$. The walk is *closed* if $v_0 = v_n$ and *open* otherwise. If $e_i \neq e_j$ for all i and j, $i \neq j$, the walk is called a *tour* or a *chain*. A closed chain is called a *circuit*. If all the vertices are distinct, a walk is called a *simple chain*, while if $v_1 = v_n$ and all other vertices are distinct, we have a *simple* circuit provided that $n \geq 3$. An example of a simple chain is given in Figure 3 by the edge sequence

$$\{e_3, e_2, e_1, e_8\} \equiv \{(v_4, v_3), (v_3, v_2), (v_2, v_1), (v_1, v_6)\}$$

Here we have replaced each edge in the sequence by the pair of vertices that are its end points as they succeed each other in the walk v_4, v_3, v_2, v_1, v_6.

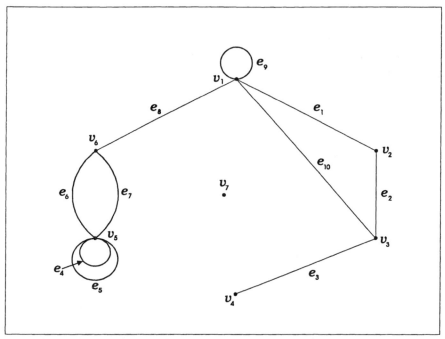

Figure 3 A Directed Graph with Seven Vertices and Ten Edges

Similar definitions may be given for directed graphs, giving attention to the direction on each arc. There we have *arc progressions*, *paths*, and *cycles*; *simple paths* and *simple cycles*.

A graph is called *connected* (strongly connected) in the undirected (directed) sense if there is a simple chain (path) between any pair of vertices. A graph of $n+1$ vertices is n-tuply connected if the removal of $n-1$ or fewer edges does not disconnect it. Two chains are said to be disjoint if they have no vertices in common, except perhaps for their end points.

A component C of a graph G is a connected subgraph which is maximal (i.e., every vertex that is adjacent to a vertex in C is also in C, and all edges of G incident with vertices in C are also in C).

A *subtree* is a connected subgraph which has no circuits. A *spanning tree* is a (maximal) subtree which contains all the vertices of the graph. An edge of the graph that is not in the tree is called a *chord*. An edge of the graph that is in the tree is known as a *branch*. When a chord is added to a spanning tree, the result is a circuit called a *fundamental circuit*. Figure 4 shows a spanning tree for a directed graph. The tree is *rooted* at v_0, from which all paths that are in the tree begin.

A special type of circuit in a graph, important for practical applications, is named after the famous Irish mathematician William Rowan Hamilton (1805-

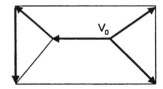

Figure 4 A Spanning Tree

1865). We call a circuit which passes through every vertex of the graph once and only once a *Hamiltonian circuit*. In contrast, the name of the Swiss mathematician Leonard Euler (1707-1783) is associated with a *Eulerian graph*, in which the edges form a chain, with each edge of the graph included in the chain once and only once. The chain may be open or it may form a circuit.

A simple graph $G = (V,E)$ having $|V| = n$ and such that every pair of vertices is joined by an edge is called a *complete graph on n vertices*. It is easily verified that a complete graph has $n(n-1)/2$ edges. Since any two complete graphs having the same number of vertices are isomorphic, we speak of the complete graph on n vertices.

A graph is called *bipartite* if its vertices can be partitioned into two disjoint sets such that the only edges in the graph are those which connect vertices from one set to those in the other (see Figure 5).

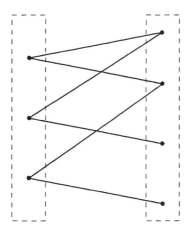

Figure 5 Bipartite Graph

An important elementary concept associated with a graph *G* on *n* vertices is that of connectedness. Intrinsically, much of algorithmic graph theory is concerned with connectivity, its redundancy and even absence in the graph.

A graph is not connected (or disconnected) when the set of vertices *V* can be separated into two sets V_1 and V_2 with no edge joining a vertex in V_1 to a vertex in V_2; otherwise it is said to be connected. Although two vertices may not be directly connected by an edge, it may be possible to reach one of them from the other by a simple chain. If there is such a chain connecting every pair of vertices, then the graph is said to be connected. Sometimes it is preferable to use the first definition, but more frequently the equivalent second definition is used. In fact, the second definition is much richer, as it opens up the entire area of problems of *reachability* or *traceability* of a graph or of subgraphs of the graph. For example, we can begin to ask for more. Can we start at a vertex and travel or trace the edges of the graph sequentially without repetition? Can we do so and still terminate at the starting vertex? Can we, by starting at a vertex, trace a simple chain through all the vertices with or without returning to our initial vertex? Can we do so if we considered only subgraphs of *n*-1 vertices?

Another type of question is concerned with how much connectivity there is in a graph. There are two ways to look at this type of question: (1) through the edges of the graph, and (2) through its vertices. A graph may be disconnected by the removal of several edges taken together. A minimum collection of such edges is known as a *cut set*, and the smallest number of edges in a cut set is called the *degree of connectivity* of the graph. A tree is connected of degree one. Clearly a tree is the weakest type of connected graph. On the other hand, in a circuit the removal of an edge leaves a connected graph (in fact a tree) behind.

There are also two ways to look at how vertices disconnect a graph. The first is associated with the concept of the *degree* of a vertex. For example, if in a tree we have a vertex of degree two and we remove it together with its incident edges, the remaining graph is disconnected. On the other hand, if the graph is a simple circuit and hence every vertex has degree two, the removal of a vertex does not disconnect the graph. It seems reasonable that the higher the degrees of the vertices, the stronger the connectivity should be. But this type of statement is too general and needs to be made specific in the context of a particular problem.

A vertex of a graph is called a *point of articulation* or *cut-vertex* if its removal disconnects or separates the graph. The *multiplicity* of a cut-vertex is the number of components which result from its deletion. More than one vertex may be a point of articulation. For example, in Figure 3 v_1 and v_6 are points of articulation. However, v_5 is not. The collection of articulation points forms a set of articulation vertices which, in the context of communication networks, may be regarded as the vulnerability set of the graph. Of course, a graph may have no point of articulation (such a graph is said to be nonseparable), but the removal of k vertices together disconnects it. Such a set is known as an *articulation set of order k*.

A graph is k-connected, for $0 \le k < n$, if the removal of k-1 vertices or fewer does not disconnect it. Any pair of vertices of such a graph can be connected by k disjoint chains (no two of which have vertices in common). A graph which has no articulation set of order k is called *k-irreducible*. Otherwise it is known as *k-reducible*.

So far we have been speaking of a general undirected graph. Connectivity questions are somewhat more complicated if a direction is assigned to the edges of the graph. Here a graph may be connected in the undirected sense, yet only *weakly connected* in the directed sense. Thus there may be a path from one vertex to another, but not conversely; i.e., it is not strongly connected. It is clear that cycles play an important role in strongly connected graphs.

THE ADJACENCY AND PATH MATRICES

The question often arises as to why raising the matrix of judgments or sometimes the supermatrix to a power determines for its entries the number of paths between the corresponding vertices, whose length is equal to that power. The vertex matrix is a first step for understanding this concept. We define a vertex (or adjacency) matrix for both directed and undirected graphs. The element in the (i,j) position of the matrix is equal to the number of edges incident with both vertex i and vertex j (or directed from vertex i to vertex j in the directed case). Thus for the directed graph of Figure 2 we have:

$$\vec{V} = \begin{array}{c} \\ v_1 \\ v_2 \\ v_3 \\ v_4 \\ v_5 \\ v_6 \end{array} \begin{array}{cccccc} v_1 & v_2 & v_3 & v_4 & v_5 & v_6 \\ \left[\begin{array}{cccccc} 0 & 0 & 0 & 0 & 0 & 0 \\ 0 & 0 & 1 & 0 & 0 & 0 \\ 0 & 1 & 0 & 0 & 0 & 0 \\ 0 & 0 & 0 & 0 & 0 & 0 \\ 1 & 1 & 0 & 1 & 1 & 1 \\ 1 & 0 & 0 & 0 & 0 & 0 \end{array}\right] \end{array}$$

In general, we have the following theorem regarding the vertex matrix $\vec{V}$ of a graph:

Theorem: The matrix $\vec{V}^n$ gives the number of arc progressions of length n between any two vertices of a directed graph.

Proof: If a_{ik} is the number of arcs joining v_i to v_k and a_{kj} is the number of arcs joining v_k to v_j, then $a_{ik}a_{kj}$ is the number of different paths each consisting of two arcs joining v_i to v_j and passing through v_k. If this is summed over all values of k, that is, over all the intermediate vertices, one obtains the number of paths of length 2 between v_i and v_j. If we now use a_{ij} to form $a_{ij} a_{jm}$, we have the number of different paths of length 3 between v_i and v_m passing through v_j, and so on. Thus if we assume the theorem is true for $\vec{V}^{n-1}$, then the coefficients of $\vec{V}^{n} = \vec{V}^{n-1} \vec{V}$ give the number of paths of length n between corresponding vertices. This completes the proof. A similar theorem holds for undirected graphs.

Sometimes when we refer to a graph with a certain property, we think of its adjacency matrix. For example, a directed graph is said to be primitive if it is strongly connected. This is reflected by the fact that $\vec{V}^{m} > 0$ for some integer $m > 0$, in which case $\vec{V}$ is primitive. A strongly connected graph $D = (V,A)$ with $n \geq 2$ vertices is primitive if and only if the greatest common divisor of the lengths of all simple cycles in D is equal to one. The concept of a vertex matrix may be generalized to that of a path matrix in which appropriate numbers are used as in a judgment matrix. Raising the matrix to powers gives the dominance of one element over another over a path whose length is equal to that power of the matrix.

References

1.   Horn, R.A., and C.R. Johnson, 1992, Matrix Analysis, Cambridge University Press, New York.

2.   Gantmacher, F.R., 1959, *Applications of the Theory of Matrices*, Interscience Publishers, New York.

3.   Lancaster, P. and M. Tismenetsky, 1985, *The Theory of Matrices*, Academic Press Harcourt Brace Jovanovich: Orlando.

4.   Berman, A., and R.J. Plemmons, 1979, *Nonnegative Matrices in the Mathematical Sciences*, Academic Press, New York.

5.   Minc, H., 1988, *Nonnegative Matrices*, John Wiley & Sons, New York.

6.   Cinlar, E., 1974, *Introduction to Stochastic Process*, Prentice-Hall; Englewood Cliffs.

7.   Leverrier, 1840, "Sur les Variations Reculaire des Elements des Orbites pour les Sept Planetes Principales," *J. de Math.* 5, 230.

8. Faddeev, D.K., 1937, "On the Transportation of the Scalar Equation of a Matrix," Leningrad: *Trudy Inst. Inzh. Prom. Stroit* 4, 78-86.

9. Cullen,C.G.,1994, *An Introduction to Numerical Linear Algebra*, PWS publishing Co., Boston.

10. Busacker, R.G., and T.L. Saaty,1965, *Finite Graphs and Networks*, McGraw-Hill Book Company, New York.

APPENDIX 2

Decline and Fall of the Invariance Principle In Decision Analysis

The Fallacy of Always Preserving Rank

1. INTRODUCTION

When does a presumed law of human nature cease to be accepted as a natural law? To show that a presumed law is not a natural law, it is sufficient to find one instance where it does not hold. One can do this either by constructing a theoretical example where the law is shown to be false, or by doing an experiment to show the contradiction, or both. Even when a law is thought to be good and is invoked by people as a normative principle for choice and action, if it is frequently and unintentionally violated in practice, it should be rejected. This is precisely what has occurred to the 'principle of invariance' in decision analysis.

The principle of invariance, sometimes known as the independence from irrelevant alternatives, encountered in decision making with utility theory has been found to be false for more than 20 years, when counterexamples were first published in the literature in 1974 [3]. Essentially, the principle of invariance says that the composite rank of a set of alternatives with respect to several criteria must stay the same if new alternatives are added or old ones deleted unless adding or deleting alternatives introduces or omits criteria. In the context of increasing the probability of changing one's choice, invariance is called *regularity*.

Why should one assume that such a principle should be true in the first place and what causes one to feel strongly that the principle should be made into a law of behavior? It is likely that the invariance principle is a consequence of one at a time kind of thinking. If one were to rate alternatives one at a time with respect to a set of criteria, each alternative would be examined by itself and obtains a score that is independent of other alternatives ranked before or after it. There would be no reason why a new alternative should affect the ranking of the old alternatives unless it adds new criteria in terms of which all the alternatives must now be additionally evaluated. But life is more complicated. We often rank alternatives by comparing them with each other on each criterion. Making comparisons is an intrinsic ability that all people have. How high we perceive an alternative to stand depends on what we already know about where other alternatives stand. We would never know how good an alternatives is on a criterion without having known about or experienced others on that criterion. This is particularly true when the criterion is not a physical property on which one can more or less measure the intensity with which every alternative possesses that criterion and then decide how desirable that intensity is. An intangible criterion requires judgment and judgment requires experience and knowledge about many alternatives. Rating alternatives one at a time is a special case of the process of paired comparisons because to create a scale of intensities for each criterion and use it to rate alternatives requires paired comparisons.

The rationalizations given by utility theorists about rank preservation are similar to the explanations people made about Euclidean geometry in the 18th century that the world is Euclidean. That belief was later shown to be simply an assumption about a geometry that obeyed Euclid's fifth postulate known as the parallel postulate than about the real world. It was believed then that God created people with prior knowledge of Euclidean geometry because no other geometry was thought to be possible. When the assumptions were challenged by Lobashevsky, Bolyai and Gauss, non-Euclidean geometries were developed that turned out to be as consistent as Euclid's geometry and more relevant to the real world as shown by the theory of relativity. The shortest distance traveled between two points was thought to always be a straight line (which on a local or microscopic scale may be true). On a sphere the shortest distance is traversed on a great circle. Relativity showed that globally, gravity pulls a beam of light causing it to travel along a curved geodesic.

The dogma of rank preservation also reminds one of the old belief that a logical system can be used to answer all questions arising within that system. But Kurt Godel showed that questions can arise in a logical theory that cannot be answered within the assumptions of that theory but may be answerable by embedding the system in another system with broader assumptions. The mechanical view arising from the need to construct utility functions led to the question as to whether independent alternatives can only be ranked one at a time but was found to be false because alternatives can be ranked in relative terms and the presence of new alternatives or deletion of old ones can change that ranking.

2. DISCUSSION

Here are two illustrations of unjustifiable rank reversal due to Corbin and Marley [3].

The first example concerns a lady in a small town, who wishes to buy a hat. She enters the only hat store in town, and finds two hats, *a* and *b*, that she likes equally well although she leans toward *a*. However, now suppose that the sales clerk discovers a third hat, a_1, identical to *a*. Then the lady may well choose hat *b* for sure (rather than risk the possibility of seeing someone wearing a hat just like hers), *a result that contradicts regularity.* The second example involves a guest being taken out to dinner, who, in deference to his host, refrains from selecting the most expensive and also most preferred dish and selects the second most expensive one, thereby increasing the chances of the second dish being chosen, *again contradicting regularity.*

Note that if instead of the hats the lady went shopping for a best PC computer, then she might well still buy the one she likes best even if there are many copies of it. Her preferences may be identical for the computers as they were for the hats. The same number of criteria may be used whose names may be different but whose priorities are the same as those used to choose the hats. In the end the numbers used are identical for the two examples but the labels are different. What should one do?

There are two lessons learnt from these examples. One is that it is we who must decide in a particular decision problem whether for that problem, rank needs to be preserved or not. It is not automatically written in the abstract structure of the real life problem itself. The other lesson is that we cannot use one and only one procedure for aggregating preferences in a multicriteria decision process once and for all. We need one procedure to preserve rank and another to allow rank to change. It is now clear that the outcome of a decision does depend on the procedure and mathematics used for the purpose. That is precisely the reason why the mathematics must derive from a deep and flexible understanding of decision making that emulates what decision making as a process in nature, rather than dictates what one should do to make a valid decision.

Some people have proposed that in the case of the desirability or the "uniqueness" of a hat, one can add such "fudge" criteria as uniqueness that would make the more preferred hat less desirable. Uniqueness and manyness are group properties and are not intrinsic attributes of any single hat. They require that one look at other hats to determine if the given hat is unique. But this implies that in ranking the hats one must assume that they are dependent on each other, violating another axiom of utility theory requiring independence among the alternatives. In passing we note that when introducing alternatives which may introduce new criteria, if one keeps adding such alternatives one would eventually run out of new criteria (and words in the dictionary to describe them) and the number of copies wins out and alters preferences. There is no way to escape this fact. In general for any decision problem, the number of alternatives can far exceed the number of criteria. To capture the effect of manyness, a procedure is required that automatically tallies how many hats there are and how desirable the given hat is. That is precisely what relative measurement to derive ratio scales does.

In the field of marketing, the effect of phantom alternatives has been observed to cause rank reversal. A car manufacturer sells two types of car–one inexpensive and not as well made as the other. To induce people to shift from the cheaper car, the manufacturer advertises that a new car with the virtues of the better car will appear on the market but the price will be much higher than that of the better made car. People are now observed to change their mind and start buying the better car. The manufacturer in fact never makes the 'phantom'. It is an advertising gimmick. There are several other generic situations of this type that can lead to rank reversal. For many decision problems ranking is made not once but three times. Once with respect to benefits, once with respect to costs, and once with respect to risks and the overall ranks are obtained by dividing (more generally taking some function of) the benefits by the costs multiplied by the risks. Thus a decision problem consists of several phases and not just one. There are situations where only the benefits or only the costs determine the outcome because one may be negligible or insignificant when compared with the other. In this framework, adding alternatives to the three structures, benefits, costs and risks, would naturally cause rank reversal.

The Analytic Hierarchy Process (AHP) is a decision making theory based on relative measurement. It derives ratio scales from paired comparisons. The AHP has a procedure that preserves rank absolutely as required by the invariance principle. In the absolute measurement mode of the AHP, one derives priorities for different intensities of each criterion. One then divides by the priority of the largest intensity in each case and then creates an ideal alternative, the best imaginable choice. In this case each alternative takes its place in the ranking and has no effect on the rank of the other alternatives. Rank is categorically preserved. But the AHP is also concerned with those cases where rank can and should change. It turns out that the two methods used to preserve the rank of the most desired alternative or to allow it to reverse give different results only 8% of the time [13]. Similar results were obtained for the two top alternatives, two lowest ranked alternatives and so on. Some experts in utility theory recently wrote the following about their own experiments with decision making:

> *"These experiments demonstrated that the MAVT and AHP techniques, when provided with the same decision outcome data, very often identify the same alternatives as 'best'. The other techniques are noticeably less consistent with MAVT, the Fuzzy algorithm being the least consistent."*

3. INVARIANCE AND RATIONALITY

One can trace the origin of the axioms of rank preservation among others to the book by Luce and Raiffa [8]. They write:

> *"Adding new acts to a decision problem under uncertainty, each of which is weakly dominated by or is equivalent to some old act, has no effect on the optimality or non-optimality of an old act.*

and elaborate it with

> *If an act is non optimal for a decision problem under uncertainty, it cannot be made optimal by adding new acts to the problem.*

and press it further to

> *The addition of new acts does not transform an old, originally non-optimal act into an optimal one, and it can change an old, originally optimal act into a non-optimal one only if at least one of the new acts is optimal.*

and even go to the extreme with:

> *The addition of new acts to a decision problem under uncertainty never changes old, originally non-optimal acts into optimal ones.*

and finally conclude with:

> *The all-or-none feature of the last form may seem a bit too stringent ... a severe criticism is that it yields unreasonable results. "*

Some people have taken this last form of invariance as the major tenet of their so called normative theory. A normative theory says that you must do it our way or you get wrong decisions. This is essentially what is called the criterion of rationality! To be a rational decision maker, one must accept and practice through the axioms of utility theory. The principle of invariance and the principle of rationality lead to a paradox because rank has been observed to reverse in practice violating invariance and suggesting that rationality as defined by utility theory is untenable. Practitioners of utility theory have insisted that their theory is the best possible; it is the norm. Reexamination of the axiomatic assumptions of utility theory is essential to be comfortable with that theory.

4. FINDINGS AND OBSERVATIONS OF DIFFERENT PEOPLE

The following are observations made by practitioners and researchers in decision theory.

Milan Zeleny [19] writes: "People's behavior has been found to deviate significantly from the "rational" axioms of utility theory. They do not maximize expected utility; they anchor their judgments in external points of reference; they often disregard prior knowledge and equally often ignore new evidence; and so on."

R. Corbin and A.A.J. Marley [3] write: "... a guest being taken out to dinner, who in deference to his host, refrains from selecting the most expensive item on the menu. Clearly, the addition of a single alternative can cause the most expensive dish to become the second most expensive, thereby increasing its chances of being chosen, again contradicting regularity. ... implicitly or explicitly, they assume that the subject is always aware of the set of potentially available alternatives T, even though, at any given time, the set of actually available alternatives A is some subset of T. Our counterexamples to regularity rely on a manipulation of the subject's knowledge of the potentially available set T....Thus, regularity tends to fail when the subject chooses on different occasions with differing knowledge of the potentially available set."

D.M. Grether and C.R. Plott [4] write: "The preference reversal phenomenon which is inconsistent with the traditional statement of preference theory remains.....No alternative theory currently available appears to be capable of covering the same extremely broad range of phenomena."

A. Tversky et. al. [16] write: "...a growing body of empirical evidence questions the assumption of invariance, which is essential to the theory of rational choice...alternative framings of the same options...produce inconsistent preferences, and alternative elicitation procedures...give rise to reversal of preferences....Because invariance - unlike independence or even transitivity - is normatively unassailable and descriptively incorrect, it does not seem possible to construct a theory of choice that is both normatively acceptable and descriptively adequate."

W.W. Pommerehne, et. al. [12] write: "Even when the subjects are exposed to strong incentives for making motivated, rational decisions, the phenomenon of preference reversal does not vanish."

A. Tversky and D. Kahneman [15] write: "The reliance on heuristics and the prevalence of biases are not restricted to laymen. Experienced researchers are also prone to the same biases–when they think intuitively. For example, the tendency to predict the outcome that best represents the data, with insufficient regard for prior probability, has been observed in the intuitive judgments of individuals who have had extensive training in statistics. Although they statistically sophisticated avoid elementary errors, such as the gambler's fallacy, their intuitive judgments are liable to similar fallacies in more intricate and less transparent problems."

D. Kahneman and A. Tversky [7] write: "The present paper describes several classes of choice problems in which preferences systematically violate the axioms of expected utility theory. In the light of these observations we argue that utility theory, as it is commonly interpreted and applied, is not an adequate descriptive model."

A. Tversky and I. Simonson [16] write: "The theory of rational choice assumes that preference between options does not depend on the presence or absence of other options. This principle, called *independence of irrelevant alternatives*, is essentially equivalent to the assumption that the decision maker has a complete preference order of all options, and that–given an offered set–the decision maker always selected the option that is highest in that order. Despite its simplicity and intuitive appeal, experimental evidence indicates that this principle is often violated."

K.M. Freeman et. al. [5] write: "Farquhar and Pratkanis find evidence for two basic effects. First, an attractive phantom can induce <u>contrast</u> effects such that other options in the choice set appear to be relatively less attractive. Second, an attractive phantom can also result in changes in the decision criteria such that those attributes and features on which a phantom excels are considered to be more important for making the decision. Depending on the magnitude and direction of these two effects, choice probabilities for the available alternatives can be dramatically altered in a manner that violates the basic axioms of classical choice theory." (See also [4].)

Tadeusz Tyszka [18] writes: "These principles contradict the foundations of utility theory, i.e. the condition of independence from irrelevant alternatives."

K.F. McCardle and R.L. Winkler [10] write: "We find that under some seemingly reasonable risk-averse utility functions, recommended behavior for the initial decision can be highly risk-taking and counterintuitive...in principle, we can model the grand world and understand fully all implications of grand-world utility functions. In practice, however, this ideal may not always be attainable and as a result we may be faced with serious modeling and assessment problems."

Mark McCord and Richard de Neufville [11] write: "In summary, the empirical result is that very different utility functions are obtained depending on the probability distribution used in the assessment. This phenomenon is quite incompatible with the axioms and places the practice of expected utility decision analysis in a quandary....the conclusion is that the justification of the practical use of expected utility decision analysis as it is known today is weak."

Mario Bunge [2] writes regarding DT (Decision Theory: von Neumann and Morgenstern 1944): "First of all, DT has been refuted experimentally ... These results contradict DT. Worse, they show that, though people have preferences, they have no utility functions. The defenders argue that the failure of DT to account for actual choice behavior only shows that people, unless guided by DT, tend to behave irrationally. However, these defenders have not bothered to put DT to the empirical test, to find out whether successful decision making does satisfy the assumptions of DT. Critics have done this and found DT inadequate as a prescriptive theory."

R.L. Keeney and H. Raiffa [8] write: "If we have assessed $k_Y = .75$ and $k_Z = .25$, we *cannot* say that Y is three times as important as Z. In fact, we cannot conclude that attribute Y is more important than Z. Going one step further, it is not clear how we would precisely define the concept that one attribute is more important than another."

As a result of the foregoing, one finds it critical to look beyond the rationality of utility theory.

References

1. Bunge, M., 1985, "Treatise on Basic Philosophy", *Vol. 7 of Epistemology and Methodology III: Philosophy of Science and Technology Part II: Life Science, Social Science and Technology.* D. Reidel Publishing Company, Boston.

2. Buede, D. and D.T. Maxwell, 1995, "Rank Disagreement: A Comparison of Multi-criteria Methodologies", Journal of Multi-Criteria Decision Analysis, Vol. 4, 1-21.

3. Corbin, R. and A.A.J. Marley, 1974, "Random Utility Models with Equality: An Apparent, but Not Actual, Generalization of Random Utility Models", Journal of Mathematical Psychology 11, 274-293.

4. Farquhar, P.H. and A.R. Pratkanis, 1993, "Decision Structuring with Phantom Alternatives", Management Science 39/10, p. 1214-1226.

5. Freeman, K.M., A.R. Pratkanis and P.H. Farquhar, 1990, "Phantoms as Psychological Motivation: Evidence for Compliance and Reactance Processes", University of California, Santa Cruz and Carnegie Mellon University.

6. Grether, D.M. and C.R. Plott, 1979, "Economic Theory of Choice and the Preference Reversal Phenomenon", The American Economic Review 69/4, 623-638.

7. Kahneman, D. and A. Tversky, 1979, "Prospect Theory: An Analysis of Decision Under Risk", Econometrica 47, pp. 263-291.

8. Keeney, R.L. and H. Raiffa, 1976, *Decisions with Multiple Objectives: Preference and Value Tradeoffs*, Wiley, New York.

9. Luce, R. Duncan, and Howard Raiffa, 1957, *Games and Decisions.* Wiley, NY.

10. McCardle, K.F. and R.L. Winkler, 1992, "Repeated Gambles, Learning, and Risk Aversion", Management Science 38/6, pp. 807.

11. McCord, M. and R. de Neufville, 1983, "Empirical Demonstration that Expected Utility Decision Analysis is Not Operational", Chapter in *Foundation of Utility and Risk Theory with Applications*, Stigun Wenstop (ed.), Reidel Publishing Company, Boston, pp. 181-200.

12. Pommerehne, W.W., F. Schneider, and P. Zweifel, 1982, "Economic Theory of Choice and the Preference Reversal Phenomenon: A Reexamination", American Economic Review 72/3, pp. 569-573.

13. Saaty, T.L., 1994, *Fundamentals of Decision Making with the Analytic Hierarchy Process*, RWS Publications, 4922 Ellsworth Avenue, Pittsburgh, PA 15213-2807.

14. Saaty, T.L. and L.G. Vargas, 1993, "Experiments on Rank Preservation and Reversal in Relative Measurement", Mathematical and Computer Modelling 17/4-5, 13-18.

15. Tversky, A. and D. Kahneman, 1974, *Judgment Under Uncertainty: Heuristics and Biases*, Science, V. 185, pp. 1124-1131.

16. Tversky, A. and I. Simonson, 1993, "Context-dependent Preferences", Management Science 39/10, pp. 1179-1189.

17. Tversky, A., P. Slovic and D. Kahneman, 1990, The Causes of Preference Reversal, The American Economic Review 80/1, 204-215.

18. Tyszka, T., 1983, "Contextual Multiattribute Decision Rules", in: Human Decision Making, Sjoberg, L., T. Tyszka and J.A. Wise (eds.), Doxa, Bodafors, Sweden.

19. Zeleny, Milan, 1982, "Multiple Criteria Decision Making, McGraw-Hill, New York.

Index